HOW TO GET A

JOB

IN

New York City
and the Metropolitan Area

Robert Sanborn and Eva Lederman

The Insider's
Guide Series

SURREY BOOKS
CHICAGO

HOW TO GET A JOB IN NEW YORK CITY AND THE METROPOLITAN AREA

Published by Surrey Books, Inc., 230 E. Ohio St., Suite 120, Chicago, IL 60611.

This book is manufactured in the United States of America.

6th Edition. 1 2 3 4 5

Library of Congress Cataloging-in-Publication data:
Sanborn, Robert, 1959-
    How to get a job in New York City and the metropolitan area / Robert Sanborn,
Eva Lederman. — 6th ed.
        p.   cm. — (The insider's guide series)
    Includes bibliographical references and indexes.
    ISBN 1-57284-018-8 (pbk.)
    1. Job hunting—New York Metropolitan Area. 2. Job vacancies—New York
Metropolitan Area. 3. Vocational guidance—Information services—New York
Metropolitan Area. 4. Industries—New York Metropolitan Area—Directories.
5. Job hunting—New York Metropolitan Area—Information services—Directories.
I. Lederman, Eva. II. Title. III. Series.
HF5382.75.U62N53   1997   97-38672
650.14'09747'1—DC21   CIP

AVAILABLE TITLES IN THIS SERIES—$17.95

How To Get a Job in Atlanta
How To Get a Job in Chicago
How To Get a Job in Dallas/Fort Worth
How To Get a Job in New York City and the Metropolitan Area
How To Get a Job in The San Francisco Bay Area
How To Get a Job in Seattle and Western Washington
How To Get a Job in Southern California

Single copies may be ordered directly from the publisher. Send check or money order for book price plus $4.00 for first book and $1.50 for each additional book to cover insurance, shipping, and handling to Surrey Books at the above address. For quantity discounts, please contact the publisher.

Editorial production by Bookcrafters, Inc., Chicago.
Cover and book design by Joan Sommers Design, Chicago.
Illustrations by Mona Daly.
Typesetting by On Track Graphics, Inc., Chicago.
"How To Get a Job Series" is distributed to the trade by Publishers Group West.

Acknowledgments

This completely revised series of books is deeply indebted to Diane Wattenbarger, who helped write and gather much of the material in chapters 1-9. Additional thanks go to Cheryl Matherly and Ann Peterson for their valuable ideas.

Robert Sanborn wishes to thank his personal support system: Ellen Sanborn and Virginia Elisabet, wife and daughter respectively.

Eva Lederman wishes to thank Faye Lederman for her exhaustive research assistance.

We also wish to acknowledge the seminal contributions of Thomas M. Camden, Editor Emeritus.

NAMES AND ADDRESSES CAN CHANGE

The authors and editors have made every effort to supply you with the most useful, up-to-date information available to help you find the job you want. Each name, address, and phone number has been verified by our staff of fact checkers. But offices move and people change jobs, so we urge you to check before you write or visit. And if you think we should include information on companies, organizations, or people that we've missed, please let us know.

The publisher, authors, and editors make no guarantee that the employers listed in this book have jobs available.

DROP US A LINE

Among the new features in this edition are "Dear Dr. Bob" letters—short notes from job seekers or workers like yourself, recounting their experiences. For this feature to be a success, we need your input. So if you have any interesting stories to share with your fellow job hunters, write to us in care of Surrey Books. We cannot guarantee publication, and letters will not be returned. Send your letters to:

Dear Dr. Bob, Job Hunting Stories
c/o Surrey Books
230 E. Ohio St., Suite 120
Chicago, IL 60611

JOB HUNTING?

These books, covering 7 major markets, can help you achieve a successful career

HOW... to get the job you want: Each book gives you more than 1,500 major employers, numbers to call, and people to contact.

WHERE... to get the job you want: How to research the local job market and meet the people who hire.

PLUS... how to use the World Wide Web, local networks, and professional organizations; how to choose a career; advice on employment services; how to sell yourself in the interview; writing power resumes and cover letters; hundreds of names and numbers, many available nowhere else!

Contents

one

So You Want To Get a Job in New York

You've decided to get a job in one of the great cities of the world. New York City and the surrounding area provide numerous opportunities for job seekers. Whether you are designing a career on Fashion Avenue, banking on a position in Wall Street, or advertising your talents on Madison Avenue, New York can be exciting and rewarding. This book will help you find the job you're looking for.

How This Book Can Help

There are, of course, other books about finding jobs and about aspects of the job search such as resume writing and interviewing. This book is a little different. We have taken an approach that will make your New York job search easier and, hopefully, successful.

How is this book any different from the rest? First, we are local. This book focuses on the New York area. We have inside information on the job market and things unique to the job search in the City, suburbs, and adjacent Connecticut and New Jersey. Second, this book combines job-search information from the World Wide Web with conventional information on how to conduct a job search. Once you have access to the Internet, you will see how your search for a career can be made easier with a wealth of information at your fingertips. Finally, this Insider's Guide is coauthored by an expert on the local job market and a national career guru; the information you'll get is cutting edge and proven effective. This book is designed to help you find and land the best job for you.

Before You Arrive

Preparation is a key to any job search, and this is especially true if you are relocating from another city to the New York area. If you're from out of town, you'll want to learn as much about the area as possible. This will help ease the transition to your new home and allow you to concentrate on your job search. This chapter will give you a head start on learning about the region and its job market.

Much of this chapter is devoted to surveying the vast array of media sources that can help you gain a better knowledge of the area. But for some readers, the first step in the job search might be to figure out their best career options. In other words, you might need to revisit the old "what do I want to do when I grow up?" question. Choosing a career direction early on will help you focus on which industries to target. Chapter 2 will help you get that part of your search behind you.

The New York Area Job Search

As unique as the area is, it is no different from any other place in the world when it comes down to finding a job. It takes work and perseverance. Chapter 4 outlines the ten steps toward seeking and securing a job. From networking to interviewing, all steps in the process are important. Chapter 5 highlights one of the most important and proven activities of the search for a career: networking. Chapter 6 will help you get your resume in shape, and Chapter 7 gets you ready to give that prospective employer the "killer" interview. Chapter 8 will help if you are looking for a summer or temporary job. And Chapter 10 is our exclusive listing of major employers in the New York area, complete with addresses, phone numbers, and contacts where available.

Going to a new city to look for a job is much different from being a tourist. You'll face not only the challenges of getting to know a new place but you'll face the task of carving a niche for yourself as well. Getting a head start on researching the city and employers will make your search much easier.

Using Local Newspapers

Learning more about New York and all it has to offer should be one of the more interesting and enjoyable parts of your preparation. There are a number of local publications that can help you learn more about the city and, of course, provide insight into the local job market.

Local newspapers are an excellent place to begin. As you start your job search, it is important to read the want ads for more than job vacancies. The classifieds can give you an idea of who the key employers are in your field and which ones are growing.

MAJOR NEWSPAPERS IN THE NEW YORK AREA

Crain's New York Business
http://www.crainsny.com
Crain Communications
220 E. 42nd St.
New York, NY 10017
(212) 210-0100
This weekly paper covers only business news about New York or national news as it affects the New York business community. Recruitment and classified ads are also included.

Newsday
http://www.newsday.com
New York News Bureau
2 Park Ave.
New York, NY 10003
(212) 251-6700
Newsday is the sixth largest metropolitan paper in the country and considered to be *the* local paper for Nassau, Suffolk, and Queens county residents. The new Monday Business Report features major business happenings, from small companies to large. A daily section covers local, national, and international business and economic development. Sunday's paper includes a section on money and careers, including employment trends and opportunities. Columnists regularly discuss small business and workplace issues.

New York Times
229 W. 43rd St.
http://www.nytimes.com
New York, NY 10036
(212) 556-1234
The *Times* is a highly respected source of business information and publishes a business section in its daily and Sunday papers, which also includes editions for Long Island, Westchester County, and New Jersey. The Sunday paper includes a huge classified ad section with opportunities for entry-level to experienced professionals in a wide range of fields. It also has a section specifically for recent college grads. Listings for opportunities in education, health care, and library work also appear in the editorial section.

The Wall Street Journal
http://www.wsj.com
200 Liberty St.
New York, NY 10281
(212) 416-2000
The *Journal* is the nation's leading newspaper for news about the business community. The paper also publishes yearly special reports on careers and small business. The *Journal* also publishes the *National Business Employment Weekly,*

which includes the classified ad sections of the paper's four regional editions. The jobs here are generally targeted to mid- to upper-level senior managers. Editorials about the business community are also included as well as articles on the job-search process, including resume writing, interviewing, networking, changing jobs, relocating, and entrepreneurial options.

LOCAL MAGAZINES AND NEWSPAPERS

Agenda New York
200 W. 57th St., Suite 202
New York, NY 10019
(212) 399-1188
Corporate arts, civic and philanthropic events in New York City.

Avenue
950 3rd Ave.
New York, NY 10022
(212) 758-9517
For and about people who live on the Upper East Side.

Barron's
200 Liberty St.
New York, NY 10281
(212) 416-2700
The Dow Jones business and financial weekly.

Brooklyn Bridge
388 Atlantic Ave.
Brooklyn, NY 11217
(718) 596-7400
Covers all subjects, from politics to art and entertainment, for Brooklynites.

City Journal
52 Vanderbilt Ave., 2nd Floor
New York, NY 10017
(212) 599-7000
New York City politics, policies, and culture.

Long Island Voice
393 Jericho Turnpike
Mineola, NY 11501
Events and topics of interest to residents of Nassau and Suffolk counties.

Manhattan File
594 Broadway, Suite 500
New York, NY 10012
(212) 219-3453
Lifestyle magazine for Manhattanites in their 20s and 30s.

Manhattan Magazine
330 W. 56th St., Suite 3G
New York, NY 10019
(212) 265-7970
Business, arts, fashion, society, and interviews with dynamic local personalities.

New York Daily News
450 W. 33rd St.
New York, NY 10001
(212) 210-2100
www.mostnews.com

New York Magazine
444 Madison Ave.
New York, NY 10022
(212) 508-0700
General interest.

New York Observer
54 E. 64th St.
New York, NY 10021
(212) 755-2400
General interest weekly paper.

New York Press
295 Lafayette St.
The Puck Building, 9th Floor
New York, NY 10012
(212) 941-1130

New York Trend
14 Bond St., Suite 176
New York, NY 11021
(212) 466-0028
Business, politics, health, arts, entertainment, and more.

Our Town
242 W. 30th St., 5th Floor
New York, NY 10001
(212) 268-8600
Local resident paper.

Paper
365 Broadway, 6th Floor
New York, NY 10012
(212) 226-4405
Guide to New York City arts, entertainment, and style.

The Resident
215 Lexington Ave., 13th Floor
New York, NY 10016
(212) 679-4970
Local resident papers for each neighborhood.

Spotlight Magazine
126 Liberty Lane
Mamaroneck, NY 10543
(914) 381-4740
Lifestyles in metropolitan New York.

Time Out New York
627 Broadway, 7th Floor
New York, NY 10012
(212) 539-4444
Covers the local beat including "around town" and "byte me."

The Village Voice
36 Cooper Square
New York, NY 10003
(212) 475-3300

The Big Picture: Business Magazines and Newspapers

The general business climate affects the local job market, no matter what career field you are in. You should keep abreast of changing trends in the economy, both regional and national. The following publications can help.

Business Week
http://www.businessweek.com
1221 Avenue of the Americas
New York, NY 10020
(212) 512-2641
Published weekly, this magazine will keep you informed as to key happenings in the business world. Special issues include: Industry Outlook (24 key industries; January), Corporate Scoreboard (ranks companies in selected industries; March), Hot Growth Companies/Best Small Companies (May), and Best Business Schools (October).

Chamber Report
NY City Partnership and Chamber of Commerce
1 Battery Park Plaza
New York, NY 10004
(212) 493-7857
A publication devoted to the organization's mission of making New York City a better place to live, work, and conduct business.

Forbes
http://www.forbes.com/
60 5th Ave.
New York, NY 10011
(212) 620-2200
Publishes 26 issues/year. Special issues include: The Annual Report on American
Industry (January), Top 500 U.S. Companies (April), International 500 (July),
800 Top U.S. Corporate Executives (personal and compensation information;
May), 200 Best Small U.S. Companies (November), and 400 Largest Private
Companies in the U.S. (December).

Fortune
http://www.fortune.com
Time-Life Building
1271 Avenue of the Americas
New York, NY 10020-1301
(212) 522-1212
Publishes 27 issues/year. Special issues include: 18-Month Economic Forecast
(January and July), America's Most Admired Corporations (February), U.S.
Business Hall of Fame (profiles selected business leaders; March), Fortune 500:
Largest U.S. Industrial Corporations (April), Service 500 (June), Global 500:
U.S. and Foreign Corporations (July), Fastest Growing 100 Public Companies
(October), Pacific Rim Survey (October), and Best Cities for Business
(November).

Inc. Magazine
http://www.inc.com/incmagazine
38 Commercial Wharf
Boston, MA 02110
(617) 248-8000
Published monthly. Special issues include: Best Cities for Starting a Business
(April), 100 Fastest Growing Public Companies (May), and 500 Fastest Growing
Private Companies (October).

Investor's Business Daily
19 W. 44th St., Suite 804
New York, NY 10036
(212) 626-7676
National daily paper focussing on marketplace trends with intensive coverage of
business and technology. Features include career management and effective job
strategies. The "Leaders and Success" column profiles successful people and
their keys to achievement.

Money Magazine
http://www.pathfinder.com/money
Time-Life Building
1271 Avenue of the Americas, Rockefeller Center
New York, NY 10020-1301
(212) 522-1212

Published monthly. Annual September issue (Best Places to Live) is especially insightful for those thinking of relocating.

Working Woman
http://www.womweb.com/sitmww.htm
135 W. 50th St., 16th Floor
New York, NY 10020
(212) 445-6100
This monthly publication is a great resource for professional women. Special issues include: Salary Survey (January), Top 50 Women in Business (May), Top 25 Careers for Women (July), and Ten Women to Watch (November).

Safer than ever—with a few caveats

A word about safety: Wear necklaces on the inside of your shirt, turn rings to face the palm of your hand, sling your purse across your shoulder (with your wallet in an inside pocket), use the ATMs inside banks rather than on street corners, and remember that crime is down across the board. The city's overall crime rate dropped 11.5% in Manhattan since 1996 in virtually all categories, from murder (down by 42%) to grand larceny. (Mayor's Management Report)

The Internet

In many ways, the World Wide Web, or the Internet, is still in its infancy. Every month the number of useful sites grows exponentially. The Web continues to be a vital information research resource. One of the key features of this book is the inclusion of numerous World Wide Web (WWW) addresses to help you learn about the local area and jump-start your job search. If you have never used cyberspace or the WWW, don't worry. In most cases it's as simple as point and click. Surfing the Internet is an excellent way to stay up-to-date on career opportunities and techniques. The Internet provides access to volumes of information and numerous contacts, all without leaving your desk.

To get started you'll need a computer, modem, and software to give you Internet access. You'll probably find it most convenient to have your own computer, but if you don't, fear not. Friends, universities, and cybercafes can provide you access to the Internet so you can join the millions now "on-line."

The "information superhighway" is really a worldwide link-up of computers and computer networks. All WWW addresses start with the letters http:// . Following this will usually be a long string of characters—often words or abbreviations—with no spaces in between. When you type that "address" into the Web browser on your computer (Netscape or Microsoft Explorer, for instance), you will be linked with the organization listed.

There are many articles and books about the Web and how to access it. We will let you explore those on your own. However, we would like to give you an idea of the type of information the Web addresses provide. For example, there are places to get career counseling, learn about careers, post your resume, find information on companies, and view the types of positions they have open. You should note the cost of each Internet-access service (America On-Line, Prodigy, or others) and other charges before signing up for any service. In addition, there are career services on the Net that will offer you some free service with hopes that you will buy others. Keep in mind that many of the best sites and homepages are free.

Let's get you started with some WWW addresses that can provide information about New York itself, careers, and the local job search.

CYBERINFO ABOUT THE NEW YORK AREA

Employment Opportunities in New York City
http://www.panix.com/clay/nyc/employment.html

New York City Information
http://www.contact.org/new_york.html
Includes links that will point you to hundreds of useful New York City resources, including The People's Green Book—an on-line guide to city services; and Clay Irving's New York Reference—a comprehensive listing of NYC Web sites, including government agencies, educational institutions, and community organizations, as well as commercial sites.

City Net-New York
http://www.city.net/countries/united_states/new_york/new_york/
Connects to information on entertainment, community organizations, restaurants, maps, other guides, parks and outdoors, sports, transportation, and more.

Netizen's Cyberstop New York City Page
http://www.columbia.edu/~hauben/nyc-guides.html
Offers a valuable section on transportation, including an interactive subway system of New York City. Feed in your origin and destination and it tells you which subway lines to use.

Net-Person's Guide to New York
http://www.k2nesoft.com/nyc/
This WWW site will link you to many others with information on business, professional organizations, libraries, transportation, and the New York City region.

City Life
http://www.sidewalk.com
Cultural events, movies, shopping, restaurants, lectures, theater and more.

State of New York
http://vote-smart.org/state/New-York
Information on New York, government, facts and statistics.

You are probably starting to get the idea of what these sites have to offer. Here are a few more sites providing general information about the New York area. Many more are interspersed throughout this book.

http://www.panix.com/clay/nyc/
lists local information on about 50 different topics.

http://emall.com/ExploreNY/NY1.html
offers information about sites in different neighborhoods.

http://www.mediabridge.com/nyc/
is the "paperless guide to New York."

New York New York
http://www.bmcc.cuny.edu/NYNY-HTML/BMCC4.HTM
Provides information on New York City, including weather, sights, politics, and business.

Your job search is unique to the New York area when . . .
You gain access to the Internet through the local coffee house. A list of cybercafes can be found on the World Wide Web at:
http://www.easynet.co.uk/pages/cafe/ccafe.html.

Here are a few local Internet cafes:

alt. coffee
139 Ave. A at 9th St.
(212) 529-2233

@cafe
12 St. Marks Place
(212) 979-5439

Cyber Cafe
273A Lafayette St.
(212) 334-5140

Ditto Internet Cafe
48 W. 20th St.
(212) 334-6436

Internet Cafe
82 E. 3rd St.
(212) 614-0747
http://www.bigmag/c.com

Newsbar No.4
107 University Place at
12th St.
(212) 260-4192

The VOID
16 Mercer St.
(212) 941-6492

CYBERSOURCES FOR YOUR JOB SEARCH—NATIONAL

Try a few of these sites on the World Wide Web to get an overview of the job search and how the Internet might help. Many of these sites will give you a multitude of other links to continue honing your job-hunt skills.

http://www.cs.purdue.edu/homes/swlodin/jobs.html
Provides a comprehensive list of major job sites including:

AT&T College Network
http://www.att.com/college
Good listing of job sites, includes advice on using technology to assist you in your job search.

Business Job Finder—Ohio State University
http://www.cob.ohio-state.edu/dept/fin/osujobs.htm
Includes job resources in finance, accounting, and consulting.

Career Resource Center
http://www.careers.org
Thousands of job, employer, and career-reference Web links. Database includes employers, professional associations, career counselors, educational and self-employment resources. Also government jobs access and employer homepages.

Career Action Center
http://199.99.204.31/CACpublic/intro.html
A good page with links to other career-related resources. Also includes job listings, resource library, employer forums, job-search information, and local business trends.

Career Channel
http://riceinfo.rice.edu:80/projects/careers
A lot of links to other career sites, as well as material on all aspects of careers and the job search, from Rice University's Career Center.

Careers.wsj.com—Wall Street Journal Careers Page
http://careers.wsj.com
Extensive career resources from the *Wall Street Journal.*

Career Magazine
http://www.careermag.com/careermag/
Internet links and career information.

Career Mosaic
http://www.careermosaic.com
Includes information on hot companies, new products and technology, benefits and employee programs, and sites and lifestyles around the world.

Career Services On-line—College of William and Mary
http://www.wm.edu/csrv/career/career.html
An excellent page with links to almost all other good career-related Internet resources, originally compiled by the College of William and Mary Career Center. Many links to other college career centers.

Interactive Employment Network (ESpan)
http://www.espan.com
Provides current resources for the job seeker: salary guides, advice from career specialists, and job listings (mostly in technical fields).

JobHunt: A Meta-list of On-Line Job-Search Resources and Services
http://www.job-hunt.org/
A well-organized list of major Internet career resource links, originally from Stanford University.

Job Safari
http://www.jobsafari.com
Well-organized list of company jobs offered on Web pages.

On-line Career Center
http://www.occ.com
A highly respected Internet jobs resource. On-line Career Center is a non-profit employer association that provides a database, job and resume files, company information and profiles, and on-line search software to assist both employers and applicants in using the Internet in their career search.

Riley Guide—Employment Opportunities and Job Resources on the Internet
http://www.dbm.com/jobguide
One of the most highly respected collections of career resource links, with extensive advice on using the Internet's resources in the career-search process.

RECOMMENDED BOOKS FOR THE ON-LINE JOB SEARCH

Gonyea, James C. *On-Line Job Search Companion: A Complete Guide to Hundreds of Career Planning and Job Resources.* New York: McGraw-Hill, 1994. A complete guide to hundreds of career-planning and job-hunting resources available via your computer.

Kennedy, Joyce Lain, and Thomas J. Morrow. *Electronic Resume Revolution.* New York: John Wiley & Sons, 1995. Provides resume information and resources via the Internet.

Kennedy, Joyce Lain. *Hook Up, Get Hired: The Internet Job Search Revolution.* New York: John Wiley & Sons, 1995. Provides job-search information via the Internet.

Riley, Margaret, Frances Roehm, and Steve Oserman. *The Guide to Internet Job Searching.* Chicago: VGM Career Horizons, 1997.

Hot Careers in the New York Area

New York's job market, according to *The New York Times*, is "alive and well." "Job hunters—chin up!" says *The Daily News*. Over the past several years, private-sector job growth has been as high or higher than at any point since 1950, following devastating job losses from 1989 to 1993. In 1996, the city experienced the single largest job gain in the past 13 years, adding 16,500 private sector jobs in one month alone. In 1998, the city is poised to add 108,000 new jobs, with strong growth in professional occupations.

In 1996, New York City produced more than half of the new jobs generated in the surrounding 27 counties while topping job growth in every large Northeastern city. Nearly every sector of the city's economy is growing, as are jobs in every borough. Even excluding the boom on Wall Street, the city still experienced more private sector growth from 1994 through 1996 than in any other three-year period during the past 40 years.

Manhattan's new media industry, which barely existed several years ago, has turned into a major force in the local economy, doubling in jobs and companies in just the last 18 months to become a "$2.8 billion juggernaut," according to a recent study by Coopers & Lybrand in conjunction with the NY New Media Association. This industry includes such positions as graphic designer, editor, Web artist/layout editor, Web site programmer/engineer, Internet operations manager, and on-line sales/marketing services. New media or interactive media departments can be found in nearly every major company across every industry, and also exist as independent businesses. Currently, the new media business employs 32,013 full-time workers in 2,128 companies (and an additional 23,960 part-time and freelance employees), ranking the industry on par with advertising (27,528 full-time jobs in 1996) and publishing (26,543). Jobs in this field are expected to grow by 79% over the next two years.

The rapid growth of new media is still dwarfed by Manhattan's flagship industries: **securities** (with 155,000 jobs), **banking, accounting, and legal services.** However, it is the service sector, concentrated mainly in the outer boroughs, that is experiencing the greatest growth. In fact, health and social services provide jobs for 315,000 employees; over one-third of those jobs are in the Bronx. These are also predicted to be the fastest growing industries through 1998.

The city's **health care** industry employs nearly 300,000 people. Home health aides, in particular, should see an increase of 10,500 employees in response to an increased demand for outpatient care as hospitals seek to cut costs, recently eliminating 1,000 jobs. Growth, though, is expected to continue at a more moderate pace as HMOs expand and new businesses form to meet industry changes. Doctors, nurses, hospital administrators, and consultants who are shut out by hospital downsizing will find positions with managed care companies. Jobs in marketing, computer technology, telecommunications, information systems, and consulting will also be plentiful since managed care is a virtual information factory.

Wall Street, which generates about 15% of all wages in the private sector, is going through a modest contraction, with the job count remaining steady after an increase of 20,000 employees between 1992 and mid-1994. The securities industry, a key sector and indicator of the city's economy, enjoyed a buoyant stock market and declining interest rates in 1997, which improved the general business climate.

The retail industry continues to expand. National chains such as Staples, OfficeMax, CompUSA, Toys 'R Us, Home Depot, Bradlees, and others have aggressively expanded their superstores in New York City. Retail has also been helped by strong tourism, the low dollar, and growth of imports.

Travel and tourism continue to play a major role in the local economy: hotels are booked, the restaurant industry is thriving, and business is booming on Broadway. Since hotel occupancy tax was cut by nearly 30% in 1994, New York has seen record years for tourism, also a result of the boom times and reduced crime rate.

Look for growth in the **printing and publishing** industries, with local periodicals doing the most hiring. Major publishers are also increasing staff to develop products for new media, including CD-ROMs and electronic versions of publications.

The face of New York City's workforce is changing as well. Asians and Pacific Islanders, the smallest minority groups, along with Hispanics are the fastest growing segments. Census reports show a labor force with no ethnic majority.

Ten Best Places to Work in the New York Area

There are a variety of factors to consider when choosing a company you want to work for. Salary, benefits, vacations, and child care are obvious ones. But there are also less tangible factors such as corporate culture, company morale, and opportunities for internal training and promotion that are equally important. No directory will tell you that Ogilvy & Mather Advertising has an in-house bar and Scholastic has an in-house gym, where people of all positions and levels socialize and network. Get as much input as you can from people on the inside who can tell you what a company's really like.

Our picks for the ten best places to work are, in alphabetical order:

AT&T
http://www.att.com/
32 Avenue of the Americas
New York, NY 10013
(212) 387-5400
1996 revenues: $52 billion; +3% from 1995
Employees: 130,400
AT&T provides telecommunication services and designs and manufactures telephone products, electrical components, and information systems. AT&T offers a tremendous number of employee benefits including: medical, dental, vision, and life insurance; pension, savings, and profit-sharing plans; tuition assistance; flexible holidays, personal and vacation days; maternity and paternity leave; counseling; smoke-free workplace; flextime, job sharing, and telecommuting options; training programs; child care and eldercare referrals.

Avis Rent A Car System
900 Old Country Road
Garden City, NY 11530
(516) 222-3000
1996 revenues: not available—privately held company
Employees: 21,000 worldwide
At Avis, the world's second largest car rental company, employees own and run the company. Its employee stock ownership plan makes it one of the largest employee-owned companies in the country. Every month employees can submit their ideas on how to improve the company, through employee participation groups. Many people describe Avis as a big family, especially since 30% of the employees have been there 10 or more years. Avis also has a strong tradition of promoting within; one-third of all managers started at entry level.

Goldman Sachs & Company
85 Broad St.
New York, NY 10004
(212) 902-1000
1996 revenues: not available—private partnership

Employees: 8,100 worldwide; 5,600 in NYC
Goldman Sachs is a leading investment bank and brokerage, buying and selling huge blocks of shares on stock exchanges around the world. Goldman Sachs is known for its competitive salaries and for its generous yearly bonuses. However, Goldman is also known for its commitment to teamwork. Job titles are not important, nor are strict dress codes. And nobody cares where your father went to school. Its workaholic atmosphere is tempered by reduced schedules for parents and an emergency drop-off child care center. Ten percent of employees are in sales, 7% are traders, and another 7% are investment bankers. Other professionals make up 22% and support staff occupy a full 53%.

IBM
New Orchard Road
Armonk, NY 10504
(914) 288-3000
http://www.ibm.com/
http://www.empl.ibm.com/
1996 revenues: $76 billion; +5.6% from 1995
Employees: 240,600 worldwide; 1,400 in NYC
In addition to IBM's position as the world's largest provider of information technology solutions, the company is also a leader in helping employees balance career and family needs. Working parents can take a three-year leave of absence while retaining benefits and have a guaranteed job upon return. The company's "individualized work schedules" program allows employees to begin their workday up to two hours before or after the regular workday, and permits up to a two-hour extended lunch break. IBM is also a leader in hiring minorities, who represent 14% of management. Engineers, scientists, accountants, and auditors make up 44% of staff. Technicians and managers account for 13% each and sales and marketing, 12%. Office personnel make up the rest.

Johnson & Johnson
One Johnson & Johnson Plaza
New Brunswick, NJ 08933
(908) 524-0400
1997 revenues (9/97): $17 billion; +5% from 1996
Employees: 81,000 worldwide; 1,500 in New Brunswick
Johnson & Johnson manufactures health care products for the consumer, pharmaceutical, and professional markets. Sales tripled between the 80s and 90s for this well-managed company that believes their employees are their greatest resource. The J&J "credo," a set of core company values, is pervasive throughout all offices. J&J is known for caring about its employees—about three-quarters of sales are devoted to employee salaries and benefits. Some of its offices have a child-care center, and J&J is a leader in family/work programs. It recently won first place in a survey conducted by the Families and Work Institute in NY. Forty percent of employees are in production, 16% are office staff, and 10% are in operations. Research and development, technicians, marketing and information service professionals, and management round out the staff.

Merck & Company
PO Box 100
Whitehouse Station, NJ 08889
(908) 423-1000
http://www.merck.com/
1997 revenues (6/97): $11.4 billion; +22% from 1996
Employees: 43,750 worldwide; approx. 60% in headquarters office.
Merck is a "worldwide human and animal health company." Merck has won
awards as the best company for women, working mothers, blacks, and
salespersons, and have won *Fortune* magazine's poll of "most admired company"
several times over. Training programs, full benefits for employees and
dependents, stock-option and savings plans, and on-site child care are among
the reasons why turnover runs at only 6.9% per year, including retirements.
Manufacturing positions make up 41% of staff, research 23%, administration
19%, sales and marketing 12%, and engineers 5%.

Morgan, J.P., and Company
60 Wall St.
New York, NY 10260
(212) 483-2323
http://www.jpmorgan.com/
1997 revenues (6/97): $6 billion; + 16% from 1996
Employees: 16,394 worldwide; 7,000 in NYC
Morgan engages in global banking, financial advising, securities underwriting,
trading, and investment fund management services. Morgan trains its own staff
through its five professional training programs and expects them to stay for the
long run. An MBA is not a requirement, nor is an undergrad liberal arts degree
frowned upon. Morgan is known for growing its own staff and encouraging
movement within its ranks. Secretaries become staff and executive assistants,
and it is not unheard of for them to become vice presidents. Indeed, the firm's
retired former chairman, Dennis Weatherstone, joined Morgan as a clerk in
London at age 16.

Seagram, Joseph E., & Sons
800 Third Ave.
New York, NY 10022
(212) 572-7000
1997 revenues (6/97): $12.5 billion; +4% from 1996
Employees: 30,000 worldwide; 650 in NYC
Seagram produces distilled spirits, wines, fruit juices, coolers, and mixers. The
company, which purchased MCA in June of 1995, is a great place for a career in
sales—trainees receive extensive training which continues throughout their
career. Reps can also be promoted to managers, regional manager, and VP of
sales. Seagram looks for outgoing, aggressive, smart people; college is not a
requirement, nor is sales experience. Benefits are plentiful including medical,
life, and disability insurance, travel allowance and company car, profit sharing,
stock purchase and retirement plans, and tuition and relocation assistance.

Viacom International
1515 Broadway
New York, NY 10036
(212) 258-6000
http://www.mcp.com/general/news5/via.html
1997 revenues (6/97): $6 billion; +10% from 1996
Employees: approx. 85,000 worldwide; 5,700 in NYC
Viacom is an entertainment and publishing company with operations in network broadcasting, video, music, and theme parks. The company is extremely progressive on gay and lesbian issues. Not only does its written policy prohibit discrimination and include gay and lesbian issues in diversity training, it also has an exceptional domestic partner benefit plan. There are also job performance guidelines for workers with chronic health problems, such as AIDS, to help them work as long as possible.

Xerox Corporation
800 Long Ridge Road
Stamford, CT 06904
(203) 968-3000
http://www.xerox.com
1997 revenues (6/97): $8 billion; +3% from 1996
Employees: 86,000 worldwide; 550 in headquarters office
Xerox is engaged in the worldwide development, manufacturing, and services of document processing products and services. Xerox is known for its social responsibility. Employees can take a one-month to one-year leave of absence, with pay, to work on a social service project. And Xerox gives employees money for the start-up of community projects identified by employees as important. Managers make up 13% of staff, professionals 20%, technicians 28%, office and clerical 21%, sales 8%, and manufacturing staff 10%.

Finding an apartment is easier if you know where to look
The *Village Voice* offers the best selection of apartments, shares, and sublets in Manhattan and the boroughs. But by the time this free paper arrives at newsstands on Wednesday, most of the good deals are long gone. That's because the paper comes out on-line on Tuesday: http://www.villagevoice.com

Ten Fastest Growing Companies in the New York Area

Based upon our research and reports from the local media, the fastest growing companies in the New York area are, in alphabetical order:

Alpine Group
1790 Broadway
New York, NY 10019
(212) 757-3333
3-year revenue growth rate: 104%
Employees: 3,809
A holding company for Superior Telecom, Alpine is a leading manufacturer
and supplier of telecommunications wire and cable products to regional Bell
operating companies. Adience, Alpine's wholly owned subsidiary, manufactures
and supplies refractory products and services to integrated steel makers and
other industries.

Cityscape Financial Corp.
565 Taxter Road
Elmsford, NY 10523
(914) 592-6677
3-year revenue growth rate: 254%
Employees: 905
Consumer finance company that originates, purchases, sells, and services
mortgage loans secured by one-to-four-family residences.

ContiFinancial Corp.
277 Park Ave.
New York, NY 10172
(212) 207-2800
3-year revenue growth rate: 79%
Employees: 1,562
CFN services home equity loans and provides financing and asset securitization
expertise to originators of a broad range of loans, leases, and receivables.

GT Interactive Software
16 E. 40th St.
New York, NY 10016
(212) 726-6500
3-year revenue growth rate: 90%
Employees: 967
GTIS creates, publishes, and merchandises interactive entertainment, "edutain-
ment" (educational entertainment), and value-priced consumer software.

The Money Store
1840 Morris Ave.
Union, NJ 07083
(908) 686-2000
http://www.themoneystore.com
3-year revenue growth rate: 53%
Employees: 3,460
The Money Store is a financial services company that sells and services
consumer and commercial loans offering home equity, home improvement,
small business, auto, and student loans.

NTL, Inc.
110 E. 59th St.
New York, NY 10022
(212) 906-8440
3-year revenue growth rate: 183%
Employees: 3,150
NTL constructs and operates broad-band communication systems which provide telecommunication, telephone, cable, and Internet services to business and residential customers.

PureTec Corp.
65 Railroad Ave.
Ridgefield, NJ 07657
(201) 941-6550
3-year revenue growth rate: 174%
Employees: 1,970
Manufactures specialty plastic products including garden hoses, medical and precision tubing, vinyl resins and compounds, wire coatings; also recycles plastic.

Superior Telecom
1790 Broadway
New York, NY 10019
(212) 757-3333
3-year revenue growth rate: 89%
Employees: 1,608
Manufactures copper telecommunications wire and cable products for the local loop segment of the telecommunications network; also manufactures data communications and electronic equipment.

Viacom
1515 Broadway
New York, NY 10036
(212) 258-6000
http://www.mcp.com/general/news5/via.html
3-year revenue growth rate: 100%
Employees: 83,500
Viacom produces programs and feature films for television. It also owns 5 television and 14 radio stations as well as Paramount Communications. Paramount engages in entertainment (television and film, theme parks, and Madison Square Garden) and publishing.

White River Corp.
777 Westchester Ave.
White Plains, NY 10604
(914) 251-0237
3-year revenue growth rate: 53%
Employees: 1,000
Through its subsidiaries, White River provides vehicle valuation and collision estimating services and software to automobile insurance companies; also designs, distributes, and sells fashion accessories.

Profiles in Bigness: Ten Largest Employers in the New York Area

Based upon our research and reports from the local media, the largest employers in the New York area are, in alphabetical order:

American International Group
70 Pine St.
New York, NY 10270
(212) 770-7000
1996 revenues: $28 billion; +9% from 1995
Employees: 36,600
AIG is a holding company and owns several insurance companies. Its subsidiaries include AIG Realty, American Life Insurance, American International Reinsurance, and others.

AT&T
32 Avenue of the Americas
New York, NY 10013
(212) 387-5400
http://www.att.com/
1996 revenues: $52 billion; +3% from 1995
Employees: 130,400
AT&T provides telecommunication services and designs and manufactures telephone products, electrical components, and information systems.

Chase Manhattan Corp.
270 Park Ave.
New York, NY 10017
(212) 270-6000
http://www.chase.com
1996 revenues: $25 billion; +4% from 1995
Employees: 67,785
In 1996, Chase merged with Chemical Bank to create a global financial services organization.

Citicorp
425 Park Ave.
New York, NY 10043
(800) 285-3000
http://www.citibank.com/
1996 revenues: $29 billion; +3% from 1995
Employees: 89,000
Citicorp owns Citibank and has numerous subsidiaries and affiliates engaged in banking and finance-related services in over 3,300 locations.

IBM
New Orchard Road
Armonk, NY 10504
(914) 288-3000

http://www.ibm.com/
http://www.empl.ibm.com/
1996 revenues: $76 billion; +5.6% from 1995
Employees: 240,600
IBM is the world's largest manufacturer of information-handling systems. Its six business units make hardware and software and service and manage networks.

Lucent Technologies
600 Mountain Ave.
Murray Hill, NJ 07974
http://www.lucent.com
1996 revenues: $23 billion; +9% from 1995
Employees: 130,400
A spin-off of AT&T, Lucent develops voice, data, and video network technologies. Its Microelectrics Group develops and manufactures power systems, optoelectric components, and integrated circuits. The company supplies infrastructure, equipment, and software to the world's top communication service providers.

Merrill Lynch & Company
World Financial Center, North Tower
250 Vesey St.
New York, NY 10281
(212) 449-1000
http://www.ml.com/
1996 revenues: $25 billion; +15.5% from 1995
Employees: 49,800
Company provides securities, commodities, futures, options, and selected insurance product brokerage services as well as economic research services.

PepsiCo Inc.
Purchase, NY 10577
(914) 253-2000
1996 revenues: $28 billion; +13% from 1995
Employees: 486,000
A leading producer and distributor of beverages, soft drinks, and syrups, PepsiCo also operates Pizza Hut, Kentucky Fried Chicken, and Taco Bell.

Phillip Morris
120 Park Ave.
New York, NY 10017
(212) 880-5000
1996 revenues: $55 billion; +3% from 1995
Employees: 154,000

Texaco Inc.
700 Anderson Hill Road
Purchase, NY 10577
(914) 253-4000

http://www.texaco.com/
1996 revenues: $46 billion; +24% from 1995
Employees: 29,713
Texaco searches for, produces, transports, refines, and markets crude oil, natural gas, and petroleum products.

Find the "500" on the Web

This address will link you to Web sites of Fortune 500 companies:
http://www.cs.utexas.edu/users/paris/corporate.real.html

Using Chambers of Commerce

Most chambers of commerce publish material that is helpful to newcomers or anyone who wants to be better informed about a community, and New York area chambers of commerce are no exception. They provide brochures and maps available free or for a nominal charge and provide much of what you'll want to know about area businesses, city services, transportation, public schools, utilities, and entertainment. Additionally, many chambers publish lists of professional organizations and other networking options within the city as well as directories and publications pertaining to the New York area.

http://www.columbia.edu/~gms18/chamber/
Lists chamber of commerce information and has a classified business section for the five boroughs as well as Long Island, Rockland County, Westchester, New Jersey, and Connecticut.

Bronx Chamber of Commerce
2885 Schley Ave.
Bronx, NY 10465
(718) 829-4111

Brooklyn Chamber of Commerce
7 Metro Tech Center, Suite 2000
Brooklyn, NY 11201
(718) 875-1000

Long Island Convention and Visitors Bureau
350 Vanderbilt Motor Parkway, Suite 103
Hauppauge, NY 11788
(516) 951-3440
Has addresses and phone numbers for chambers of commerce in Suffolk County cities and townships.

Nassau County Chamber of Commerce
125 S. Cottage St.
Valley Stream, NY 11580
(516) 872-9400

New York City Chamber of Commerce
1 Battery Park Plaza
New York, NY 10004
(212) 493-7400

Queens Chamber of Commerce
75-20 Astoria Blvd., Suite 140
Jackson Heights, NY 11370
(718) 898-8500

Staten Island Chamber of Commerce
130 Bay St.
Staten Island, NY 10301
(718) 727-1900

Westchester Chamber of Commerce
235 Mamaroneck Ave.
White Plains, NY 10605
(914) 948-2110
Has names and numbers of county offices in Putnam, Orange, Sullivan,
Dutchess, Ulster, and Rockland counties.

Choosing a Career

Choosing a career or making a decision about which direction you wish to take in the world of jobs is certainly important, but it also can be one of the most difficult processes we go through in life. Ever since we learned to speak as two-year-olds, aunts, uncles, and other assorted adults have asked us, "What do you want to be when you grow up?" Now we ask ourselves that same question. So how do we choose that career, anyhow?

The first step in choosing a career is to learn who you are and what you want. In other words, start with self-assessment. We've outlined a few tools for you to use in assessing yourself and your abilities. It is important to remember that it is very difficult to get a job if you do not know what you want to do. Self-assessment will enable you to start with a goal in mind. After you figure out who you are, it is much easier to find a compatible career.

A Few Facts about Career Decision Making

According to a recent Gallop poll, most people don't have goals when starting to think about the job search. No real planning goes into what is arguably the most important decision of their lives. The poll shows that:

- 59% of us work in an area or career in which we never planned to work.
- 29% of us are influenced by another person to go into a career. It's like the advice given to Dustin Hoffman in *The Graduate*. Someone says, "Plastics—that's where you should be. Try working in plastics." So we consider plastics.
- 18% of us fall into jobs by chance. You're looking for a job in banking and someone mentions that they know of a job in consulting. Sure you're willing to look at it. Next thing you know, you're a consultant.
- 12% of us took the job because it was available. You're walking by the local GAP store and see a "management trainee" sign. You take it!

This same Gallop poll indicated that we fail to properly assess ourselves and our career options. If we had to do it over, the poll indicates, 65% of the American public would get additional information on career options early on. Other polls show that up to 80% of the working public is dissatisfied with one or more aspects of their career and have seriously considered changing.

All of these facts and figures certainly bode poorly for those who jump into a career haphazardly. And, conversely, the statistics bode well for those who delve into a little career exploration before taking the plunge. This is especially true in light of the fact that the average American emigrates through seven to ten jobs and three to four careers in a lifetime. Thus, we will probably need to assess ourselves more than once as our own life changes with the changing job market. Self-assessment is a tool we will use throughout our professional lives.

Strategies in Self-Exploration

Practically everyone wants a job that provides personal satisfaction, growth, good salary and benefits, a certain level of prestige, and a desirable location. But unless you have a more specific idea of the kind of work you want, you probably won't find it. You wouldn't take off on your big annual vacation without some kind of destination in mind. Given that your job will take up much more of your time than your vacation, a little planning is certainly in order.

There are several strategies that can help you learn who you are. Among them are talking with friends and family, self-assessing, and getting help from a career professional.

Friends and family sometimes know you better than you think. They can also provide great support throughout the job search. Try the self-assessment exercises in this chapter, then discuss your results with those who know you best. They may have some insight that you overlooked. However, it is important to follow your own desires and not the dreams of family and friends when choosing a career.

Everyone can benefit from a thorough self-appraisal. The insight gained from self-appraisal is valuable not only in deciding on a career but also in articulating this knowledge in the resume and interviewing process. Perhaps you want to be a little more scientific in your appraisal of yourself. Try career testing. Professionals in vocational planning have literally dozens of tests at their disposal designed to assess personality and aptitude for particular careers.

Getting Started with Self-Assessment

What follows is a list of highly personal questions designed to provide you with insights you may never have considered and to help you answer the Big Question, "What do I want to do?"

To get the most from this exercise, write out your answers. This will take some time, but it will force you to give each question careful thought. The more effort you put into this exercise, the better prepared you'll be for the tough questions you'll be asked in any job interview. The exercise also can be the basis for constructing a winning resume—a subject we'll discuss in more detail in Chapter 6.

QUESTIONS ABOUT ME

Here are some questions to get you started. The answers will indicate what kind of person you are. Be honest. Take as much time as necessary.

1. Describe yourself in less than 500 words. Address these questions: Do you prefer to spend time alone or with other people? How well disciplined are you? Are you quick-tempered? Easygoing? Do you prefer to give orders or take orders? Do you tend to take a conventional, practical approach to problems? Or are you imaginative and experimental? How sensitive are you to others?
2. What accomplishment are you most proud of?
3. What are the most important things you wish to accomplish?
4. What role does your job play in those achievements?
5. Why do you (or don't you) want your career to be the most important thing in your life?
6. What impact do you have on other people?
7. Describe the kind of person others think you are.
8. What role does money play in your standard of values?
9. What do you enjoy most/dislike most?
10. What do you want your life to be like in 5 years?
11. What are your main interests?

What Job Attributes Do You Value Most?

After answering the above questions, it is important to match the job attributes you value to your career. Job burnout usually happens when people are in jobs that don't allow them to do and get the activities and rewards they want. But job satisfaction will occur if a person follows his or her motivations into a career. The following ranking will assist you in beginning to match the job attributes you value with careers that are in step with them.

Rank the following in order of importance to you:

- Leadership
- Creativity
- High Salary
- Helping Others
- Job Security
- Variety
- Physical Activity
- Self-development
- Recognition
- Working with My Mind

- Competition
- Taking Risk

- Prestige
- Independence

Once you've ranked the above, you should begin to get an idea of what's important to you. Compare your priorities to those of the workplace in your potential career/job. Values of the workplace can be determined in several ways. One method is to interview current employees of the company. Another is to research the company through articles and publications to determine its values and beliefs.

QUESTIONS ABOUT MY JOB

Questions about your job can also help in your self-assessment.

1. Describe in detail each job you have had. Begin with your most recent employment and work back toward graduation. Include your title, company name, responsibilities, salary, achievements and successes, failures, and reason for leaving. If you're a recent college graduate and have little or no career-related work experience, you may find it helpful to consider your collegiate experience, both curricular and extracurricular, as your work history for questions 1, 2, 3, 7, 8, 9, and 10.
2. What would you change in your past, if you could?
3. In your career thus far, what responsibilities have you enjoyed most? Least? Why?
4. How hard are you prepared to work?
5. What jobs would allow you to use your talents and interests?
6. What have your subordinates thought about you as a boss? As a person?
7. What have your superiors thought about you as an employee? As a person?
8. If you have been fired from any job, what was the reason?
9. Does your work make you happy? Should it?
10. What do you want to achieve by the time you retire?

Answering these questions will help clarify who you are, what you want, and what you realistically have to offer. They should also reveal what you don't want and what you can't do. It's important to evaluate any objective you're considering in light of your answers to these questions. If a prospective employer knew nothing about you except your answers to these questions, would he think your career objectives were realistic?

One way to match who you are with a specific career is to refer to the *Dictionary of Occupational Titles (DOT)*. The *DOT* is an encyclopedia of careers, covering hundreds of occupations and industries. For the computer buff, *The Perfect Career* by James Gonyea (3444 Dundee Rd., Northbrook, IL 60062) has a database of over 600 occupations for IBM and compatibles.

Professional Testing

As mentioned earlier, professionals in career counseling (see list below) have literally dozens of tests at their disposal designed to assess personality and aptitude for particular careers. Here are a few of the most commonly used career tests.

Strong Interest Inventory

This test looks at a person's interests to see if they parallel the interests of people already employed in specific occupations. It is used chiefly as an aid in making academic choices and career decisions. It continues to be one of the most researched and highly respected counseling tools in use.

Myers-Briggs Type Indicator

This test is based on Carl Jung's theory of perception and judgment and is a widely used measure of personality dispositions and preferences. Used in career counseling, it helps to identify compatible work settings, relate career opportunities and demands to preferences in perception and judgment, and gain insight into personality dimensions, all of which provide the opportunity for greater decision-making ability.

16 PF (Personality Factor) Questionnaire

This test measures 32 personality traits of a normal adult personality along 16 dimensions. Used frequently in counseling, the computerized printout and narrative report show how personality traits may fit into various career fields.

Career Counseling

Although the terms are often used synonymously, there is a difference between a career counselor and consultant. Most professionals use the title "counselor" if they have an advanced degree in psychology, counseling, social work, or marriage, family, and child counseling and are licensed by the state.

Need a list of certified counselors?
The National Board for Certified Counselors provides a list of professional "certified career counselors" in local areas. Certification requires a master's degree and three years of supervised counseling experience. For further information call (800) 398-5389 or send a self-addressed 55-cent stamped return envelope to:

The National Board for Certified Counselors
599 Stevenson Ave.
Alexandria, VA 22304

Also check out the Journal of Career Planning and
Development, which has articles on career counseling.

Professionals who are not licensed often call themselves "career consultants."
This field attracts people from a variety of backgrounds, education, and levels of
competency. It's important, then, to talk to others who have used a given service
before committing yourself.

Because most career counseling and consulting firms are private, for-profit
businesses with high overhead costs, they usually charge more for testing than
local colleges or social service agencies, which are listed later in this chapter.

What can you expect from a career counselor? For one thing, counselors
offer an objective viewpoint. One licensed professional career counselor puts it
this way: "You may not be able to discuss everything with family, friends, and
especially coworkers if you happen still to be working. A trained professional can
serve as a sounding board and offer strategies and information that you can't get
elsewhere. We can essentially help a person become more resourceful."

This particular career counselor usually spends four sessions with individuals who want to establish a sense of direction for their careers. Here's what sessions cover:

- Exploring problems that have blocked progress and considering
  solutions.
- Establishing career objectives and determining strengths and areas
  to work on.
- Writing a career plan that outlines a strategy to achieve goals.
- Preparing an ongoing, self-directed plan to explore career goals.

"A counselor should help people develop methods and a framework on
which to base continual exploration about what they want from a career, even
after they are employed," our counselor friend says.

All too often people look for "quick fixes" in order to get back to work, she
says. "In haste, they may not take time to reflect on where their career is going, to
make sure they look for a job that will be challenging and satisfying."

CAREER COUNSELORS AND CONSULTANTS
IN THE NEW YORK AREA

What follows are a few counselors and consultants who may be able to help you
in your job search. Keep in mind, though, that a listing in this book does not constitute an endorsement of any consulting firm or testing service. Before embark-
ing on a lengthy or expensive series of tests, try to get the opinion of one or more
persons who have already used the service you're considering. To check out a particular practitioner, you can contact the following:

http://www.igc.apc.org/bbb/
This is the homepage of the Better Business Bureau. It offers a geographic directory of offices, list of publications, reliability reports on businesses, scam alerts, and more. Following are phone numbers of consumer-protection offices in the area:
Better Business Bureau of Long Island (516) 420-0500
Better Business Bureau of Metropolitan New York (212) 533-6200
Better Business Bureau of Westchester (914) 428-1230
Nassau County Office of Consumer Affairs (516) 571-2600
New York City Department of Consumer Affairs (212) 487-4398
New York State Attorney General's Office of Consumer Protection
    (800) 771-7755
Westchester County Office of Consumer Complaints (914) 285-2155
    The NY Public library offers free referrals and short-term career counseling.
For information, contact:

Brooklyn Public Library
Grand Army Plaza
Eastern Parkway at Flatbush Ave.
(718) 780-7777
Brooklyn, NY 11201
Offers a one-hour session, including editing of written resume. Monthly series
of workshops is available focussing on various job topics.

The Mid-Manhattan Library
Job Information Center
455 5th Ave.
New York, NY 10018
(212) 340-0849
DISCOVER, an interactive computer career choice program, is available
by appointment.
Many public libraries offer free referrals and short-term career counseling. For
information, contact:

Janice Moore
Learner's Advisory Service
2556 Bainbridge Ave.
NY Public Library, Fordham Center
Bronx, NY
(718) 220-6583

Nassau County Public Library
Hempstead Branch
115 Nichols Court
Hempstead, NY 11550
(516) 481-6990
Offers a seven-week "job club" addressing job-search topics.

Queens Borough Public Library
89-11 Merrick Blvd.
Jamaica, NY 11432
(718) 990-0746
Offers career counseling (no appointment needed), which includes a resume critique and introduction to the library's career services; holds monthly workshops on interview techniques and crafting resumes.

Westchester Library Systems
Educational Brokering Service
410 Saw Mill River Road
Ardsley, NY 10502
(914) 674-3600
Holds a biannual eight-week group counseling seminar at various library locations, which includes aptitude testing and a one-on-one session. Individual counseling is available sporadically. Half-hour resume clinics are also offered.

PRIVATE CAREER COUNSELORS

Career Mentors
989 6th Ave.
New York, NY 10010
(212) 947-3180
Programs are tailored to meet individual needs and combine consulting with homework over a period of 4 to 12 sessions at $100 per hour. Evening hours are available and initial consultation is free.

Crystal-Barkley Corporation
152 Madison Ave., 23rd Floor
New York, NY 10016
(800) 333-9003
The proprietary "life/work design" process allows individuals to assess their unique qualities and integrate personal and professional needs. The 40-hour course held over two weekends costs $1,400 and includes 5 hours of follow-up consultation. Counseling alone is also available at an hourly rate.

Downtown Professional Consultants
150 Broadway
New York, NY 10005
(212) 732-5570
Programs designed to assess interests, develop leadership abilities, sharpen interview skills, and write an effective resume.

The Five O'Clock Club
16 W. 16th St.
New York, NY 10011
(212) 255-6458
Voted "Top Career Expert" by *Fortune* magazine, Dr. James Borland provides

comprehensive services to executives, recent grads, freelancers, career changers, and entrepreneurs.

Heris, Toni
353 W. 56th St.
New York, NY 10019
(212) 245-6042
Counseling to begin, change, or advance career and deal with workplace issues. Sessions are $110 per hour.

Personnel Sciences Center
276 5th Ave., Suite 704
New York, NY 10001
(212) 683-3008
Initial 90-minute meeting, 12 hours of testing, and follow-up program is available for $450. Further consultations are $80/hr.

The Prager-Bernstein Group
441 Lexington Ave., Rm 1404
New York, NY 10017
(212) 647-0645
Offers a testing program, including 4 personality and vocational tests as well as counseling to assess skills, interests, experience, and accomplishments. Career transition management is also available, as are support groups. Fees are $100-125 per hour.

Remba, Claire, Associates
340 E. 93rd St.
New York, NY 10128
(212) 289-9478
A package of 6-8 sessions runs $90 per session, and evening and weekend hours are available.

Shapiro, Ruth, Associates
290 9th Ave., Suite 11A
New York, NY 10001
(212) 633-6149
Sessions run from $75-125 each; a 10-session program is available for career changers.

The Vocare Group
101 W. 55th St., Suite 13L
New York, NY 10019
(212) 581-5334
Career and life-transition counseling, testing and assessment, job-search and interview training.

Career Assistance at Colleges and Universities

Students often don't realize how much help is available through college and university career and placement centers. Career and placement centers provide assistance in choosing a program of study as well as career testing to current students. After graduation, many colleges and universities continue to work with alumni through their career centers. Check with your school and others to find out what's available and who is eligible for assistance.

While most colleges and universities don't permit the general public to use their counseling and placement services, some will offer programs to the public for a fee. The extent of assistance varies from campus to campus.

Some colleges and universities offer non-credit and credit courses as well as special lectures and seminars to help individuals prepare for the job hunt and explore options in the work world. In recent years, schools also have offered more practical courses that are designed to help individuals acquire job skills or brush up on ones they already have.

Try on a career with an internship

Internships are more popular today than ever before—with both new grads and seasoned workers interested in changing careers. It's a form of on-the-job training that lets both you and your employer determine your potential in a specific work environment.

If you're about to graduate, check the career services office at your college, where lists of available internships usually abound. If you're already in the workforce, get in touch with the same office at the college you attended or try the career offices in nearby colleges. When applying, be sure to stress what you can offer an organization and express your enthusiasm for the field.

For more information, look into resources listed in Chapter 8.

NEW YORK AREA COLLEGES OFFERING CAREER GUIDANCE

The International Association of Counseling Centers accredits college and university counseling centers and provides regional referrals. Contact them at 101 S. Whiting St., Suite 211, Alexandria, VA 22304, (703) 823-9840 for further information.

Brookdale Community College
Career Clinic

Newman Springs Road
Lincroft, NJ 07738
(908) 224-2581
Career counseling package includes 10 hours of testing, two interviews, and a written report for $295.

Columbia University Teacher's College
The Center for Psychological Services
525 W. 120th St.
New York, NY 10027
(212) 678-3262
The Center is a combined teaching, service, and research facility staffed by graduate students in psychology under the direct supervision of Teacher's College faculty. Career counseling is available on a low-cost sliding scale fee of $2-30.

Fairfield University
Fairfield, CT 06430
(203) 254-4000
Career counseling is available at $50/session and a series of three tests is $175. A half-hour free orientation describes the center's services.

Hofstra University Career Counseling Center
Saltzman Community Services Center, Room 120
Hempstead, NY 11550
(516) 463-6787
Career counseling and testing is offered for $360, which requires approximately 10 hours over a period of time and includes evaluation, testing, and review sessions.

LaGuardia Community College
Division of Adult and Continuing Education
31-10 Thomson Ave.
Long Island City, NY 11101
(718) 482-5300
Individual career counseling, resume preparation, job interview workshops.

Long Island University
University Center, Northern Blvd.
Greenvale, NY 11548
(516) 299-2000
Testing runs $25-50 and counseling is also available. Evaluation is free.

New York University
Career & Life Planning
50 W. 4th St., Room 327
New York, NY 10012
(212) 988-7060
Counseling is available at the rate of $60/hr. Testing is available at an additional charge.

State University of New York
Education Opportunity Center
470 Vanderbilt Ave.
Brooklyn, NY 11238
(718) 636-7900
Job assistance, counseling, outplacement, referrals.

Cybertips for career testing and counseling

Try this site to determine your Myers-Briggs (MBTI) type and to get more information on your MBTI personality type:

http://sunsite.unc.edu/jembin/mb.pl

For more information on personality types try:
http://www.yahoo.com/Science/Psychology/Personality/

Career Action Center (http://WWW.GATENET.COM/cac/) offers extensive services in interest and skills testing, test interpretation, and career counseling.

Tests of all kinds
(http://www.2h.com/Tests/personality.phtml) can be found on the Internet.

America On-Line and eWorld both provide career information and on-line career counseling services.

Social Service Agencies with Job Resources

Unlike independent career counselors and consultants, social service agencies are not-for-profit. They offer a wide range of services, from counseling and vocational training to job placement and follow-up, and their services are either low cost or free. Keep in mind, though, that a listing in this book does not constitute an endorsement of any agency.

The *New York City Greenbook* lists social service agencies.
http://www.pubadvocate.nyc.gov/~advocate/greenbook/greenbook.html

The Sourcebook: Social and Health Services in the Greater NY Area is compiled by United Way of New York City and published by Oryx Press, 1996.

Agudath Israel of America
84 William St.
New York, NY 10038
(212) 797-9000
Job counseling, professional
aptitude testing, job training,
and placement.

**American Institute for
Creative Living**
2295 Victory Blvd.
Staten Island, NY 10314
(718) 698-0300
Vocational and career counseling
on a sliding scale of $25-75.

Central Long Island Family
Counseling Services
226 Jericho Turnpike
Floral Park, NY 11101
(516) 354-8926

Federation Employment and
Guidance Service (FEGS)
114 5th Ave.
New York, NY 10011
(212) 366-8400

Flatbush Development Corp.
1035 Flatbush Ave.
Brooklyn, NY 11226
(718) 856-4600

Goodwill Industries of Greater NY
4-21 27th Ave.
Astoria, NY 11102
(718) 728-5400
http://www.ocgoodwill.org/
gii/good3.html

Jewish Board of Family and
Children's Services
120 W. 57th St.
New York, NY 10019
(212) 582-9100

Just One Break
373 Park Ave. S., 7th Floor
New York, NY 10016
(212) 725-2500
Vocational and career counseling for
disabled adults.

New York Urban League
204 W. 136th St.
New York, NY 10030
(212) 926-8000
http://drum.ncat.edu/~league/ul.html

New York Women's
Employment Center
45 John St., Suite 605
New York, NY 10038
(212) 964-8934

92nd St. YM-YWHA
1395 Lexington Ave.
New York, NY
(212) 996-1100

The Salvation Army
120 W. 14th St.
New York, NY 10011
(212) 337-7200
http://www.webnet.com.au/salvos/

Selfhelp Community Services
440 9th Ave.
New York, NY 10001
(212) 971-7600

Vera Institute of Justice
377 Broadway
New York, NY 10003
(212) 334-1300

Women's Counseling Center
of Queens
112-11 68th Drive
Forest Hills, NY 11375
(718) 268-3077

YMCA of Greater New York
333 7th Ave.
New York, NY
(212) 630-9600
http://www.interaccess.com/
users/dhayward/

YWCA
610 Lexington Ave.
New York, NY 10022
(212) 735-9728
http://www.pmedia.com/Avon/
ywca.html

YWCA of Brooklyn
30 3rd Ave.
Brooklyn, NY 11217
(718) 875-1190

YWCA of White Plains and
Central Westchester
515 N. White Plains Road
White Plains, NY 10603
(914) 949-6227

Career Change: Reality Bites

One morning you wake up, put on your $200 sunglasses, and head to work in your new Lexus. When you get to the office the doors are locked. To your surprise a sign on the door says "Filed for Bankruptcy." At this point you are probably saying, "I must be dreaming." Well, in today's work world, downsizing, mergers, and cost-cutting are all real—and sometimes reality bites!

Dramatic setbacks can often be your best opportunity for considering a career change. However, most people changing careers tend to believe they lack the skills for another career field. Maybe and maybe not. Self-assessment, defining your aptitudes and values, and possibly vocational testing can assist you in deciding on a career change.

There are three main reasons why people change careers:

1. A desire for a better fit among occupation, interests, and values is the primary reason that managers and professionals change careers. People want more career satisfaction and are usually willing to change careers to get it. Those who were coerced into that first career either by parents, misguided ambition, or lack of career information are highly likely to be dissatisfied. In time, they seek change.

2. Job loss. People that are laid off or fired make up a significant portion of those deciding to change careers rather than just replace the job that was lost. Appropriately, it is these people who may experience depression in their search because they feel they have been forced into the change.

3. A smaller group of career changers comprise those who at mid-career decide to turn a passion or hobby into an occupation.

The ability to transfer your skills is crucial in a career change. Many people feel their experience is only relevant to the previous job. In reality, most skills may be applied to a wide variety of jobs. Below are a number of commonly transferable skills. How many do you have?

administering	operating
analyzing	organizing
assisting	persuading
calculating	planning
creating	problem-solving
distributing	recommending
editing	researching
gathering	speaking
instructing	supervising
monitoring	trouble-shooting
motivating	writing

From customer service to fund-raising

After working for a year in customer service for a large retail chain, Sharon decided to make a career change when the company was faced with financial difficulties and had to downsize. Having been a music major in college, Sharon was not sure if she had acquired enough useful job skills to transfer into a new career. She became interested in a fund-raising job at a local university when one of her business contacts mentioned an opening in the development office.

"I volunteered for the annual tele-fund-raising campaign at the university to find out if I could handle development activities. I discovered that I really enjoyed the work. Best of all, many of my skills from my previous job, especially in communication, writing, and computer literacy, were well suited for it. I interviewed for the job and got it, with the additional help of a recommendation from my business contact."

Starting Your Own Business

Perhaps your self-assessment results lead you away from employment altogether and toward starting your own business. If so, a wealth of information is provided through the U.S. Small Business Administration, which provides free information on a variety of topics, including loan programs, tax preparation, government contracts, and management techniques. Although simple questions can be answered by telephone, you'll learn more by dropping by one of the main offices to meet with staff members or volunteers from SCORE (Service Corps of Retired Executives).

Small Business Administration
26 Federal Plaza
New York, NY 10278
(212) 264-4354
http://www.sbaon-line.sba.gov/
and
35 Pinelawn Road
Melville, NY 11747
(516) 454-0750
You can also contact Small Business Administration Web sites at:
http://www.sbaon-line.sba.gov

SMALL BUSINESS CENTERS

SCORE (Service Corps of Retired Executives) is a federally funded organization of retired executives who volunteer their time and expertise to assist small business owners. They, in turn, receive support and advice from ACE (Active Corps of Executives). SCORE has offices located at:

Small Business Administration
26 Federal Plaza
New York, NY 10278
(212) 264-4507
http://www.sbaon-line.sba.gov/business_management/score.html

Office of the Borough President, Room 333
120-55 Queens Blvd.
Kew Gardens, NY 11424
(718) 263-8961

400 County Seat Drive
Mineola, NY 11501
(516) 571-3303

The Small Business Administration also supports university small business development centers staffed by full-time professional consultants. One-on-one counseling is available to focus on business plan development.

http://www.smallbiz.sunycentral.edu/nysbdc.htm

Provides information on NY State small business development centers.

The following universities offer courses, seminars, workshops, and counseling designed to keep the small business owner informed of educational, economic, and research trends and developments.

Baruch College, City University of New York
360 Park Ave. S.
New York, NY 10010
(212) 802-6610

Bronx Community College
McCracken Hall
West 181st St. and University Ave.,
Room 14
Bronx, NY 10453
(718) 563-3570

Bronx Outreach Center
560 Cortlandt Ave.
Bronx, NY 10451
(718) 563-9204

Central Harlem Outreach Center
163 W. 125th St., Room 1307
New York, NY 10027
(212) 346-1900

College of Staten Island
2800 Victory Blvd.
Staten Island, NY 10314
(718) 982-2560

**Downtown Brooklyn
Outreach Center**
395 Flatbush Ave.
Brooklyn, NY 11201
(718) 260-9783

East Harlem Outreach Center
145 E. 116th St., 3rd Floor
New York, NY 10029
(212) 346-1900

Kingsboro Community College
2001 Oriental Blvd., Bldg. T4204
Brooklyn, NY 11235
(718) 368-4619

Mercy College
555 Broadway
Dobbs Ferry, NY 10522
(914) 674-7485

**New York University's Stern School
of Business**
44 W. 4th St., Room 5-61
New York, NY 10012
(212) 995-4404

Pace University
1 Pace Plaza, Room W483
New York, NY 10038
(212) 346-1900
Pace affiliates: West Harlem (212)
865-4299; East Harlem (212) 534-
2729. Offers an initial seminar and
one-on-one counseling.

Rockland Community College
145 College Road
Suffern, NY 10901
(914) 356-0370

Rutgers University
49 Bleecker St.
Newark, NJ 07102
(973) 353-5950

Small Business Resource Center
222 Bloomingdale Road, 3rd Floor
White Plains, NY 10605
(914) 644-4116

**State University College of
Technology**
2350 Route 110
Farmingdale, NY 11735
(516) 420-2765

State University of New York
Harriman School, Room 109
Stony Brook, NY 11794
(516) 632-9070
Holds and advertises seminars on an
as-needed basis.

Ulster County Community College
Business Resource Center
1 Development Court
Kingston, NY 12401
(800) 724-0833
Small Business Center:
(914) 339-0025

**York College, City University
of New York**
Small Business Development Center
94-50 159th St., Science Bldg.,
Room 107
Jamaica, Queens, NY 11451
(718) 262-2880

Business Resources for Women and Minorities

The following resources for women and minorities may also be of help. Refer to
the networking organizations listed in Chapter 5 for additional support groups
and information.

Women's Organizations: A New York City Directory is the most comprehensive
listing of women's organizations in New York City. It is published by The New

York City Commission on the Status of Women, located at 1 Centre St., Suite 2358 South, New York, NY 10007. The 200-page directory lists 400+ local women's organizations across a wide variety of categories including education, child care, counseling, employment, health, and many more. The Commission can be reached at (212) 788-2738.

Women's Web sites

http://www.sbaon-line.sba.gov/womeninbusiness/
is the SBA's homepage for women in business. Links are provided to the National Women's Business Council and other related sites.

http://www.intac.com/~kgs/bbpw/meta.html
lists sites related to businesswomen's issues and organizations, employment, and more.

http://www.igc.apc.org/womensnet/
links you to services and resources for women.

The following selection of organizations provides assistance specific to women-owned and minority-owned businesses:

Access for Women
New York City Technical College
300 Jay St., Room M-407
Brooklyn, NY 11201
(718) 260-5730
Vocational training program and information about career options in technical fields.

American Women's Economic Development Corp.
71 Vanderbilt Ave.
New York, NY 10169
(212) 692-9100
(800) 222-AWED
http://www.sbaon-line.sba.gov/business_management/score.html
Offers courses for all levels of business development and provides support services to help women sharpen their business skills. Counseling by business experts is available in person or by phone, and a special hotline service answers urgent questions. Financial aid is available.

Brooklyn Chamber of Commerce
7 Metrotech Center, Suite 2000
Brooklyn, New York 11201
(718) 875-1000
(718) 875-1003

http://www.columbia.edu/~gms18/chamber/Bklyn/bklyntoc.html
Contact: Georgia Karaban
The Minority and Women Business Development Committee holds seminars, provides information on procurement, and aids in shaping the Chamber's small-business agenda.

Empire State Development Corporation
633 3rd Ave.
New York, NY 10017
(212) 803-3100
Offers a variety of programs and services for minority- and women-owned businesses, including the following:
The Business Development and Lending Program provides financial, bonding, and technical assistance to state-certified businesses owned by women and minorities and low-interest loans and guarantees to construction firms: (212) 803-3618; contact Nicholas Torrens.
The Puerto Rican/Latino Business Development Center offers advice on government and private sector financing from legal, financial, and marketing experts. Also provides assistance in bidding for government contracts: (212) 803-3238; Director: Marcus Doron.

Fashion Institute of Technology Small Business Center
7th Ave. at 27th St., Room C110
New York, NY 10001
(212) 217-7250
Contact: Elaine Stone
Offers workshops for women and minorities to assist in the start-up of small businesses and to expand existing businesses.

National Association for Female Executives (NAFE)
135 W. 50th St., 16th Floor
New York, NY 10020
(212) 445-6235
Founded in 1972, NAFE is the oldest national women's business association. It has 200,000 members and functions as a networking and educational group for women executives in all phases of business. It offers a resume service and aptitude testing and publishes a bi-monthly magazine.

National Association of Women Business Owners, NY Chapter
245 5th Ave., Suite 2103
New York, NY 10016
(212) 779-7504
(516) 829-6060
Provides management and technical assistance, business contacts, leadership training, and advice on business strategies to advance women in their fields. Hosts monthly evening program and networking forum. Acts as a referral service.

New York City Department of Business Services
Minority- and Women-Owned Business Enterprise Program
110 Williams St., 2nd Floor
New York, NY 10038
(212) 513-6470
Provides minority- and women-owned business access to the full array of the
City's programs and their participation in the New York City procurement
process. Holds workshops, seminars, and conferences.

New York City Technical College
Access for Women
300 Jay St., M-407
Brooklyn, NY 11201
(718) 260-5730
Provides women with programs and support services to assist them in entering
non-traditional fields and trades.

New York State Department of Economic Development
163 W. 125th St., 17th Floor
New York, NY 10027
(212) 961-4100
The Minority and Women's Development Division certifies businesses as
minority- or women-owned, provides management and training seminars,
assists with financing, and advises on government contracts and international
trade. The Regional Technical Assistance Program provides free technical
assistance to loan applicants.

New York University Stern School of Business
44 W. 4th St., Room 561
New York, NY 10012
(212) 995-4404
Contact: Michelle Anton
The not-for-profit Urban Business Assistance Corporation provides low-cost
consulting services and education programs, including business plan development, marketing guides, and organizational analysis. Courses range from $45-80.

Non-Traditional Employment for Women
243 W. 20th St.
New York, NY
(212) 627-6252
Trains women with high school diplomas to establish a trade such as carpentry,
electronics, construction, and blue collar work.

Opportunity Program for Women
415 7th St.
Brooklyn, NY 11215
A community-based organization that provides free job-readiness programs,
career counseling, and vocational and education referrals to unemployed
women.

Small Business Administration
26 Federal Plaza, Room 3100
New York, NY 10278
(212) 264-1485
The SBA's 8A nine-year program for "socially disadvantaged" U.S. citizens serves as a middleman and helps procure contracts for small businesses. Contact the office for information on certification.

Suffolk County Office of Economic Development
Hauppauge Office Park, PO Box 6100
Hauppauge, NY 11788
(516) 853-4738
Contact: Sylvia Diaz
Provides services to assist with financing. Offers individual counseling, workshops, and seminars.

Women, Inc.
335 Madison Ave., 4th Floor
New York, NY 10017
(212) 503-7752
(800) 930-3993 (membership information)
A national non-profit organization designed to help improve the working environment for women business owners and those interested in starting a small business. A loan program is available for start-up and expanding businesses. Membership is $29/yr. and includes a business plan kit, discounts on business services, and special events and conferences.

Women's Advisory Board
The Chamber of Commerce and Industry
1 Battery Park Plaza
New York, NY 10004
(212) 493-7400
Fosters initiatives that will attract women to participate in the New York business community.

Women's Center for Education and Career Advancement
New York Women's Employment Center
45 John St., Suite 605
New York, NY 10038
(212) 964-8934
Contact: Carolyn Johnson
Offers career, personal development, and cultural workshops as well as skill development courses for members and the general public. Provides a network of career advisors and a free daytime program for displaced homemakers and single parents.

Great Books to Help You Figure Out Your Life

People who are entering the job market for the first time, those who have been working for one company for many years, and those who are considering a career change can usually use a little more help than we have supplied here, and certainly the more help the better. To get that little extra boost, we can refer you to some excellent books. If you have access to college resources, be sure to take advantage of the career libraries as well as the counseling and career planning services that are available on most campuses.

Cybertip: Buy books on-line

While the number of small independent bookstores seems to be declining, the number of large superstores is increasing. However, if you prefer to shop for your career books on-line, the number of on-line booksellers is also growing, and these booksellers can often get you those hard-to-find books you might have given up on. Try the following sites for on-line book sales:

http://www.amazon.com/
http://www.barnesandnoble.com/

CAREER STRATEGY BOOKS

Baldwin, Eleanor. *Three Hundred New Ways to Get a Better Job*. Holbrook, MA: Adams Publishing, 1991.

Beatty, Richard H. *Get the Right Job in 60 Days (or Less)*. New York: John Wiley & Sons, 1991.

Boldt, Laurence G. *Zen and the Art of Making a Living: A Practical Guide to Creative Career Design*. New York: Penguin Books, 1993.

Bolles, Richard N. *What Color Is Your Parachute?: A Practical Manual for Job-Hunters & Career-Changers*. Berkeley, CA: Ten Speed Press, 1997. The bible for job hunters and career changers, this book is revised every year and is widely regarded as one of the most useful and creative manuals on the market.

Bolles, Richard N. *The Three Boxes of Life and How to Get Out of Them: An Introduction to Life/Work Planning*. Berkeley, CA : Ten Speed Press, 1981.

Clawson, James G., et al. *Self Assessment and Career Development*. New York: Prentice-Hall, 1991. A very thorough guide with self-assessment worksheets and a good bibliography.

Criscito, Pat. *Resumes in Cyberspace: Your Complete Guide to a Computerized Job Search*. Woodbury, NY: Barrons Educational Series, 1997.

Dorio, Marc A. *The Complete Idiot's Guide to Getting the Job You Want*. New York: MacMillan General Reference, 1995.

Dubin, Judith A., and Melonie R. Keveles. *Fired for Success: How to Turn Losing Your Job into an Opportunity of a Lifetime*. New York: Warner Books, 1990.

Harkavy, Michael. *One Hundred One Careers: A Guide to the Fastest Growing Opportunities*. New York: John Wiley & Sons, 1990.

Jackson, Tom. *Guerrilla Tactics in the Job Market*. New York: Bantam Books, 1993. Filled with unconventional but effective suggestions.

Kanchier, Carole. *Dare to Change Your Job and Your Life*. Indianapolis, IN: Jist Works, Inc., 1996.

Kleiman, Carol. *Career Coach: Carol Kleiman's Inside Tips to Getting and Keeping the Job You Want*. Berkeley, CA: Berkeley Publishing Group, 1995.

Krannich, Ronald L. *Change Your Job, Change Your Life: High Impact Strategies for Finding Great Jobs in the 90's*. Manassas, VA: Impact Publications, 1997.

Morin, William J., and James C. Colvena. *Parting Company: How to Survive the Loss of a Job and Find Another Successfully*. New York: Harcourt Brace, 1991.

Munschauer, John L. *Jobs for English Majors and Other Smart People*. Princeton, NJ: Peterson's Guides, 1991.

Roper, David H. *Getting The Job You Want . . . Now: 50 Winning Moves for Spotting Hot Companies, Identifying Hiring Patterns, and Landing a Great Job*. New York: Warner Books, 1994.

Washington, Tom. *The Hunt: Complete Book to Effective Job Finding*. Bellevue, WA: Mount Vernon Press, 1992.

Weinstein, Bob. *Resumes Don't Get Jobs: The Realities and Myths of Job Hunting*. New York: McGraw-Hill, 1993.

Yate, Martin. *Jobs with a Future*. New York: Ballentine Books, 1997.

Yate, Martin. *Knock `Em Dead 1997: The Ultimate Job Seeker's Handbook* (10th ed.). Holbrook, MA: Adams Publishing, 1995.

Books for Students and Recent Graduates

Combs, Patrick. *Major in Success: Make College Easier, Beat the System, and Get a Very Cool Job*. Berkeley, CA : Ten Speed Press, 1995.

Farr, J. Michael. *America's Top Jobs for College Graduates*. Indianapolis, IN: Jist Works, Inc., 1996.

Fry, Ron. *Your First Job*. Hawthorne, NJ: Career Press, 1993.

Kravetz, Stacy. *Welcome to the Real World*. New York: Norton & Co., 1997.

Krueger, Brian D. *College Grad Job Hunter: Insider Techniques and Tactics for Finding a Top-Paying Entry Level Job*. Milwaukee, WI: Quantum Leap, 1997.

La Fevre, John L. *Resumes Don't Get Jobs; The Realities and Myths of Job Hunting: The Inside Story from a College Recruiter*. New York: Prentice-Hall, 1993.

Mitchell, Joyce Slayton. *The College Board Guide to Jobs and Career Planning.* Princeton, NJ: College Board, 1994.

Richardson, Bradley G. *Jobsmarts for Twenty-Somethings.* New York: Vintage Books, 1995.

Sears, Susan Jones. *Building Your Career: A Guide to Your Future.* Scottsdale, AZ: Holcomb Hathaway, 1995.

Steele, John, and Marilyn Morgan. *Career Planning & Development for College Students and Recent Graduates.* Lincoln, IL: VGM Career Horizons, 1991.

Sutcliffe, Andrea. *First Job Survival Guide.* New York: Owl Books, 1997.

Tolliver, Cindy, and Nancy Chambers. *Going Part-Time: The Insider's Guide for Professional Women Who Want a Career and a Life.* New York: Avon Books, 1997.

Books for Mid-Life Career Changers

Birsner, E. Patricia. *The Forty-Plus Job Hunting Guide: Official Handbook of the 40-Plus Club.* New York: Facts on File, 1997.

Byron, William J. *Finding Work Without Losing Heart: Bouncing Back from Mid-Career Job Loss.* Holbrook, MA: Adams Publishing, 1995.

Haldane, Bernard, and Peter F. Drucker. *Career Satisfaction and Success: A Guide to Job and Personal Freedom.* Indianapolis, IN: Jist Works, Inc., 1995.

Holloway, Diane, and Nancy Bishop. *Before You Say "I Quit": A Guide to Making Successful Job Transitions.* New York: MacMillan, 1990.

Logue, Charles H. *Outplace Yourself: Secrets of an Executive Outplacement Counselor.* Holbrook, MA: Adams Publishing, 1995.

Moreau, Daniel. *Kiplinger's Survive and Profit from a Mid-Career Change.* Washington, DC: Kiplinger Books, 1995.

Stevens, Paul. *Beating Job Burnout: How to Turn Your Work into Your Passion.* Lincoln, IL: VGM Career Horizons, 1996.

Books for Seniors and Retirees

Bird, Caroline. *Second Careers: New Ways to Work After 50.* New York: Little Brown, 1992.

Burkhardt, Margo. *How to Find a Job When You're over 50, Don't Have a Resume, and Don't Know What to Look For.* San Leandro, CA: Bristol Pub. Enterprises, 1991.

Kerr, Judy. *The Senior Citizen's Guide to Starting a Part-Time, Home-Based Business.* New York: Pilot Industries, 1992.

Strasser, Stephen, and John Sena. *Transitions: Successful Strategies from Mid-Career to Retirement.* Hawthorne, NJ: Career Press, 1990.

Books for People with Disabilities

Allen, Jeffrey. *Successful Job Search Strategies for the Disabled: Understanding the ADA.* New York: John Wiley & Sons, 1994.

Driedger, Diane. *Across Borders: Women with Disabilities Working Together.* Charlottetown, Prince Edward Island, Canada: Gynergy Books, 1996.

Hawking, Stephen. *Computer Resources for People with Disabilities: A Guide to Exploring Today's Assistive Technology* (2nd ed.). Alameda, CA: Hunter House, 1996.

Kissane, Sharon. *Career Success for People with Physical Disabilities.* Lincoln, IL: VGM Career Books Horizons, 1996.

Books for Women and Minorities

Littman, Barbara. *Women's Business Resource Guide.* Chicago: Contemporary Books, 1996.

Lunnenborg, Patricia. *Women Changing Work.* New York: Bergin & Garvey Publishers, 1990.

McKenna, Elizabeth Perle. *When Work Doesn't Work Anymore.* New York: Doubleday, 1997.

Thompson, Charlotte E. *Single Solutions—An Essential Guide for the Single Career Woman.* Brookline, MA: Branden Publishing, 1991.

Woods, James D., with Jay H. Lucas. *The Corporate Closet: The Professional Lives of Gay Men in America.* New York: MacMillan, 1994.

How to find real-time job openings

Daniel Lauber's "Job Finder" books describe in detail thousands of on-line and off-line sources for finding job vacancies. Besides information on general ads, each book includes job-listing periodicals, job hotlines, job-matching services, and salary surveys. Books cover "Professionals," "Non-Profits and Education," and "Government." All are published by: Planning/Communications, 7215 Oak Ave., River Forest, IL 60305; phone (708) 366-5200; fax (708) 366-5280.

three

If I Can't Find a Job, Should I Go Back to School?

" 'm having a real hard time finding a job. Maybe I'll just go back to school."
The rationale seems logical: more schooling equals better job. The facts,
however, don't always show the "more schooling" route to be the best one,
as we will discuss below. Sometimes, however, getting another degree or a
bit more education can make the difference between a job and a great career.

When To Go Back to School

Admittedly, additional education can enhance your marketability. But as you
weigh the pros and cons of committing time and money to the classroom, you
should never consider additional education a panacea for all of your career woes.

A myth people want to believe is that an advanced degree, a different degree,
or even a bit more education will automatically translate into a better job. People
considering law school or an MBA frequently fall prey to this myth. The reality is
that the job market is very tight, especially for lawyers, and employers are resis-
tant to hire people who may have entered a particular field on a whim and don't
have any real long-term commitment to the profession. It is less risky for employers to hire someone with a proven track record than someone with a new
advanced degree. Those pursuing graduate work in the liberal arts, not wishing
to teach, are also in for a big surprise when they realize that they often end up in
the same predicament they were in upon graduating with a B.A.: undecided upon
a career and having very few options.

Despite the negatives, though, there are several good reasons for returning to
school for additional education. These include:

To Acquire Additional Skills.
If you find that your skills are not keeping pace with the demands of your career, you may consider returning to school. Learning accounting, computer systems, or a foreign language, for example, may be the boost your career needs.

To Prepare for a Career Change.
Frequently, job changers will realize that they want to leave their current field altogether. If after talking with a career counselor, assessing your goals, and weighing your options, you decide that a career change is the right choice, additional education—a different degree—may be a requirement.

To Advance in Your Career.
For certain fields, such as investment banking, an MBA is necessary to advance. In other fields, the standards for additional education may be more subtle. Another degree or merely additional course work toward a degree may translate into a salary increase or consideration for a promotion.

Some people may be intimidated at the thought of acquiring additional education because they associate it with spent time and money. In reality, professional education can take many forms and carry a wide range of price tags. Other options to graduate school with varying cost-benefit trade-offs include community college courses, evening classes at a university, professional training for certification, or even executive education programs offered by many business schools. The bottom line is that when you consider additional education, do not limit your thinking only to formal degree programs at a university.

Tips on Considering Additional Schooling

There are many issues to consider before returning to school. First, determine how an additional degree or professional training will fit into your long-term goals. As you prepare to invest money, time, and energy on education, it is essential to know how you will benefit one year, five years, or even ten years later. Additionally, in order to select your best educational alternative, you must be able to articulate what benefit it will offer your career.

Second, many graduate schools require work experience before you can apply. For example, top business schools require two years of work experience. Thus, it is important to be familiar with the requirements of your proposed field of study.

Third, ask yourself whether you've really done your homework when weighing alternatives. Your watchword should be research. If you are changing career fields, avoid any post-degree surprises by researching the market, employment trends, and major employers. When evaluating professional training programs, be sure you have researched the schools to know who is offering accredited and respected courses. Make your decisions based on facts and figures and not on the suggestions of well-meaning friends and family members—and certainly not on the advice of admission representatives from graduate schools.

Finally, the biggest obstacle to returning for more education may be yourself. Saying that you're too old, you don't want to invest the money, or you don't want to take time off from your current job may merely be excuses to justify your refusal to take the plunge. Alternatively, you may have valid reasons for staying put for the time being. Be honest with yourself; only you can decide.

Law school at sixty—you're never too old!
One of our favorite stories is about a man who decided at the age of 60 to go to law school. "That will take three years," his friends and family moaned. "You'll be 63!" "So what?" Ed replied. "If I don't go to law school, in three years I'll still be 63." In Ed's way of thinking, he couldn't put three years to better use than to accomplish a lifelong goal.

In considering additional education, ask yourself, "If I do not choose to pursue additional education now, will I be satisfied with my career progress in a year?... five years?" This may be the best measure of how you might benefit from additional education.

Education and Income

Most of us have heard of the guy down the street who flunked out of college or failed to complete high school and is now a millionaire. *Forbes* magazine listed Bill Gates, a Harvard dropout and the founder of Microsoft computers, as the country's richest individual. In 1997 he had a net worth of $40 billion and counting. Howard Hughes flunked out of Rice University and still managed to gain genius status and amass an empire. The fact is that there are many such success stories among the not-so-educated.

What we don't hear are stories about the many failures. According to the Bureau of the Census, when salaries of all working people over the age of 25 were examined, on average those with the most education had the highest annual incomes. People who failed to enter high school averaged a salary of $15,223 a year. These figures include those with large amounts of experience. Those with less than a high school diploma but with some high school education increased on average to $18,012 per year, and high school graduates earned $23,410 per year.

In terms of income, even some college education is better than none. Americans who have completed some college average incomes of $27,705. Those completing a bachelor's or four-year degree earn an average of $35,900 per year, some $12,000 higher per year than the high school graduate.

Finally, there are those that strive for more than a bachelor's degree. For those who complete graduate, professional, or other college work beyond the bachelor's, the extra education will garner them an average of $43,032 per year. This will, of course, vary with the type of graduate study pursued. Law or medical school will almost certainly give you a higher income than one year of graduate study in a less marketable area.

Dear Dr. Bob

I recently heard that a doctor who is a general practitioner makes on average $117,000 a year and that internal medicine specialists make $181,000 a year. Should I change careers to become a doctor? Signed, Curious Career Changer

Dear Curious Career Changer

Certainly, becoming a doctor can seem like a wonderful choice. The drama of the emergency room, a good salary, knowing that you're making a difference in people's lives. However, you should consider the hard work, high cost, and many years it takes to become a doctor. Since there are three times as many applicants as there are slots for med school, I recommend exploring all your options in the medical field.

First, make sure that the health field is the field you are most interested in, then look into all the options. Options such as medical physics, physicians' assistants, pharmacy, and occupational and physical therapy are a few alternatives in the health field that may be a good fit and more time and cost effective for you.

However, don't do anything drastic! Being in medicine isn't exactly what you see on TV. You ought to talk to a few real health professionals or a career counselor before leaping into anything.

Getting Organized for Graduate School

If you decide that graduate or professional school is definitely what you need in your life and you've weighed the pros and cons, then get ready for the graduate school application process, which can be "The Nightmare on Elm Street."

However, organization can make your life much easier and good preparation can eventually land you in the school of your choice. Here are some tips to help you:

- Request application materials around September of the year prior to the year you want to enroll.
- Know each school's application time line (exam results, application due date, etc.).
- Establish a time frame for yourself, setting goals to complete tests and prepare paperwork and other relevant information well before the actual due date.
- Take practice tests, and learn what to expect on the tests, how answers are scored, whether you lose points for wrong answers, and so on.
- Take the actual tests.
- Forward exam results to selected schools.
- Get transcripts from schools attended.
- Obtain letters of recommendation.
- Write essays.
- Use certified mail to deliver materials to schools. This insures receipt of the materials by the school.
- Visit schools you are interested in attending, if possible.

Preparing for graduate school admissions tests

Graduate schools, law schools, and medical schools all require test scores before admitting anyone. The standardized tests include the GMAT (Graduate Management Admission Test), LSAT (Law School Admission Test), and MCAT (Medical College Admission Test). Prep courses can help ready you for these tests. Such courses help familiarize you with the contents of the tests and question types. They also offer strategies of test taking to help you improve your scores. Below are two services that provide test preparation courses.

Kaplan (1-800-KAP-TEST)
Princeton Review (1-800-2-REVIEW)

Selecting a Graduate School

Selecting a graduate school requires much consideration before committing money and two to three years of your life. The task of making the best selection in a graduate school is one that will have a significant impact on subsequent job placement, starting salary, and career potential. Here are some criteria to help in evaluating potential graduate schools: the school's reputation, both academically and among the employment community; curriculum, specialization(s), geographic location, department size, selectivity of admissions, faculty reputations and areas of expertise, and level of financial aid/support for students.

CYBERTIPS ON GRADUATE SCHOOLS

The Career Channel
http://riceinfo.rice.edu/projects/careers/
Provides information on graduate school application deadlines; rankings of top professional, medical, and graduate schools; test prep courses; and test examples.

CollegeNET Page for New York
http://www.collegenet.com:80/cn/geograph/ny.html
Find information about colleges and universities in New York, including
Web addresses.

Educational Testing Service
http://hub.terc.edu/ra/ets.html
Provides test dates.

Graduate & Professional Schools from the University of Virginia
http://minerva.acc.virginia.edu/~career/grdsch.html

Jobtrak
Offers advice on grad school: applying, testing, and financing; also has links to grad school sites by topic.

Peterson's Guide to Graduate and Professional Study
http://www.petersons.com/graduate
Links to over 1,500 universities on the Net that offer grad programs; arranged by geography.

The Best Graduate Programs for Your Success

There are many resources to help you select graduate programs such as *Peterson's Guides* and *Barron's Guide, Gorman's, Business Week's* annual "Best B Schools" edition and the follow-up book, and *U.S. News and World Reports'* issue on best graduate schools. All of these give some type of information on graduate schools.

We encourage you to look at all these sources. However, we have compiled a list, along with Web addresses, of programs from around the country that consistently show up at the top of national rankings. Additional lists outline programs in the professional, trade, and continuing studies areas available in this city and its environs.

The WWW addresses for business and law schools listed below will provide information on each university listed, its faculty and students, admission requirements, financial assistance, and general information about its graduate school. Entries are listed alphabetically and are not intended to imply any ranking.

TOP BUSINESS SCHOOLS

Harvard University
http://www.hbs.harvard.edu/

Massachusetts Institute of Technology (Sloan)
http://www-sloan.mit.edu/

Northwestern University
http://www.nwu.edu/graduate/

Stanford University
http://www-gsb.stanford.edu/index.html

University of Pennsylvania (Wharton)
http://www.wharton.upenn.edu/

TOP LAW SCHOOLS

Columbia University—New York City
http://www.janus.columbia.edu/

Harvard University Law School
http://www.law.harvard.edu/

Loyola University of Chicago
http://www.luc.edu/schools/law

Stanford University
http://www-leland.stanford.edu/group/law/

University of California—Los Angeles School of Law
http://www.law.ucla.edu

Yale University
http://www.yale.edu/lawweb/lawschool/ylshp.htm

Further Education in the New York Area

Below is a partial list of programs in the New York area. Most of the following graduate programs listed are nationally ranked in their field.

Columbia University
116th St. and Broadway
New York, NY 10027
(212) 854-1754
Medicine (preparatory program
for medical school also offered),
law, education (Teacher's College),
business, political science.

Cornell University
1300 York Ave.
New York, NY 10021
(212) 746-5454
Medicine.

CUNY Graduate School
33 W. 42nd St.
New York, NY 10036
(212) 642-1600
English, history.

Fordham University
E. Fordham Road
Bronx, NY 10458
(212) 636-6000
Graduate School of Social
Services, law.

Hofstra Univerity
200 Hofstra University
Hempstead, NY 11550
(516) 463-6600
Business administration; offers a
total of 88 Master's programs.

Hunter College
695 Park Ave.
New York, NY 10021
(212) 772-4000
Social work, urban planning.

Long Island University
University Center, Northern Blvd.
Greenvale, NY 11548
(800) LIU-PLAN
Pharmacy, taxation.

New School for Social Research
66 W. 12th St.
New York, NY 10011
(212) 229-5600
Political and social science,
management, and urban policy.

New York University
32 Washington Place
Washington Square

New York, NY 10003
(212) 998-1212
Law, business (Stern College).

Pace University
1 Pace Plaza
New York, NY 10038
(212) 346-1200
Business, law, computer science, and
information systems.

Queens College
65-30 Kissena Blvd.
Flushing, NY 11367
(718) 997-4455
Biology, chemistry, biochemistry.

Rutgers University
New Brunswick, NJ 08903
(908) 445-3770
Engineering, law, political science.

Sarah Lawrence College
1 Meadway
Bronxville, NY 10708
(914) 395-2510
Women's history, health advocacy.

**State University at Stony Brook
(SUNY)**
Nicolls Road
Stonybrook, NY 11794
(516) 689-6000
Ecology and evolution, math, physics.

St. John's University
Grand Central and Utopia Parkways
Jamaica, NY 11439
(718) 990-1865
Psychology, business, pharmacy
(largest school in the country).

VOCATIONAL/TRADE SCHOOLS IN THE NEW YORK AREA

If you need to update your skills, such as computing or accounting, you may want
to consider an apprenticeship program. An apprenticeship program is less costly
than a full-time graduate program and may provide just the current skills you need.

If you want to try a new career such as chef, real estate agent, or medical assistant, vocational schools can provide the skills necessary. Below are a few resources for vocational schools in the New York area.

Job Information Center
Mid-Manhattan Library
455 5th Ave., 2nd Floor
New York, NY 10017
TRAIN, a computerized on-line database of educational and vocational training programs, provides a comprehensive and easily accessible listing of program information for public and private agencies throughout New York City.

The Vocational Foundation
902 Broadway
New York, NY
(212) 777-0700
Publishes *Vocational Training in New York City: Where to Find It.*

Career Success (Target Marketing, Liberty, MO) is a newsletter covering vocational career opportunities, job outlook, and financial aid. Also see *Vocational Careers Sourcebook* (Gale Research, Detroit, MI) and *American Trade Schools Directory* (Croner Publications, Jericho, NY), which organizes trade schools geographically and has a special section for New York City, arranged by borough as well as by subject.

NEW YORK CITY'S TOP TRADE SCHOOLS

American Institute of Banking
80 Maiden Lane
New York, NY 10038
(212) 349-8440

Berlitz Language Center
40 W. 51st St.
New York, NY 10022
(212) 765-1000

Carpenters Apprenticeship School
395 Hudson St.
New York, NY 10014
(212) 727-2224

Center for Book Arts
626 Broadway, 5th Floor
New York, NY 10012
(212) 460-9768

Christine Valmy International School
437 5th Ave.
New York, NY 10016
(212) 779-7800
Beauty, cosmetology.

Culinary Center of NY
100 Greenwich Ave.
New York, NY 10011
(212) 255-4141

Dun & Bradstreet—Business Education Division
99 Church St.
New York, NY 10007
(800) 445-1382
http://www.dnb.com/
Accounting, sales training.

Evening School of World Trade
One World Trade Center, 55W
New York, NY 10011
(212) 435-2558
Banking, stock market trading, foreign trade, business management.

French Culinary Institute
462 Broadway
New York, NY 10013
(212) 219-8890
http://plaza.interport.net/fci/

H&R Block Income Tax School
370 7th Ave.
New York, NY 10001
(212) 594-5480
http://www.gate.net/~gwieser/
hrbhome.html

Hill School of Insurance
139 Fulton St.
New York, NY 10038
(212) 732-1468

Institute of Allied Medical Professionals
405 Park Ave.
New York, NY 10010
(212) 758-1410
Medical imaging.

Institute of Design and Construction
141 Willoughby
Brooklyn, NY
(718) 855-3661
Architecture, engineering, building construction, drafting.

Interboro Institute
450 W. 56th St.
New York, NY 10019
(212) 399-0091
Accounting, business management, optical assistants.

International Bartending School
500 8th Ave.

New York, NY 10018
(800) TOP-BARS
http://www.bartending.com/

Jean Louis David Training Center
141 E. 61st. St.
New York, NY 10022
(212) 838-8303
Hair cutting.

New York Food and Hotel Management School
154 W. 14th St.
New York, NY 10011
(212) 675-6655

New York Real Estate Institute
347 5th Ave.
New York, NY 10010
(212) 683-5518

New York School of Dog Grooming
248 E. 34th St.
New York, NY 10016
(800) 541-5541

New York School of Interior Design
170 E. 70th St.
New York, NY 10021
(212) 472-1500

New York School for Medical and Dental Assistants
116-16 Queens Blvd.
Forest Hills, NY
(718) 793-2330

On the Record School of Reporting
225 Broadway
New York, NY 10007
(212) 571-2004
Court reporting.

Peter Kump's New York Cooking School
307 E. 92nd St.
New York, NY 10128
(212) 410-4601

Technical Career Institute
320 W. 31st St.
New York, NY 10001
(212) 594-4000

Travel Institute
15 Park Row
New York, NY 10038
(212) 349-3331

CONTINUING EDUCATION PROGRAMS IN THE NEW YORK AREA

Many professionals opt to take short courses in specific technology to stay abreast of their field. Some fields, such as nursing, require a certain amount of course-work each year to maintain a license. And for all of us, education is a personally enriching lifelong process. Whatever the reason, there are many good continuing education classes being offered. Below are a few schools providing continuing education courses.

Adelphi University—Main Campus
South Ave.
Garden City, NY 11530
(516) 877-3400
http://www.adelphi.edu/
Offers the ABLE program for working adults 21 years and older to earn an undergraduate degree by attending evening and weekend courses.

Baruch College Continuing Studies
17 Lexington Ave.
New York, NY 10010
(212) 802-5600
http://bbweb.sitea.baruch.cuny.edu/

Bergstraum Adult Education Center
411 Pearl St.
New York, NY 10038
(212) 233-1533
Business, computer, languages, real estate, self-improvement.

Bronx Community College
181st and University Ave.
Bronx, NY 10453
(718) 220-6424
Continuing education and certificate programs in computers and electronics.

Columbia University
116th St. and Broadway
New York, NY 10027
(212) 854-2820
http://www.cc.columbia.edu/
Offers continuing education and certificate programs.

Cooper Union Continuing Education
130 Cooper Square
New York, NY 10003
(212) 353-4195
http://www.cooper.edu/
Arts, design & technology, languages.

Fashion Institute of Technology
227 W. 27th St.
New York, NY 10001
(212) 217-7675
Offers Associate-level programs and competency-based certificate programs.

Iona College
715 North Ave.
New Rochelle, NY 10801
(914) 633-2590
Offers certificate programs in medical coding, legal assistance, insurance, and certified employee benefits.

LaGuardia Community College
Division of Adult and Continuing Education
31-10 Thomson Ave.
Long Island City, NY
(718) 482-7244

Long Island University
University Center, Northern Blvd.
Greenvale, NY 11548
(516) 299-2238
http://www.liunet.edu/
Offers a large number of continuing education courses and certificate programs, including financial planning, real estate, art and antiques, and more.

New School for Social Research
66 W. 12th St.
New York, NY 10011
(212) 229-5600
http://dialnsa.edu/homenice.html
Offers over 800 courses; certificate programs available in 10 subjects, including film production, graphics and desktop publishing, computers in business, and culinary arts. Offers on-line education program which enables students to "attend" courses via computer conferencing.

New York University
School of Continuing Education
32 Washington Place
Washington Square

New York, NY 10003
(212) 998-7080
http://www.nyu.edu/
Offers more than 2,000 courses, 100 certificate programs, and advanced professional certificates; also sponsors free career nights covering a variety of topics.

NY Institute of Finance
2 Broadway, 5th Floor
New York, NY 10004
(212) 859-5000
http://nestegg.iddis.com/nestegg/nyif/catalog/homepage.html
coursecat_pubnyif@prenhall.com
Courses and executive seminars; licensing preparation, independent study, and certificate programs.

Pace University
Adult Resource Center
1 Pace Plaza
New York, NY 10038
(212) 346-1288
http://www.pace.edu/

Pratt Institute
200 Willoughby Ave.
Brooklyn, NY 11205
(718) 636-3453
Offers a wide range of continuing education courses, including computers, art, and interior design. Offers a 2-year Associate Certificate program.

Queens College
Mid-Manhattan Extension Center
25 W. 43rd St.
New York, NY
(212) 633-1646 (24 hrs.)
(212) 633-1717
http://www.cs.qc.edu/Queens/
Broad liberal arts, labor, and urban studies.

St. John's University
Grand Central and Utopia Parkways
Jamaica, NY 11439
(718) 990-6101
http://sjuvm.stjohns.edu/index.html
Offers certificate programs in computers, recreation and health, real estate, health care, small business management, medical billing, and health management; continuing education courses also available.

St. Joseph's College
265 Clinton Ave.
Brooklyn, NY 11205
(718) 399-0068
Offers degrees and certificates in human resource management, community health, health administration, and nursing. Classes in Brooklyn, Queens, Staten Island, Nassau, and Suffolk are available days, evenings, and weekends.

On-line Education

No need to pack those bags or leave your job and friends to head off for school. Today's technology brings the teachers, ideas, books, and dialogue to the student electronically. The advantages are that correspondence study is dependable, low cost, and can be done anywhere. Still it is important to check out what credits, degree, or credentials you may receive. Additionally, consider all costs associated with on-line education and don't forget to inquire about financial aid.

Although on-line education is convenient, some people may not do well outside a typical classroom environment where you see the teacher and take part in dialogue. Think about the kind of study environment that works best for you. It is also important to note that the field of on-line education is constantly changing, and new possibilities certainly will pop up after the publication of this book.

If you would like to learn more about on-line or long-distance learning programs, the following resource can assist you:

The National University Continuing Education Association (NUCEA) provides comprehensive guides to long-distance learning ranging from correspondence programs to programs delivered through various electronic media. Contact them at One Dupont Circle, Suite 615, Washington, DC 20036, (202) 659-3130, www.nucea.edu

Also, check out the following books and on-line resource:
Bear, John and Mariah. *Bear's Guide to Earning College Degrees Non-traditionally.* Bericia, CA: C & B Publishing, 1997.
Dixon, Pam. *Virtual College.* Princeton, NJ: Peterson's Guides, 1996.
Duffy, James P. *How to Earn a College Degree without Going to College.* New York: John Wiley & Sons, 1994.
The Electronic University: A Guide to Long-distance Learning Programs. Princeton, NJ: Peterson's Guides, 1993.
Peterson's Guide to Independent Study. Princeton, NJ: Peterson's Guides, 1992.
Yahoo—Distance Learning
    http://www.yahoo.com/Education/Distance_Learning/

Did you know that you can also take courses offered by certified teachers and professional experts on-line? Typical courses offered include: History, English,

Sociology, Languages, Math, Science, the Arts, and Computer Science. However, no college credit or certificates are awarded for these courses. For further information contact The Electronic University Network (Sarah Blackmun, Director of Instruction, 1977 Colestin Rd., Hornbrook, CA 96044, (415) 221-7061). This network consists of organizations that work with groups of colleges to provide long-distance learning programs.

College credit by Internet

The following site has links to all SUNY and CUNY schools:

http://bio444.beaumont.plattsburgh.edu/
SUNYInternetResources.html

This site has pages on schools offering continuing education, vocational schools, electronic courses, and executive development programs:

http://www.petersons.com

four

The 10-Step Job Search

Almost everything can be broken down into steps. The job search is no different. If you take the process one step at a time and follow our basic rules, you are more likely to find a job. As you begin, it is important to remember that you are in control, and in the end it is you who must land the job. To get there you need to be proactive; companies will not come looking for you. Rather, you have to search out the companies, the jobs, and the people that are in a position to hire.

The 10-Step Job Search

1. Know Thyself—Where Are You Going?
2. Research the Job Market.
3. Organize Your Search.
4. Network.
5. Persistence and Follow-Up.
6. Prepare Your Resume.
7. Mail Your Resume.
8. Use Your Career Resources.
9. The Killer Interview.
10. Make Sure This Is the Job for You.

Step 1: Know Thyself—Where Are You Going?

Hopefully, Chapter 2 has set you on the right path to choosing a career. To get somewhere you need to decide where it is you are going, what you want to do, and what you are capable of doing. Other items to assess include the characteristics of your ideal work environment, the type of experience you wish to gain from the job, and how much money you intend to make. To a large extent, your happiness with your job coincides with how closely it meets your needs and motivates you.

Once you've answered these questions you will be able to articulate why you are interviewing for a particular position and why you are right for that position.

Step 2: Research the Job Market

The alarm clock rings, and you slowly get out of bed and head downstairs for your morning jolt of java along with the want ads from the daily paper. Tempted to read the comics, you resist the urge and resume your job search with the want ads. After all, this is how people find jobs. Wrong! According to *Forbes* magazine, only about 10 percent of professional and technical people find their jobs through want ads.

Your best bet is not to send a resume to every ad in the paper. Instead, try to identify who's hiring and where the opportunities may be. How do you learn these things? Research.

Libraries

Libraries provide vast amounts of resources for job searching, ranging from company information (ranking, annual sales, product information, number of employees, who's running the show) to resume writing guides, business newspapers and magazines, salary statistics, and, of course, directories such as *Standard and Poor's Register of Corporations, Directors, and Executives*. To save precious time in your research, the reference desk is invaluable in locating materials for your job search.

Local university and community college libraries may also offer resources for job seekers. Many local schools have reference libraries that are well equipped with career resource information and job directories that you can use even if you are not an alumnus. Some libraries also offer vocational testing and career guidance, often in conjunction with the school's career planning office.

TOP THREE BUSINESS LIBRARIES

The three most useful libraries, each housing a wealth of information on business and career resources, are:

The Central Research Library/Center for the Humanities
5th Avenue at 42nd St.
New York, NY 10018
(212) 930-0830
http://gopher.nypl.org/research/research.html
The General Research Division stores 88 miles of shelves beneath the Main Reading Room with over two million volumes. The public Catalog Room

contains on-line catalogs, CD-ROM databases and Internet access (free of charge). The Economic and Public Affairs Divisions contains a large selection of business databases and CD-ROMs as well as access to on-line sources such as Lexis/Nexis. It also houses 11,000 current periodical titles, including virtually every major business journal published in the Western World.

The Mid-Manhattan Library
455 5th Ave. (at 40th St.)
New York, NY 10018
(212) 340-0833
http://gopher.nypl.org/branch/central_units/mm/midman.html
The library now has computers with Internet access and E-mail capability on every floor. The Job Information Center, located on the 2nd floor, offers business directories and industry-specific career directories as well as books on resume writing and job-search strategies. Seminars and workshops are often offered on topics such as resume writing, job hunting, and dealing with job-search stress.

Science, Industry and Business Library (SIBL)
188 Madison Ave. at 34th St.
New York, NY 10016
http://gopher.nypl.org/research/sibl/index.html
SIBL is the world's largest public information center devoted solely to science and business. Library technology includes CD-ROMs and on-line services, as well as access to electronic databases, journals, and bulletin boards via 100 networked workstations which feature ABI/Inform, General Business File, and Dun & Bradstreet's *Million Dollar Directory* with business and financial data, among many others. An electronic training center is available to educate the public in the use of electronic resources. While 500 seats are wired for laptop connections, SIBL is also designed to be a "library without walls"; 24-hour dial-in remote access and e-mail allows off-site users to search for, access, and request library material.

CYBERRESEARCH AT NEW YORK AREA LIBRARIES

The following WWW addresses provide general information on library programs, references and abstracts from journals and books, and much more. For a longer list of Internet job resources, see the section on "Internet Job Listings" farther on in this chapter.

CUNY Libraries
http://www.panix.com/clay/nyc/libraries.html
Provides links to a directory of all CUNY libraries, among other library sites.

Libraries on the Web (compiled by University of Washington)
http://weber.u.washington.edu/~tdowling/libweb/usa.html
An extensive list of national and international library Web sites.

The Mid-Manhattan Library
http://gopher.nypl.org/branch/central_units/mm/midman.html

New York Public Libraries
http://gopher.nypl.org/
Provides links to the New York Public Library, branch and neighborhood
libraries, and the research libraries.

New York City University Libraries
(gopher://metro.org:70/11/region)
Lists and provides links to all of New York City's university libraries on the
Internet.

Science, Industry and Business Library
http://gopher.nypl.org/research/sibl/index.html

Queens Borough Public Library
gopher://vax.queens.lib.ny.us/

OTHER LIBRARIES WITH JOB INFORMATION CENTERS

Bronx Public Library
2556 Bainbridge Ave.
Bronx, NY 10458
(718) 579-4200

Brooklyn Public Library
280 Cadmen Plaza West
Brooklyn, NY
(718) 722-3333
Brooklyn's main business library.

Brooklyn Public Library
Grand Army Plaza
Eastern Parkway at Flatbush Ave.
(718) 780-7777
Brooklyn, NY 11201

Nassau County Public Library
Hempstead Branch
115 Nichols Court
Hempstead, NY 11550
(516) 481-6990

Queens Borough Public Library
89-11 Merrick Blvd.
Jamaica, NY 11432
(718) 990-0746

Westchester Library System
(914) 674-3600
Consists of 38 branch libraries, 14 of which have job information centers.

Directories

Directories provide you with corporate structures, company financial figures, company rankings, best companies to work for, best places to live, who's making what salary, and top careers. When you're beginning your homework, whether you're researching an entire industry or a specific company, there are four major directories with which you should be familiar.

OUR FOUR FAVORITE DIRECTORIES

The Directory of Corporate Affiliations (National Register Publishing, New Providence, NJ) is an organized business reference tool covering public and private businesses in the U.S. and throughout the world. This six-volume directory allows the user to examine the parent company and all subsidiaries of the parent company, categorized by geographic area or S.I.C. (Standard Industrial Classification) codes that identify the company's product or service. If you want to know the corporate reporting structure, the company's subsidiaries, or the company's banking, legal, or outside service firms, this is the directory to use.

Standard and Poor's Register of Corporations, Directors, and Executives (Standard and Poor's Publishing, 25 Broadway, New York, NY 10004) is billed as the "foremost guide to the business community and the executives who run it." This three-volume directory lists more than 50,000 corporations and 70,000 officers, directors, trustees, and other bigwigs.

Each business is assigned an S.I.C. number. Listings are indexed by geographic area and also by S.I.C. number, so it's easy to find all the companies in a local area that produce, say, industrial inorganic chemicals.

You can also look up a particular company to verify its correct address and phone number, its chief officers (that is, the people you might want to contact for an interview), its products, and, in many cases, its annual sales and number of employees. If you have an appointment with the president of XYZ Corporation, you can consult Standard and Poor's to find out where he or she was born and went to college—information that's sure to come in handy in an employment interview. Supplements are published in April, July, and October.

Ward's Business Directory of U.S. Private and Public Companies (Gale Research Inc., New York, NY) is the leading source for hard-to-find information on private companies. This six-volume publication lists more than 142,000 companies in alphabetic, geographic, and industry arrangements. It also provides rankings and analyses of the industry activity of leading companies. If you want to determine parent/subsidiary relationships, merger and acquisition positions, or general information on private and public companies, this is the directory to use.

The Million Dollar Directory (Dun & Bradstreet, 3 Century Drive, Parsippany, NJ 07054) is a three-volume listing of approximately 160,000 U.S. businesses with a net worth of more than half a million dollars. Listings appear alphabetically, geographically, and by product classification and include key personnel. Professional and consulting organizations such as hospitals and engineering services, credit agencies, and financial institutions other than banks and trust companies are not generally included.

So much for our favorite directories. The following listings contain more than 30 additional directories and guides that may come in handy. Many of these, as well as other directories, are available at area libraries.

NATIONAL/REGIONAL DIRECTORIES

Be sure to check out the industry-specific directories listed with each employment category in Chapter 10.

American Almanac of Jobs and Salaries
Avon Books
1350 Ave. of the Americas
New York, NY 10019
Information on wages for specific occupations and job groups, many of which are professional and white collar. Also presents trends in employment and wages.

American Salaries and Wages Survey
Gale Research Co.
835 Penobscot Building
Detroit, MI 48226
Detailed information on salaries and wages for thousands of jobs. Data is subdivided geographically.

Brands and Their Companies
Gale Research Co.
835 Penobscot Building
Detroit, MI 48226
Index of more than 200,000 trade, brand, product, and design names.

Business Organizations, Agencies, & Publications Directory
Gale Research Co.
835 Penobscot Building
Detroit, MI 48226
Lists contact and descriptive information to guide users to more than 30,000 business-related information resources, associations, chambers of commerce, government agencies, and publications.

Career Guide: Dun's Employment Opportunities Directory
Dun and Bradstreet
3 Sylvan Way
Parsippany, NJ 07054
Employment information on companies with at least 1,000 employees, including hiring practices and disciplines hired geographically.

College Placement Annual
College Placement Council Directory
62 Highland Ave.
Bethlehem, PA 18017
Occupational needs of more than 2,300 corporations and government employers.

Corporate Technology Directory—High-Tech Firms
Corporate Technology Information Services
12 Alfred St., Suite 200
Woburn, MA 01801
Profiles of high-tech corporations, including address, phone, ownership, history, brief description, sales, number of employees, executives, and products. Indexed by company names, geography, technology, and product.

Dictionary of Occupational Titles
U.S. Dept. of Labor
200 Constitution Ave., N.W.
Washington, DC 20210
Occupational information on job duties and requirements; describes almost every conceivable job.

Directories in Print
Gale Research Co.
835 Penobscot Building
Detroit, MI 48226
Contains detailed descriptions of all published directories: what they list, who uses them, and who publishes them.

Directory of Companies Required to File Reports with the SEC
U.S. Securities and Exchange Commission
450 5th St., N.W.
Washington, DC 20549
To find out if shares of stock in a company are publicly traded.

Directory of Foreign Manufacturers in the U.S.
Georgia State University Business Press
35 Broad St.
Atlanta, GA 30303
About 10,000 companies in the United States that have 10 percent or more foreign ownership.

Directory of Leading Private Companies
National Register Publishing Co.
New Providence, NJ
Profiles about 7,000 large private firms whose annual sales are more than $10 million.

Directory of Publications
Gale Research Co.
835 Penobscot Building
Detroit, MI 48226
Lists national, local, and trade magazines alphabetically and by state.

Dun and Bradstreet State Sales Guide
Dun and Bradstreet
430 Mountain Road
New Providence, NJ 07974
Covers all businesses in each state that are included in Dun and Bradstreet's
Reference Book.

Employment Outlook 1994–2005
U.S. Department of Labor's Bureau of Labor Statistics
200 Constitution Ave., N.W.
Washington, DC 20210
Detailed projections of the U.S. economy and labor force.

Encyclopedia of Associations
Gale Research Co.
835 Penobscot Building
Detroit, MI 48226
Directory of state and national associations, indexed by topic, key word,
organization name, and geography.

Encyclopedia of Business Information Sources
Gale Research Co.
835 Penobscot Building
Detroit, MI 48226
Lists each industry's encyclopedia, handbooks, indexes, almanacs, yearbooks,
trade associations, periodicals, directories, computer databases, research centers,
and statistical sources.

Engineering, Science, and Computer Graduates: Peterson's Job Opportunities
Peterson's Guides
202 Carnegie Center
Princeton, NJ 08543
Lists specific companies within these industries.

Fortune Double 500 Directory
Time, Inc.
Time & Life Building
Rockefeller Building, Rockefeller Center
New York, NY 10020
Lists the 500 largest and the 500 second-largest industrial corporations, along
with the 500 largest commercial banks, utilities, life insurance companies,
diversified financial companies, retailers, transportation companies, and
diversified services.

Job Openings—Publication #510K
Consumer Information Center, Dept. G
Pueblo, CO 81009
Free 80-page booklet, revised monthly, highlights occupations with large
numbers of openings and indicates where they are located.

Job Seeker's Guide to Private and Public Companies
Gale Research Co.
835 Penobscot Building
Detroit, MI 48226
Lists over 15,000 firms, including products and services, size, human resource
contacts, and application procedures.

National Directory of Minority-Owned Business Firms
Business Research Services
4201 Connecticut Ave., N.W., Suite 610
Washington, DC 20008
Lists company name, size, description, and address.

National Directory of Women-Owned Business Firms
Business Research Services
4201 Connecticut Ave., N.W., Suite 610
Washington, DC 20008
Lists company name, size, description, and address.

National Trade & Professional Associations of the United States
Columbia Books
1212 New York Ave., N.W., Suite 330
Washington, DC 20005
Alphabetical profiles of associations, including address, phone, affiliations,
history, publications, meetings, and annual budget. Indexed by subject,
geography, budget, and acronym.

Occupational Outlook Handbook
U.S. Department of Labor's Bureau of Labor Statistics
200 Constitution Ave., N.W.
Washington, DC 20210
Describes what people do in their jobs, training and education needed,
earnings, working conditions, and employment outlook.

Occupational Outlook Quarterly
U.S. Department of Labor's Bureau of Labor Statistics
200 Constitution Ave., N.W.
Washington, DC 20210
Gives an overview of the outlook for different sectors of the economy and
individual occupations.

State and Metropolitan Area Data Book
U.S. Department of Commerce
The Herbert C. Hoover Building

14th St. and Constitution Ave., N.W.
Washington, DC 20230
Compiles statistical data from many public and private agencies. Includes
unemployment rates, rate of employment growth and population growth for
every state. Also presents a vast amount of data on employment and income for
metropolitan areas across the country.

Ward's Business Directory of U.S. Private and Public Companies
Gale Research Co.
835 Penobscot Building
Detroit, MI 48226
Covers nearly 85,000 privately owned companies, representing all industries.

Who Owns Whom: North American Edition
Dun & Bradstreet
430 Mountain Road
New Providence, NJ 07974
Shows the ownership of subsidiaries and associate companies and how they fit
into their parent groups.

DIRECTORIES WITH LOCAL DATA

Burrelle's New York Media Directory
Burrelle's Information Systems
75 E. Northfield Road
Livingston, NJ 07039
Print and electronic media companies in New York.

Dalton's New York Metropolitan Directory of Business and Industry
410 Lancaster Ave.
Haverford, PA 19041
(800) 221-1050
15,000 firms in Manhattan, Bronx, Queens, Brooklyn, Nassau, Suffolk, and
Putnam counties as well as Hudson, Essex, and Bergen counties in NJ.

Hoover's Guide to Top New York Companies
Hoover's, Inc.
1033 la Posada Drive, Suite 250
Austin, TX 78752
(800) 486-8666
1,350 leading public and private New York City companies.

Industrial Directory—New York State
Harris InfoSource International
2057 Aurora Road
Twinsburg, OH 44087
(800) 888-5900
Lists nearly 11,000 companies in New York, their product or service, gross sales,
imports and exports.

Long Island Business/Long Island Executive Register Issue
Long Island Business News
2150 Smithtown Ave.
Ronkonkoma, NY 10779
(516) 737-1700
Lists over 3,000 Long Island-based government agencies, corporations, non-profits, trade and professional organizations, minority and women's business groups, and labor unions.

Long Island Business/Tech Directory Issue
Long Island Business News
2150 Smithtown Ave.
Ronkonkoma, NY 10779
(516) 737-1700
969 high-tech companies, laboratories, and universities.

Metro New York Directory of Manufacturers
Commerce Register Inc.
190 Godwin Ave.
Midland Park, NJ 07432
(800) 221-2172
7,000 industrial firms with 6+ employees in New York, Orange, Putnam, Rockland, and Westchester counties.

NYNEX Fast Track Digital Directory
NYNEX Information Technologies
100 Church St.
New York, NY 10017
(212) 513-9405
Ten CD-ROMs covering 100 million businesses and residences.

New York Business Directory
American Business Directories
5711 S. 86th Circle
Omaha, NE 69127
(800) 555-6124
http://www.abii.com
Lists 734,000 businesses in New York state; Volume 1 covers New York City. Lists name, address, phone, number of employees, name of owner or manager, and sales volume. Available on-line through Business America Online.

New York Publicity Outlets
Public Relations Plus
Box 1197
New Milford, CT 06776
(800) 999-8448
New York consumer media including 300 radio/TV/cable stations, 900 radio and TV interview shows, 475 daily and weekly newspapers, 1,150 consumer magazines, and 65 ethnic media outlets.

Trade Magazines

Every industry or service business has its trade press—that is, editors, reporters, and photographers whose job it is to cover an industry or trade. You should become familiar with the magazines of the industries or professions that interest you, especially if you're in the interviewing stage of your job search. Your prospective employers are reading the trade magazines; you should too.

Many of the magazines we've included are available at the libraries listed earlier in this chapter. Most of the following magazines have editorial offices in the area, reporting area news about the people and businesses in their industry. The majority carry local want ads and personnel changes. Additional trade magazines are listed in Chapter 10 under specific career categories. For a complete listing of the trade press, consult the *Ayer Directory of Publications* at the library.

REGIONAL TRADE MAGAZINES

ABA Banking Journal
345 Hudson St.
New York, NY 10014
(212) 620-7200

Across the Board
The Conference Board
845 3rd Ave.
New York, NY 10022
(212) 339-0451
Business management magazine.

Adweek/East
1515 Broadway
New York, NY 10036
(212) 536-5336

AIGA Journal of Graphic Arts
American Institute of Graphic Arts
1059 3rd Ave.
New York, NY 10021
(212) 752-0813

American Lawyer
600 3rd Ave.
New York, NY 10016
(212) 973-2800

ARTnews Magazine
48 W. 38th St.
New York, NY 10018
(212) 398-1690

Back Stage
1515 Broadway
New York, NY 10036
(212) 764-7300

Barron's National Business and Financial Weekly
200 Liberty St.
New York, NY 10281
(212) 416-2700

Beauty Fashion
530 5th Ave.
New York, NY 10036
(212) 687-6190

Chamber Report
NY City Partnership and
Chamber of Commerce
1 Battery Park Plaza
New York, NY 10004
(212) 493-7400

Chief Civil Service Leader
150 Nassau St.
New York, NY 10038
(212) 962-2690

The City Journal
Manhattan Institute
52 Vanderbilt Ave.
New York, NY 10017
(212) 599-7000
Politics, policies, and culture.

City Limits
40 Prince St.
New York, NY 10012
Urban issues.

Data Communications
1221 Avenue of the Americas
New York, NY 10020
(212) 512-2699

D&B Reports Magazine
Dun and Bradstreet
299 Park Ave.
New York, NY 10171
(212) 593-6723
Small business management.

Downtown Express
80 8th Ave., Suite 312
New York, NY 10011
(212) 242-6162
For executives of lower Manhattan.

Editor and Publisher
11 W. 19th St.
New York, NY 10011
(212) 675-4380

Electronic News
475 Park Ave. S., 2nd Floor
New York, NY 10017
(800) 883-6397

Equities Magazine
160 Madison Ave., 3rd Floor
New York, NY 10017
(212) 213-1300

The Exporter
90 John St.
New York, NY 10038
(212) 587-1340

Financial World
1328 Broadway
New York, NY 10001
(212) 594-5030

The International Executive
John Wiley & Sons
605 3rd Ave.
New York, NY 10158
(212) 850-6000

Investment Dealer's Digest
2 World Trade Center
New York, NY 10048
(212) 227-1200

Management Review
American Management Association
135 W. 50th St., 15th Floor
New York, NY 10020
(212) 903-8393

Manhattan Magazine
330 W. 56th St., Suite 36
New York, NY 10019

Manhattan Spirit
242 W. 30th St., 5th Floor
New York, NY 10001
(212) 268-8600

New York Apparel News
110 E. 9th St.
Los Angeles, CA 90079
(213) 627-3737

New York Construction News
1221 6th Ave., 41st Floor
New York, NY 10020
(212) 512-4770

New York Law Journal
345 Park Ave. S.
New York, NY 10010
(212) 779-9200

New York Public Library News
5th Ave. at 42nd St.
New York, NY 10009
(212) 221-7676

Official City Guide
350 5th Ave., Suite 2420
New York, NY 10118
(212) 315-0800

Printing News/East
245 W. 17th St., 7th Floor
New York, NY 10011
(212) 463-6759

Real Estate Weekly
1 Madison Ave.
New York, NY 10010
(212) 679-1234

Showbiz/Model
40 E. 34th St.
New York, NY 10011
(212) 969-8715

Small Business Opportunities
1115 Broadway, 8th Floor
New York, NY 10010
(212) 807-7100

**Standard & Poor's, NYSE
Stock Reports**
25 Broadway

New York, NY 10004
(212) 208-8392

TV News
80 8th Ave.
New York, NY 10011
(212) 243-6800

Wall Street Technology
1515 Broadway
New York, NY 10036
(212) 869-1300

Wall Street Transcript
100 Wall St.
New York, NY 10005
(212) 747-9500

Westchester Commerce
235 Mamaroneck Ave.
White Plains, NY 10605
(914) 948-2110

Women's Wear Daily
7 W. 34th St.
New York, NY 10003
(212) 630-4600

Job Listings

Cover all your bases and respond to promising job advertisements in your field. The following resources contain only job listings and job-related information and advice. The job-related publications preceded by an asterick (*) are all available at the Job Information Center on the second floor of New York City's Mid-Manhattan Library, located at 455 5th Ave. at 40th St. For specific trade-related publications, check out the periodical desk in the business department.

*AAR/EEO Affirmative Action Register
8356 Olive Blvd.
St. Louis, MO 63132
(314) 991-1335
Academic, professional, and administrative jobs for women, minorities, veterans, and people with disabilities. Monthly magazine consists totally of job listings.

Black Employment & Education
2625 Piedmont Road 56-282
Atlanta, GA 30324
(404) 469-5891

Magazine lists career opportunities nationwide. Your resume may be placed on their database for employer access.

Career Pilot
Future Aviation Professionals of America
4959 Massachusetts Blvd.
Atlanta, GA 30337
(409) 997-8097
Monthly magazine outlines employment opportunities for career pilots.

Community Jobs
30 Irving Place, 9th Floor
New York, NY 10003
(212) 475-1001
Monthly nationwide listings of jobs with community organizations and advocacy groups.

Contract Engineer Weekly
PO Box 97000
Bothell, WA 98041
(206) 823-2222
Weekly magazine of job opportunities for contract engineers.

*Federal Jobs Digest
Breakthrough Publications
310 N. Highland Ave.
Ossining, NY 10562
Civil service job listings (semi-monthly).

International Employment Hotline
Cantrell Corp.
PO Box 3030
Oakton, VA 22124
(703) 620-1972
Monthly listing of overseas jobs. Features current job openings & helpful advice.

*National and Federal Legal Employment Report
Federal Reports
1010 Vermont Ave., N.W.
Washington, DC 20005
(202) 393-3311
Monthly in-depth listings of attorney and law-related jobs in federal government and with other public and private employers throughout the U.S.

Opportunities In Non-profit Organizations
ACCESS: Networking in the Public Interest
50 Beacon St.
Boston, MA 02108

(212) 475-1001
Monthly listings of community jobs around the country, organized by type of non-profit.

QUICK-LIST OF JOB PUBLICATIONS

Asterisked items are available at the New York City Mid-Manhattan Library, 455 5th Ave. If you wish to contact the publishers, call the library for specific information at: (212) 340-0849.

*ARTJOB/BANK
(semi-monthly): Includes internships and administrative positions.

*ArtSEARCH
(semi-monthly): Lists jobs in a wide range of performing arts; also includes internships.

Athletics Employment Weekly
Lists openings for directors, coaches, and assistants.

*Aviso
(monthly): Jobs in museums, galleries, and archives.

*AWIS Newsletter
(bi-monthly): Academic jobs, published by the Association for Women in Science.

Career Connections
Contains job listings in media, marketing, sales, health and fitness, facility management, sporting goods, event management, college athletics, and sports law.

*Career Opportunity News
(semi-monthly): Job trends, statistics, and news.

*Career Woman
(3 issues/yr.): Articles and recruitment ads for women.

*The Chief
(weekly): Information and listings of city, state, and federal civil service jobs.

*Chronicle of Higher Education
(weekly): Academic jobs.

*Community Jobs
(monthly): Job opportunities with non-profit and social change organizations.

Employment News
Provides career opportunities and job-search advice for banking industry.

*Environmental Opportunities
(monthly): Lists 80-120 positions in each issue including administrative, consulting, research, teaching, internships, seasonal positions, and more; schedule of conferences also included.

*Equal Opportunity
(3 times/yr.): Recruitment ads.

*Federal Career Opportunities
(semi-monthly): Civil service job listings; also available on-line.

*Federal Times
(weekly): Ads, articles on federal civil service trends.

Forty Plus Newsletter
(quarterly): Provides assistance to executives over 40 seeking employment in the NY metropolitan area.

Help Wanted Magazine
(bi-weekly): Covers large employers and job openings for job seekers in New York.

Hot Line News
(bi-monthly): Opportunities in the music industry.

*International Career Employment Opportunities
(bi-weekly): Private, government, and non-profit positions.

Job Express
(bi-weekly): Contains listings of open assignments and contracts, and situations wanted in computer consulting.

JobMart
(semi-monthly): Lists jobs in planning, urban opportunities, community development, and transportation.

*Job Openings for Economists
(several times/yr.).

*Job Opportunities Bulletin
(monthly): Professional and paraprofessional jobs in day care.

*MLA Job Information List
(quarterly): Published by the Modern Languages Association.

*National Ad Search
(weekly): Professional and management jobs listed in the nation's newspapers.

*National Business Employment Weekly
(weekly): Lists professional and management jobs as well as articles on job-search strategies and salaries. Non-profit job listings every first and third week.

O'Dwyer's PR Marketplace
(bi-weekly): Lists public relations jobs.

Public Interest Employment Service Jobs Alert
(bi-monthly): Openings in legal aid offices, public interest law, and non-profit organizations.

*Public Sector Jobs Bulletin
(bi-monthly): Jobs with local governments.

Social Service Jobs
Listings of openings for social workers, psychologists, and counselors.

The Source
(monthly): Features employment opportunities in advertising, PR, marketing, and journalism. Includes industry-specific executive recruiters, job banks, job hotlines, and trade associations.

*Teaching Opportunities
(9 issues/yr.): Lists openings in public schools.

*Technical Employment News
(weekly): Engineering and technical service jobs.

United Nations Jobs Newsletter
(monthly): Lists vacancy notices at the U.N.

VOICE-BASED JOB HOT LINES

"Let your fingers do the walking!" Just dial any one of the numerous telephone job banks and listen to the taped recordings that describe available positions and how to apply. Many are available at no charge other than what you might spend for the telephone call. Some company-oriented job information lines include:

AT&T (800) 562-7288 (non-management, communications)
   (800) 858-5417 (management, communications)
Avis (516) 222-3399
Bankers Trust (212) 250-9955
Chase Bank (718) 242-7537
Citibank (718) 248-7072
Continental Airlines (201) 961-8505
Daily News (212) 210-6300
Dime Savings Bank (800) 932-2995
Federal Job Information Center (212) 264-0422
Fleet Bank (800) 358-5627
Flushing Hospital Medical Center (718) 670-5627
Gay Men's Health Crisis (212) 337-1910
Hilton Hotel (212) 586-7000; ask for jobline
Hotel Macklowe (212) 789-7000
Hotel Parker Meridien (212) 708-7351
IBM (914) 288-5700
ITT (212) 258-1768
Metropolitan Life Insurance (212) 578-4111
NY Library Association (800) 252-6952

NY Telephone (212) 395-2800
  ext. 1—Service & Technology
  ext. 2—Management
Newsday (516) 843-2076; (718) 575-2498
The New York Times (212) 556-1383
Pace University (212) 346-1893
Pepsicola Company (914) 767-6300
Pfizer (212) 573-3000
Pratt Institute (718) 636-3742
Prudential Insurance (201) 802-6000
Sheraton Centre Hotel and Tower (212) 621-8523, ext. 1
Sloan Kettering Memorial Hospital (212) 629-5627
Starbucks (212) 978-9595
Staten Island University Hospital (718) 226-9270
SUNY Stony Brook (516) 632-9222
Visiting Nursing Service (212) 560-3342
Waldorf Astoria (212) 872-4717

INTERNET JOB LISTINGS

Use the Net as another source of job listings. Below are a few places to begin.

America's Job Bank
http://www.ajb.dni.us/
A federal program that may eventually include the jobs posted with state unemployment offices (euphemistically called Job Service, Employment Security, etc.) nationwide.

Career Channel
http://riceinfo.rice.edu/projects/careers/
Rice University lists jobs, links, and a wealth of other job-search information.

Career Magazine
http://www.careermag.com/careermag/
A comprehensive resource that includes job-opening database, employer profiles, articles, and news to assist in the career search and career forums.

Career Resource Center
http://www.careers.org/
An excellent source, with links to many other job-listing and job resources organizations.

Career Services On-line—College of William and Mary
http://www.wm.edu/csrv/career/career.html
Excellent starting point for career service practitioners and students, covering topics from resumes to job listings.

CareerWeb
http://www.cweb.com/
Job seekers can browse worldwide career opportunities, including the *Wall Street Journal National Business Employment Weekly.*

EINet Galaxy Career and Workplace Resources
http://galaxy.einet.net/galaxy/Community/Workplace.html
A guide to worldwide information and services.

E-Span: Interactive Employment Network
http://www.espan.com
Provides a searchable database of high-tech job openings as well as a wide variety of resources for the job seeker.

JobCenter
http://www.jobcenter.com
Matches job searcher's skills with employer's needs.

MedSearch America
http://www.medsearch.com/
This Washington-based firm maintains an extensive health-jobs database nationwide.

Monster Board
http://www.monster.com/
Companies around the country list jobs along with employer profiles. Search for jobs by location, industry, company, and discipline.

National Business Employment Weekly
http://www.nbew.com/
A Dow Jones publication featuring articles from the print edition.

Online Career Center
http://www.occ.com/
Includes job listings from over 300 U.S. companies. Browse by job title, company name, or geographic region.

JOB LINKS SPECIFIC TO THE NEW YORK AREA

JobNet—Private Sector Jobs from New York State Employment Security
(http://www.careers.org/html/s-ny.htm)
Jobs posted at New York State Job Service Centers. Updated weekly. Details about the job listings are available through the local Job Service Center at no charge. Simply provide the listed job order number to receive a referral.

Federal Jobs in New York
(http://www.careers.org/text/ny.txt)
Jobs with the federal government within New York, updated several times per week.

RECOMMENDED READING

Dixon, Pam, and Sylvia Tiersten. *Be Your Own Headhunter Online*. New York: Random House, 1995.

Kennedy, Joyce Lain. *Hook Up, Get Hired! The Internet Job Search Revolution*. New York: John Wiley & Sons, 1995.

Mehler, Mark, and Gerry Crispin. *Careerxroads: The 1997 Directory to Jobs, Resumes and Career Management on the World Wide Web*. Washington, DC: IEEE, 1996.

Small Companies

Today's job market has changed. Big business is no longer the biggest employer. Today, 80% of new jobs created in the United States are by small and medium-sized firms that are four or five years old.

Small and medium-sized businesses, those that employ less than 500 people, are good bets for employment opportunities. These companies are expected to expand. Small businesses employ 48% of the American workforce. Two-thirds of all first jobs come from these growing businesses. The big boys of business may still provide better benefits and pay to their employees, but they only manage to provide 11% of the jobs sought by first-time job seekers.

Searching for jobs with small businesses is not, however, as easy as the traditional job search at the large corporation. Small business is less likely to advertise for a position, use an agency, or post a listing at a local college. They generally use the networking method of knowing someone who knows someone. Thus, you may need to be creative when searching out small companies. Use your resources, such as chambers of commerce (see Chapter 1), to help you in your search.

RECOMMENDED READING

Colton, Kitty, and Michele Fetterolf. *1995: A Job Seeker's Guide to America's 2000 Little-known, Fastest-Growing High-Tech Companies*. Princeton, NJ: Peterson's Guides, 1994.

Step 3: Organize Your Search

The most difficult part of any job search is getting started. The next most difficult is staying organized. Preparing a resume, sending it out, scheduling interviews, and returning phone calls is enough to cause anyone to grab for the extra-strength aspirin! Organize your job search and you'll have fewer headaches.

Don't Get Caught Without Your Daily Planner

Have you ever noticed how many people carry around those little black "Daily Planners"? In this case, what's good for the crowd is also good for you, the job searcher. You need to keep a written record of every person you contact in your job search and the results of each contact. This will prevent a job lead from falling through the cracks. It may even come in handy for future job searches.

Your Daily Planner should serve as a way of organizing your efforts for greatest efficiency. Much of your job search will be spent developing your network of contacts. Still, you should allocate a portion of each week for doing research on companies that interest you and for pursuing other means of contacting employers.

As you go through your contacts and begin to research the job market, you'll begin to identify certain employers in whom you're interested. Keep a list of them. For each one that looks promising, start a file that contains articles on the company, its annual report, product brochures, company profile, and any other interesting information. Every so often, check your "potential companies" list against your planner to ensure that you stay in contact with them.

Step 4: Network

While Chapter 5 will give you the essentials of networking, it is important to remember that it's "who you know" that gets you ahead in the job search. Professional organizations are a great source for networking and gleaning vital information about employment. Get involved in organizations in your field of interest to keep abreast of opportunities as they become available. And don't forget to stay abreast of the business world in general through business magazines and newspapers (see Chapter 1 for listings).

If you are just starting your network, use the information interview (see Chapter 5) to find out more about a particular career field and to acquaint yourself with professionals in that field. People like to hire individuals they know, so the more potential employers you meet, the better your odds for landing a job.

Dear Dr. Bob

Is there job-search etiquette I should know about?
—Proper Etiquette Job Searcher

Dear Proper Etiquette Job Searcher

As everywhere else, there exists proper etiquette in the job search. For example, the telephone is a wonderful tool by which an assertive job seeker can make contact with employers and follow-up on job applications and leads. However, reminding the employer of your interest in a position is not tantamount to badgering him or her into interviewing you. Follow every letter you mail with a phone call, but allow ample time for the employer to receive and review your credentials. One to two weeks is the usual rule of thumb.

Manic Monday mornings are a particularly unpleasant time for employers to receive phone calls. A better time is between 10 a.m. and 2 p.m. Tuesdays, Wednesdays, or Thursdays. And always check to see if you have called at a convenient time.

The fax machine can be a dangerous beast and should be used cautiously by the job searcher. Certainly it does offer instant communication with an employer. But unsolicited faxes are annoying to employers. Not only does it tie up the fax line and use expensive paper but it is likely that the hiring authority will not even see it. However, my advice is to fax only when requested to do so by a hiring authority.

Finally, treat the potential employer with the utmost respect. Be sure to keep meetings at the time you both agreed on. Follow up with a thank-you letter, reiterating your qualifications and thanking your host for his or her time. Try to keep everyone in your network informed of your status in the job search.

Step 5: Persistence and Follow-Up

Persistence is one of the key strategies in the job search. Whether you are pursuing job leads, sending out resumes, scheduling interviews, or contacting a hiring authority, you need to be persistent. The passive job searcher relies upon the want ads as his or her only source of job leads. The persistent job searcher is proactive, using resources such as networking groups, newspapers, professional organizations, and directories. The passive job searcher will accept "no" without questioning or pursuing the hiring authority. The persistent job searcher will make a few more calls. Being persistent can help you accomplish the ultimate goal— landing the job.

Persistence is also a state of mind. It's important to remain enthusiastic, to keep going, and to make calls. It is only too easy for the job searcher to lose energy and conveniently forget to make those important follow-up calls. Remember you most likely are just one of many applicants for a job, and persistence is the key to success. Plenty of rejection will probably come your way. It is up to you to keep going and put rejection behind you.

Follow-up all promising contacts with calls and letters. Whether you're networking or actually talking with someone in a position to hire you, it is important to stay in touch with whomever can assist you in your job search. If someone takes the time to give you a lead, it is only proper for you to inform the individual of the outcome.

Follow-up resumes with a phone call to ensure that your resume was received. It is impossible to get an interview if your resume got lost in the mail. Likewise, a thank-you note after an interview will keep your name foremost with the interviewer and less likely to be lost in the shuffle.

Our "silent" president speaks

Nothing in this world can take the place of persistence. Talent will not; nothing is more common than unsuccessful men with great talent.

Genius will not; unrewarded genius is almost a proverb. Education will not; the world is full of educated derelicts. Persistence and determination alone are omnipotent.
—Calvin Coolidge

Step 6: Prepare Your Resume

Writing a good resume and a cover letter to accompany it is important in marketing yourself and lining up interviews. Chapter 6 goes into detail on resume writing. It is important to remember that this step can be crucial to your other steps.

Remember that most resumes get about 20 seconds of the employer's time. Therefore, it is vital to keep the resume to one page and skimmable enough to grab the reader's attention. The following guidelines should help you develop a well-written resume:

- Tailor your resume to the potential job as much as possible.
- Information should be easy to skim and locate.
- Length should be one page and no more than two.
- Proofread your final version; then have someone else proofread it.
- The overall appearance should be professional.
- Printing should be done on a laser printer.

A cover letter should always accompany your resume. The purpose of the cover letter is to persuade the employer to read your resume and invite you for an interview. The cover letter should be sent to a specific person. It should be brief but provide enough information to entice the employer. The following information should be in the cover letter:

- The first paragraph should identify who you are, whether you were referred by someone, and what your objective is.

- The second paragraph is your chance to sell yourself. It should tell the employer why you are good for the company and what you can offer. Use facts and figures to describe your qualifications.
- The last paragraph is where you request an interview and state how you will follow-up with the employer.

The cover letter and the resume are often the first impression the employer will have of you. Do your best in preparing them!

Step 7: Mail Your Resume

When sending your resume out, the Personnel Department is probably not your best target since their job is to screen out rather than welcome applicants. Understand that Personnel or Human Resources can help your career once you're in the company. However, your best initial target is the decision-maker who is the "hiring authority."

Mass Mailing

A common job-search technique is to research a list of companies and send off as many resumes and cover letters as possible. Then you wait for your hard work and many dollars in postage to pay off with a call back and an interview. Sometimes mass mailings work, but mostly they don't. We recommend the targeted mailing technique.

Targeted Mailing

A targeted mailing is one that focuses only on companies with jobs you know you are qualified for and in which you have names of specific hiring authorities. Most importantly, in a targeted mailing you must be prepared to follow-up with phone calls.

In doing your research about prospective companies you have come up with the names of many that you are interested in working for. Prioritize these companies and target the top 15—those you are most interested in. Send these a resume and carefully written cover letter directed to the individual who can help or hire you. Follow-up with a phone call. When you take a company off your list, add a new one.

Various directories and networking contacts will help you come up with names of individuals who could be in a position to help or hire you. Or a phone call to the company can sometimes secure the name of the right person to mail to. Never be afraid to mail letters to more than one person at a firm, especially at some of the larger companies, where the more people who see your resume and are in a position to do something about it, the better.

A targeted mailing cannot work without follow-up phone calls. Let the employer know you will be calling so that the resume remains on his or her desk, and make sure you call within 10 to 14 days after you send the letter.

Although we make this sound easy, contacting the hiring authority could require talking with two or three people in order to determine who the decision-maker is. It could take many phone calls and much follow-up, but don't get discouraged. The important thing is to get your resume in front of the right person and away from the resume graveyard.

Treat the secretaries/assistants with all the respect possible since they are essentially gatekeepers. They often have the power to grant or deny you access to a hiring authority. Getting off on the right foot with the secretary enhances your chances of talking directly with the more influential person. Treating the secretary/assistant as a professional is crucial since he or she often knows everything going on in the office and can give you access to the boss.

Step 8: Use Your Career Resources

Finding a good job is difficult and today the traditional job search is insufficient. You need to use every resource available, including employment agencies, executive search firms, social service agencies, government agencies, career consultants, college career centers, and career fairs. Let's examine these resources one by one.

Employment Agencies

Your first impulse may be to turn the job hunt over to a professional employment service. However, if you're a recent college graduate or offer no special or high-demand skills, employment agencies can be less than helpful. Those that specialize in temporary jobs are even less likely to lead you to your dream job. We recommend taking charge of your own job search since you know yourself and your goals better than anyone else. If you do decide to use employment services, become familiar with their operations and limitations. This will save you a lot of time, effort, and possibly money.

Employment agencies act as intermediaries in the job market between buyers (companies with jobs open) and sellers (people who want jobs). Agencies are paid either by the employer or the worker for placing people. Find out the total cost beforehand and how the fee is handled.

Employment agencies seldom place a candidate in a job that pays more than $50,000 a year. Most employment agencies concentrate on support jobs rather than middle or upper-management positions. A company will do a job search on their own or utilize an executive search firm to fill top management positions. However, if you are in the secretary/assistant field, it may be worth your while to look at employment agencies. To many companies, it's worth the agency fee to avoid the hassle of prescreening dozens, if not hundreds, of applicants.

If you decide to use an agency, be sure it's a reputable firm. Ask people in your field to recommend a quality agency, and consult the Better Business Bureau or the Consumer Fraud Unit to see if there have been any complaints about the agency you're considering. Most important, read the contract thoroughly, including all the fine print, before signing anything. Remember, the agency is loyal to its source of income—usually the company. Also remember that if a company has to pay a fee to hire you, you may be at a disadvantage over other candidates not using an agency. Finally, the job-search strategies an agency provides are all outlined in this book and you can implement most of them yourself.

A listing in this book does not constitute an endorsement of any agencies or firms. Before using a service, try to get the opinion of one or more people who have already used the service you're considering. You can also contact the following:

Better Business Bureau of Long Island
(516) 420-0500

Better Business Bureau of Metropolitan New York
(212) 533-6200

Better Business Bureau of Westchester
(914) 428-1230

Nassau County Office of Consumer Affairs
(516) 571-2600

New York City Department of Consumer Affairs
(212) 487-4398

New York State Attorney General's Office of Consumer Protection
(800) 771-7755

Westchester County Office of Consumer Complaints
(914) 285-2155

Better Business Bureau via the Net
http://www.igc.apc.org/bbb/
This is the homepage of the Better Business Bureau. It offers a geographic directory of offices, list of publications, reliability reports on businesses, scam alerts, and more.

Below is a list of some local employment agencies, including their areas of specialty.

SELECTED NEW YORK AREA EMPLOYMENT AGENCIES

Able Associates
280 Madison Ave.
New York, NY 10017
(212) 689-5500
Traditional and new-media positions in entertainment, publishing, interactive advertising.

Accent Multilangue
274 Madison Ave., Suite 906
New York, NY 10016
(212) 779-3333
Bilingual positions.

Action Fashion Personnel
1707 69th St.
North Bergen, NJ
(212) 575-1964
Fashion industry.

Alert Decisions
1171 Madison Ave.
Patterson, NJ 07503
(973) 742-2600
http://www.alertdecisions.com
MIS, telecommunications, computer programming in NY, NJ, and CT. Offers on-line job registration.

Bank Personnel Resources
575 Madison Ave.
New York, NY 10017
(212) 605-0250

Bocelli, Nadine & Company
420 Madison Ave.
New York, NY 10017
(212) 644-8181
Legal support staff.

Brownstone Sales and Marketing Group
312 E. 22nd St.
New York, NY 10010
(212) 254-8700

Clark, Toby Associates
405 E. 54th St.
New York, NY 10022
(212) 752-5670
Public relations, marketing, communications.

Cunningham, Dale Agency
14 E. 60th St.
New York, NY 10022
(212) 223-0277
Advertising.

Gardner Associates
300 Madison Ave.
New York, NY 10017
(212) 687-6615
Printing and publishing.

The Gromwell Group
30 E. 42nd St.
New York, NY 10017
(212) 972-9300
General.

Hartline Associates
305 Madison Ave.
New York, NY 10017
(212) 297-0600
Computer-related positions.

Huberman, Arnold & Associates
51 E. 25th St.
New York, NY 10010
(212) 545-9033
Public relations.

Jay Gee Personnel
2 W. 45th St.
New York, NY 10036
(212) 921-4830
Art direction, photography.

Kalus, Lisa, & Associates
26 Broadway
New York, NY 10004
(212) 837-7889
Engineering and construction.

Locke, Norman Personnel
310 Madison Ave.
New York, NY 10017
(212) 661-3520
Banking and finance.

Macinnis Ward & Associates
551 5th Ave.
New York, NY 10017
(212) 808-8080
Real estate.

Ribolow Employment Agency
230 Park Ave.
New York, NY 10169
(212) 808-0580
Publishing, education, non-profit, finance.

Smith Personnel
41 E. 42nd St.
New York, NY 10017
(212) 370-5400
Music business.

Stamm Personnel
27 Whitehall St.
New York, NY 10004
(212) 509-6600
Wall Street positions.

Waldron, Don & Associates
450 7th Ave.
New York, NY 10123
(212) 239-9110

Sales managers, executives, and
trainees.

Winston Medical
535 5th Ave.
New York, NY 10017
(212) 687-7890
Technical, administrative, and
executive positions in clinics,
private facilities, and hospitals.

Winston Personnel
535 5th Ave.
New York, NY 10017
(212) 557-5000
General.

Executive Search Firms

Executive search firms are paid by companies to locate people with specific qualifications to meet a precisely defined employment need. Most reputable executive search firms belong to an organization called the Association of Executive Recruiting Consultants (AERC). A search firm never works on a contingency basis. Only employment agencies do that. Because the company has to pay a large fee, they may opt to forgo using an executive search firm during hard times.

Yet, if you choose to use an executive search firm, as specialists who know the market they can be very helpful in providing advice and leads. Keep in mind that you are only useful to the search firm if there is an assignment that matches your background and qualifications exactly.

Dear Dr. Bob
I have recently graduated and was considering using an executive search firm to simplify my job search. What do you recommend?—Recently Confused Graduate

Dear Recently Confused Graduate
Unless you are middle to upper-management, the search firm will not be interested in helping you. Since the search firm looks for candidates with highly developed skills in a particular area, your experience may seem inadequate compared to the candidate with 15 years of work history. For the present time, try the techniques in this book to land a job on your own.

Below is a list of local executive search firms, including their areas of specialty. For a full listing of executive search consultants, see *The Directory of Executive Recruiters* (Kennedy Publications, Fitzwilliam, NH).

NEW YORK AREA EXECUTIVE SEARCH FIRMS

Accountants Executive Search
535 5th Ave., Suite 1200
New York, NY 10017
(212) 682-5900

Artisan
10 E. 40th St., Suite 2901
New York, NY 10016
(212) 448-0200
www.artisan-inc.com
Desktop publishing, graphic design, multimedia production, Web page designers.

The Bankers Register
500 5th Ave., Suite 414
New York, NY 10010
(212) 840-0800

Davis, Bert
425 Madison Ave., Suite 14A
New York, NY 10017
(212) 838-4000
Publishing.

Design Recruiters Group
211 E. 43rd St.
New York, NY 10017
(212) 687-1161
Interior design.

Donnelly, J.P., Associates
420 Lexington Ave., Suite 300
New York, NY 10170
(212) 972-9696
Computer-related and Wall Street positions.

Evans, Allen
157 E. 57th St.
New York, NY 10022
(212) 486-6626
Communication, technical publishing.

Fields, Jerry, and Associates
353 Lexington Ave., 11th Floor
New York, NY 10016
(212) 661-6644
Advertising and graphic arts.

Fortune Personnel Consultants
505 5th Ave., Suite 1100
New York, NY 10017
(212) 557-1000
http://www.databahn.net/fortune/
Technical fields including engineering, manufacturing, quality control, materials management, purchasing.

The Fry Group
369 Lexington Ave.
New York, NY 10017
(212) 557-0011 Contact: John Fry
PR, advertising, marketing.

Gould McCoy & Chadick
300 Park Ave.
New York, NY
(212) 688-8671
General.

Hotel World Management & Executive Recruitment
305 Madison Ave.
New York, NY 10017
(212) 986-2000
Hospitality.

Kalus, Lisa, & Associates
26 Broadway, Suite 400
New York, NY 10004
(212) 837-7889
Construction and environmental work.

Koller, Howard Group
353 Lexington Ave.
New York, NY 10016
(212) 661-5250
Magazine and book publishing, direct
marketing, legal.

Korn/Ferry International
237 Park Ave.
New York, NY 10017
(212) 687-1834
General.

London & Company
360 Lexington Ave., Suite 1902
New York, NY 10017
(212) 599-2200
Legal.

Management Recruiters
295 Madison Ave., 36th Floor
New York, NY 10017
(212) 972-7300

Manasia Inc.
29 John St.
New York, NY 10005
(212) 285-1011
Physical and occupational therapists

The McConnell Group
500 5th Ave., Suite 4815
New York, NY 10110
(212) 997-0112
Financial services, all levels.

Paul, Joel H., and Associates
352 7th Ave.
New York, NY 10001
(212) 564-6500
Non-profit industry.

Perez, Arton
300 Lexington Ave.
New York, NY 10016
(212) 986-1630
Higher education.

Pinnacle Group
130 Water St., Suite 4F
New York, NY 10005
(212) 968-1200
Financial services, investment and
commercial banking, capital markets.

Plessner, Rene, Associates
375 Park Ave.
New York, NY 10152
(212) 421-3490
Cosmetics, fashion.

Russell Reynolds Associates
200 Park Ave. 10017
New York, NY
(212) 351-2000
General, with emphasis on finance,
technology, and telecommunications.
Serves Fortune 500 and smaller
entrepreneurial businesses.

Spencer Stuart & Associates
277 Park Ave., 29th Floor
New York, NY 10178
(212) 336-0200
General.

Spring Associates
10 E. 23rd St.
New York, NY 10010
(212) 473-0013
Communications, marketing,
advertising, sales promotion.

Stuhl, Michelle, & Associates
51 E. 25th St.
New York, NY 10010
(212) 545-1234
Graphic arts, architecture, interior
design.

Thompson, Alexander, & Co.
521 5th Ave., 17th Floor
New York, NY 10175
(212) 599-2055
MIS, finance, accounting.

Social Service Agencies

Unlike professional employment agencies, career consultants (see farther on), and executive search firms, social service agencies are not-for-profit. They offer a wide range of services, from counseling and vocational testing to job placement and follow-up—and their services are either low cost or free. Below is a list of social service agencies in the area.

One-stop shopping for social services

There are hundreds of social service agencies in New York City. To help you find the services, fees, and client qualifications that meet your specific needs, consult *The Sourcebook: Social and Health Services in the Greater New York Area*. The directory is indexed by topic as well as agency name. Address, phone, fees (if any), qualification requirements, and description of services offered are listed. This book is particularly useful for finding programs for people with disabilities, hearing, or sight impairments, veterans, immigrants, displaced homemakers, and others with specific needs.

NEW YORK AREA SOCIAL SERVICE AGENCIES

http://www.pubadvocate.nyc.gov/~advocate/greenbook/greenbook.html is the *New York City Greenbook,* which lists social service agencies.

Central Long Island Family Counseling Services
226 Jericho Turnpike
Floral Park, NY 11101
(516) 354-8926

Federation Employment and Guidance Service (FEGS)
114 5th Ave.
New York, NY 10011
(212) 366-8400

Flatbush Development Corp.
1035 Flatbush Ave.
Brooklyn, NY 11226
(718) 856-4600

Goodwill Industries of Greater NY
4-21 27th Ave.
Astoria, NY 11102
(718) 728-5400
http://www.ocgoodwill.org/gii/good3.html

Jewish Board of Family and Children's Services
120 W. 57th St.
New York, NY 10019
(212) 582-9100

New York Urban League
204 W. 136th St.
New York, NY 10030
(212) 926-8000
http://drum.ncat.edu/~league/ul.html

New York Women's Employment Center
45 John St., Suite 605
New York, NY 10038
(212) 964-8934

92nd St. YM-YWHA
1395 Lexington Ave.
New York, NY
(212) 996-1100

The Salvation Army
120 W. 14th St.
New York, NY 10011
(212) 337-7200
http://www.webnet.com.au/salvos/

Selfhelp Community Services
440 9th Ave.
New York, NY 10001
(212) 971-7600

Women's Counseling Center of Queens
112-11 68th Drive
Forest Hills, NY 11375
(718) 268-3077

YMCA of Greater New York
333 7th Ave.
New York, NY
(212) 630-9600
http://www.interaccess.com/users/dhayward/

YWCA
610 Lexington Ave.
New York, NY 10022
(212) 735-9728
http://www.pmedia.com/Avon/ywca.html

YWCA of Brooklyn
30 3rd Ave.
Brooklyn, NY 11217
(718) 875-1190

YWCA of White Plains and Central Westchester
515 N. White Plains Road
White Plains, NY 10603
(914) 949-6227

Government Agencies

Whether your passion is photography or journalism or finance, don't rule out a job in the public sector. City, state, and federal job listings cover nearly as many fields as the private sector. Stop in the following offices and check out the local listings.

GOVERNMENT AGENCIES

Civil Service Division of Nassau County
140 Old Country Road
Mineola, NY 11501
(516) 571-2511

Nassau County Department of Social Services
Employment Programs Information
County Seat Drive
Mineola, NY 11501
(516) 571-5757

Nassau County Office of Employment and Training
9000 Ellison Ave.
Westbury, NY 11590
(516) 683-3320

New York City Department of Personnel
18 Washington St.
New York, NY 10004
(212) 487-5627

New York City Housing Authority
Dept. of Social and Community
Services
250 Broadway, Room 1901
New York, NY 10007
(212) 306-4141

**New York State Civil Service
Department**
Announcement and Application
2 World Trade Center
New York, NY 10048
(212) 487-6455

Office of Personnel Management
Federal Job Information and
Testing Center
201 Varick St.
New York, NY
(212) 337-2142
http://www.jobweb.org/index/gjobs.htm
http://http2.sils.umich.edu/~awood/
725/govern.html

**United States Government
Department of Labor/Job Corps**
201 Varick St.

New York, NY 10014
(212) 337-2287

**Westchester County Department
of Employment and Training**
150 Grand St.
White Plains, NY 10603
(914) 285-3910

**Westchester County Office
of Personnel Planning**
148 Martine Ave.
White Plains, NY 10601
(914) 285-2117

**Westchester County Operation
Talent Bank**
Office for Women
112 E. Post Road, Room 216
White Plains, NY 10601

**Women's Office for Information
and Referral**
150 Grand St., 6th Floor
White Plains, NY 10601
(914) 285-5972

NEW YORK STATE JOB SERVICE

The New York State Job Service is a state-run agency that screens applicants and
fills positions for jobs in the private sector. The agency has offices throughout all
five boroughs and you can visit any of them. The 54th St. location has a running
video of jobs available and interactive terminals that allow you to select fields of
interest and view the available openings, which change daily.

**NY State Employment Service and
Professional Placement Center**
247 W. 54th St.
New York, NY 10019
(212) 265-2700

New York State Department of Labor
New York City Job & Career Center
225 W. 54th St.
New York, NY 10019

(212) 247-5650
http://ny.jobsearch.org/

NY State Dept. of Labor
Manhattan Clerical Sales Office
Personnel
247 W. 54th St.
New York, NY 10019
(212) 265-2700

NY State Dept. of Labor
345 Hudson St.
Brooklyn, NY 10014
(718) 352-6555

NY State Dept. of Labor
25-01 Queens Plaza North

Long Island City, NY 11101
(718) 706-5590

NY State Dept. of Labor
1139-1141 Hylan Blvd.
Staten Island, NY 10305
(718) 447-2931

Career Consultants

Career consultants vary greatly in the kind and quality of the services they provide. Some may offer a single service, such as vocational testing or preparing resumes. Others coach every aspect of the job search and stay with you until you accept an offer. The fees vary just as broadly and range from $100 to several thousand dollars. You, not your potential employer, pay the fee.

A qualified career consultant can be an asset to your job search. But no consultant can get you a job. A consultant can help you focus on an objective, develop a resume, teach you to research the job market, decide on a strategy, and provide interviewing techniques. But in the end, the consultant can't interview for you. You are responsible.

The only time you should consider a consultant is after you've exhausted all the other resources we've suggested here and still feel you need expert and personalized help with one or more aspects of the job search. The key to choosing a career consultant is knowing what you need and verifying that the consultant can provide it.

Check references. A reputable firm will gladly provide them. Check the Better Business Bureau and get referrals from friends who have used a consultant. Before signing anything, ask to meet the consultant who will actually provide the services you want. What are their credentials? How long have they been practicing? What does the consultant promise? What is required from you? How long can you use the consultant's services? Be sure to shop around before selecting a consultant. Refer to Chapter 2 for a list of possible counselors.

College Career Centers

If you are in college and are not acquainted with your school's career center, make a point to stop by and check out the services available. Colleges and universities usually provide services to their alumni and members of the local community also.

There is more to a college career center than just job postings. It's a great resource for building your network, researching the job market, and seeking counseling to establish a career strategy. And most colleges and universities also offer services such as vocational testing and interpretation and the use of the resource library to the general public. Refer to Chapter 2 for a listing of local colleges and universities and the career services provided to students, alumni, and the general public.

Career Fairs

Another job-search resource that can help is the ubiquitous career fair. Career fairs are the shopping malls for job searchers. Employers line up to market their companies and job opportunities. Job searchers browse the aisles, often stopping when a particularly glitzy brochure or big company name catches their eye. And like the shopping mall, employers want to sell, sell, sell their opportunities while job searchers want to snatch up great deals.

Career fairs are a job shopper's delight. The large number of employers in one place makes it easy to research many companies. Additionally, career fairs afford the job searcher a chance to meet face-to-face with company representatives, often an advantage for people who make a better impression in person than on paper. Finally, at some career fairs candidates can actually interview for jobs with prospective employers during the event.

Career fairs are most often advertised in the classified section of the newspaper. Professional associations will also frequently receive announcements. Colleges and universities often sponsor career fairs and post announcements of these and other events. Some coordinators of career fairs will even put up billboards and advertise on television.

As more and more employers rely on career fairs to meet qualified applicants, the savvy job searcher must be comfortable attending these events. These few tips will help you more effectively use a career fair.

- Prior to the fair, get a list of the companies attending in order to begin researching potential employers. Knowing what a company does allows you to use the precious few minutes you will have with a company representative to sell yourself rather than ask basic questions about the company's products.

- Plan a strategy. Use your research to prioritize the companies you want to talk with. Sequence the companies according to which companies you must, without a doubt, talk with before the end of the fair.

- Arrive early the day of the fair in order to scope out the facilities and meet with company representatives before lines get too long. Familiarize yourself with the location of employers, the flow of traffic, and the layout of the building.

- Avoid wasting time in long lines to talk to big-name employers, even if they have great company give-away goodies. Smaller employers and their representatives will have less traffic, which means that you may be able to spend more time talking with him or her and making a positive impression.

- Take the initiative in approaching employers. Prepare a short two-to-three-minute "infomercial" about yourself so that you can quickly acquaint employers with your background. Have a list of questions ready for employers so that you don't have to suffer angst while trying to decide what to say to him or her.

- Bring lots of resumes and be prepared to leave them with any employer who interests you. Before leaving the career fair, revisit your favorite employers and leave your resume with them again to make sure your name does not get lost in the pile.

The shopping mall was created as a convenience to vendors who want lots of consumers and consumers who want lots of vendors in one easy place; the career fair provides the same convenience to job searchers and employers. A successful strategy will help you avoid lost time and hopefully get you inside the company for a proper interview later.

CAREER FAIR ORGANIZATIONS

There is no one-stop-shopping list or single source of information on job and career fairs in the New York City area. However, here are some suggestions:

http://www.espan.com/js/jobfair.html
Lists career fairs geographically.

http://starbase.ingress.com/nyworks/ecal.html
Lists career-related events happening in NYC.

The New York City Public Library hosts various career fairs and seminars throughout the year. "Marketing Yourself" and "Your Career and You" are two of their current workshop titles.

Job Expo International hosts four yearly technical career fairs for computer professionals and four sales and management fairs in New York, New Jersey, and Connecticut and can be reached at (212) 505-1780.

The Lendman Group, located in Florida at (804) 473-2450, is a major national organizer of career fairs and has been in business for 32 years. They hold 14-16 Technical Fairs, which include computer and engineering positions, and Sales and Retail Management fairs per year in the New York metropolitan area. While most organizers charge between $2 and $20, entrance here is free.

Jonathan Ladd Co. holds 4 sales fairs per year in the NY and NJ area and can be reached at (800) 752-6343 for schedule information.

The New York Times hosts a Systems Information Technology career fair 3-4 times per year. Other topics currently in the works are health care and diversity. Also check out the classified section of the *Sunday Times* for listings of company career fairs.

New York Newsday hosts the Career Forum Expo in the fall.

Call the **Jacob Javits Center** at (212) 216-2100 and **Madison Square Garden** at (212) 465-6741 to inquire about upcoming career events.

Hotel Pennsylvania (212) 736-5000, **The Hilton Hotel** (212) 586-7000, and **The Park Central Hotel** (212) 247-8000 are favorite spots for career fairs. Call for schedule information.

Companies that hire seasonal employees or companies that are opening a new branch location often hold career fairs. **Radio City Music Hall** holds an annual career fair in September to recruit employees for the Christmas season.

Step 9: The Killer Interview

The killer interview consists of three parts: preparation, success during the interview, and follow-up. We'll highlight key aspects of this process. However, Chapter 7 discusses the interview in greater detail.

Preparation

Before any interview, you need to prepare and practice in order to do the best job possible in selling yourself to the employer. Follow this procedure for best results:

- Identify your strengths, skills, goals, and personal qualities. Self-assessment is crucial to knowing what you have to offer an employer and to conveying it effectively. Try to come up with five unique strengths. Have examples of how you have used them professionally.
- Research the company in order to ask intelligent questions. An interview is suppose to be a dialogue; you want to learn about them just as they want to learn about you.
- Rehearse what you plan to say during the interview. Practice answers to commonly asked questions and determine how you will emphasize your strengths and skills.
- Dress professionally and conservatively. If you make a negative first impression, you may not be fairly considered for the job. Refer to Chapter 7 for dressing tips in the interview.

Success During the Interview

Chapter 7 covers what interviewers are looking for. Below are some additional tips to help you succeed in your interview.

- Arrive on time or ten minutes early. This will ensure you the full amount of time allotted and show that you are enthusiastic about the position.
- The first five minutes of the interview can be extremely important. To start your interview off right, offer a firm handshake and smile, make good eye contact, and say something to break the ice. "Nice to meet you," or something of that sort, should clear your throat nicely and prepare you for more substantive conversation.
- As you begin the interview, be aware of non-verbal behavior. Wait to sit until you are offered a chair. Look alert, speak in a clear, strong voice, try

to stay relaxed, avoid nervous mannerisms, and try to be a good listener as well as a good talker.

- Be specific, concrete, and detailed in your answers. The more information you volunteer, the better the employer gets to know you and thereby is able to make a wise hiring decision. But don't be long-winded.
- Always have questions for the interviewer.
- Don't mention salary in a first interview unless the employer does. If asked, give a realistic range and add that opportunity is the most important factor for you.
- Offer examples of your work and references that will document your best qualities.
- Answer questions as truthfully as possible. Never appear to be "glossing over" anything. If the interviewer ventures into ticklish political or social questions, answer honestly but try not to say more than is necessary.
- Never make derogatory remarks about present or former employers or companies. Make sure you look very positive in the interviewer's eyes.

Follow-Up

The following suggestions will help you survive the "awful waiting" time after the interview.

- Don't get discouraged if no definite offer is made or specific salary discussed.
- If you feel the interview isn't going well, don't let your discouragement show. Occasionally an interviewer who is genuinely interested in you may seem to discourage you to test your reaction.
- At the end of the interview, ask when a hiring decision will be made. This is important not only because it reconfirms your interest in the position but also so you'll know when to expect a response.
- Send a thank-you letter to the interviewer: thank him or her for the time and effort; reiterate your skills and qualifications for the position; and make clear your interest in the job.
- Make notes on what you feel you could improve upon for your next interview and on what you feel went particularly well. After all, experience is only valuable to the extent that you're willing to learn from it.
- If offered the position, up to two weeks is a reasonable amount of time to make your decision. All employment offers deserve a written reply, whether or not you accept them.

You will learn a great deal about patience during the waiting period that follows an interview. The important point to remember during this time is that all your hopes shouldn't be dependent on one or two interviews. The job search is continuous and shouldn't stop until you have accepted an offer. Keeping all your options open is the best possible course.

Keep in contact with the company if they haven't responded by the date they indicated in the interview. Asking the status of your application is a legitimate question. This inquiry should be stated in a manner that is not pushy but shows your continued interest in the company.

Step 10: Make Sure This Is the Job for You

Start celebrating! You have received a job offer after working so diligently on the job search. But before you accept or decline, consider the offer carefully. Make sure the details of the offer are clear; preferably, get them in writing. Details should include starting date, salary and benefits, location, job description and responsibilities, and the date by which you must respond. Evaluating a job offer can be both exciting and difficult. We have provided the following information to assist you in making a job decision.

Negotiating Salary

Be aware of what other people in similar positions are making before accepting any offer. *The Occupational Outlook Handbook,* put out by the U.S. Department of Labor every two years, cites salary statistics by field. Another good source of information is *The American Almanac of Jobs and Salaries* by John Wright, published by Avon. Professional societies and associations frequently provide this sort of information too. It's one more good reason to belong to one.

When negotiating salary, proceed with care to prevent jeopardizing a positive relationship with your new employer. Here are some points in negotiating salaries:

- Be prepared with salary research before discussing any figures.
- Approach the session with trust and a willingness to compromise.
- Know when to stop. Don't push your luck.
- Be open to substituting other benefits in exchange for a higher salary.

The end result should be that both parties are happy with the outcome. For advice on how to get the salary you want, we recommend these books:

BOOKS ON SALARY NEGOTIATION

Chapman, Jack. *Negotiating Your Salary: How to Make $1000 a Minute.* Berkeley, CA: Ten Speed Press, 1996.

Farr, J. Michael. *Getting the Job You Really Want.* Indianapolis, IN: Jist Works, Inc., 1994.

Fisher, Roger, and William Ury. *Getting to Yes: Negotiating Agreement Without Giving In.* New York: Penguin USA, 1991.

Krannich, Ronald L., and Caryl Krannich. *Dynamite Salary Negotiations: Know What You're Worth and Get It.* Manassas, VA: Impact Publications, 1997.

Compare the Offers on Paper

Don't blindly accept the first offer you receive. You've put a great deal of effort in the job search, so spend a little more time in comparing the relative merits of each offer. Below is a sample checklist to assist you in this endeavor. The idea is to list the factors that you consider important in any job, and then assign a rating for how well each offer fills the bill in each particular area.

We've listed some factors that should be considered before accepting any offer. Some may not be relevant to your situation. Others that we've left out may be of great importance to you. So feel free to make any additions, deletions, or changes you want. Assign a rating (1 being the lowest and 5 the highest) for each factor under each offer. Then total the scores.

The offer with the most points is not necessarily the one to accept. The chart doesn't take into account the fact that "responsibilities" may be more important to you than "career path," or that you promised yourself you'd never punch a time clock again. Nevertheless, looking at the pros and cons of each offer in black and white should help you make a much more methodical and logical decision.

Factor	Offer A	Offer B
Responsibilities	_____	_____
Company reputation	_____	_____
Salary	_____	_____
Vacation leave	_____	_____
Insurance/Pension	_____	_____
Profit sharing	_____	_____
Tuition reimbursement	_____	_____
On-the-job training	_____	_____
Career path advancement	_____	_____
Company future	_____	_____
Product/service quality	_____	_____
Location (housing market, schools, transportation)	_____	_____
Boss(es)	_____	_____
Co-workers	_____	_____
Travel	_____	_____
Overtime	_____	_____
Other _____	_____	_____
TOTAL POINTS	_____	_____

Evaluating Job Offers

A job involves more than a title and salary. Before you accept any offer, be sure you understand what your responsibilities will be, what benefits you'll receive besides salary (insurance, profit sharing, vacation, tuition reimbursement, etc.), how much overtime is required (and whether you'll be paid for it), how much travel is involved in the job, who your supervisor will be, how many people you'll supervise, and where the position could lead (do people in this position get promoted?). In short, find out anything and everything you can to evaluate the offer.

The cost of living is essential in comparing job offers in different cities. The difference in the cost of living can mean living like royalty in Indianapolis or struggling in New York, even if the salaries offered seem relatively close. To compare cost of living, check the Consumer Price Indexes provided by the Bureau of Labor Statistics.

It seems obvious that it's unwise to choose a job solely on the basis of salary. Consider all the factors, such as your boss and colleagues and the type of work you'll be doing, before making any final decision.

Corporate Cultures

Every company has a different corporate culture (philosophies and management style) and some fit better with your own personality than others. Thus it is important to research the company's culture in your career search. Specific companies are discussed in the following books:

BOOKS ON CORPORATE CULTURE

Levering, Robert, and Milton Moskowitz. *The 100 Best Companies to Work for in America.* New York: Plume, 1994.

Peters, Thomas J., and Robert H. Waterman, Jr. *In Search of Excellence: Lessons from America's Best-Run Companies.* New York: Warner Books, 1988.

Peters, Thomas J., and Nancy Austin. *Passion for Excellence: The Leadership Difference.* New York: Random House, 1985.

Plunkett, Jack. *The Almanac of American Employers.* Boerne, TX: Corporate Jobs Outlook, 1994.

It is also possible to decipher a company's culture during the interview. The following are factors worth examining:

- What is the environment like? Look at the appearance of the office, the company newsletter, brochures, and bulletin boards.
- Who is on board? How does the company greet strangers, what kind of people work for them, and why is the company a success (or failure)?
- How are employees rewarded? Look at the benefits, awards, compensation, and recognition given to employees.

- What is the fashion statement? Look at the dress code. Are there different dress styles for levels of employment?
- How do people spend their time? Look at the ambience of the workplace and what an average day is like.
- How do managers behave? Look at the history of the company, how things get done, and the management style.

Is the Job a Dream or a Nightmare?

Dream jobs sometimes do turn into nightmare employment. It happens all the time. How do you avoid this possibility? Look for the eight danger signs of the "job from hell."

Financial problems and corporate turmoil. Prospective employees rarely do financial or management research on a company in which they are interested. It will behoove you to find out if the firm is financially sound and if there has been much turmoil within the company.

Layoffs indicate danger. Many companies try to convince new employees that recent layoffs will have no effect on their position. Don't believe it! A good indication of a job about to go bad is that mass layoffs have recently occurred.

Recent mergers or acquisitions can be another danger signal. Companies that have bought or merged with another company are usually trying to reduce expenses. And the easiest way for the corporate world to reduce expenses is to cut employees and reorganize. The chances of you working in the position you interviewed for will diminish with reorganization. Being new, you may also be one of the first to be laid off or transferred.

Word on the street. What is the informal word about your new potential workplace? Word of mouth is often a good source of inside information about the reality of working for a particular company. Try to eliminate gossip and scuttlebutt from those who are naturally and overly negative. But if a general consensus exists that a company is not good to its employees or that people are unusually unhappy, carefully weigh your decision.

Turnover within your position. How many people have worked in your new position during the last couple of years? Is your particular job one that experiences a great deal of turnover? High turnover should alert you to the possibility that either the job is horrible and no one can stand it or that no one is really capable of doing this job, including you. Percentages show that those who take jobs with high turnover rates are very likely to become a statistic as well.

Elusive or vague job description. A key danger signal is the absence of or vagueness in your job description. Look for a job where the duties are known up front. It's fine for some things about a job to be determined later, and you certainly want your responsibilities to be increased, but don't take a job in which you are not sure what your primary duties will be or to whom you will report.

"Bad boss" potential. Don't discount the boss's influence on your job performance or your satisfaction within a job. Most employees spend more waking time with a boss than with their spouse. Try to meet your boss before you accept the job and ask yourself if you are ready to live with him or her on a daily basis. As we have mentioned before, your boss should be a role model. He or she should help you grow and develop in your career. If you have doubts about your boss, you should have doubts about the job.

That gut feeling. Finally, you can never discount that deep-down feeling you get about your job offer. Even when the pay and benefits are great, you still might have mixed emotions about a particular job. Explore those emotions and find out why they are "mixed." They may be more than a premonition.

Even if a job looks like a winner, if you see one or more of these danger signs, do a little more research before you accept. Don't wind up a major loser.

five

Network, Network, Network: The Best Job-Search Technique

What's the difference between knowing a lot of people and having an influential network? If you're a smart job searcher, you will realize that knowing a lot of people is just the start. It is the process of staying in touch with people and building strong connections that creates an influential and powerful network. While the old axiom "it's not what you know but who you know" may be an overstatement for all job searches, savvy job seekers combine ingenuity and creativity to use who they know to help them find jobs in which they can use what they know.

For many people, networking has a negative connotation. It implies cocktail parties, insincere conversation, and golf games with people you don't really like. In reality, however, job networking is simply asking people you know for information about careers and employment. You may already be networking and not know it!

The Six Myths of Networking

In order to encourage more networking, let's start by debunking some common myths.

MYTH #1: People get jobs through ads and other formal announcements. The truth is that fewer than 20 percent of available jobs are ever advertised. The majority of jobs are in the "hidden job market." Mark S. Granovetter, a Harvard sociologist, reported to *Forbes* magazine that informal contacts, or networks, account for almost 75 percent of successful job searches. Agencies find about

9 percent of new jobs for professional and technical people, and ads yield about another 10 percent.

If those figures don't convince you to begin networking, how about these. A recent study found that employers preferred using networks to hire new employees because it reduced recruiting costs and decreased the risks associated with hiring a new, unknown employee. Furthermore, people who use networking are generally more satisfied with the job they land and tend to have higher incomes.

MYTH #2: Networking is so effective, you can ignore more traditional means of job searching, such as responding to ads. This is simply not true. As important as networking is to your job search, you will shorten the time you spend looking for a job if you use more methods. The average job seeker only uses a few of the available job-search techniques. No wonder job searches take so long! Networking complements your other techniques, not replaces them. Don't put all your eggs in one basket; use as many options as possible.

MYTH #3: Networking is only effective for people who are very assertive. If you were asking people for jobs, this might be true. However, networking is just asking people for information for your job search, which requires you to be polite but not overly assertive.

If you are uncomfortable contacting people, start your network with people you know well or with whom you have some connection: you go to the same church, you are both members of the same alumni association, etc. Talking with friends and family is less intimidating than approaching strangers. Networking in friendly territory will help you develop confidence in your approach and know what questions to ask.

MYTH #4: The job hunter's most important networking contacts within a company are in the HR department. If you limit your network to human resources personnel, you will be waiting a long time for a job. Only one person in four gets their job by relying strictly on personnel offices. Human resources people are there to help others hire. Find those "others."

The purpose of networking is to talk to as many people as possible. Sometimes people only tangentially related to the hiring process can provide you with valuable information about your industry, tips on companies that may be hiring, or names of other contacts.

MYTH #5: No one knows enough people to network effectively. Most people know an average of 200 people. Even if only 20 people you know can help you with your job search, those 20 can refer you to 400 additional people, and your network has taken off.

Certainly if you're moving to a new town, your list of contacts will be small. You must act to develop it. Find out about your local alumni association, join a church, join professional associations, and attend as many social functions as possible. Meet people!

MYTH #6: Once you've found a job, there is no need to keep up with your network. Absolutely false. Write a thank-you note immediately after meeting with someone who was helpful with your job search. Once you've landed a job, let your network know and periodically touch base with them.

Networking as a waiter

Eric, a recent college graduate, was interested in getting a job in the very competitive field of advertising. While waiting for interviews to roll in, he waited tables at a local pub in order to pay the bills.

One night, several months and part-time jobs after graduation, Eric struck up a conversation with a group of people that had stopped by after work. After learning that they worked for a large advertising agency, Eric told them about his job search, collected their business cards, and contacted the office the following week. Eric's personality, resume, and samples impressed the office staff so much that they invited him for an interview. He got the job.

Step-by-Step Guide to Networking

To begin the networking process, draw up a list of all the people you know who might help you gain access to someone who can hire you for the job you want. Naturally, the first sources, the ones at the top of your list, will be people you know personally: friends, colleagues, former clients, relatives, acquaintances, customers, and club or church members. Just about everyone you know, whether or not he or she is employed, can generate contacts for you.

Don't forget to talk with your banker, lawyer, insurance agent, dentist, and other people who provide you with services. It is the nature of their business to know lots of people who might help you in your search. Leave no stone unturned in your search for contacts. Go through your holiday-card list, college yearbook, club membership directories, and any other list you can think of.

The next step is to expand your network to include new people who can help you. The easiest way to do this is to ask each of the people you do know for the names of two or three other people who might be helpful in your job search.

Professional organizations are another resource. If you are changing careers, you should view professional organizations as essential to your job search. Most groups meet on a regular basis and are an excellent way to contact other people in your field. Some professional associations offer placement services to members. Many chambers of commerce publish directories of the professional and trade associations that meet in your area. Local business magazines and newspapers also publish times and locations for meetings of professional associations.

Your college alumni association is another resource to expand your network. Alumni club meetings provide opportunities to catch up on happenings with your alma mater and meet other professionals in your area. Additionally, some schools maintain alumni databases for the express purpose of networking. This is a valuable resource for both seasoned professionals and recent college grads looking for a job lead and a friendly face. Still other alumni associations offer resume referral services that you can join for a small fee.

The Information Interview

There are situations, however, when your existing network simply won't be adequate. If you're changing careers, you may not know enough people in your new field to help you. If you've just moved to a new location, your network may still be in Iowa. Your situation may require you to creatively build a new network. One of the best techniques for doing this is the "information interview."

Information interviewing is a technique for developing contacts by interviewing people for job-search information. This technique acknowledges that names of contacts are easy to find but relationships that can help you find a job require additional action on your part.

First, telephone or write to possible contacts whom you've identified through lists of acquaintances, professional associations, your alumni organization, or simply a cold call. Explain that you are very interested in his or her field, and arrange a twenty-minute appointment. Be very clear that you are not asking him or her for a job but only for information. Also, never ask new people out to lunch. It is too time consuming and lunch isn't as important to the business person as it may be to the job searcher. Don't give someone a reason to turn you down. Twenty minutes is enough time for you to get information without imposing on your host.

The information interview is the time to ask your contact questions about the field, the job market, and job-hunting tips. Ask your contact to review your resume and make recommendations about how to present yourself or fill in gaps in your experience. Most importantly, ask your contact for the names of two or three other people to talk with, thus expanding your network. And always follow up with a thank-you letter.

QUESTIONS TO ASK IN AN INFORMATION INTERVIEW

Job Function Questions

What do people with a job like yours do?

What does your typical day consist of?

What do you like/dislike about your work?

Who are the key people in your field?

What skills are necessary for your position?

Company Questions

What has been the major achievement of this organization?

How often do you interact with top management?

What trends do you foresee for this organization and in the field?

What is the company's corporate culture like?

Who are your major competitors?

Career Field Questions

What is the growth potential in your field for the next five years?

What journals or magazines should I read?

What professional organizations do you recommend?

Who else would you recommend that I talk with?

Information interviews not only help build your network but they can identify career paths, potential employers, worthwhile professional associations, and weaknesses in your work or educational background. Most importantly, learning to glean information is a skill that will serve you throughout your life.

Example of an Information Interview Letter

66 W. 57th St.
New York, NY 10038
(212) 555-3367
April 11, 1998

Dr. David Hart
President
Environmental Research

Dear Dr. Hart:
Dr. Young, with whom I have studied these past two years, suggested that you might be able to advise me of opportunities in the environmental engineering field.

I am about to graduate from the university with a B.S. in civil engineering, and I am a member of Phi Beta Kappa. For two of the last three summers, I have worked as an intern with the Air Pollution Control Association.

I am eager to begin work and would appreciate a few minutes of your time to discuss trends in environmental research and, as a newcomer, gain the benefit of your advice regarding a career. Exams are finished on June 6, and I would like to arrange a meeting with you shortly thereafter. I look forward to hearing from you and in any case will be in touch with your office next week.

Sincerely,

Rich Smith

Information interview letter tips:
- Keep it short and direct.
- Tell enough about yourself to demonstrate that you are sincere and qualified.
- Always conclude with a date when you'll call, and always call if they haven't called you by that date.

Admittedly, networking will not work in every situation. No amount of networking will help you land a job for which you do not have the minimum qualifications. Nor will networking work if you try to meet with people at a much higher professional level than your own. A CEO will likely be unwilling to help someone looking for an entry-level position. You can also make people unwilling to help you by being pushy and demanding. But if you avoid these pitfalls, you should develop a great network.

Do You Know Your Networking Net Worth?

To determine the net worth of your networking ability, take the following quiz to assess how you approach people at professional meetings, social events, and community functions. For each statement, circle Y for yes or N for no.

Y   N   1. I belong to at least one professional or trade association in which I can meet people in my field.

Y   N   2. In the past year, I have used my contacts to help at least two people meet someone of importance to them.

Y   N   3. In the last month, I have attended at least two functions in order to meet people who are potential professional contacts.

Y   N   4. When I meet new professional contacts, I ask them for a business card and make notes on the back about our conversation.

Y   N   5. When asked, "What kind of job are you looking for?" I can answer in two sentences or less.

Y   N   6. I keep in touch with former classmates and workmates.

Y   N   7. I have given colleagues information to help them solve a problem.

Y   N   8. I always know at least 10 professionals in my field well enough to call and say, "Hi, this is (my name)," and they know who I am.

Y   N   9. When attending professional or social functions, I introduce myself to new people and show interest in their careers.

Y   N   10. I am involved in at least one community or social organization outside work.

Count how many times you circled Y, then analyze your score:

0-4   You can make your job search easier by learning the basics of networking.

5-8   You can give and get even more out of your professional networks.

9-10   You're well on your way to feeling the power of networking in your job search!

Networking Etiquette

There are, of course, many ways in which to network, and for each method you must know the rules, or the etiquette, of networking.

On the Telephone. Since the purpose of networking is to establish a personal relationship with people who can help you with your job search, you will find that the telephone is more effective than letters to contact people. When calling, clearly state the purpose of your call and explain how you found the person's name and telephone number. Be sensitive about the time you call. In one study, employers indicated that Monday mornings and Friday afternoons were the worst times to try to reach them, for obvious reasons. The best times to call business people, this same survey said, are Tuesdays, Wednesdays, and Thursdays between 10:00 a.m. and 2:00 p.m.

The Twenty-Minute Meeting. When you make an appointment to meet with someone for information, many of the same rules apply as when interviewing for a job. Arrive a few minutes early; bring a copy of your resume; and be prepared with questions to ask. It is best not to ask to meet someone for the first time over lunch.

Thank-You Notes. The thank-you note is more than just a polite gesture. A well-written thank-you note enhances your credibility with your interviewee. In your thank-you note, reiterate key points of your conversation and explain how you intend to act on your contact's advice. Include a copy of your resume for his or her files. Make sure that your contact has your correct phone number and address so that he or she can contact you with additional information.

Networking On-line. On-line computer services can help you expand your network to mind-boggling numbers. Many of the main on-line services such as CompuServe and America On-line have discussion groups that can be useful for job searchers. Prodigy offers a careers bulletin board that is another way to do information interviews.

One caution, however, about using these services. Be careful about providing too much personal information such as your address, phone number, social security number, and so on, because you never know who is lurking on the Net. Additionally, people can easily misrepresent themselves, and you may not be corresponding with whom you think you are.

E-mail has become commonplace in the corporate world and presents another way to make networking contacts. "Netiquette," or etiquette on the Net, however, suggests that this is not always the best way to conduct informational exchanges. It is, however, a great way to confirm appointments and send thank-you notes.

CYBERTIPS ON NETWORKING

A few sources for networking on the Net include:

ESPAN
http://www.espan.com/library/asso.html
Provides networking advice.

Training Forum—Search Associations Web Pages
http://www.trainingforum.com/assoc.html
Information includes contacts, descriptions, addresses, and events data.

Professional Organization Home Pages. Many local and national professional organizations are developing sites on the Internet for their members. Often these include times of meetings and information on job openings or careers in that particular field. Ask your contacts if such sites exist within your field and look them up.

List-Serves. Many professional organizations also maintain list-serves, or e-mail mailing lists that members use to maintain on-going dialogues on issues within the field. This is an excellent way to get up-to-date information and to learn of people who can help you in your job search. Do not, however, ask people for jobs over the list-serve. Find their e-mail address and write to those you are interested in talking to individually.

NETWORKING HANGOUTS

While many fields such as fashion and finance still have districts, others such as advertising and publishing are spreading out and migrating to new grounds—many funky new advertising agencies are setting up shop in Soho. Check out the bars and restaurants near a particular company. For instance, employees at Skadden Arps Slate Meagher & Flom, a top New York law firm, frequent P.J. Clarke's Bar, located in their building at 915 3rd Ave.

Netparty is a local group that organizes and sponsors frequent get-togethers for young professionals to network in a low-key, social atmosphere. Networking parties take place at fashionable clubs and bars around the city, such as Le Bar Bat. Admission is $8 and includes light food. Netparty can be reached at (212) 969-0293 and by e-mail at netparty@bway.net to receive notices of upcoming events.

Here are some good hangouts to hit during happy hour, where you'll rub shoulders with people in advertising, media, accounting, law, finance, and business.

American Festival Cafe
Rockefeller Center
20 W. 50th St.
New York, NY
(212) 332-7620

The Beer Bar at Cafe Centro
MetLife Building
45th St. at Vanderbilt
New York, NY 10166
(212) 818-1222

Bryant Park Grill
40th St. and 5th Ave. behind
the library in Bryant Park
(212) 840-6500

Campagna
24 E. 21st. St.
New York, NY 10010
(212) 460-0900
Music industry.

Divine Bar
244 E. 51st St.
New York, NY 10022
(212) 319-9463

El Rio Grande
160 E. 38th St.
New York, NY
(212) 867-0922
Accountants, lawyers.

Film Center Cafe
635 9th Ave.
New York, NY 10036
(212) 262-2525
Film makers.

La Cite Grille
120 W. 51st.

New York, NY 10020
(212) 956-7100
Media, advertising.

Monkey Bar
60 E. 54th St.
New York, NY 10021
(212) 838-2600

Moran's Bar & Grill
4 World Financial Center
New York, NY 10281
(212) 945-2255
Investment bankers.

Park Avalon
225 Park Ave. S.
New York, NY 10003
(212) 533-2500

Starbucks Coffee
13-25 Astor Place
New York, NY 10003
(212) 982-3563
Writers, artists.

Union Bar
204 Park Ave. S.
New York, NY 10003
(212) 674-2105

Networking After You Land the Job

Networking doesn't end when you land the job. Keep people who are part of your network informed about your job search, and let them know when you finally land a job. Periodically touch base and let them know how things are working out with the new job.

Maintaining your network requires that you contribute as much as you receive. After you find your job — or even while you are looking for it — remember that your ideas, information, and contacts can help other people in your network. Often we have to train ourselves to offer such information because we don't think of ourselves as resources.

Sometimes people seem to walk into successful jobs or successful career changes. If you asked them how they did it, they would probably say they were in the right place at the right time. No doubt, some people do just get lucky, but others have high career awareness, or an idea of what their next career move or career change might be. Developing high career awareness means knowing what your next move is, planning for it, knowing who might be involved in helping you, and positioning yourself for it.

In other words, networking should become a part of your life and a part of your plans for your next career move. Knowing people in all types of career areas allows you to keep up with the possibilities and helps you position yourself to take the next step up the career ladder.

BOOKS ON NETWORKING

Numerous books have been written on job searching and networking. Here are a few good ones.

Boe, Anne. *Networking Success*. Deerfield Beach, FL: Heath Communications, 1994.
Krannich, Ronald L., and Caryl Rae. *The New Network Your Way to Job and Career Success: Turn Contacts into Job Leads, Interviews, and Offers.* Manassas, VA: Impact Publications, 1993.
Metzler, Ken. *Creative Interviewing: The Writer's Guide to Gathering Information by Asking Questions*. Needham Heights, MA: Allyn & Bacon, 1997.
Petras, Kathryn and Ross. *The Only Job Hunting Guide You'll Ever Need: The Most Comprehensive Guide for Job Hunters & Career Switchers*. New York: Fireside, 1995.
Stoodley, Martha. *Information Interviewing: How to Tap Your Hidden Job Market*. Deerfield Beach, FL: Ferguson Pub., 1996.

Networking Resources in the New York Area

There follows a list of more than 115 organized groups, ready-made for networking, forming relationships, and gathering inside information about business, commerce, and jobs in the New York area.

SELECTED NEW YORK AREA PROFESSIONAL ORGANIZATIONS, TRADE GROUPS, NETWORKS, CLUBS, AND SOCIETIES

Advertising Club of New York
235 Park Ave. S., 6th Floor
New York, NY 10003
(212) 533-8080
AdclubNY@aol.com
Contact: Kerstin Santa
Members are professionals in advertising, publishing, marketing, and business. The Young Professionals Division for members under thirty has its own Board as well as educational, programming, and social committees. Members receive

an Adweek subscription, invitations to all monthly events, seminars, and functions, and a quarterly newsletter containing job listings.

Advertising Women of New York
153 E. 57th St.
New York, NY 10022
(212) 593-1950
Exec. Dir.: Ms. Terry Player
Organization of women whose members are executives in the communications industry: advertising, marketing, merchandising, research, promotion, public relations, and the media. Offers seminars and luncheon programs. Holds support sessions twice a month for members and acts as a job-search clearing-house. Sponsors annual career conference for professionals and students; awards scholarships and runs public service programs.

American Association of Advertising Agencies
405 Lexington Ave.
New York, NY 10174
(212) 682-2500
Pres.: O. Burtch Drake
Organization of advertising agencies. The association acts as an information clearinghouse, gathers statistics and conducts surveys on public relations, media, and related subjects. Operates a secondary research library containing information on the advertising industry.

American Association of Exporters and Importers
11 W. 42nd St.
New York, NY 10036
(212) 944-2230
Pres.: Eugene J. Milosh
Members are customs brokers, freight forwarders, trading companies, banks, attorneys, insurance firms, and manufacturers. Conducts seminars and workshops. Publishes weekly trade alert and special information bulletins.

American Bureau of Shipping
2 World Trade Center, 106th Floor
New York, NY 10048
(212) 839-5000
Pres.: Robert Somerville
Comprised of ship owners and builders, naval architects, marine underwriters, and others in the marine industry.

American Institute of Aeronautics and Astronautics
85 John St.
New York, NY 10038
(212) 349-1120
Publishes a variety of materials and abstracts. Contact the office in Reston, VA, for information on career services and counseling: (800) 639-2422.

American Institute of Architects
200 Lexington Ave., Suite 600
New York, NY 10016
(212) 683-0023
Contact: Bill Gray
Hosts various meetings and seminars each month. Offers preparatory course for
the Architectural Registration Exam.

American Institute of Certified Public Accountants
1211 Avenue of the Americas
New York, NY 10036
(212) 596-6200
Pres.: Barry Melancon
Association of practicing certified public accountants in the private, government, and educational sectors. Offers seminars and workshops. Local chapters
publish weekly newsletters; national association publishes bulletins and letters.
Holds annual meeting.

American Institute of Chemical Engineers
345 E. 47th St.
New York, NY 10017
(212) 705-7338
Exec. Dir.: Glenn Taylor
Professional society of chemical engineers. Offers employment services,
sponsors competitions, maintains speakers' bureau and numerous committees
including career guidance. Publishes monthly magazine, bi-monthly journal,
and quarterly progress reports.

American Institute of Graphic Arts
545 W. 45th St.
New York, NY 10036
(212) 246-7060
http://www.aigany.org
Focused on graphic design professionals and students and related arts such as
photography, illustration, and the printing industry. The NY Chapter focuses on
business seminars, job fair & other major design-related programming.

American Insurance Association
85 John St.
New York, NY 10038
(212) 669-0400
Pres.: Richard Boehning
Association of individual property and casualty insurance companies. Offers
seminars and workshops to members; holds annual meeting.

American Management Association
1601 Broadway
New York, NY 10019
(212) 586-8100

Pres. & CEO: David Fagiano
Organization of professional managers. Provides members with the latest information about their fields; offers educational and training courses in the area of management development. Members include individuals as well as companies. Publishes newsletters and books; operates a management bookstore and information systems library.

American Marketing Association
60 E. 42nd St., Suite 1765
New York, NY 10165
(212) 687-3280
Hosts conferences and seminars on marketing issues including job hunting and resume preparation. Offers on-line service for job listings and a mentoring program run by the career advisory board.

American Society of Civil Engineers
345 E. 47th St.
New York, NY 10017
(212) 705-7496
Director: James E. Davis
National association of civil engineers; provides publications.

American Society of Composers, Authors and Publishers (ASCAP)
1 Lincoln Plaza
New York, NY 10023
(212) 595-3050
Pres.: Marilyn Bergman
National association of composers, lyricists, and publishers. Publishes newsletter and directory.

American Society of Interior Designers (ASID)
200 Lexington Ave.
New York, NY 10016
(212) 685-3480
New York chapter of association of practicing professional interior designers and associate members in allied design fields. Largely a networking organization; local chapters maintain placement services and job round-ups. Publishes bi-monthly report and student career guide.

American Society of Magazine Editors
919 3rd Ave.
New York, NY 10022
(212) 872-3700
Exec. Dir.: Marlene Kahan
Hosts speaker luncheons and seminars for senior-level editors.

American Society of Mechanical Engineers
345 E. 47th St.
New York, NY 10017
(212) 705-7722

Contact: Julia Crislip
Offers short courses, seminars, and conferences as well as an employment assistance program and bi-monthly regional job bulletin. Member can access all association news on ASME Net and post a resume in the on-line career fair.

American Society of Travel Agents
18 W. Marie St.
Hicksville, NY 11801
(516) 822-4602

American Society of Women Accountants
1 Battery Place
New York, NY 10033
Contact: Joan Clark (212) 837-6600
Professional society of women accountants, educators, and others in the field. Publishes monthly and quarterly newsletter; holds semi-annual conference.

American Women in Radio and Television
234 5th Ave., Suite 403
New York, NY 10016
(212) 481-3038
Pres.: Chickie Bucco
Hosts frequent networking events and leadership roundtable discussions as well as entertainment events and workshops with speakers.

You've already got lots of contacts

Networking paid off for Liz, a young woman eager to make her way in banking or a related industry. She told us why she's glad she took the time to talk with her friends and neighbors about her job search.

"I was having dinner with close friends and telling them about my job search," says Liz. "During the conversation, they mentioned a banker friend they thought might be hiring. As it turned out, the friend didn't have a job for me. But he suggested I come in, meet with him, and discuss some other possibilities. He put me in touch with an independent marketing firm, servicing the publishing industry. The owner of the firm was looking for someone with my exact qualifications. One thing led to another, and pretty soon I had landed exactly the position I wanted."

Architectural League of New York
457 Madison Ave.
New York, NY 10022
(212) 753-1722

Contact: Rosalie Genezro
National association of architects and architectural firms. Largely an educational organization that sponsors lectures and exhibitions. Focuses on contemporary architecture in the areas of city planning, mural decoration, sculpture landscape, interior design, and photography.

ArtTable Inc.
270 Lafayette St., Suite 608
New York, NY 10012
(212) 343-1735
Executive director: Aleya Saad
Invitational membership of women in leadership positions in the visual arts.

Asian Women in Business
1 W. 34th St., Suite 1202
New York, NY 10001
(212) 868-1368
Executive Director: Bonnie Wong
Workshops, discounts to AWIB-sponsored events & programs, free quarterly newsletter on business topics.

Association of Authors' Representatives
10 Astor Place, 3rd Floor
New York, NY 10003
(212) 353-3709
Contact: Ginger Knowlton
Publishes brochure and directory of members.

Association of Computer Professionals
9 Forest Drive
Plainview, NY 11803
(516) 938-8223
Pres.: Seymour Bosworth

Association for Computing Machinery
1515 Broadway
New York, NY 10036
(212) 869-7440
Exec. Dir.: Joseph DeBlasi
125 professional chapters and 500 student chapters of computer scientists, engineers, physical scientists, business system specialists, analysts, and social scientists interested in computing and data processing. Holds 60 special-interest group meetings per year; offers resume referral service and career counseling.

Association of Consulting Chemists and Chemical Engineers
40 W. 45th St.
New York, NY 10036
(212) 983-3160

A national association that acts to advance the practice of independent consultants and their organizations in the fields of chemistry and chemical engineering. Refers members to companies interested in hiring engineering consultants. Publishes membership directory that includes resumes and histories.

Association of Graphic Communications
330 7th Ave., 9th Floor
New York, NY 10001-5010
(212) 279-2100
http://www.agcomm.org
Education, training, discount programs for equipment & supplies, employment services, insurance programs, trade show, awards competition, buyer's guide & directory.

Association of Group Travel Executives
c/o Arnold Light
The Light Group
424 Madison Ave., Suite 705
New York, NY 10017
(212) 486-4300

Association of Investment Brokers
49 Chambers St., Suite 820
New York, NY 10007
Contact by mail only.
Publishes newsletter 10 times per year. Holds annual meeting.

Association of Managing Consultants
521 5th Ave., 35th Floor
New York, NY 10175
(212) 697-8262
Pres.: Ed Hendricks
Operates a job referral service; firms inquiring about availability of consulting services are furnished with a list of members indicating their location and special skills.

Association of Real Estate Women
15 W. 72nd St., Suite 31G
New York, NY 10023
Eileen Brumback, President
(212) 787-7124
Membership in AREW is open to men as well as to women. Through seminars, workshops, on-site tours, luncheons, and a monthly newsletter, AREW provides members with vital information on real estate-related issues and trends.

Association of Travel Marketing Executives
257 Park Ave. S.
New York, NY 10010
(212) 598-2472

Exec. Dir.: Kristin Zern
Conducts "Certified Travel Marketing Executive" educational program.

Association for Women in Computing/NYC
214 Riverside Drive, Apt. 505
New York, NY 10025
(212) 662-0909
E-mail: 71331,3476@compuserve.com or awcnyc@dorsai.org
Quarterly meetings featuring expert speakers on diverse topics, monthly
newsletter, annual conference, networking, free passes to PC Expo & UNIX
Expo, discounts on training, software, and services from sponsors.

Bronx Board of Realtors
1867 Williams Bridge Road
Bronx, NY 10461
(718) 892-3000
Exec. VP: Nunzio Del Greco
Sponsors networking seminars and educational forums; provides health
insurance program and listing service.

Career Apparel Institute
1156 Avenue of the Americas
New York, NY 10036
(212) 869-0670
Contact: Jackie Roffelli

Chemists Club
40 W. 45th St.
New York, NY 10036
(212) 626-9300
Social club for people in the field. Hosts seminars; publishes monthly newsletter.

Consultants' Network
57 W. 89th St.
New York, NY 10024
(212) 799-5239
Director: Stan Berliner
Operates a clearinghouse for independent consultants. Houses resource center
on the Net with resume listings.

Cosmetic Executive Women
217 E. 85th St., Suite 214
New York, NY 10028
(212) 759-3283
A non-profit organization comprising women in the beauty, cosmetics, and
fragrance industries and related fields such as fashion, finance, and communications. Membership open to established women with 2 years' experience in field;
however, referrals and guidance for young women interested in the field is available on a limited basis.

Direct Marketing Association
1120 6th Ave.
New York, NY 10036
(212) 768-7277
Members are creators and producers of direct mail and direct response advertising. The Direct Marketing Educational Foundation sponsors several three-day Basic Direct Marketing courses and offers career guidance brochures.

Drug, Chemical and Allied Trades Association
2 Roosevelt Ave., Suite 301
Syosset, NY 11791
(516) 496-3317
Exec. Dir.: Richard Lerman
Organization of manufacturers and distributors of drugs, chemicals, cosmetics, toiletries, essential oils, flavors, and fragrances. Offers seminars for management development. Publishes bi-monthly newsletter; holds frequent meetings.

Environmental Action Coalition
625 Broadway, 9th Floor
New York, NY 10012
(212) 677-1601
Exec. Dir.: Stephen Richardson
Educates the public about the nature and scope of major environmental issues and houses a resource center. Provides volunteer and intern programs as well as job listings, which are also posted on the Net. Maintains library including archival material and periodicals.

Environmental Defense Fund
257 Park Ave. S.
New York, NY 10010
(212) 505-2100
Exec. Dir.: Frederic D. Krupp

Fashion Group International
597 5th Ave., 8th Floor
New York, NY 10017
Director of Membership Services: Patricia Maffei
Members include top-level executives in the fashion industry.

Financial Women's Association of New York
215 Park Ave. S., Suite 1713
New York, NY 10003
(212) 533-2141
Exec. Dir.: Nancy Sellar
Organization of women and men involved in investment and commercial banking, securities research, sales and trading, portfolio management, corporate financial analysis and planning, business journalism, and investor relations. Provides monthly job listings, internship program for college students, and career-guidance seminars.

Fragrance Foundation
145 E. 32nd St., 14th Floor
New York, NY 10016
(212) 725-2755
Pres.: Annette Green
Holds seminars on trends in the industry; maintains information center and
library; runs sales programs; provides listing of major companies.

Fur Industry Council of America
224 W. 30th St., 2nd Floor
New York, NY 10001
(212) 564-5133
Director, Fashion Promotions: Sandy Blye
Association of fur manufacturers and retailers. Operates consumer hotline.
Publishes various booklets and quarterly newsletter.

Graphic Arts Professionals
PO Box 3139
New York, NY 10165
(212) 644-8085
Contact: James W. Prendergast
Holds monthly luncheons and dinners with instruction and education as the
theme. Membership open to all associated with or interested in the graphic
arts industry.

Greater Independent Association of National Travel Services
2 Park Ave., Suite 2205
New York, NY 10016
(212) 545-7460
Pres.: Susan Shapiro
Holds regional workshops and showcases.

Healthcare Businesswomen's Association
333B Route 46 West, Suite B201
Fairfield, NJ 07004
(973) 575-0606
Executive: Carol Davis Grossman
Marketing, research and development, operations, sales, law, finance, and
managed care professionals.

Human Resources Planning Society
317 Madison Ave., Suite 1509
New York, NY 10017
(212) 490-6387
Exec. Dir.: Walter Cleaver
National association of human resource planning professionals including
staffing analysts, business planners, and others concerned with employee
recruitment, development, and utilization.

IEEE Aerospace and Electronics Systems Society
c/o Institute of Electrical and Electronics Engineers
345 E. 47th St.
New York, NY 10017
(212) 705-7900
A society of the Institute of Electrical and Electronics Engineers involved in
the development and installation of electronics for the aerospace industry.
Publishes monthly magazine.

Institute of Electrical and Electronics Engineers
345 E. 47th St.
New York, NY 10017
(212) 705-7900
Engineers and scientists in electrical engineering, electronics, and allied fields;
membership includes 47,000 students.

Institute of International Education
809 United Nations Plaza
New York, NY 10017
(212) 883-8200
Fosters international education programs; encourages business and educational
partnerships.

Institute of Management Accountants
10 Paragon Drive
Montvale, NJ 07645
(201) 573-9000, (800) 638-4427
Contact: Gloria Mellone
Keeps members abreast of changes and trends in the accounting and finance
professions. Offers employment networking, review courses, self-study
programs, and in-house education.

Institute of Public Administration
55 W. 44th St.
New York, NY 10036
(212) 730-5480
Pres.: David Mammen
A private research, educational and consulting agency addressing public
administration, public policy, and government organization.

Institute of Real Estate Management
1975 Linden Blvd.
Elmont, NY 11003
(516) 285-3800
Pres.: Perry Finkleman

Insurance Society of New York
c/o The College of Insurance
101 Murray St.

New York, NY 10007
(212) 815-9217
Pres.: Ellen Thrower
Parent organization of the College of Insurance. Houses the largest
insurance-related library in the country.

International Academy of Health Care Professionals
70 Glen Cove Road, Suite 209
Roslyn Heights, NY 11577
(516) 621-0620
Association of psychologists, social workers, and medical and health care
professionals.

International Association of Printing House Craftsmen
c/o Herst Lithographers
620 12th Ave.
New York, NY 10036
(212) 245-4666
Pres.: Ralph Locascio
Open to anyone in the graphic arts field. Holds educational meetings to update
members about trends in the field. Offers weekend seminars, job postings in
monthly bulletin, and a scholarship program.

International Federation of Women Lawyers
186 5th Ave.
(212) 686-6608
New York, NY 10010
Contact: Eleanor Brown
Multinational association of female lawyers in 70 countries.

Ladies Apparel Contractors Association
450 7th Ave.
New York, NY 10123
(212) 564-6161
Established to handle labor relations for apparel contractors. Hosts seminars
and workshops on labor relations; offers internships; publishes newsletter.

League of Professional Theatre Women/New York
300 E. 56th St.
New York, NY 10022
(212) 583-0177
President: Shari Upbin
Producers, managing & casting directors, choreographers, designers, general &
stage managers, talent, literary & press agents, playwrights, attorneys,
insurance, accountants, public funding executives, administrators, dramaturgs,
critics & musical directors. Must be sponsored by 2 League members. Offers
seminars, awards, salons, festivals, and educational programs.

Long Island Board of Realtors
300 Sunrise Highway
West Babylon, NY 11704
(516) 661-4800
Pres.: Joseph Canfora
Promotes education and professional standards in the field.

Magazine Publishers Association
919 3rd Ave., 2nd Floor
New York, NY 10022
(212) 752-0055
Publishes booklet on "careers in magazine publishing." Holds seminars and meetings.

Men's Fashion Association of America
475 Park Ave. S., 17th Floor
New York, NY 10016
(212) 683-5665
Exec. Dir.: Eric Hurtz
Organization of textile mills, apparel manufacturers, yarn producers, and retailers of men's and boys' apparel. Brings together the fashion press, designers, and manufacturers through two annual press previews. Offers in-house internships.

Metropolitan Black Bar Association
1204 3rd Ave., Suite 141
New York, NY 10022
Contact: Kim Wilson
(212) 330-0387

Multimedia Publishers Group
60 Cutter Mill Road, Suite 502
Great Neck, NY 11021
(516) 482-0088
Pres.: Harry Fox
Promotes education and understanding of CD-ROM technologies and products.

NYZS/The Wildlife Conservation Society
2300 Southern Blvd.
Bronx, NY 10460
(718) 220-5100
Contact: Michelle Margan
Operates Bronx Zoo/Wildlife Conservation Park, Aquarium for Wildlife Conservation, and three other wildlife centers in New York. Education department offers classes and internships.

National Academy of Sports
220 E. 63rd St.
New York, NY 10021

(212) 838-2980
Pres.: Howard Hillman

National Academy of Television Arts and Sciences
111 W. 57th St., Suite 1020
New York, NY 10019
(212) 586-8424
Pres.: John Cannon
Members are persons engaged in almost all facets of television performing and production. Sponsors workshops and seminars; publishes bi-monthly newsletter (*NATAS News*).

National Alliance of Sales & Marketing Executives
350 5th Ave., Suite 5408
New York, NY 10118
(212) 714-1244
Executive Director: Bruce Colwin
http://www.nasme.com
A dynamic & fast-growing organization open to sales, marketing & management executives, representing large multinational corporations to small, fast-track companies. Monthly programs feature new ideas to increase sales & market more effectively and provide networking opportunities.

National Association of Black Social Workers
1969 Madison Ave.
New York, NY 10035
(212) 348-0035
Pres.: Robert Knox
Supports, develops, and sponsors community projects to serve the interest of the black community.

National Association for Female Executives
30 Irving Place, 5th Floor
New York, NY 10003
(212) 477-2200
http://www.nafe.com
Career-minded women in both the corporate arena and the entrepreneurial sector. Annual dues: $29. Publishes the award-winning publication *Executive Female*, offers insurance and financial planning programs, business start-up guides, career development events, and corporate and travel discount programs.

National Association of Social Workers, NYC Chapter
15 Park Row, 20th Floor
New York, NY 10038
(212) 577-5000
Exec. Dir.: Dr. Robert S. Schachter
Organization of professional social workers. Offers seminars on employment, a book of available jobs, and a mentoring program.

National Health Career Association
350 5th Ave., Suite 3304
New York, NY 10118
(212) 259-9412

National League for Nursing
350 Hudson St.
New York, NY 10014
(212) 989-9393
Contact: Dr. Patricia Moccia
Membership includes individuals, agencies, and nursing educational institutions.
The center for career advancement offers guidance on educational programs.
Councils on various topics meet throughout the year.

National Resource Center for Paraprofessionals in Education
25 W. 43rd St., Room 620N
New York, NY 10036
(212) 642-2948
Director: Anna Lou Pickett
Resource center for administrators of state and local education agencies,
colleges, and universities.

Newswomen's Club of New York
15 Grammercy Park S.
New York, NY 10003
(212) 777-1610
Largely a social group focused on networking. Members are journalists with the
daily newspapers, wire services, syndicates, national news and news/feature
magazines, and radio and television stations. Publishes monthly bulletin; holds
monthly workshops.

The friendly networker

Steve, an electrical engineer, interviewed with NASA. He
realized during the interview that the position was not
something he was cut out for or interested in. However, it
was just the sort of thing that a friend of his would be
perfect for. He admitted to the interviewer that he was the
wrong person for the job and spent the next ten minutes
describing how perfect his friend would be for the position. The interviewer was so impressed at this act of altru-
ism that he actually followed up and called the person. He
eventually offered her the job. Steve didn't land a job for
himself, but he did enhance his network relationships by
demonstrating his own quick thinking, integrity, and team
spirit—qualities any employer can appreciate.

New York Alliance of Black School Educators
PO Box 100-499
Brooklyn, NY 11210
Pres.: Ronald Frye

New York American Marketing Association
60 E. 42nd St., Suite 1765
New York, NY 10165
(212) 687-3280
http://www.nyama.org
60+ annual educational programs, monthly magazine, bi-monthly newspaper,
career networking events, awards program, directory of marketing research firms.

New York Association of Black Journalists
PO Box 2446
New York, NY 10185
Pres.: Sheila Stainback

New York Biotechnology Association
c/o Coopers & Lybrand Kurz
225 Broadhollow Road
Melville, NY 11747

New York Clothing Manufacturers Association
(212) 754-3100
Contact: Sidney Orenstein
Networking group for manufacturers of men's tailored clothing. Holds
frequent meetings.

New York Council of Defense Lawyers Educational Services
530 5th Ave.
New York, NY 10036
(212) 334-3555

New York County Lawyers Association
14 Vesey St.
New York, NY 10007
(212) 267-6646
Contact: Harrie Astor
Offers lawyer placement service and continuing legal education courses. Hosts
monthly "lunch with a judge."

New York Credit and Financial Management Association
49 W. 45th St., 5th Floor
New York, NY 10036
(212) 944-2400
Organization of credit and financial executives of manufacturing firms,
wholesalers, banks, advertising agencies, insurance companies, and accounting
firms. Maintains resume file for use by member companies; holds seminars
and workshops.

New York Hotel and Motel Trades Council
707 8th Ave.
New York, NY 10036
(212) 245-8100
Pres.: Peter Ward

NY New Media Association
55 Broad St.
New York, NY 10004
(212) 785-7898
http://www.nynma.org
Members work in diverse fields from broadcasting, publishing, Web site
development and design to musicians & venture capitalists. Offers monthly
newsletter, semi-annual membership directory, discounts on conferences and
subscriptions, discounts on exhibition space at New York-area trade shows.
Holds "cybersuds" networking parties for its 1,700 individual and 1,300
company members.

New York Society of Independent Accountants
509 Westchester Ave.
Ryebrook, NY 10573
(800) 696-9742
Contact: Tom Langtry

New York Society of Security Analysts
1 World Trade Center, Suite 4447
New York, NY 10048
(212) 912-9249
Members include analysts employed by brokerage houses, banks, insurance
companies, mutual funds, and other financial institutions. Holds seminars,
workshops, and classes. Posts job offerings; maintains a career development
committee.

New York State Bankers Association
99 Park Ave., 4th Floor
New York, NY 10017
(212) 949-1170
Organization of commercial banks and financial institutions. Holds seminars
and classes. Also open to non-members.

New York State Restaurant Association
505 8th Ave.
New York, NY 10018
(212) 714-1330
Pres.: Fred G. Sampson
Keeps members of food service operations informed about issues affecting the
industry. Holds annual convention and trade show.

New York State Society of Certified Public Accountants
530 5th Ave.
New York, NY 10036
(212) 719-8300, 944-5650
Exec. Dir.: Robert L. Gray
Offers CPA job bank, committee for career services, mentoring program, and career days; holds numerous workshops and seminars.

New York State Trial Lawyers Association
132 Nassau St.
New York, NY 10038
(212) 349-5890
Pres.: John Cherundolo
Holds seminars; maintains a library.

New York Women in Communications
355 Lexington Ave., 17th Floor
New York, NY 10016
(212) 679-0870
Administrator: Ellen Shapiro
Sponsors career development and informational programs as well as mentoring opportunities.

New York Women's Bar Association
234 5th Ave., Suite 403
New York, NY 10016
(212) 889-7873
The organization's committee on women's advancement runs workshops, classes, and a mentoring program. Job listings are posted in the monthly newsletter.

The One Club
32 E. 21st St.
New York, NY 10010
(212) 979-1900
The One Club is strictly for copywriters, art directors, and wannabes. The club offers free lectures and seminars to its 650 members, and junior membership is free the first year. Four portfolio reviews are held throughout the year for members of any level.

People-to-People Sports Committee
80 Cutter Mill Road
Great Neck, NY 11021
(516) 482-5158
Pres.: Rand Milton
Comprised of prominent persons in the sports promotion field; organization promotes international sports exchanges, donates sports equipment, and provides sports coaches to developing countries.

Plastic Soft Materials Manufacturers Association
330 W. 58th St., Suite 413
New York, NY 10019
(212) 489-5400
Exec. Dir.: Sheldon Edelman

Professional Women in Construction
342 Madison Ave., Room 451
New York, NY 10173
(212) 687-0610

Promotion Marketing Association of America
257 Park Ave. S.
New York, NY
(212) 979-0085
Contact: Scott Levy
Organization of promotion service companies, sales incentive organizations, and companies using various promotion programs. Associate members include manufacturers of premium merchandise, consultants, and advertising agencies.

Public Art Fund
1 E. 53rd St., 11th Floor
New York, NY 10022
(212) 980-4575
Serves as resource center and information clearinghouse on public arts programs and opportunities available in the public art field.

Public Relations Society of America
33 Irving Pl., 3rd Floor
New York, NY 10003
(212) 995-2230
Director: Ray Gaulke
Professional society of public relations practitioners in business and industry, counseling firms, government, associations, hospitals, schools, and non-profit organizations. Conducts professional development programs. Maintains job referral service, speakers' bureau, and research information center.

Risk and Insurance Management Society
655 3rd Ave., 2nd Floor
New York, NY 10017
(212) 286-9292
Exec. Dir.: Linda Lamel
Sponsors educational forums; maintains speakers' bureau and electronic bulletin board.

Security Traders Association
1 World Trade Center, Suite 4511
New York, NY 10048

(212) 524-0484
Pres.: John Watson
Conducts educational programs for brokers and dealers.

Society of Cosmetic Chemists
120 Wall St.
New York, NY 10005
(212) 668-1500
Maintains job listings and publishes a career guidance booklet. Holds monthly meetings; offers continuing education courses.

Society of Motion Picture and Television Engineers
595 W. Hartsdale Ave.
White Plains, NY 10607
(914) 761-1100
Exec. Dir.: Fred Motts
Non-profit organization of professional engineers and technicians in motion pictures, television, and allied arts and sciences. Sponsors lectures, exhibitions, and conferences to advance the theory and practice of engineering. Organizes technical courses at universities. Job listings posted in monthly journal.

Society of the Plastics Industry
355 Lexington Ave.
New York, NY 10017
(212) 351-5425
Exec. Dir.: Fran Lichtenberg

Society of Women Engineers
120 Wall St., 11th Floor
New York, NY 10005
(212) 509-9577
Exec. Dir.: Elaine Osterman
Educational service society of women engineers. Membership is also open to men. Offers career guidance, a "shadowing" program, networking services, and resume database. Publishes national magazine with job listings. Provides scholarships for advanced degrees and re-entry into the field.

Special Interest Group on Programming Languages
c/o Association for Computing Machinery
1515 Broadway
New York, NY 10036
(212) 869-7440
Association of computer professionals interested in programming languages. Publishes monthly newsletter.

Type Directors Club
60 E. 42nd St., Suite 721
New York, NY 10165

(212) 983-6042
Exec. Dir.: Carol Wahler
Professional society of typographic designers, type directors, teachers of typography, and those with an interest in typographic education. Offers job referral and placement, resume bank, monthly meetings with industry updates, seminars, and conferences.

Wings Club
52 Vanderbilt Ave., 18th Floor
New York, NY 10017
(212) 867-1770
Contact: Margie Gewirtz
Maintains a meeting place for persons connected with aviation and foreign and domestic aeronautics. Hosts monthly luncheons with guest speakers.

Women in Production
347 5th Ave., Suite 14086
New York, NY 10016
(212) 481-7793
Organization of individuals involved in all phases of print and graphics, including those working in magazine and book publishing, agency production, print manufacturing, print-related vending and buying, and advertising production. Funds scholarships for graphic arts education and offers continuing education programs.

Women's Media Group
PO Box 2119, Grand Central Station
New York, NY 10163
Provides members in publishing, journalism, film, television and other media with outlets for mentoring, career development and advocacy activities.

Women's National Book Association
160 5th Ave., Room 625
New York, NY 10010
(212) 675-7805
A networking organization offering a job referral service and mentoring program as well as meetings and seminars.

Women's Sports Foundation
Eisenhower Park
East Meadow, NY 11554
(516) 542-4700
Exec. Dir.: Donna Lopiano
The foundation educates the public about athletic opportunities available to women and provides educational guides, travel, and training grants and offers an internship program. The organization also maintains an information clearinghouse on women's sports and fitness.

Young Menswear Association
1328 Broadway
New York, NY 10001
(212) 594-6422
Established to encourage young people to explore the potential of the menswear industry. Offers scholarships to young people in the field; circulates resumes among members.

six

Developing the Perfect Resume

I t seems almost impossible to write the imperfect resume, with over 125 books on the market today pertaining solely to resume writing. However, we still anguish over the process, believing it will secure us a job. Keep in mind that no one ever secured a job offer on the basis of a resume alone. The way to land a good position is to succeed in the interview. You have to convince a potential employer that you're the best person for the job. No piece of paper will ever do that for you—but having an excellent resume is a necessary first step.

The resume is an invitation enticing the employer to interview you. With a little success, and some luck, the employer will want to meet you after reading your resume. However, the most effective method of resume delivery is for you to first meet the employer in person; then provide your resume. We understand that this is not always possible.

The French word *résumé* means "a summing up." Thus the purpose of a resume is not to catalogue, in exact detail, your entire biography. You should be concise with your work experience, education, accomplishments, and affiliations. Your goal is to pique the employer's interest. A good rule of thumb is that the resume should be kept to one or at most two pages.

The Basics of a Good Resume

To develop a resume that entices a potential employer to want to meet you, we suggest the following tips:

1. *Tailor your resume to the potential job opening.* The astute job searcher should always research a potential employer and find out as much information as possible on the qualifications needed for a particular job and then tailor his or her

141

resume to match the qualifications. When listing your experience and education, concentrate on those items that demonstrate your ability to do the job you are applying for. Using a computer will facilitate this process of customizing each resume.

2. *Be concise.* Most employers don't have time to read a two-page resume and usually scan a resume within 10-20 seconds. Thus, you want to capture the reader's attention quickly. Only then will you get a more careful reading. This is not the time to demonstrate your impressive vocabulary. Instead, describe your experience in short, pithy phrases. Give figures and facts when describing your accomplishments. Your resume should read more like a chart than a chapter in a textbook. And it should look more like an ad than a legal document.

3. *Be honest.* Never lie, exaggerate, embellish, or deceive. Be honest about your education, accomplishments, and work experience. A deliberate lie can be grounds for termination and will likely turn up in a background search. If you have gaps between jobs, and gaps are not always as negative as some would have you believe, you may consider listing years worked rather than months.

4. *Have a professional presentation.* Today's high quality computers allow you to prepare your own resume with the same professional results as paid resume preparers. A good rule of thumb: make your resume professional enough to send out on the potential employer's letterhead. If it isn't, it's probably not sharp enough.

Your resume should cover your most current work experiences (three to four jobs), with the name, location, and dates of employment plus a summary of your responsibilities relevant to the qualifications of the job you are seeking. Be sure to state your accomplishments on each job. Present your work history chronologically. Begin with your present position and work backward to your earlier jobs. If you haven't had that many jobs, organize your resume to emphasize the skills you've acquired through experience.

There are no hard and fast rules on what to include in your resume besides work experience, education, and special skills pertinent to the job for which you are applying. Professional affiliations may also be of interest to the employer. Do not list anything personal (such as marital status, date of birth, etc.) that could potentially screen you out. Salary history and references should not be included in your resume; these should be discussed in person during the interview.

Keep in mind that a resume is a sales tool. Make sure that it illustrates your unique strengths in a style and format you can be proud of. Be brief, tailor your experiences to the job you are seeking, and provide figures and facts to support your accomplishments.

Elements of a Resume

Here are the five main elements of a resume, with a brief description of each. All need not appear in the same order in every resume, and sometimes one or two are combined or left out, as you'll see in the sample resumes that follow.

NAME
Address
City, State, Zip
Phone
E-Mail Address (optional)

Objective: Employers use this information as a screening device or to assess a job match. It should grab the reader's attention and motivate him or her to read further. Make this relevant to the job for which you are applying!

Experience: The more impressive your work history, the more prominently you should display it. Use facts and figures to support accomplishments and goals reached.

List employment in reverse chronological order, putting the most promotable facts—employer or job title—first.

Give functional description of job if work history is strong and supports job objective.

List dates of employment last. They are the least important of all your information.

Skills: You may want to embed these in the employment section. Or, for career changers, list the skills section first. Highlight skills that are relevant to the potential job opening. Give short, results-oriented statements to support skills. Position your most marketable skills first.

Education: List in reverse chronological order, putting the most salable facts—school or degree—first. Mention honors or achievements, such as a high GPA or Dean's List.

Miscellaneous: Call this section anything applicable: Interests, Activities, Achievements, or Accomplishments.

Give only information that promotes your candidacy for the position for which you are applying.

References: Available upon request. Don't waste space on names and addresses. Have ready on a separate sheet.

Choosing a Resume Format

There are many different but equally acceptable ways to organize your resume. Every resume compiler and career counselor has his or her favorite method and style. The format you use should best present your strongest points and best convey your message to the potential employer. Resume books will use different terms for the various styles, but here are the three most popular types.

1. *The Chronological Resume* is the traditional style, most often used in the workplace and job search. It is also the resume style favored by most employers. That does not mean, however, that it is the most effective. A positive aspect of the chronological resume, aside from it being the traditional approach that employers may expect, is that it emphasizes past jobs that you wish your potential employer to notice. This resume is also very adaptable, with only the reverse chronological order of previous employment an essential ingredient.

2. *The Functional Resume* is most common among those reentering the job market after an absence, career changers, and those wishing to emphasize skills gained through non-work experience. This resume focuses on the many skills gained from employment and the accomplishments one has achieved. It shows a potential employer that you can do and have done a good job. What it doesn't necessarily emphasize is where you have done it and when.

3. *The Combination Resume* merges features of the functional and chronological resumes. This allows job seekers to emphasize accomplishments and skills while still maintaining the traditional format of reverse chronological order of positions held and organizations worked for. This format is perfect if your most current work is not your most impressive.

Sample After-College Chronological Resume

The Chronological Resume format is ideal for someone just graduating with little work experience. Here is a sample:

Michael King
26 E. 75th Street
New York, NY 10012
(212) 555-0007

EDUCATION: New York University, New York, NY
BA, Political Science, May 1998.
Courses include: Business Law, Applied Probability,
Statistics, Calculus, Economics, English, Creative
Writing, French.

WORK   SALES MANAGEMENT INTERN. Summers 1996-1997.
EXPERIENCE: **Bloomingdale's.** New York, NY.
Managed the sales, distribution, pricing, shelving, and display of all shoes in the main store. Intensive on-the-job
and educational training through the store's management
training program.

CAMPUS REPRESENTATIVE. School years 1995-1998.
Office of Admissions, New York University. New York, NY.
Organized and implemented an entire recruiting campaign
for qualified high school minority students. Received a
record number of minority student acceptances and
matriculates.

ACTIVITIES   President, Black Student's Association
AND HONORS: Recipient, Minority Student Scholarship
Freshman Advisor
Tutor for high-risk high school students
National Collegiate Minority Leadership Award

REFERENCES: Available upon request.

Sample Career-Changing Functional Resume

The Functional Resume format is ideal for someone changing careers since it emphasizes skills rather than past employment. Here is a sample:

Kathy Lawrence
55 W. 72nd Street
New York, NY 10012
(212) 555-2436

OBJECTIVE   To obtain a position as an administrative assistant.

AREAS OF EXPERTISE
Administrative
- Independently analyzed a major client's account for an advertising agency.
- Maintained and managed funds in excess of $50,000 for a non-profit organization.
- Managed two rental properties.

Organizational
- Set up procedures for assigned experiments and procured equipment for a research laboratory.
- Planned course syllabi to facilitate learning for students with assessed weaknesses.

Computer
- Managed data input and generated monthly reports.
- Completed courses in Excel spreadsheets and Pagemaker.
- Designed and produced monthly newsletter.

WORK HISTORY   Computer Operator, IBM Corp., New York, NY (1996-present)
                    Trouble-shooter in accounting, Cargill, Wilson, and Acree, New York, NY (1992-95)
                    Instructor, Math Department, Brookdale Community College (1989-92)

EDUCATION   New York University, MS, Mathematics (1991)
                    New York University, BA, Mathematics (1987)
                    GPA 3.7/4.0

HONORS/   Dean's List, three semesters
ACTIVITIES   Treasurer for non-profit organization

REFERENCES   Available upon request.

Sample Combination Resume

The Combination Resume allows you to use aspects of both the chronological and functional formats. This type is good for someone whose present work perhaps does not reflect his or her most impressive skills. Here is a sample:

Paul Wheaton
49 E. 57th Street
New York, NY 10012
(212) 555-0011

EDUCATION
Long Island University, Greenvale, NY; GPA 3.7/4.0
MS, Information and Computer Science, December 1991
New York University; GPA 3.4/4.0
AB, Mathematics, May 1986

QUALIFICATIONS
Career-related Projects:
- Designed and implemented multi-tasking operating system for the IBM-PC.
- Implemented compiler for Pascal-like language.
- Designed electronic mail system using PSL/PSA specification.

Languages and Operating Systems:
- Proficient in Ada, Modula-2, Pascal, C+
- Thorough knowledge of IBM-PC hardware.
- Experienced in UNIX, MS-DOS, CP/M operating systems.

Hardware:
- IBM-PC (MS-DOS), Pyramid 90x (UNIX), Cyber 990 (NOS)

WORK EXPERIENCE
Simms Programming Services, New York, NY 3/92-present
UNIX Programmer
- Responsible for porting MS-DOS database applications to IBM-PC/AT running Xenix System V. System administration.

IBM Corp., New York, NY 10/89-12/91
Computer Programmer
- Performed daily disk backup on Burroughs B-1955 machine. Executed database update programs and checks. User assistance.

Computer companies in the New York area 6/86 - 8/89
Computer Operator
- Held full-time positions. Responsible for maintaining computers.

REFERENCES   Available upon request.

Sample Combination Resume for Liberal Arts Major

As mentioned earlier, the Combination Resume allows you to use parts of both the chronological and functional formats. This type is good for liberal arts majors who have several career fields to select among because of their broad educational background. Since Laura (example resume follows) wanted to apply for jobs in broadcasting, magazine publishing, and writing speeches for a congressman, she used the combination style to avoid writing several different resumes. Here is the sample:

Laura Chic

49 W. 57th Street

New York, NY 10012

(212) 555-0011

EDUCATION   Columbia University, New York, NY; GPA 3.7/4.0
AB, May 1998
Major in English literature. Minor in psychology.
Participated in Columbia University-in-Italy Program (Rome).
Member of Columbia University's Women's Cross
Country Running.
Editor *Running Notes.* Reporter for student newspaper.
Member of Chi Omega sorority. Rush Co-Chairperson and
Panhellenic Society representative.

EXPERIENCE   **Columbia University Sports Information Office,**
New York, NY
Administrative Intern, Spring 1995 to present.
Reported on all school sports events. Managed post-game
football press box operations. Published stories about school
athletes. Wrote press releases.
Football Statistician, Fall 1996 and fall 1997.
Compiled statistics. Wrote game summaries and
weekly reports.
IBM Computers, New York, NY
Public Relations Intern, Summers 1995 and 1996.
Researched information for IBM Computer's student
advertisements and special publications. Proofread copy and
checked facts. Replied to reader correspondence. Coordinated
IBM Computer's School Visitation Program.
Salesperson, Summer 1994.
Completed nightly closings, and maintained various
departments in manager's absence. Rotated throughout
store as needed. Highest sales for two months.

INTERESTS   Enjoy playing the piano and guitar, oil and watercolor painting. Avid runner. Have traveled in Europe and throughout the western U.S.

REFERENCES   Available upon request.

Resume Checklist

- Brainstorm a list of the skills and talents you want to convey. These may include character traits such as persistence and assertiveness; work skills such as fluency in languages and computer literacy; and transferable skills such as managing, motivating, and leading people, manipulating data, evaluating and analyzing systems.
- Prepare your resume on a computer and printer that give you the same results as a professionally typeset resume.
- Use heavyweight (at least 20 lb.), high-quality paper and a laser printer if at all possible. White, off-white, or light gray papers (8½ x 11 inches) are usually safe, conservative bets. However, if you are in theater, arts, or advertising, you can be a little more daring. If you have the budget, consider buying 9½ x 12½-inch envelopes so you won't have to fold your resume and cover letter.
- Be concise and brief in your wording.
- Avoid personal pronouns.
- Use active verbs to describe your accomplishments rather than your assigned duties.
- Arrange information in descending order of importance within each section of your resume.
- Be consistent in format and style.
- Tailor your skills and experience as much as possible to each potential job opening.
- Proofread your resume, and then have a few friends proofread it as well.
- Be selective in sending out your resume. Mass mailings usually only result in spending unnecessary time and money.

Using the Computer to Design Your Resume

Welcome to the high-tech world of resume writing. Even if you don't own your own computer, many libraries have them available, and copy stores such as Kinko's rent computer time. So there is no excuse to rule out the computer in designing your resume. There are certain advantages:

- You have the ability to save your resume on a disk, which simplifies editing it for a specific company or position. Revises and updates become simple.
- Computers offer a wide range of type faces, styles (bold, italics, and so on), and sizes. Combined with a laser printout, you can achieve a professional-looking resume at modest expense.

No matter what method you use to prepare your resume, proofread it before printing. Misspelled words or typing errors reflect badly on you even if it's not your fault. Recruit a friend to help read your resume, word for word and comma for comma. And don't make last minute changes after everyone has proofed it. Somehow, you will end up with an error.

Professional Resume Preparers

It is always better to prepare your own resume, as long as you have reasonable writing skills. However, if you have trouble condensing your writing style and you have no friends who can help, no access to a university career office or books on resumes, then a professional may be able to assist you.

Before choosing a professional resume service, try to get a recommendation from someone whose judgment you trust. Find out the minimum and maximum costs before employing any service. Ask whether the price includes only writing, or typesetting and printing as well. If changes are needed, will it cost extra? Finally, always shop around for the best services available. Don't forget that many career counselors and consultants also provide resume preparation; refer to Chapter 2.

The following are firms that will assist you in preparing your resume. Keep in mind that a listing in this book does not constitute an endorsement.

The laughing stock of the company

Make sure that you don't end up as fodder for employer levity as did the following unfortunates:

One candidate wrote under Job Responsibilities: "Assassinated store manager during busiest retail season." What she meant to write was "assisted."

"Education: College, August 1890 — May 1994."

"Here are my qualifications for you to overlook."

"Please call me after 5:30 p.m. because I am self-employed and my employer does not know I am looking for another job."

Reason for leaving last job? The candidate replied: "No special reason." Another replied: "They insisted that all employees get to work by 8:45 every morning. Couldn't work under those conditions."

One applicant submitted a seven-page resume and stated, "This resume is fairly long because I have a lot to offer you."

SELECTED PROFESSIONAL RESUME PREPARERS IN THE NEW YORK AREA

Below are a list of writers certified by the Professional Association of Resume Writers, as well as others who are well recognized in the industry. Remember that working with them is a collaborative effort.

The Bakos Group
420 Lexington Ave.
New York, NY
(800) 370-6641 (All business conducted by fax)
http://empire.na.com/bakos/bakoshp.html
Since 1981, Bakos has helped 250,000 job seekers worldwide, from entry-level to professional Fortune 500 positions. They are open 24 hours a day, 7 days per week, have a staff of 100 writers, and guarantee that if you do not receive a position they will rewrite your resume for free. Bring in their ad in the *Yellow Pages* and receive six months of free on-line access to over 140,000 subscribers, including 80% of the Fortune 500.

Career Blazers Resume Service
590 5th Ave.
New York, NY 10036
(212) 719-3232
http://www.cblazers.com/
President: Bill Lewis
Career Blazers has 50 years of experience in the employment industry and 22 books to their credit. It is also the only service with an on-site employment service. Director George Gruber believes that this affiliation helps to service their clients better because they are in constant contact with potential employers and better understand their needs. Resumes can be listed in the National Resume Bank and the Executive Search Firm Registry. Customized mailings are also available, utilizing the company's own database network of 9.5 million employers.

Career Crafters
310 Madison Ave.
New York, NY 10016
(212) 687-7500

Boasts over 25 years of service to job seekers and employers. Offers resume and cover letter assistance with rush service as well as free placement assistance. Free consultation and resume critique.

Career Pro Resume Services
150 Nassau St., #1024
New York, NY 10038
(212) 227-1434
Contact: Judith Friedler
Judy Friedler is a certified professional resume writer who works closely with clients to determine career goals, accomplishments, and skills. Prices for full development and preparation of a resume for individuals with under 10 years of experience range from $125-195; original cover letters are $35. For those with over 10 years experience, the cost is $195-295. Targeted direct mail campaigns are also available. Consultation is free.

CompuCraft
124 E. 40th St., Suite 403
New York, NY
(212) 697-4005
Contact: Eta Barman, David First
Compu-Craft does not use "cookie-cutter" resumes and works individually with entry-level, professional, and executive job searchers as well as career changers to develop a resume that specifically meets their needs. Career workshops, counseling, and interview training is also available. Saturday and evening appointments are available and evaluation is free. Call for prices.

Executive Resumes International
20 W. 38th St., 4th Floor
New York, NY 10018
(800) 669-0359
This agency specializes in highlighting transferable skills in a format they've termed the "concept resume," which is particularly useful for career changers. It runs from $95-295 and includes an in-depth interview. Traditional resumes are $55-95. Career counseling and interview training is available, as well as a data-base of employers, from small business owners to multinational corporations.

Gilbert Career Resumes
275 Madison Ave.
New York, NY 10016
(212) 661-6878
(800) 967-3846
career @TIAC.com
Director Marty Weitzman, with 30 years of experience in the field, is on the Board of the Professional Association of Resume Writers and conducts work-shops for its members. The agency, with clients nationwide, specializes in resumes for retail, fashion, hospitality, and financial industries, though they work with people in every field. Fees, charged at an hourly rate of $100, average $200 but can run from $100-1,000. Mass mailing and direct mail are also available.

Key-Rite/Resume-Riter
180 Broadway, 12th Floor
New York, NY 10038
(212) 385-9363
Key-Rite is a less individual, less personal, and less expensive resume service. Resumes start at just $10 per page for a standard corporate format: clients complete a questionnaire and then speak with a writer who completes the resume. Custom-written cover letters are $5 each. Evaluation is free, as are their job bank and help-wanted list. Other useful services include fax accounts, mail accounts for responding to ads, and an answering service. Consulting and counseling is also available starting at $25/hr.

National Professional Writers Group
450 7th Ave.
New York, NY
(212) 695-6950
Handles resumes in addition to business and professional writing. Works with executives, self-employed, and everyone in between.

Network Resumes
301 Madison Ave., 3rd Floor
New York, NY 10017
(212) 687-2411
http://starbase.ingress.com/nyworks/
Director: John Aigner
Network Resumes at The Livelihood Center is a one-stop shopping center where you can mix and match services to meet your needs and budget. Resume writing, which includes a complete interview draft, review session(s), proofs as required, laserset, and 50 copies is $120-145 for a recent college grad and $190 for professionals. Editing and rewriting of drafts is also available. The Center also provides interview coaching and rehearsal, access to the Internet, industry seminars, workshops, and support groups. Free review and evaluation.

Professional Resumes
60 E. 42nd St., Suite 839
New York, NY
(212) 697-1282
Contact: David Klot
David Klot has written over 20,000 resumes in his 25 years in business. He works with recent college grads as well as middle and upper-level managers to put together a one-page accomplishment-oriented resume. Free writing updates are offered on all resumes, which run $150-300, including the evaluation. Interview training is also available.

Electronic Resume Issues

Tom Washington, author of *Resume Power: Selling Yourself on Paper,* provides some hints for preparing electronic resumes.

The term "electronic resumes" refers to the fact that more companies are electronically scanning resumes and storing information in computer databases. These resumes are then available in seconds when managers seek a person with just the right background. It also refers to the ability to send resumes electronically to electronic bulletin boards, enabling employers from all over the world to "discover" you.

Interviewer: Does an electronic resume have to be different from a traditional resume?

Tom: Yes and no. No, in the sense that the things that make any resume effective will make a scanned resume effective. Visually it still has to be easy to skim and read, and it should include results and contributions rather than just duties. Your results and contributions are the things that cause employers to want to meet you.

But, yes, the resume also needs to be different. To be effective your resume must be easy to scan into the computer database, and it needs to be easy to retrieve. Without being properly composed, some words or whole lines can become scrambled and thus difficult to read. You should do everything you can to avoid that.

In order to prevent your resume from getting "scrambled," it helps to understand how a resume is scanned. First the resume is placed within an electronic scanner, which sends a "picture" of the document to a computer with optical character read (OCR) software. The software then translates the picture into words.

To ensure that your resume is properly scanned, just follow these simple rules. Laser printed resumes scan best. Avoid nine-pin dot matrix printers, although 24-pin dot matrix printers will produce acceptable quality. Avoid the use of italics and fancy fonts. Some scanners cannot read them properly. Stick with Times Roman, Bookman, Arial, Helvetica, Courier, or fonts that are closely related to these. Avoid the use of shading, columns, boxes, vertical lines, or underlining. All of these things can confuse scanners.

Inter.: What can people do to get their resume read?

Tom: The answer is to understand the importance of key words. When a job becomes available, decisions are made as to what kind of experience and knowledge is required. Then certain "key words" are selected. These key words are chosen because it is believed that virtually all highly qualified people will use these words in their resumes. For example, a manager needing a programmer in COBOL on a UNIX operating system, using an IBM AS400, would request that the computer search its database for resumes with those terms. Then a human will need to skim each resume selected by the database to determine if the person does in fact have the desired background. If so, a key will be punched, the resume will be printed out, and an interview will be arranged.

Inter.: How do people make sure their resumes contain the right key words?

Tom: Put yourself in the shoes of an employer who is looking for someone with your experience. If you were looking for someone like you, what key words would you look for? Then simply make sure those words appear somewhere in the resume. The computer doesn't care if they appear at the beginning or at the end; it will find them and cause these resumes to appear on the computer screen.

Inter.: Any other hints?

Tom: Try to think of the different ways an employer might look for key words. If you are an RN, make sure the acronym *RN* appears, but also find a place to spell it out—registered nurse. Be aware of synonyms. If you are an attorney, make sure the word *lawyer* also appears. Find ways to bring in the buzz words and jargon that are used in your field.

Here is a checklist for preparing the ideal scannable resume:
- Use 8½ x 11-inch paper, light color.
- Avoid dot matrix printouts. Laser prints scan easier.
- If using a computer, use the 12 point font size, and do not condense spacing between letters.
- Avoid using a newspaper-type format, columns, or graphics.
- Be sure to include your name at the top of the second page if your resume is two pages.
- Key words or accomplishments are often scanned; make sure your resume contains words related to the position for which you are applying. Use "hard" vocabulary: "computer skills," "software packages," etc. Also avoid flowery language.

Resumix provides a brochure, "Preparing the Ideal Scannable Resume." If you are interested, call Resumix at (408) 988-0444.

The Cover Letter Adds a Custom Touch

Never, never send your resume without a cover letter. Whether you are answering a want ad or following up an inquiry call or interview, you should always include a letter with your resume. Use your researching skills to locate the individual doing the hiring. Using the personal touch of addressing your cover letter to a real person will save you the headache of having your resume sent to H.R.'s stack of resumes, or possibly even being tossed out.

A good cover letter should be brief and interesting enough to grab the reader's attention. If you've spoken with the individual, you may want to remind him or her of the conversation. Or, if you and the person to whom you are writing know someone in common, be sure to mention it.

In the next paragraph or two, specify what you could contribute to the company in terms that indicate you've done your homework on the firm and the industry. Use figures and facts to support your accomplishments that are relevant to the job opening.

Finally, in the last paragraph, either request an interview or tell the reader that you will follow-up with a phone call within a week to arrange a mutually convenient meeting.

Sample Cover Letter

Mary Baker
52 W. 72nd Street
New York, NY 10012

August 12, 1998

Ms. Jacqueline Doe
Wide World Publishing Company
22 Central Park Blvd.
New York, NY 10012

Dear Ms. Doe:

As an honors graduate of New York University with two years of copy editing and feature-writing experience with the *New York Weekly*, I am confident that I would make a successful editorial assistant with Wide World.

Besides my strong editorial background, I offer considerable business experience. I have held summer jobs in an insurance company, a law firm, and a data processing company. My familiarity with word processing should prove particularly useful to Wide World now that you have become fully automated.

I would like to interview with you as soon as possible and would be happy to check in with your office about an appointment. If you prefer, your office can contact me between the hours of 11 a.m. and 3 p.m. at (212) 555-6886.

Sincerely,

Mary Baker

Sample Cover Letter in Reply to Want Ad

Stacy Barnes
34 Central Park Blvd.
New York, NY 10012
(212) 555-2468

May 15, 1998

Mr. Tom White
Anderson Consulting
24 Wall Street
New York, NY 10012

Dear Mr. White:

My background seems ideal for your advertisement in the May 13 issue of the *New York Times* for an experienced accountant. My five years of experience in a small accounting firm in Brooklyn has prepared me to move on to a more challenging position.

As you can see from my resume, enclosed, my experience includes not only basic accounting work but also some consulting with a few of our firm's larger clients. This experience combined with an appetite for hard work, an enthusiastic style, and a desire to succeed makes me a strong candidate for your consideration. I assisted the company in expanding its clientele by 30%.

I would appreciate the opportunity to discuss how my background could meet the needs of Anderson Consulting. I will call you within a week to arrange a convenient time to meet.

Sincerely,

Stacy Barnes

Sample Networking Cover Letter

Jose Ramirez
560 Central Park Blvd.
New York, NY 10012
(212) 555-6886

December 2, 1997

Mr. James King
3-Q Inc.
45 Houston St.
New York, NY 10012

Dear James:

Just when everything seemed to be going smoothly at my job, the company gave us a Christmas present that nobody wanted: management announced that half the department will be laid off before the new year. Nobody knows yet just which heads are going to roll. But whether or not my name is on the list, I am definitely back in the job market.

I have already lined up a few interviews. But knowing how uncertain job hunting can be, I can use all the contacts I can get. You know my record—both from when we worked together at 3-Q and since then. But in case you've forgotten the details, I've enclosed my resume. I know that you often hear of job openings as you wend your way about New York and Long Island. I'd certainly appreciate your passing along any leads you think might be worthwhile.

My best to you and Susan for the Holidays.

Cordially,

Jose

Enclosure

Do's and don'ts for cover letters
Do:

- Send a resume with every cover letter.
- Use high-quality, high-rag-content paper.
- Target an individual person about the job opening.
- Be brief and interesting enough to capture the reader's attention.
- Tailor your experiences to meet the potential job opening.
- Use acceptable business format; letter should be well spaced on the page.
- Have someone check your letter for grammar, spelling, and formatting mistakes.
- State an agenda in the letter and follow-up in the amount of time you specified.

Don't:

- Send your first draft of a letter just so you can meet the deadline.
- Send your letter to the president of the company simply because you don't know the name of the hiring authority.
- Include information that can be found on your resume.
- Give only one possible time to meet.
- Call the company four times a day after you have sent the letter.

CYBERTIPS FOR RESUME AND COVER LETTER WRITING

Using the Net to find more sample resumes and cover letters is a good place to start. Many of the job-search services or college career center homepages also have tips on resume and cover letter writing. Some on-line services will also post your resume for employer perusal.

Career Channel
http://riceinfo.rice.edu/projects/careers/
Rice University lists jobs, links, and a wealth of other job-search information.

Career Services On-line—College of William and Mary
http://www.wm.edu/csrv/career/career.html
Excellent starting point for career service practitioners and students, covering topics from resumes to job listings.

Cover Letters by the Rensselaer Polytechnic Institute Writing Center
http://www.rpi.edu/dept/llc/writecenter/web/text/coverltr.html

E-Span: Interactive Employment Network
http://www.espan.com

Resumes from Yahoo
http://www.yahoo.com/Business/Employment/Resumes/

Resumes On-Line
http://199.94.216.72:81/online.html

BOOKS ON RESUME AND COVER LETTER WRITING

The following books are full of all the how-to information you'll need to prepare an effective resume and most are available from bookstores or your local library.

Besson, Taunee. *National Business and Employment Weekly Resumes.* New York: John Wiley & Sons, 1994.

Downe, Robert P. *The Better Book for Getting Hired: How to Write a Great Resume, Sell Yourself in the Interview, and Get That Job* (3rd ed.). North Vancouver, BC: Self Counsel Press, 1993.

Fournier, Myra, and Jeffrey Spin. *Encyclopedia of Job-Winning Resumes.* Ridgefield, CT: Round Lake Publishers, 1991.

Hahn, Harley, and Rick Stout. *The Internet Yellow Pages.* Berkeley, CA: Osborne McGraw-Hill, 1994.

Jackson, Tom, with Ellen Jackson. *The New Perfect Resume.* New York: Anchor/Doubleday, 1996.

Kennedy, Joyce Lain, and Thomas J. Morrow. *Electronic Resume Revolution.* New York: John Wiley & Sons, 1994.

Krannich, Ronald L., and Caryl Krannich. *High Impact Resumes and Letters: How to Communicate Your Qualifications to Employers* (7th ed.). Manassas, VA: Impact Publications, 1997.

Lewis, Adele. *How to Write a Better Resume.* Woodbury, NY: Barron's, 1993.

Nadler, Burton Jay. *Liberal Arts Power: What It Is and How to Sell It on Your Resume* (2nd ed.). Princeton, NJ: Peterson's Guides, 1990.

Parker, Yana. *The Damn Good Resume Guide: A Crash Course in Resume Writing* (3rd ed.). Berkeley, CA: Ten Speed Press, 1996.

Podesta, Sandra, and Andrea Paxton. *201 Killer Cover Letters.* New York: McGraw-Hill, 1995.

Provenzano, Steven. *Top Secret Resumes and Cover Letters.* Chicago: Dearborn Publishing, 1995.

Smith, Michael H. *The Resume Writer's Handbook.* New York: Harper and Row, 1994.

Weinstein, Bob. *Resumes Don't Get Jobs: The Realities and Myths of Job Hunting.* New York: McGraw-Hill, 1994.

Yate, Martin. *Resumes That Knock 'em Dead.* Holbrook, MA: Bob Adams, 1995.

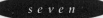

seven

The Killer Interview

Your networking paid off and your resume was a success. You are now ready to take the next step in your job search. Unfortunately, though, your resume won't automatically grant you a job, and all the contacts in the world won't do you any good if you don't handle yourself well in an interview. All interviews have the same goal: to convince the interviewer that he or she should hire you or recommend that you be hired. That is what counts. Remember, this interview is all that stands between you and the job, so make it a killer interview. This chapter will guide you through the steps and give you an idea of what to expect and what to avoid when interviewing.

Dr. Bob's Six Steps to a Killer Interview

STEP 1: Preparing for the Interview

Good preparation shows ambition and zeal and is a key part of interviewing that is often forgotten. The more you prepare, the more you will be relaxed and comfortable with the interview. Additionally, the more you prepare, the greater your chance of impressing someone with your knowledge of the company and the interview process.

Researching the company before the interview is a must in your preparation. You should be familiar with the following company information before your interview begins:

- The interviewer's name.
- General information about the company, such as the location of the home office, number of plants/stores and their locations, names of parent company, subsidiaries, etc.
- Organizational structure, type of supervision, type of training program.
- Philosophy, goals, and image.

- Financial details, including sales volume, stock price, percent of annual growth in earnings per share, recent profits, etc.
- The competition in the industry and the company's place in it.
- The products or services marketed by the company, including recent media coverage of them.
- Career path in your field.
- Recent news items regarding the company or the industry. It is especially important to check the *Wall Street Journal*'s business section to see if the company you are interviewing with is mentioned on the morning of the interview. Be prepared to speak on many aspects of the company.

Researching the company via the World Wide Web

One of the easiest ways to research a company or organization is to do so over the Net. While not every organization has a WWW address, more and more companies are beginning to see the benefits of a homepage. Increasingly, companies are posting employment opportunities on their Web pages. Library Net addresses, mentioned in Chapter 4, are also a good place to check. Try a few of these sites for starters:

Computer-Related Companies
http://www.xnet.com/~blatura/computer.shtml
An excellent list of U.S. computer-related company Web pages.

Hoover's Company Profiles
http://www.hoovers.com/bizreg.html
Links to over 1,100 corporate Web sites, combined with extensive information about many corporations, including history, current business, personnel, and office locations. A wonderful resource.

Hot 1000 List
http://techweb.cmp.com/techweb/ia/hot1000/hot1.html
This list includes any homepages officially established by or for the company among companies comprising the Fortune 1,000.

Industrial Companies
http://www.xnet.com/~blatura/industry.shtml
A fine list of U.S. industrial company Web pages.

Another part of preparation is constructing a list of questions to ask the interviewer at the end of the meeting. Producing a list of questions and asking intelligent questions about the company indicates that you're prepared and that you did your research. We include a list of possible questions for you to ask later in this chapter.

Practicing Before Your Interview

Another key part of preparation and of conducting the most successful of interviews is to practice the interview as much and in as many ways as possible. This can take many forms. However, the best way is to build a list of the questions you feel will be asked and to make sure that you know how to answer them and have answered them out loud to yourself or to someone helping you with a mock interview. Practice your answers and multiple variations of them and you will be much better prepared for the interview.

STEP 2: Dressing Right: Interviewing Fashion Do's and Don'ts

Never underestimate the power of a sharply dressed man or woman during an interview. Proper attire is a key ingredient to a good first impression with your prospective employer. Hygiene is equally important. Shaving should be done the morning before the interview. Perfume and cologne should be low key. Keep the hair trimmed, fingernails clean, and let your credentials and charm do the rest.

The Career-Dressed Woman

Within reason, a variety of conservative colors are appropriate for most interview situations. Many tasteful suits are available in black, brown, teal, taupe, olive, forest, maroon, burgundy, and plum. When selecting a suit, especially if you are on a limited budget, focus on classic cuts and styles. The proper fit is just as essential as the suit itself. A good suit should last at least five years. Try to select a high-quality fabric such as wool or wool gabardine. These are the coolest fabrics—making them appropriate not only for the stress of interviewing but also for everyday wear year-round.

If the shoe fits wear it! We see countless well-dressed women with shoes with run-down heels and scraped up toes. Don't brainwash yourself by thinking that they are only shoes and nobody looks at your feet anyway. Shoes are one of those make-or-break elements of your wardrobe. Make sure the local shoe repair has done a good job at keeping yours new looking.

Keep it feminine: a lot of women still hold the idea that professional means masculine. Not true. Women's professional attire has come into its own since the late '80s and early '90s, when stiffly tailored dark suits paired with floppy bows and ties were all the rage. These have been replaced with soft scarves, unique pins, and more attractive colors and styles.

Keep in mind when selecting professional clothing that "feminine" in no way means "sleazy." Tight skirts, too high heels, and low-cut blouses are never appropriate, no matter how conservative their color or casual the office.

The bottom line is that much of business is influenced by image. You may not get that job because you look great, but not looking good may be a reason why you don't get hired.

The Career-Dressed Man

On your big shopping spree for the proper suit, try to be conservative, not flashy. Stick with darker colors like navy blue, dark gray, or black. Single-breasted vs. double-breasted? Whatever you look best in is what you should buy. Usually single-breasted is more conservative and probably best for interviewing.

Shirts and ties are very important in the construction of the perfect suit. Your dress shirts should be comfortable and fit properly around the neck. Tight shirts in the neck area tend to make you resemble Baby Huey or the Pillsbury Doughboy.

The tie can say a lot about the individual, so when choosing your tie be careful and take your time. Try to steer yourself toward the 100% silk ties; they tend to portray a more professional look. Don't allow the tie to overpower your suit with loud colors and crazy patterns. The proper length is also vital in choosing the right tie. Too short a tie makes you look silly. Once knotted, a tie should reach over your belt buckle. Anything higher is not acceptable.

Dress socks are a must. No thick socks and no athletic socks; this is your career, not a gymnasium. Coordinated color socks are essential and they should come over the calf so that when you sit down, you aren't flashing skin between the top of the sock and trouser cuff.

Polished wing-tip shoes are always safe. Make sure that your shoes are as shiny as a new dime. As is the case with women's shoes, your shoes can say a lot about you and should not be in a state of disrepair.

Common Dressing Mistakes Made by Men

Now that you are an expert on career dressing, here are a few mistakes made by men in their quest to dress to impress:

- The belt and suspenders faux pas. You only need one or the other to keep your pants up.
- Make sure that you are not wearing high-water pants. The length of the pant leg should reach the middle of your shoe.
- No knit ties. They went out some years ago with leisure suits.
- Iron your shirt. Wrinkles are not in style.
- No gaudy rings or chains. Save them for bar hopping or the discos. The fact remains that clothes make a difference in our society. One might wish that impressions did not count, but they do!

How to dress

A friend of ours who wanted to break into investment banking finally landed her first big interview with Merrill Lynch. It was fairly easy for her to do her homework on a company of that size. Two days before the interview, however, it suddenly dawned on her that she had no idea how to dress. How did she solve her problem?

"It was pretty easy, actually, and fun, too," says Laura. "All I did was go and hang around outside the office for 15 minutes at lunch time to see what everybody else was wearing."

However, we recommend that even if the office attire is casual, one should still dress professionally. One career counselor recommends that one should "always dress one step above the attire of those in the office where you are interviewing."

STEP 3: The First Impression

The first impression, whether we like it or not, is important in a successful interview. Start off the interview right! Arriving at least ten minutes early helps you relax a little rather than rushing into the meeting all tense and harried. Remember to treat the receptionist, secretary, and anyone else you meet the same way you would treat any potential boss. Be friendly and professional. They often have input into the selection of candidates.

The beginning of the interview is crucial. Many experts feel that the decision to hire you is made during the first four minutes. The rest of the interview is used to justify this earlier decision. Four things are important in creating that first impression. First, a firm handshake, for both men and women, is important. Second, try to make eye contact with the interviewer as much as possible—but don't have a staredown. Third, try to convey a positive attitude with a friendly smile; never underestimate yourself—past jobs and education have equipped you with valuable skills. And finally, say something simple early on to get those first words out of your mouth: "Very nice to meet you" should suffice. It is also important to address your interviewer by last name unless instructed to do otherwise.

STEP 4: Express Yourself

The bulk of the interview is designed for you to answer questions posed by the interviewer. Here are a few tips:

- Be aware of your non-verbal behavior. Wait to sit until you are offered a chair. Look alert, speak in a clear, strong voice, and stay relaxed. Make good eye contact, avoid nervous mannerisms, and try to be a good listener as well as a good talker. Smile.

- Follow the interviewer's lead, but try to get the interviewer to describe the position and duties to you fairly early in the interview so that you can later relate your background and skills in context.
- Be specific, concrete, and detailed in your answers. The more information you volunteer, the better the employer gets to know you and thereby is able to make a wise hiring decision.
- Don't mention salary in a first interview unless the employer does. If asked, give a realistic range and add that the opportunity is the most important factor for you.
- Offer examples of your work and references that will document your best qualities.
- Answer questions as truthfully and as frankly as you can. Never appear to be "glossing over" anything. On the other hand, stick to the point and don't over-answer questions. The interviewer may steer the interview into ticklish political or social questions. If this occurs, answer honestly, trying not to say more than is necessary.
- Never make derogatory remarks about present or former employers or companies.

QUESTIONS YOU MAY BE ASKED DURING AN INTERVIEW

Bear in mind that all questions you are asked during an interview serve a specific purpose. Try to put yourself in the interviewer's shoes. Imagine why he or she is asking the questions, and try to provide the answers that, while never dishonest, present you in the most desirable light. Direct your responses toward the particular position for which you are applying. What follows are some questions that employers often ask during interviews. As we mentioned earlier, it is advisable to rehearse answers to these questions prior to your interview so you can appear relaxed and confident.

Ice Breakers
These are designed to put you at ease and to see how well you engage in informal conversation. Be yourself, act natural, and be friendly.
  a. Did you have any trouble finding your way here?
  b. How was your plane flight?
  c. Can you believe this weather?
  d. I see you're from Omaha. Why do you want to work here?

Work History and Education
These are to assess whether your background and skills are appropriate for the position. Talk about your skills coherently and relate them to the job to be filled.

*Note: Questions marked with an asterisk (*) are among the toughest to answer. Further on in this chapter, the "15 Toughest Interview Questions" are treated in some depth so you can "ace" them when the time comes.

Give specific examples of how you used certain skills in the past. Remember that questions you are asked concerning your past will help the employer determine how you might react and make decisions in the future.

a. *Tell me about yourself.
b. Tell me about the most satisfying job/internship you've ever held.
c. Tell me about the best boss you ever had. The worst.
d. What have you learned from some of the jobs you've held?
e. For what achievements were you recognized by your superiors at your last position?
f. What are you looking for in an employer?
g. What are you seeking in a position?
h. Why did you choose to get a degree in the area that you did?
i. In what activities have you participated outside of work (or class)?
j. How did you finance your education?
k. *What do you like/dislike about your current (or last) job?

Ambitions and Plans

These are questions to evaluate your ambition, how clearly you have thought about your future goals, their feasibility, and how actively you seek to meet them.

a. Are you a joiner or more individually centered? A leader or a group member? A committee member or chairperson? (There isn't necessarily a wrong answer to this type of question. Keep in mind that a ship full of captains will flounder just as badly as a ship with none at all.)
b. What job in our company would you choose if you were free to do so?
c. What does success mean to you? How do you judge it?
d. Assuming you are hired for this job, what do you see as your future?
e. What personal characteristics do you think are necessary for success in this field?
f. How far will you go to get ahead in your career?
g. Are you willing to prove yourself as a staff member of our firm? How do you envision your role?
h. Are you willing to work overtime?
i. *Where do you see yourself five years from now?
j. How much money do you hope to earn in five years? Ten years?

Company or Organization

These questions are to determine if you have conscientiously researched the company and if you would be a "match" for them. They also indicate your interest in the company.

a. Do you prefer working for a small or large organization?
b. Do you prefer a private or non-private organization? Why?
c. What do you know about our organization?
d. *Why are you interested in this company?

 e. What kind of work are you interested in doing for us?

 f. What do you feel our organization has to offer you?

 g. *Why do you think you can contribute to our company?

Values and Self-Assessment

These help the interviewer get to know you better and to determine how well you understand yourself. They also help to inform the interviewer of what motivates you.

 a. What kinds of personal satisfactions do you hope to gain through work?

 b. If you had unlimited funds, what would you do?

 c. *If you could live during any time in history, when and where would you live?

 d. What motivates you?

 e. What are your strengths and weaknesses?

 f. How would you describe yourself?

 g. What do you do with your free time?

 h. What kind of people do you like to work with?

 i. How do you adapt to other cultures?

 j. *What is your greatest achievement?

 k. *How do you manage stress?

How to Handle Objections During the Interview

It is not uncommon to face objections in an interview. It may be that the interviewer believes you lack some skills required. Don't panic! If you keep a level head, you will be able to recover. For example, one woman was applying for an assistant buyer position in the fragrance department of a retail operation although she had never sold perfumes. Her background was in shoes. The interviewer didn't feel she had enough knowledge of perfumes. But by the end of the interview, she had swayed the interviewer with facts of her past achievements as a salesperson, convincing him that skilled people are capable of learning any product line. She even discussed trends in the fragrance industry, which she had researched in a trade magazine—surprising the interviewer, who didn't expect her to know much about the subject.

 If an interviewer appears to have an objection to hiring you, ask what it is. With this knowledge, you may be able to change the interviewer's mind or redefine the job description to fit your qualifications.

STEP 5: Questions, You Must Have Questions

A typical interviewer comment toward the close of an interview is to ask if you have any questions. Never just say "no." Keep a list of questions in mind to ask. Sometimes even the worst of interviews can be salvaged by good questions. If you believe that most of your questions were answered during the interview, try the "not-really-a-question" tactic. This might be a statement such as, "As I mentioned, I believe that my creativity and attention to detail are my strengths. How do you think these would fit into the organization?" Here are a few other questions you might ask.

QUESTIONS TO ASK INTERVIEWERS

- What would a normal working day be like?
- About how many individuals go through your program each year?
- How much contact is there with management?
- During training, are employees transferred among functional fields?
- How soon could I expect to be advanced to the next level in the career path?
- How much travel is normally expected?
- Will I be expected to meet certain deadlines? How frequent are they?
- How often are performance reviews given?
- How much decision-making authority is given after one year?
- Does the company provide any educational benefits?
- How frequently do you relocate professional employees?
- Have any new product lines/services been announced recently?
- What are the essential skills/qualities necessary for an employee to succeed in this position?
- Where are the last two people who held this position (did they leave the company or get promoted)?
- What role would my job play in helping the company achieve its corporate mission and make a profit?
- What are the five most important duties of this job?
- Why did you join the company? What is it about the company that keeps you here?
- What has the company's growth pattern been over the past five years?

At the conclusion of the interview, ask when a hiring decision will be made. This is important not only because it reconfirms your interest in the position but also so you'll know when, realistically, to expect a response. Don't forget, of course, to thank your interviewer for his or her time and to make clear your interest in the position if you feel there may be any doubt about this point.

STEP 6: The Aftermath

As soon as you leave the interview and have a chance, take notes on what you feel you could improve upon for your next interview and on what you feel went particularly well. After all, experience is only valuable to the extent that you're willing to learn from it. It also helps to make a note of something in the interview you might use in your thank-you letter.

The All Important Thank-You Letter

Always follow up each interview with a prompt thank-you letter—written the same day, if possible. The purpose of the letter is to supplement the presentation you made. Thank the interviewer for his or her hospitality. Express continued interest in the position, and mention up to three additional points to sell yourself further. Highlight how your specific experience or knowledge is directly applicable to the company's immediate needs, and if you forgot to mention something important in the interview, say it now. If possible, try to comment on something the interviewer said. Use that comment to show how your interests and skills perfectly match what they're looking for.

The thank-you letter should be sent A.S.A.P.! Your name should remain in front of the interviewer as much as possible. Sending the letter immediately will demonstrate how serious you are about the position. It may well be the final factor in helping you land the job.

Get the most from your references

References should remain confidential and never revealed until a company is close to making you an offer and you want to receive one.

Always brief your references before you supply an interviewer with their names and numbers. Tell the references what company you're interviewing with and what the job is. Give them some background on the company and the responsibilities you'll be asked to handle.

Your references will then be in a position to help sell your abilities. Finally, don't abuse your references. If you give their names too often, they may lose enthusiasm for your cause.

Waiting

Now the waiting begins. Try not to be too impatient, and remember that for the time being no answer is better than a rejection. There could be many reasons why you haven't heard from the company. It could be that the interview process hasn't concluded, or that other commitments have kept the company from making a decision. The most important point to remember during this time is that all your hopes shouldn't be pinned on one or two interviews. The job search is continuous and shouldn't stop until you have accepted a job offer. Keeping all your options open is the best possible plan.

However, if much time has passed and you haven't heard anything from a company in which you are particularly interested, a telephone call or letter asking about the status of your application is appropriate. This inquiry should be stated in a manner that is not pushy but shows your continued interest in the firm. Remember that waiting is an integral part of the job hunt, but a demonstration of your continued interest is appropriate.

Many job seekers experience a kind of euphoria after a good interview. Under the impression that a job offer is imminent, a candidate may discontinue the search. This is a serious mistake. The hiring decision may take weeks or may not be made at all. On average, about six weeks elapse between the time a person makes initial contact with a company and receives a final answer. If you let up on your job search, you will prolong it. Maintain a constant sense of urgency. Get on with the next interview. Your search isn't over until an offer is accepted and you actually begin your new job.

15 Toughest Interview Questions—and How To Answer Them

1. Tell me about yourself. This question, in one form or another, is one of the most likely to be asked. It is also one of the most likely questions to be answered poorly. Answer it without going into your personal life or family background. Stick to your professional and educational background and how it applies to the job you are interested in. Focus on your strengths and—especially with this question—remember to keep your response brief.

2. Teach me how to do something. This question is sometimes used in a consulting or sales company interview. One candidate responded by verbally teaching the interviewer how to play tennis. The subject of the lesson isn't what matters but, rather, the teaching presentation. The interviewer is assessing how well you would do in front of a client. Do you have the skills to impress or persuade a person, and are you articulate and sophisticated in your presentation? Most importantly, can you think on your feet?

3. Should city buses be free? You are probably wondering what free buses have to do with you getting the job. Nothing! Instead, the interviewer wants to see how you think the question through. The interviewer doesn't expect you to have expertise in this area and wants dialogue to occur. Don't be afraid to ask questions to determine whether you are heading in the right direction. Always modify your thinking with whatever information the interview may provide to you. Keep in mind that analytical ability is important but so are enthusiasm and creativity.

4. Do you know how to operate a Macintosh computer? On your resume you listed PC knowledge, but you have no experience with the Mac. Then why did the interviewer ask this question? Either the company uses Macs or the interviewer wanted to pull a weakness from your resume. Rather than bluntly saying "no," rephrase your response as: "I have gained a good deal of experience on the PC and with many programs. I feel comfortable with computers, and the transition to the Mac should be fairly easy."

5. Why do you think you can contribute to our company? Most candidates will answer in a typical manner that they are energetic, motivated, and a hard worker. This may or may not be true, but every interviewer has heard this response. What is more effective is to respond with examples or facts from your past experiences that draw the interviewer a picture of how you are a go-getter. This is an excellent question to prepare for, as it gives you an idea of what makes you unique from all other qualified candidates on the market.

6. If you could live during any time in history, when and where would you live? This is an off-the-wall question but it will occur sometimes. The interviewer probably doesn't expect a specific answer. And he may not let you off the hook after you give your answer. Feel free to give yourself time to think before answering; a pensive pause can sometimes even help an interview. Whatever your answer, have a reason for choosing it because almost certainly the interviewer will follow up with, "Why did you choose that?" At work the unexpected happens, and the interviewer wants to see how you deal with it.

7. What is your greatest achievement? This question allows the interviewer to assess both values and skills. What you select as your achievement will express what is important to you. And at the same time your narrative will reveal skills you have acquired. The interviewer will be interested in listening for skills necessary for the job opening.

8. Do you think your grades were a good indication of your academic achievement? If you were an A student, you can respond enthusiastically, "Yes!" However, those of us who had less than fantastic grades will respond differently. There are many reasons you may not have had high grades. For example: you worked full time while attending school or you were involved in many outside organizations. Turn the answer into a positive by explaining the benefits you received from the trade-offs of working and attending school. Emphasize your common sense and creativity rather than your grades. Besides, grades are not everything.

9. Why are you interested in this company? If you've done your homework on the company, you shouldn't sweat over this question. This is your opportunity to show how well your skills and values match that of the company's.

10. What do you like/dislike about your current (or last) job? You need to be alert when answering this question. Criticizing a former employer could send the message that you are a troublemaker or have a negative attitude, which could spell the end to your prospects with this company. Be as positive about your work experience as possible. Emphasize what you contributed and learned from the company. Even a negative experience can be translated into challenges and learning opportunities.

11. Describe how you dealt with a difficult problem. Try to be as positive as you can, and focus on the approach you used rather than any negative outcomes. For example, describe how you examined the problem, developed several alternative solutions, and implemented the solutions. Emphasize any positive outcomes from your solutions.

12. Where do you see yourself five years from now? Be realistic in your answer rather than trying to impress the interviewer. You can reiterate your goals to advance while still being a team player. And you can add that new opportunities are bound to arise within the company, which will also affect what you would like to be doing five years from now. Emphasize how the current job you are interviewing for will prepare you for five-year goals.

13. How do you manage stress? Listen carefully to the question. This isn't asking "can" you manage stress, but rather "how." The basic answer to this question involves giving an example of how you maintained your cool, pulled everyone together, and came up with a positive result, all without becoming overwhelmed.

14. What can you do for our company that someone else cannot? Similar to Question 5, this question usually will come after a description of the job has been provided. You need to reiterate what skills you have that pertain to the position and the company overall. Reemphasize those qualities that you feel are unique and how they might help the organization.

15. Could you explain these gaps in your work history? You may have gaps in your work history for many legitimate reasons. What you want to express is that you enjoy working and that when things aren't going as planned (maybe you were laid off) you are challenged to learn and overcome. Be sure to describe any studying or volunteer work that you may have done while unemployed.

9 Interview Styles to Watch For

The interviewing process can be tricky at times. Most applicants are clueless as to how the interview will go or what it will entail. Many job seekers and career changers will eventually encounter some of these interview types. Knowing a little about each of them is certainly advantageous. Knowing what to expect will boost your confidence and dry out those nervous, sweaty palms.

Behavioral Interviewing. A new technique for interviewing, behavioral interviewing assumes that past behavior predicts future performance. You can easily recognize when an interviewer is using "behavioral interviewing" because you will be asked questions about how you have worked in the past. For example, "Tell me about a time when you successfully learned a new software package"; or, "Tell me about a conflict you had with a co-worker and how you dealt with it." The employer expects you to tell short stories about yourself to give more insight into how you behave at work.

The best strategy to use when answering behavioral interview questions is the STAR technique. STAR stands for situation, task, action, result. First, describe the situation and task you were assigned in order to set the stage. Next, review the action you took. Plan to spend the most time on this part of the answer because your past performance is what the employer is most interested in. Finally, emphasize the results, the outcome of your actions.

Situation: "I was assigned sales manager for a new product my company was introducing."

Task: "I was to develop a marketing plan to determine best sales techniques."

Action: "I created a market survey instrument and conducted a campaign to assess consumer preference. I also conducted blind taste tests at local supermarkets."

Result: "The result was a successful marketing campaign that saw sales of our product skyrocket by 42%."

With STAR, you are able to convince the employer that you are capable of performing the open job by demonstrating your past success.

The Analytical Interview. The analytical interview is designed to let the interviewer see you think on your feet. The interviewer will ask you challenging questions to see how you analyze and perform under pressure. You may hear some off-the-wall questions like the examples below. In some cases you may be given a pen and paper, but don't be surprised if you're not. Most of the time the interviewer is looking for an answer that is simply in the ball park. If you are totally stumped and caught off guard by the question, think creatively. You also are better off answering humorously than not at all. Remember, the interviewer is interested in your thinking process, not just in how you derived the answer. Here are some questions that may put you on the spot.

- Why are manhole covers round?
- What are the number of square yards of pizza eaten in the U.S. each year?
- How many gas stations would you estimate there are in the United States?

How much does a 747 weigh?

D. N. Meehan, a senior scientist at a large firm, was interviewing a young man. Meehan asked the candidate to estimate the weight of a fully loaded 747 at takeoff. It's pretty obvious that coming up with the correct answer would be very difficult for almost anyone. Since the applicant was not versed in aviation, he felt he would have to come up with something creative and unique in order to leave a lasting impression on the interviewer. The candidate asked if he could use anything in the room and then proceeded to use Meehan's computer. It was a surprise to Meehan when the candidate turned on the "flight simulator" game and came up with the correct answer.

Tennis, anyone?
Theo Kruijssen, a student at Columbia University, was asked "How many matches need to be played in a single elimination tennis tournament if there are 256 participants?" Eagerly, Theo began using his math background and developed an equation to solve the problem. Several minutes later, he had his answer. The interviewer, however, was not as impressed as Theo was. The interviewer said that it was quite simple: "There are 255 matches. Each match has one loser and everyone loses once except the winner."

Stress Interviewing. The stress interview is like a horror film. It is more interesting to see than to be in. The intent of the interviewer is to determine how well you can handle pressure or a crisis situation.

Usually, the interviewee doesn't recognize a stress situation. For example, a candidate was taken to lunch by two recruiters. The recruiters informed the candidate that he didn't have the qualifications for the job, and then they began talking among themselves. In reality, they were seeing how he would respond to rejection since the position was in sales, which required dealing with stress and rejection.

Your best strategy for the stress interview is to recognize questions in disguise. Rather than becoming hostile, relax and attempt to present your case to the employer. There are endless cases where the interviewee allows the discussion to get under his skin and make his blood boil. Instead, be humble and try to ignore anything that offends you. Even though questions are designed to insult you, view this as a challenge and answer candidly.

No stress interviewing information would be complete without at least one horror story. A director of a business school placement office told us one that injects new meaning into the word stress. A candidate was interviewing with a Wall Street firm that was known for challenging interviews. He walked into a large boardroom, and at the end of the table, a partner, holding a newspaper in front of his face, said, "Get my attention." Thinking quickly, the candidate took out his lighter and set the newspaper on fire. We're not sure if he got the job, but he did get the partner's attention.

The Manhattan, Kansas, Interview. This type of interview occurs more often than you are aware of since it forms a hidden agenda within the interview itself. We often hear interviewers talk about how they would feel about a candidate if they were stuck with him or her in the airport in Manhattan, Kansas, or anywhere else for that matter, for twenty-four hours. Would you be pals or get on each other's nerves? Many times this assessment is based solely on personality and fit with the interviewer's personality. However, it does serve as a reminder that it is the interviewer who is recommending you for the job, not someone else in the company. You must impress your interviewer while also showing that you're a pretty good person to have around.

Stream of Consciousness Interviewing. This interview goes something like this: "Well let me tell you something about the company, we are located downtown, which is a great place for lunch, as a matter of fact I found a wonderful little restaurant last week that served wonderful pasta, it tasted just like something I had in Italy last year, Italy, now that's a great place to visit, I went there with my sister and we had a blast, Milan, Rome, and Florence, the art is wonderful."

Are you starting to get the picture? Just because you know how to interview doesn't mean your interviewer does. Sometimes you need to learn how to control the interview. For first timers this can be extremely difficult. You also need to be sure that you do not embarrass or insult your interviewer. One way to insert yourself into the stream of consciousness interview is to ask questions about the company and quickly follow up with statements about how your particular strengths would work well in that environment. This type of interview is a real challenge. Make sure that the interviewer leaves with a positive impression of who you are rather than just a feeling of having told a good story.

The Epicurean Interview. If you are in an all-day interview and someone offers to take you to lunch, it may not be as relaxing as it sounds. This is not your moment to put your interviewing skills on the back burner. When going to lunch during the interview process, never let your killer interview guard down. While conversation may be informal, evaluation is still present. Here are some Epicurean hints for the lunch interview:

- Don't order the most expensive item simply because you are not paying. It is best to order something in the medium price range. Also, don't worry about saving money by ordering the cheapest item; order what you want within reason.
- Stay away from spaghetti, spinach, and shrimp dishes or any other dish that could give you embarrassment. It can be extremely awkward trying to work a piece of food out from between your teeth or slurping up a long pasta noodle.
- If you don't drink alcohol, this is not the time to begin. And if you do drink, we recommend you wait until you have the job. If you must drink, limit yourself to just one. It is best to be as alert as possible during the lunch interview.
- Try to relax. Finding common interests between the interviewer and yourself will help lighten the conversation.

Dear Dr. Bob

How about sharing an interesting Epicurean experience with us.— Sincerely, The Epicurean Club.

Dear Epicurean Club

A student I worked with told me a story about going to a classy restaurant with a potential employer. Having talked a great deal and eaten only a little during the meal, the student decided to order what she thought was a simple dessert. But being a classy restaurant where swank desserts were served, she received a large, flaming confection. In fact, it was such a large, flaming dessert that the waiter set the plant hanging over the table on fire. Needless to say, the student made a burning impression on the employer. Bon appétit!

The Athletic Interview. From time to time athleticism, or at least some degree of fitness, can help during an interview. I recall one interview where I was told to meet my potential employer on a popular street corner in New York City. We were to meet and then go someplace to talk. As my luck would have it, by the time the interviewer showed up, he was late for a train at Penn Station. However, he was still interested in talking with me, so in business suits and briefcases we jogged to the station. He made his train and I got a second interview. Always be ready for the unexpected, even if it takes a little more out of you than you expected.

The Grunge Interview. We have talked about proper dress during the interview. There are still those, however, who believe that the best way to interview is to feel comfortable with yourself and your dress. In other words, be yourself and the job is bound to come. Wrong! Take this one opportunity to blend in with those that are interviewing you, and do not make an issue or statement with your clothes. Once you get the job and they see what a great employee you are, they will better understand your dressing desires and requirements. No matter how cool it looks to grunge dress and no matter how comfortable you feel, take our advice and hang up the blue jeans for a few hours.

Dr. Bob's Friendly Interview. As I finished up this section on interviewing, a staff member alerted me to the fact that I had not included my own style of interviewing: the "friendly interview," in which the employer is quite pleasant and lulls you into thinking that he likes everyone. The idea is to catch you off guard with a simple question that might reveal more than you planned about who you are. The way to handle this (and every interview) is to understand that your interview face must be on at all times, always presenting your best side. We all know that everyone has weaknesses; the interview, however, is not the time to let people know about them.

A Few Final Tips on Interviewing

In many ways an interview is like a first date. You can't predict how it will turn out. However, like a date, you can prepare yourself to make the best impression possible. You can also assess whether the company is a good match for you. Just as your first date may not be your best, likewise your first interview may not be your best.

However, you can learn from your mistakes and correct them in future interviews. Most importantly, don't forget to follow-up. If you had the dream date, you wouldn't forget to call again—so must you write the "thank-you letter" to the potential employer.

Rejected? How Can It Happen?

Remember that the world is full of rejections and failures. What would motivate us to improve if we didn't have past failures? Everybody flunks at some point in their life; nobody is perfect. To give you a flavor of how to really fail an interview, here are some major employer turn-offs (provided by the Lindquist-Endicott Report, Northwestern University):

Sloppy appearance. Like it or not, people form lasting impressions of you within the first seconds of the interview. When dressing for an interview, pay close attention to details.

Arrogant attitude. If employers had to sum up the qualities they are looking for in candidates in two words, they would likely be "team player." They want people whose first loyalty is to the company and who are willing to work for the good of the group. Arrogant individualists have no place in this environment.

Limited knowledge about the company or the field. No greater turn-off exists than to expect the employer to tell you about his or her company. One of Procter and Gamble's favorite interview questions is, "Which of the P&G products is your favorite?" Simple question, but it surprises many.

Asking about the salary or benefits too early. Asking about the salary too early in the interview says nothing about what you can do for the company, only what you want from them. You don't want the employer to think that you are selfish with a one-way mind.

Lack of clarity in long-range goals. Employers want to know why you want a particular job and where you want to go with it. Demonstrate that you have some sort of career plan and that that plan fits in with the company's goals.

Failure to ask for the job. Interviewing is like a sales presentation. After you have spent time marketing yourself, don't forget to close the deal. Ask for the job and let them know you are interested.

How to Bounce Back from Rejection

Do these lines sound familiar? "You're really not the right one." "We liked you, but we've decided not to hire right now." "You really don't have the experience we are looking for." "You are overqualified." These phrases occur more often than we would like. It's important to keep your sanity and courage during the interview process.

Anger, stress, guilt, fear, and anxiety are unfortunate companions to any job search. The strategy, therefore, is to learn to deal with rejection in a healthy and constructive manner and not let it distort your judgment. Develop methods to compensate for the beating your ego may take during the job search. Family and friends can be an excellent source for encouragement and positive support. Don't forget to eat well and exercise to relieve the stress involved in the job search. Be persistent and don't give up! Eddie Rickenbacker once said, "Try like hell to win, but don't cry if you lose." This should be one of your mottoes.

What Do Interviewers Really Want To See?

General Personality. Ambition, poise, sincerity, trustworthiness, initiative, and interest in the firm. (General intelligence is assumed.) Different firms look for different kinds of people, personalities, style, appearance, abilities, and technical skills. Always check the job specifications. Don't waste time talking about a job you can't do or for which you don't have the minimum qualifications.

Personal Appearance. A neat, attractive appearance makes a good impression and demonstrates professionalism.

Work Experience. Again, this varies from job to job, so check job specifications. Be able to articulate the importance of what you did in terms of the job for which you are interviewing and in terms of your own growth or learning. Even if the work experience is unrelated to your new field, employers look upon knowledge of the work environment as an asset.

Verbal Communication Skills. The ability to express yourself articulately is very important. This includes the ability to listen effectively, verbalize thoughts clearly, and express yourself confidently.

Job Skills. The interviewer will evaluate your skills for the job, such as organization, analysis, and research. It is important to emphasize the skills that you feel the employer is seeking and to give specific examples of how you developed them. This is the main reason why it is important to engage in self-assessment prior to the interview.

Goals/Motivation. Employers will assess your ability to articulate your short-term and long-term goals. You should seem ambitious yet realistic about the training and qualifications needed to advance. Demonstrate your interest in the functional area or industry and a desire to succeed and work hard.

Knowledge of the Interviewer's Company and Industry. At a minimum, you are expected to have done some homework on the company. Don't waste interview time asking questions you could have found answers to in printed material. Know the firm's position and character relative to others in the same industry. General awareness of media coverage of a firm and its industry is usually expected.

CYBERTIPS ON INTERVIEWING

As with most aspects of the job search, the Internet is full of sites with tips on interviewing and the latest in interviewing news. We have listed a few below:

Career Channel
http://riceinfo.rice.edu/projects/careers/Channel

Career Magazine
http://www.careermag.com/careermag/newsarts/interviewing.html

Espan—Career Library
http://www.espan.com/library/index.html

BOOKS ON INTERVIEWING

Allen, Jeffrey G. *The Complete Q & A Job Interview Book.* New York: John Wiley & Sons, 1988.

Biegelein, J. I. *Make Your Job Interview a Success.* New York: Arco, 1994.

Corcodilos, Nicholas. *Ask the Headhunter: Reinventing the Interview to Win the Job.* New York: Plume, 1997.

Fear, Richard A. *The Evaluation Interview.* New York: McGraw-Hill, 1990.

Hammond, Bruce R. *Winning the Job Interview Game: New Strategies for Getting Hired.* Liberty Hall, 1990.

Kador, John. *The Managers Book of Questions.* New York: McGraw-Hill, 1997.

King, Julie Adair. *The Smart Woman's Guide to Interviewing and Salary Negotiation.* Chelsea House Publishing, 1997.

Krannich, Caryl Rae and Ronald L. *Interview for Success: A Practical Guide to Increasing Job Interviews, Offers, and Salaries* (6th ed.). Manassas, VA: Impact Publications, 1996.

Marcus, John J. *The Complete Job Interview Handbook.* New York: Harper & Row, 1994.

Medley, H. Anthony. *Sweaty Palms: The Neglected Art of Being Interviewed.* Berkeley, CA : Ten Speed Press, 1992.

Smart, Bradford D. *The Smart Interviewer.* New York: John Wiley & Sons, 1990.

Stewart, Charles J., and William B. Cash. *Interviewing Principles and Practices.* Dubuque, IA: William C. Brown Publishers, 1993.

Washington, Tom. *Interview Power: Selling Yourself Face to Face.* Bellevue, WA: Mt. Vernon Press, 1995.

Yate, Martin John. *Knock 'Em Dead 1997: The Ultimate Job Seeker's Handbook* (10th ed.). Holbrook, MA: Adams Publishing, 1996.

eight

Summer Jobs, Internships, Temporary and Part-Time Jobs

For some, getting a job is seen as a summer only or as a temporary job. If that is the case, this is the chapter for you. First, summer jobs.

Summer Jobs—Findable and Rewarding

Summer provides the unique opportunity for students to brainstorm about careers that strike their interest. This is an experimental time in which the employer takes only a limited risk. But, how does one go about finding a summer job?

Finding a summer job is very similar to finding a permanent job. Persistence and positive attitude are keys for the high school or college job seeker just as they are for the full-time worker. Here are a few simple hints for prospective summer job seekers.

Set realistic expectations. Don't expect to get rich with summer work and, most importantly, realize that you won't get to the top after a week's work. Some progress can be expected, but summer jobbers should realize that they aren't on the same totem pole as permanent workers.

Have the right attitude. Nothing impresses an employer more than the right attitude. What do they want in an employee? Someone who is loyal, respectful, polite, punctual, enthusiastic, and hardworking. Remember that the number of people who really have all these qualities is small. If you can demonstrate your willingness to be the right person, you may get the job.

Dress right. Dress is a real issue with the summer job seeker. The best way to dress for summer jobs is somewhere between a suit and tie, as parents might encourage, and jeans and T-shirt, as friends might suggest. A collared shirt with slacks or khakis for guys, and slacks or skirt for young women are certainly acceptable. Additionally, wear leather shoes, not sneakers.

Be persistent. As a job seeker you can't be persistent enough. A true key to success in a summer job search is to keep trying, often with the same employer. Many summer success stories come from young people who visit their top five summer job sites of choice once a week until they get a job. One common mistake made by summer job seekers is to stop looking once they think they have a job. Even if an interview goes well or an employer says they like you, you must keep going until you have an actual job offer.

Interview well. Hopefully, after all your searching and preparation, your final challenge will be the interview. But don't be too worried; after all, if you get the interview, you do have a good chance of getting the job, or else the company wouldn't be wasting their time with you. For a successful interview, keep in mind these familiar guidelines: (1) Give specific reasons why you are right for the job; (2) Try to relate every question to your strengths of being loyal, enthusiastic, and other desirable qualities; (3) Inject a little humor into your otherwise serious and hardworking nature—but don't overkill on the comedy; and finally (4) Ask lots of questions to demonstrate your interest in the position.

As you go out into the summer job market, there are a few areas that can present stumbling blocks to your search. These include fear of risk; failing to contact the right person within the company; and taking no for an answer. (In other words, not being persistent enough.) If, on the other hand, you avoid these common traps, you will most likely find yourself on your way to a rewarding summer job experience.

If you are hesitant about working during the summer because you would rather be sitting by the pool, consider the many non-indoor summer opportunities. A summer job doesn't have to be inside an office or fast-food restaurant. There are paid internships offered by non-profit organizations that are not the typical office job environment.

As with any summer job, finding a good one requires starting your search as early as possible. The application process alone takes time, not to mention the research portion.

Dr. Bob's Six-Step Summer Job System

How do you get a job for the summer? Our tried and true system has worked for students and others for years.

1. Know what you want to do. Try to make a decision about what you want to do as early as possible. The sooner you decide, the sooner you can begin your search. Don't forget, the Career Center at your school provides resources and counseling to students. (See Chapter 2 for information on choosing a career.)

2. Develop a resume. It is important to accomplish this as early as possible since companies and application deadlines are as early as December for some summer jobs. (See Chapter 6 for details on resume and cover letter writing.)

3. Write a cover letter. A good cover letter is essential—it directs attention to your resume. Don't forget to have your resume and cover letter critiqued by a friend and career counselor, if possible.

4. Do research and make contacts. This step takes the longest, but hard work here can really pay off. Information interviews (see Chapter 5) with people in your field can help develop contacts. Don't forget your Alumni Office to develop a list of prospective employers. Make as many contacts as possible, and as soon as you have your contact list, begin mailing letters and resumes. A helpful tip is to send your letters in batches so you can track them efficiently and follow up each one with a letter.

5. Follow-up and Persistence. This is the most important step! Make sure that for every letter you send out, for every person you talk to, and for every potential job site you visit, you continue to call back and let them know you are interested. Failure to follow up is disastrous for many a summer job searcher.

6. Schedule interviews. As part of your follow-up, try to schedule interviews. Give your letters time to arrive, then follow up with a phone call. This will keep you a step ahead of most college students, who don't start looking for summer jobs until school is out. Finally, make sure you know how to perform the "killer" interview discussed in Chapter 7.

Jobs without salaries

Americorps is a national service program aimed at alleviating poverty in America's cities and towns. They produce a bi-weekly electronic bulletin featuring immediate assignment openings, program updates, and national service news of interest to career centers, volunteer offices, libraries, professional groups, and potential volunteers. To request an information brochure or application, call (800) 942-2677.

Top Summer Internships in the New York Area

The following is a list of paid summer internships in New York that generally accept applicants from all walks of life—from recent college grads to career changers to people re-entering the workforce.

Christie's
502 Park Ave.
New York, NY 10022
(212) 546-1079
Christie's is the world's oldest fine-art auctioneer with 77 offices in 30 countries. Interns work with specialists in over 12 Fine and Decorative Art departments as well as marketing, PR, and information systems. Over the past 20 years, Christie's has consistently retained about 15% of interns for full-time positions.

Circle in the Square Theatre
1633 Broadway, 6th Floor
New York, NY 10012
(212) 581-6371
Contact: Nicholas Nagler, Manager and Intern Coordinator
Production interns assist in casting, costumes and props, crew, and stage and theater management. Openings are available year-round and during the summer for college grads and grad students, mid-career changers, people with work experience, and those re-entering the workforce.

Cooper-Hewitt National Museum of Design
Peter Krueger Summer Internship
2 E. 91st St.
New York, NY 10128
(212) 860-6977
Contact: K. MacIntosh, Intern Coordinator
Interns are assigned to curatorial, education, or administrative departments and assist with special research or exhibition projects. Summer interns receive a $2,500 stipend.

Great Projects Film Co.
584 9th Ave.
New York, NY 10036
(212) 581-1700
Contact: Daniel Polin, President
Great Projects produces historical, scientific, and public affairs documentaries for public broadcasting and accepts college grads, grad students, mid-career changers, and people re-entering the workforce. Interns' responsibilities include office management research, proposal writing, and apprentice film editing.

Harper's Magazine
666 Broadway
New York, NY 10012
(212) 614-6500

Contact: Internship Coordinator
Open to undergrads, recent grads of any age. Program alumni have gone on to positions at Random House, Esquire, Details, New York Times Magazine.

NOW Legal Defense and Education Fund
99 Hudson St., 12th Floor
New York, NY 10013
Contact: Martha Davis, Staff Attorney
Internships are available for those with an interest in education, public policy, fund-raising, public relations, social science research, marketing, and writing. Openings during the summer and year-round.

Rainforest Alliance
65 Bleecker St.
New York, NY 10012
(212) 677-1900
Open to high school and college grads, students, and career changers. Available internships include "smart wood program," "certification program," and "natural resources and rights program." Possibility of full-time employment.

Ruder Finn
301 E. 57th St.
New York, NY 10022
(212) 593-6400
Requirements: College grads of any age. As the third largest PR firm in the city, Ruder Finn is known for its corporate communications, science and health campaigns, environmental marketing, and support for the arts. It also represents foreign governments, such as the breakaway republics of Croatia and Bosnia. Recent college grads of any age are eligible to be trainees, are assigned to an account group, and are encouraged to participate in creative meetings. During the first week of the program, they attend full-day classes on the public relations industry, featuring lectures by experts in the field and discussions on journalistic writing skills. Classes meet once per week for the remainder of the twelve weeks. About 50% of participants are later hired as employees.

Saks Fifth Avenue
611 5th Ave.
New York, NY 10022
(212) 753-4000
Open to undergrads, grads of any age, and international applicants. Programs include weekly seminars with executives and field trips to vendor showrooms.

Smithsonian Institution, Office of Museum Programs
Internships in Museum Practices, Arts and Industries Bldg.
900 Jefferson Drive, S.W., Room 2235
Washington, DC 20560
(202) 357-3101
Contact: Elana Piquer-Mayberry, Coordinator, Intern Services
Summer positions are available in New York, which include work in public

relations, curatorial, educational programming, collections management, and museum design and production. Over 700 college grads, grad students, midlife career changers, and people re-entering the workforce are accepted.

Vera Institute of Justice
377 Broadway
New York, NY 10013
(212) 334-1300
Contact: Susan Rai, Sr. Planner and Attorney
College grad and grad student interns participate in investigations and preparation for trials and work on research projects for this agency, which places defendants in alternative incarceration programs.

RECOMMENDED SOURCES AND GUIDES FOR INTERNSHIPS

The Academy of Television Arts and Sciences
Student Internship Program, 5220 Lankershim Blvd., North Hollywood, CA 91601, (818) 754-2830 (provides internships in the media field).

The American Institute of Architects
Director, Education Programs, 1735 New York Ave., N.W., Washington, DC 20006 (provides information on architectural internships).

Inroads, Inc.
100 South Broadway, PO Box 8766, Suite 700, St. Louis, MO 63102 (African-American, Native American, and Hispanic-American students can intern in the areas of business, engineering, and science).

National Audubon Society
Government Affairs Internship Program, 666 Pennsylvania Ave., S.E., Washington, DC 20003, (202) 861-2242; contact Greg Plowser (provides internships in resource conservation and wildlife management).

National Directory of Internships
National Society for Internships and Experiential Education, 122 St. Mary's St., Raleigh, NC 27605 (provides information on internships in a variety of areas).

National Institutes of Health
Summer Internship Program, Office of Education, Bldg. 10, Room 1C129, 9000 Rockville Pike, Bethesda, MD 20892, (301) 402-2176 (provides internships working alongside influential scientists).

RECOMMENDED READING ON INTERNSHIPS

Gilbert, Sara Dulaney. *Internships 1997: The Hotlist for Job Hunters* (2nd ed.). New York: Arco Publishing, 1997.

Gilbert, Sara Dulaney. *Internships: A Directory for Career-Finders.* New York: Arco Publishing, 1995.

Oldman, Mark, and Samer Hamadeh. *The Princeton Review: America's Top 100 Internships.* New York: Villard Books, 1995.

Peterson's editors. *Peterson's Internships 1997: Over 40,000 Opportunities to Get an Edge in Today's Competitive Job Market* (17th ed.). Princeton, NJ: Peterson's Guides, 1996.

Summer Job and Internship Hunting on the Net

Be sure and use your computer in your summer job search. Below are a few sources to get you started.

Career Mosaic
http://www.careermosaic.com
Lists job opportunities for cooperative education and internships.

Career Resource Center
http://www.careers.org
Be sure to look to CRC for links to current jobs, employer sites, newsgroups, and government sites throughout the year.

JobTrak
http://www.jobtrak.com
An excellent place to look for jobs posted at member colleges and universities. You'll need a password, however. Check with your college placement or career office.

Online Career Center
http://www.occ.com/
Try a keyword search on "internship" to get a list of these.

Peace Corps
http://www.peacecorps.gov

Peterson's Education Center
http://www.petersons.com
Check this resource for internship opportunities at colleges and universities nationwide. You will also find information on summer job opportunities.

Temporary/Part-Time Jobs

Locating part-time work in your chosen field is ideal since you can continue to develop your network of contacts. Many professionals can freelance. An administrative assistant, for example, might be able to find part-time work at a law firm. An accountant might be able to do taxes on a part-time basis and still gain access to new referrals.

Another option is independent contracting. For example, if you're a computer programmer and the company you're interviewing with can't justify hiring someone full time because there isn't enough work, suggests that they hire you on a temporary basis for specific projects. Or offer to come in one or two days a week. Or suggest that you work on an as-needed basis. The advantage to the company is that they don't have to pay you benefits (except those you're able to negotiate). The advantage to you is income and experience in your chosen field.

People with technical skills can work themselves into becoming full-time freelancers in precisely this manner. They might even talk an employer OUT of hiring them full time and negotiate contract work in order to maintain the freedom of their self-employed status.

SELECTED EMPLOYMENT AGENCIES FOR TEMPORARY AND PART-TIME JOBS

Accountemps
565 5th Ave.
New York, NY 10017
(212) 687-7878
Accounting, bookkeeping, finance.

Cantor Concern Services
330 W. 58th St.
New York, NY 10019
(212) 330-3000
PR and communications.

Career Blazers Temporary Service
590 5th Ave.
New York, NY 10017
(212) 719-3232
General.

Carlyle Consulting Services
1 Penn Plaza
New York, NY 10119
(212) 629-6565
Computer networking, mainframe support.

Ecco Staffing Services
1139 Broadway
New York, NY
(212) 741-3977
Food services, hospitality.

Eden Personnel
280 Madison Ave.
New York, NY 10016
(212) 685-4666
General.

Interim Personnel
227 E. 45th St.
New York, NY 10016
(212) 983-8800
http://www.interim.com
Word processing, data entry, secretarial.

International Bank Temps
10 E. 39th St., Room 524
New York, NY 10016
(212) 226-5377

MacSpecialists
19 W. 21st St.
New York, NY 10011
(212) 924-3979
Graphic arts, Web design, multimedia, editors, and proofreaders.

Medi-Temps
19 W. 44th St.
New York, NY 10036
(800) 856-9727
Physicians, nurses, lab and X-ray techs.

New Boston Systems
61 Broadway
New York, NY 10005
(212) 269-8400
Information system consultants.

Norrell Staffing
420 Lexington Ave.
New York, NY 10016
(212) 697-7267
Computer programmers, network
engineers, systems analysts.

Wall Street Services
11 Broadway, Suite 1065
New York, NY 10004
(212) 509-7200
Legal and financial support,
MBA temporaries.

Olsten Staffing Services
500 5th Ave., Suite 910
New York, NY 10110
(212) 391-7000
General.

Winmar Temporary Service
535 5th Ave.
New York, NY 10017
(212) 687-8977
General.

Smith Personnel
41 E. 42nd St.
New York, NY 10017
(212) 370-5400
Desktop publishing, proofreading,
artists.

Word Processing Professionals
505 5th Ave., 18th Floor
New York, NY 10017
(212) 557-2788
Word processing, computer
instructors, desktop publishers.

Temping in Today's Market

Temporary help receipts grew 11% in 1996 to a record high of $44 billion, according to the National Association of Temporary Staffing Services. Payroll rose 13 percent to $32 billion and the number of people working in temporary positions in 1996 rose by 7%. Temporary hires, independent contractors, leased employees, and part-timers constitute about 20% of today's workforce. If this trend continues, nearly one-third of all employees may be working on an as-needed basis within the next ten years.

One recent survey of 150 human resource executives conducted by the Office Team found that 78% viewed a consistent record of temporary employment equivalent to full-time work. And more than one-third of the temps surveyed at one agency were offered jobs as a result of temp assignments.

Temping is not only a means to pay the bills while looking for a full-time job but it can also be a way to get your foot in the door. A temp position gives you the opportunity to demonstrate your initiative and skills while also allowing you to test the waters of a company before committing to them.

The sheer number of temp agencies in New York is overwhelming and you will probably only want to work with several. Consult the following Web site, which offers lists of local agencies, advice on working with them, and reviews of people's personal experiences with particular agencies.

http://www.best.com:80/~ezy/redguide.html/

RECOMMENDED READING ON TEMPORARY/PART-TIME JOBS

Beusterien, Pat. *Summer Employment Directory of the United States.* Princeton, NJ: Peterson's Guides, 1997.

Canape, Charlene. *The Part-Time Solution: The New Strategy for Managing Motherhood.* New York: Harper Collins, 1990.

Hassett, Brian. *The Temp Survival Guide.* Seacaucas, NJ: Citadel Books, 1997.

Landes, Michael. *Back Door Guide to Short-Term Job Adventures: Internships, Extraordinary Experiences, Seasonal Jobs, Volunteering, Work Abroad.* Berkeley, CA: Ten Speed Press, 1997.

Levinson, Jay Conrad. *555 Ways to Earn Extra Money: Revised for the '90s.* New York: Henry Holt, 1991.

Paradis, Adrain A. *Opportunities in Part-Time and Summer Jobs.* Lincoln, IL: VGM Career Horizons, 1997.

nine

How To Handle a New Job and Workplace

A new job, new colleagues, and a new desk — this is what the job search was all about. How do you handle the new job? Well, let the job experts give you some advice.

Walking into your new everyday life, seeing all those new colleagues, and concentrating on fitting into the atmosphere can be overwhelming. But it is important to keep your cool, stay focused, and be yourself. It is natural to be nervous, but how that nervousness manifests itself is important. Showing too much apprehension or bumbling about a bit too much can give others, and cost you, a bad first impression.

How Significant Is the First Day on the Job?

The first day at work can certainly be one of the most important days during your time at a particular company. This is the day that you begin to establish who you are and what you can contribute to the organization. The first day can show your employer a lot. It will give him or her an idea of what you are like as an employee and how you will fit into the workplace.

In order to ease some of the restraint you may be feeling or cure some of those first-day butterflies, here are some tips that will enable you to feel more comfortable. For starters, promptness is essential and says a lot to the employer. This is important for more than just the first day. If you are constantly late, it reveals a sense of irresponsibility and may cause you some grief down the road.

Once you arrive at work on time, determining your duties and what is expected of you is vital. Take a little time to settle in, but try to get on the job soon, and show enthusiasm and contentment with your new job.

You might want to meet with your boss early in the day. This will show motivation and eagerness and will contribute early on to a good first impression. It will also give you an idea of some of the expectations that the company has for you. This and subsequent meetings should help you determine what drives the company and your superiors.

Learn the chain of command and assess the importance of teamwork. Ask about the long-term goals of the company so you can assess your role in it. Keep in mind on your first day that the old saying is true: you never get a second chance to make a first impression.

First Day Do's and Don'ts

It is important to keep in mind some rudimentary but very significant factors in terms of your on-the-job performance. We have formed a Top Ten list that should guide you through a successful first day on the job.

1. **DON'T** expect the red carpet to roll out for you. Employees may not even be expecting you, and special treatment may not be forthcoming.

2. **DON'T** imagine rewarding accomplishments and important responsibilities to await you on your first day. Be prepared for paperwork and orientations.

3. **DON'T** stress. Just take it one step at a time. The company knows you are new and will help you get acclimated; they want you to perform well.

4. **DON'T** be afraid to ask questions, and make sure you realize that no question is a stupid question.

5. **DON'T** be overwhelmed with all the new information. Concentrate on grasping the major points or the most urgent.

6. **DO** enjoy yourself. Think of your job as a challenge and a way to gain new skills for the future.

7. **DO** be prepared. Show everybody that you have your head on straight, can plan ahead, and know what you are doing.

8. **DO** get involved. Interpersonal communication within a company is very important. Be a part of the team, and show other employees that you have some good ideas.

9. **DO** be confident. You were hired because you are qualified. Don't let anything get in your way and make you think otherwise. If the company believes in you, then by all means you should believe in yourself.

10. **DO** stay focused. Try to maintain a working attitude throughout the day. Daydreaming and other distractions will hinder your professional image. Try not to incorporate your personal life with your professional life for the security of your career.

Adjusting Over the Long Run

A new job can be very intimidating and can fill you with mixed emotions about a career. Here are some helpful hints that will enable you to adjust to the company, fit in, and, most importantly, make an impact as a valuable employee.

Develop good communication skills. Has it come to your attention that most top-notch people in a company seem to know one another? Interpersonal communication is a key ingredient in making your job more productive and pleasant. Listen as well to everybody's input, not just those higher up on the career ladder. Keep in mind that you spend a large portion of your life with your workmates, and most of them have something to offer.

Take risks. Don't be afraid to take risks. A leader will have developed enough self-confidence so that taking a few calculated risks is worth the possible payoff. Overcoming skepticism and taking risks can even be the turning point of a career. Just remember to weigh all the options and be prepared for negative as well as positive results.

Work hard. A hard worker always seems to have a brighter future than someone who settles for being just adequate. Let the company know that you are the "go to" person. If you portray that hard-working image, the next step for most supervisors is to trust you with additional duties.

Honesty is the best policy. Try not to make excuses to bail yourself out of hot water. You are better off apologizing and admitting the fact that you made a mistake. Most importantly, never point your finger at other employees. You will only look foolish and cowardly. You want to set a good example, not be the bad example.

Maintaining a Good Relationship with the Boss

Here are some helpful tips to assist you in maintaining a good relationship with your boss.

- Think of your boss as a customer for the product you are trying to sell: yourself. Keep in mind that there is no such thing as impressing your boss too much.
- Value and respect your boss' time. Managers must handle a number of things all at once. If you see that your boss is busy, try to solve the problem yourself or seek assistance from another employee. Freeing your boss from trivial concerns will make everyone's life easier.
- Be open to advice. Don't be offended when your supervisor tries to steer you in the right direction. Make room for criticism, and view it as information that can make you a more effective employee.
- Never make your boss look foolish. Don't challenge his or her judgment in front of other employees. If you feel that you're right, talk to the boss privately. Involving others will just result in dispute and cause havoc.

- Always make your boss look good. Try to keep him/her informed of new issues and ideas. Remember that the better you do, the better the boss looks; and the better the boss looks, the better your career will be.
- Tell your boss about your career objectives or plans for the future. Inform him/her about your ideas and goals of accomplishment. Be optimistic, not skeptical, when discussing career plans with the head person.
- When confrontation with the boss is necessary, try to find an ice-breaking technique to reduce tension. Try to find a common goal or interest in solving the problem. This brings people together and makes them more open to discussion and less defensive.
- Always listen to your boss, but never let him/her walk all over you. Even though you may not have the final say, your judgments deserve to be heard.

A good professional relationship with the boss is vital in terms of job happiness and success. But don't look for the boss to be either perfect or your good buddy. A boss should be a role model and a leader, the person we answer to and respect.

Dear Dr. Bob

Lately, I've noticed my boss taking all the credit for my hard work. He never mentions my name when receiving glowing remarks about a project. What should I do?—Unrecognized Employee

Dear Unrecognized Employee
Your situation is an age-old one. We are supposed to make our bosses look good and hope they will return the favor. Unfortunately, that hasn't happened in your case. I am one that believes "what goes around, comes around" and eventually your efforts will be rewarded. You will have other jobs and other bosses, but your ability will stay with you. In the meantime, use subtle techniques for claiming what is due. Make sure your name appears on written reports. When people praise your boss, mention how hard the whole department has worked as well. In due time, you will receive your just recognition.

Creativity and Innovation in Your Career

Corporations want individuals that can be assets and contribute to the company. New ideas and different approaches are always encouraged. Be creative. Show the company that you have the zeal and ability to bring new concepts to the company. Try not to be a routine employee who comes to work, takes care of her responsibilities, and leaves work exactly on time everyday.

Don't hesitate when you think you have a new idea that might help the company. The reality is that many companies do not recognize the value of the creative process but only the "bottom line" result. Here are a few tips for breaking your own barriers to creativity.

Postpone judgment. Explore an idea before promoting or nixing it. Even a patently unrealistic idea may lead to a workable solution to a problem.

Look for the second right answer. Avoid the trap of committing too soon to a single solution to a problem. Always look for the second, less obvious answer.

Take risks. How many models for an airplane did Orville and Wilbur Wright fail with before they found one that worked? Think about that the next time you are hesitant in something.

Look for unlikely connections. Computer guru Steve Jobs once said that when he worked for Atari he applied what he learned about movement from a modern dance class in college to the development of video games. Talk about an unlikely connection!

Allow yourself to be foolish. Kids have a leg up on us when it comes to creativity because they are encouraged to be foolish. Creativity flourishes when you allow your mind to romp. Some experts even suggest keeping toys in your office or home to encourage your playful side.

Creativity is within everyone's grasp. It comes out not when you do something that no one has done before but when you do something that you have never done before. Recognizing the barriers you yourself have erected to the creative process is the first step to unleashing your potential. Your career and success can only be enhanced once this is done.

Romance in the Office: A Definite Don't

Many dedicated corporate types have found Cupid's arrow piercing their briefcases and setting their hearts aflutter under their banker pinstripes. What's a person to do when love hits in the workplace? The logical, reasonable answer is, "Don't do it!" But rarely is romance logical or reasonable.

Let's face it. Being in proximity with others for an extended period of time makes the workplace fertile ground for romance to blossom. You share common interests, talk frequently, and may even have similar problems. Next thing you know, you find Mr. or Ms. Right directly under your nose. If you are indeed smitten by a coworker, we offer a few words of advice about relationships in the workplace.

- Know the company's policy on dating coworkers. Some companies consider it unprofessional or even a conflict of interest. However, it is unlikely that your organization will have a written policy prohibiting such relationships.
- Remember that the workplace is for work. Heated romances should remain outside the workplace.
- Be prepared for people to gossip. Romance is juicy stuff — especially for those who don't have it. There are no easy answers about how to handle gossip. It's best to ignore harmless gossip and to confront people spreading malicious stories (there is harm in a rumor that you or your significant other is pregnant!).
- Think about how to handle the break-up. No one wants to think about the end of a relationship, especially when it is just beginning. However, the number-one workplace hazard is a vindictive ex. Understand that if things don't work out, it is likely that you will still work together. Make sure you are ready for that possibility.
- Finally, never date the boss. Regardless of how professionally you conduct yourself in the office, every action or decision you make will be viewed by others through the lens of your relationship. Additionally, having an ex-significant other for a boss can be terribly awkward.
- If a romance goes sour, there is always the risk of sexual harassment. When one person in a relationship has greater authority over the other, the possibility of sexual harassment exists.

The easiest course is to avoid workplace romances altogether. However, love is capricious, and you may well find that one special person just across the hall. If that's the case, even Cupid understands the importance of separating love and work.

Keeping Your Career on the High Road

Becoming successful and happy is the ultimate dream of those who are trying to get their foot in the door. A true success story involves hard work and a positive professional attitude. Here are some tips that will enable you to take that first step toward a new and fulfilling life.

1. Always maintain a good professional relationship with your coworkers and peers. Knowing a wide array of people is certainly advantageous and can become very helpful when you need a favor or some assistance.
2. Find a mentor, somebody who can develop the best in you and advance your interests in the company.
3. Try to concentrate on small, easy projects at first. Conquering your first assignment will give the company a good initial vision of your work abili-

ties. This will also alleviate the pressures a little and add to your self-esteem and believability.

4. Cater to your clients. Be straightforward and candid with them. Make them see that you are fair and treat them as people not profit figures. Try to value their time by being flexible with your schedule.

5. Never assume that a certain issue is not your job. Try to do whatever you can to make your department and the company work. Even if you are not responsible for certain areas, it won't hinder your career if you attempt to find answers when a problem affects you.

6. Take on as many responsibilities and as much work as you can handle. The operative phrase here, however, is "as much work as you can handle." Willingly accepting additional projects and assignments can ingratiate you with your boss only if you complete them in a timely and professional manner.

7. Accept criticism as a form of information that can make you a better employee. When constructively criticized, determine and take the actions that can correct the problem.

8. Never get stuck in one job. Always look to move forward. If you feel that you don't have a future at a certain company, keep your eyes open for other opportunities. Make sure you gain more and more skills and credibility as you progress.

9. Be a leader. Emphasize your willingness to help others. Gaining leadership status can be challenging, but it will definitely broaden your career in the long run.

10. Stay current on issues in your field. Keeping current enables you to assess the stability of your current job and to predict your next career move.

11. Good people are hard to find. No matter how cliché, it's true. If you excel, you will be in an elite group and in demand by employers.

Keep Your Network Alive

Ideally, this book will help you achieve your dream job. But remember that the average person changes jobs five to eight times in their career. Thus, after you've landed a job, it is important that you notify your network people of your new position and thank them for their assistance. Don't throw away those business cards you worked so hard to accumulate. After all, you never know when you may need to ask them for help again. You've spent months building up a network of professional contacts. Keep your network alive.

Make a "New Year's Resolution" to weigh all aspects of your job annually. Evaluate your current situation and the progress you are making (as measured by increased salary, responsibilities, and skills). Compare the result with what you want from your life's career. Even though you may be completely satisfied in your new job, remember that circumstances can change overnight, and you must always be prepared for the unexpected.

We hope you make good use of the job-search techniques outlined in this book. Perhaps the next time you talk to an unemployed person or someone seeking a new job, you will look at that person with new insight gained from your own job search and career successes. We hope you'll gladly share what you've learned from these pages about how to get a job.

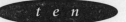

ten

Employers in the New York Metropolitan Area

This chapter contains the names, addresses, and phone numbers of the New York area's top 1,500 employers of white-collar workers. The companies are arranged in categories according to the major products they manufacture and the major services they provide.

Entries contain the name of the human resources director or other contact, where possible, and a brief description of the company's business, where appropriate. This listing is intended to help you survey the major potential employers in fields that interest you. It is selective, not exhaustive. We have not, for example, listed all the advertising agencies in the area as you can find that information in the *Yellow Pages*. We have simply listed the top twenty-five or so, that is, the largest ones potentially offering the most jobs.

Most big firms have offices in the suburbs, too
Many of the corporations listed in this chapter have offices in the suburbs as well as Manhattan. Because of space limitations, we have sometimes listed only the Manhattan location. If you'd like to work in the suburbs, check with the personnel departments in Manhattan about additional offices. They are usually located in new industrial parks in Long Island and Westchester County as well as northern New Jersey and southern Connecticut.

In addition, we've included many firms whose corporate headquarters are in the Tri-State area outside of Manhattan just in case commuting is not a factor in your job search.

The purpose of this chapter is to get you started, both looking and thinking. This is the kickoff, not the final gun. Browse through the whole chapter, and take some time to check out areas that are unfamiliar to you. Many white-collar skills are transferable. People with marketing, management, data processing, accounting, administrative, secretarial, and other talents are needed in a huge variety of businesses.

Ask yourself in what area your skills could be marketed. Use your imagination, especially if you're in a so-called specialized field. A dietitian, for instance, might look first under Health Care, or maybe Hospitality. But what about financial companies, museums, banks, or the scores of other places that run their own dining rooms for employees or the public? What about food and consumer magazines? Who invents all those recipes and tests those products?

The tips and insider interviews that are scattered throughout this chapter are designed to nudge your creativity and suggest additional ideas for your job search. Much more detailed information on the area's top employers and other, smaller companies can be found in the directories and other resources suggested in Chapter 4. We can't stress strongly enough that you have to do your homework when you're looking for a job, both to unearth places that might need a person with your particular talents and to succeed in the interview once you've lined up a meeting with the hiring authority.

A word about hiring authorities: if you've read Chapter 7, you know that the name of the game is to meet the person with the power to hire you, or get as close to that person as you can. You don't want to go to the chairman or the personnel director if the person who actually makes the decision is the marketing manager or customer service director.

Just Where Are Those Employers Located, Anyway?

New York's system of street addresses is very confusing to newcomers. Numbers on the north-south streets, such as Fifth Avenue, do not correspond to the numbers of the cross streets. An out-of-towner would expect a building at Fifth and 53rd Street to have an address such as "5300" or "5301." Not so! Nor do the numbers on the north-south Avenues follow any pattern. A good map or pocket guide is essential if you are new to New York.

To help you become more familiar with the various business districts and industry locations in the New York area, we've described some of the most important ones below.

The Garment District: Most apparel retailers and wholesalers are located in this district, from 30th to 40th Streets between Seventh Avenue and Broadway. Apparel wholesalers maintain offices in the 1300s and 1400s on Broadway. There are also many apparel retailers and wholesalers scattered throughout Brooklyn and Queens.

Publisher's Row: Many publishing houses are located on either Avenue of the Americas or Lexington Avenue. You'll find a few on Madison Avenue and Fifth Avenue and others in lower Manhattan. When people refer to Publisher's Row, they are talking about a section of the Midtown area from 40th Street to 50th Street on Avenue of the Americas.

Ad Agencies: The advertising business is to Madison Avenue what the apparel business is to Seventh Avenue. Many of New York's most prestigious advertising firms can be found on or near Madison Avenue in the Midtown area.

Broadcasting: The main offices of the three major television networks are located on or near Avenue of the Americas in the 50s. NBC has studios in its corporate headquarters. Other television studios and production facilities are located in the 60s, on or near Broadway. There is now a large cable production facility in Astoria, Queens. The Astoria Studios house several radio and TV channels, among them WFAN Radio.

Electronics, Telecommunications, and Office Automations Systems: Most of these companies have offices in Long Island and Westchester. Virtually every one of the leaders in the industry has office space outside of New York City as well as recruiting offices in Manhattan. Usually, recruiting for the suburban jobs is done separately from recruiting in New York. Use a suburban directory if you wish to work in a particular suburb, or call the numbers we've provided to ask about suburban recruiting.

Federal Plaza: You'll find most U.S. government offices in lower Manhattan's Federal Plaza, which is near City Hall Park. You'll find most of the buildings between Broadway and Lafayette Streets, two main avenues that run north and south and are easy to locate.

Hotels: Central Park South is the address of some of New York's grandest hotels that overlook Central Park from the south side of the park. You can stroll along the park and pass such fine hotels as the St. Moritz and the Plaza. You'll find four- and five-star hotels on Fifth, Madison, and Park Avenues.

Insurance: A large number of the insurance firms in New York are located in a small area in lower Manhattan. If you're looking for a job in the insurance business, you will be spending time in this small area in the vicinity of William Street, John Street, Maiden Lane, and Nassau Street. These are small, winding streets that can confuse even the most experienced New Yorker. Try to find an address on a map, or get explicit directions from the company by phone.

Wall Street: New York's financial district, home to the New York Stock Exchange and the nation's largest investment firms, banks, brokerage houses, and financial advisors, is located on the southern tip of Manhattan Island. Also in the neighborhood are the World Trade Center and the World Financial Center complexes. The towers are bordered by West Street and Vesey Street and are a main tourist attraction as well as a financial and trade center.

Manufacturing: Queens County is just over the 59th Street bridge, a short trip from the east side of Manhattan. Here you will find Long Island City, where hundreds of general manufacturers and production plants are located. If we have not listed a manufacturing company you'd like to work for, check the local Queens *Yellow Pages*. You may find the company in or near Long Island City.

Museums and Galleries: New York's museums are numerous, and they are located all over the city rather than in one area or district. But most art galleries are concentrated in one of two locations: 57th Street in the Midtown area, or SoHo and TriBeCa below Greenwich Village in lower Manhattan.

New Media: The New York Information Technology Center at Broad and Center Street is the hub of New York's "Silicon Alley," and new companies are springing up on nearby Broadway, John, and William Streets. A youthful cadre of entrepreneurs has also invaded SoHo and established this artsy neighborhood as the new breeding ground for high-tech startups specializing in multimedia, Web design, and computer services.

Obviously, we can't list every possible hiring authority in the New York area's "Top 1,500." If we tried, you'd need a wagon to haul this book around. Besides, directories go out of date—even those that are regularly and conscientiously revised. So always *double-check* a contact whose name you get from a book or magazine, including this one. If necessary, call the company's switchboard to confirm who heads a particular department or division.

Here, then, are the New York area's greatest opportunities. Note that in most cases, nearby New Jersey and Connecticut employers are listed after the New York employers.

The New York area's top 1,500 employers are arranged in the following categories:

Accounting/Auditing

Advertising Agencies

Aerospace/Aviation

Apparel/Textiles

Architecture

Automotive

Banking

Broadcasting: TV and Radio

Chemicals

Computers: Hardware/Software

Computers: Information Services/Multimedia

Construction

Cosmetics/Perfume/Toiletries

Educational Institutions

Electronics/Telecommunications

Engineering

Entertainment

Environmental Services

Food/Beverage Producers and Distributors

Foundations/Philanthropies

Government
Health Care
Hospitality: Hotels and Restaurants
Human Services
Insurance
Law Firms
Management Consultants
Market Research Firms
Museums/Art Galleries
Oil/Gas/Plastics
Paper and Allied Products
Pharmaceuticals/Biotechnology
Printing
Public Relations
Publishers, Book/Literary Agents
Publishers, Magazine and Newspaper
Real Estate
Retailers/Wholesalers
Sports, Fitness, and Recreation
Stock Brokers/Financial Services
Travel/Shipping/Transportation
Utilities

Accounting/Auditing

WEB SITES:

AccountingNet
http://www.accountingnet.com/

Accountants Home Page
http://www.computercpa.com/

FinanceNet
http://www.financenet.gov/

PROFESSIONAL ORGANIZATIONS:

For networking in accounting and related fields, check out these local professional organizations listed in Chapter 5. Also see "Banking" and "Stock Brokers/Financial Services."
American Institute of Certified Public Accountants
American Society of Women Accountants
New York State Society of Certified Public Accountants
For additional information, you can contact:

American Accounting Association
http://www.rutgers.edu/Accounting/raw/aaa/associat.htm
5717 Bessie Drive,
Sarasota, FL 34233
(941) 921-7747

American Institute of Certified Public Accountants
http://www.rutgers.edu/Accounting/raw/aicpa/home.htm
1211 Ave. of The Americas
New York, NY 10036
(800) T0-AICPA

American Society of Women Accountants
1255 Lynnfield Road, Suite 257
Memphis, TN 38119
(901) 680-0470

CPA Associates
201 Route 17 North, 4th Floor

Rutherford, NJ 07070-2574
(201) 804-8686

Institute of Certified Management Accountants
10 Paragon Drive
Montvale, NJ 07645
(201) 573-9000

Institute of Internal Auditors
http://www.rutgers.edu/Accounting/raw/iia
249 Maitland Ave.
Altamonte Springs, FL 32701-4201
(407) 830-7600

National Association of Black Accountants
7249A Hanover Parkway
Greenbelt, MD 20770
(301) 474-6222

National Society of Public Accountants
http://www.nspa.org
1010 N. Fairfax St.
Alexandria, VA 22314
(703) 549-6400

New Jersey Society of Certified Public Accountants
425 Eagle Rock Ave.
Roseland, NJ 07068
(201) 226-4494

New York Society of Independent Accountants
6 Glenwood Drive
Darien, CT 06820
(203) 357-1463

PROFESSIONAL PUBLICATIONS:

Accountant, The
Accounting and Business Review
Accounting Education News
Accounting Horizons
Accounting Review
Accounting Technology
Accounting Today
Bowman's Accounting Report

Corporate Accountant, The
CPA Digest
CPA Journal
Journal of Accountancy, The
Management Accounting
National Public Accountant
Practical Accountant, The

DIRECTORIES:

Accountants Directory (American Business
   Directories, Inc., Omaha, NE)
Accounting Firms and Practitioners
   (American Institute of Certified Public
   Accountants, New York, NY)
Career Opportunities Handbook (New York
   State Local Public Accounting Firms,
   New York, NY)
Emerson's Directory of Leading U.S.
   Accounting Firms (Gale Research,
   Detroit, MI)
National Directory of Certified Public
   Accountants (Peter Norback Publishing
   Co., Princeton, NJ)
Who Audits America (Data Financial Press,
   Menlo Park, CA)

New York Employers:

Anchin, Block & Anchin
1375 Broadway
New York, NY 10018
(212) 840-3456
Director of Recruiting: David Finkelstein

Andersen, Arthur, and Company
1345 Avenue of the Americas
New York, NY 10105
(212) 708-4000
Director of Recruiting: Loraine MacInnis

BDO Seidman
330 Madison Ave.
New York, NY 10017
(212) 885-8000
Director of Recruiting: Angela Street

Berdon, David, & Co.
415 Madison Ave.
New York, NY 10017
(212) 832-0400
Director of Recruiting: Lisa Edelstein

Buchbinder Tunick & Co.
1 Pennsylvania Plaza
New York, NY 10119
(212) 695-5003

Cohn, J.H., & Co.
400 Park Ave.
New York, NY 10022
(212) 563-4200
Director of Human Resources: Howard
Fishman
Corporate Headquarters in Roseland, NJ

Coopers and Lybrand
1301 Avenue of the Americas
New York, NY 10019
(212) 259-1000
Regional Director of Recruiting: Joseph S.
Rorro

Deloitte & Touche
1633 Broadway
New York, NY 10019
(212) 489-1600
Director of Recruiting: Melissa Holland-
Forde
Corporate Headquarters in Connecticut.

E&Y Leventhal, Kenneth, Group
1285 Avene of the Americas
New York, NY 10036
(212) 773-3000
Personnel Director: Al Frazia

Eisner, Richard A., & Co.
575 Madison Ave.
New York, NY 10022
(212) 355-1700
Partner, Human Resources: Richard Fisher

Ernst and Young
787 7th Ave.
New York, NY 10019
(212) 773-3000
Director of Personnel: Cindy Hirsch

Friedman Alpren & Green
1700 Broadway
New York, NY 10019
(212) 582-1600
Director of Personnel: Cindy Hirsch

Goldstein Golub Kessler & Co.
1185 Avenue of the Americas
New York, NY 10036
(212) 372-1000
Partner, Director of Human Resources:
Warren Gurtman

Grant Thornton
605 3rd Ave.
New York, NY 10158
(212) 599-0100
Director of Human Resources: Edward
McCann

Isaacs, Edward, & Co.
380 Madison Ave.
New York, NY 10017
(212) 297-4800
Director of Human Resources: Laura
Stonbely

KPMG Peat Marwick
345 Park Ave.
New York, NY 10154
(212) 758-9700
Director of Recruitment: Jorge Ribalaigua

Lopez, Edwards, Frank & Co.
1 Penn Plaza
New York, NY 10119
(212) 629-8833
Personnel Director: Abby Lucrezia
Headquarters in Valley Stream, NY:
(516) 872-3400

Mahoney Cohen Rashba & Pokart
111 W. 40th St.
New York, NY 10018
(212) 490-8000
Director of Human Resources:
Christopher Zarbo

Marcum Kliegman
130 Crossways Park Drive
Great Neck, NY 11797
(516) 390-1000

Margolin, Winer & Evens
400 Garden City Plaza
Garden City, NY 11530
(516) 747-2000

Director of Human Resources:
Stanley Stempler

Marks Shron & Co.
111 Great Neck Road
Great Neck, NY 11021
(516) 466-6550
Director of Human Resources: Cheryl Tell

McGladrey & Pullen
555 5th Ave.
New York, NY 10017
(212) 697-0606
Contact Director of Human Resources

Mitchell Titus & Co.
1 Battery Park Plaza
New York, NY 10004
(212) 709-4500
Director of Human Resources: Dianne
Edey

Moore Stephens
331 Madison Ave.
New York, NY 10017
(212) 682-1234
Partner: Kathleen Clayton

Pannell Kerr Forster and Company
420 Lexington Ave.
New York, NY 10170
(212) 867-8000
Personnel Director: Richard Stewart

Price Waterhouse
1177 6th Ave.
New York, NY 10036
(212) 596-7000
Contact: Director of Recruiting

Rosen Seymour Shapes Martin & Co.
757 3rd Ave.
New York, NY 10018
(212) 303-1800
Personnel Director: Ellen Burke

Weiser, M.R., & Co.
135 W. 50th St.
New York, NY 10020
(212) 641-6700
Director of Personnel: Ellis Abramson

Connecticut Employers:

Coopers & Lybrand
1 Canterbury Green
P.O. Box 10108
Stamford, CT 06904
(203) 326-8400
Recruiting Manager: Laura Fox

Deloitte & Touche
10 Westport Road
Wilton, CT 06897
(203) 761-3000
Personnel Representative: Laurie Tripoli
Corporate headquarters.

KPMG Peat Marwick
3001 Summer St., Stamford Square
Stamford, CT 06905
(203) 356-9800
Primary Recruiter: Jeannie Precioso

Price Waterhouse
300 Atlantic St.

P.O. Box 9316
Stamford, CT 06904
(203) 358-0001

New Jersey Employers:

Cohn, JH, and Company
75 Eisenhower Parkway
Roseland, NJ 07068
(201) 228-3500
Director of Human Resources:
Howard Fishman

Rothstein Kass & Co.
85 Livingston Ave.
Roseland, NJ 07068
(201) 994-6666

Wiss and Company
354 Eisenhower Parkway
Livingston, NJ 07039
(201) 994-9400
Human Resources Director:
Leonard Michielli

Accounting firms big and small

We talked with Richard Craig, a Certified Public Accountant, now a Senior Vice President in finance at a leading data processing firm. We asked how he began his career in accounting and about the advantages and disadvantages associated with the size of the firm you work for.

Said Craig, "I started at Touche Ross (now Deloitte & Touche), one of New York's big eight (now the big six) accounting firms. Usually, working for a larger firm means learning a specific task. Staffs are larger, so each job is more specialized. You don't usually handle as many components of a job as you would in a smaller firm. You sometimes have more opportunity for hands-on experience in a smaller firm and gain more general management experience," Craig advised.

"But regardless of the size of the firm where you begin your career, if you wish to advance you should remain flexible through the first five years. If your job is not what you expected, be willing to make a change.

"Also, if you want a manager's position, you may have to move around to gain general managerial experience.

Sometimes, that will mean a transfer to a department that would not necessarily be your first choice. But if the position rounds out your background, it is usually worth at least a temporary stay."

Advertising Agencies

WEB SITES:

Advertsing Age
http://www.adage.com

Advertising World
http://www.utexas.edu/coc/adv/world/index.cfml

American Association of Advertising Agencies
http://www.commercepark.com/AAAA/AAAA.html

PROFESSIONAL ORGANIZATIONS:

For networking in advertising and related fields, check out the following local professional organizations listed in Chapter 5. Also see "Market Research" and "Public Relations."
Advertising Club of New York
Advertising Women of New York
American Association of Advertising
    Agencies
Direct Marketing Association
The One Club

For additional information, you can contact:

Advertising Council
http://www.adcouncil.org
261 Madison Ave., 11th Floor
New York, NY 10016
(212) 922-1500

Advertising Mail Marketing Association
http://www.amma.org

1333 F St., Suite 710
Washington , DC 20004
(202) 347-0055

American Advertising Federation
1400 K St., NW, Suite 1000
Washington, DC 20005
1-800-999-2231

American Marketing Association
http://www.ama.org
250 S. Wacker Drive, Suite 200
Chicago, IL 60606
(312) 648-0536

Direct Marketing Association
11 W. 42nd St.
New York, NY 10036
(212) 768-7277

PROFESSIONAL PUBLICATIONS:

Adcom Magazine
AD-vertiser, The
Advertising Age
http://www.adage.com
Adweek
Agency Magazine
American Demographics Magazine
Business Marketing
Catalog Age
Creativity Magazine
Direct Marketing Magazine
Direct Marketing News
http://www.dmnews.com
Direct Marketing World
http://www.dmworld.com
Promo Magazine

DIRECTORIES:

Advertisers and Their Agencies (Engel Communications, West Trenton, NJ)

Advertising Agencies Directory (American Business Information, Inc., Omaha, NE)

Advertising Career Directory (Gale Research, Detroit, MI)

Adweek Directories (BPI Communications, Inc., New York, NY) Includes directories of ad agencies and public relations firms as well as guides to media, advertising, and marketing services.

Bacon's Business Media Directory (Bacon's Information International, Ltd.—Chicago, IL)

Standard Directory of Advertisers (National Register Publishing Co., New Providence, NJ)

Standard Directory of Advertising Agencies (National Register Publishing Co., New Providence, NJ) For those interested in the advertising field, the industry's Red Book, or *Standard Directory of Advertising Agencies*, is useful in finding a specific contact in your area of interest. For example, an artist would contact the agency's Art Director or Creative Director. The directory is available at most libraries.

New York Employers:

Ammirati & Puris/Lintas
885 2nd Ave.
New York, NY 10017
(212) 605-8000
Senior VP, Director of Human Resources and Public Relations: Andrea Fessler

Ayer, NW, and Partners
825 8th Ave.
New York, NY 10019
(212) 474-5000
Exec. VP, Human Resources: Donna Milch

BatesUSA
405 Lexington Ave.
New York, NY 10174
(212) 297-7000
Senior VP, Director of Personnel:
Nancy Smith

BBDO NY
1285 Avenue of the Americas
New York, NY 10019
(212) 459-5000
Executive VP, Human Resources: Ron Mason

Bozell Worldwide
40 W. 23rd St.
New York, NY 10010
(212) 727-5000
Exec. VP, Human Resources: Joanne Conforti

D'Arcy, Masius, Benton and Bowles
1675 Broadway
New York, NY 10019
(212) 468-3622
Director of Personnel: Leslie Engel

DDB Needham
437 Madison Ave.
New York, NY 10022
(212) 415-2000
Director of Human Resources: Judson Saviskas

Deutsch Inc.
215 Park Ave. S.
New York, NY 10003
(212) 995-7500
Director of Human Resources: Jean Gellert

FCB/Leber Katz Partners
150 E. 42nd St.
New York, NY 10017
(212) 885-3000
Director of Human Resources: Judith Kemp

Grey Advertising
777 3rd Ave.
New York, NY 10017
(212) 546-2000
Director of Human Resources: Kevin Bergin

Griffin Bacal
130 5th Ave.
New York, NY 10011
(212) 337-6300
Director of Human Resources: Mary Cioffi

Jordan McGrath Case & Taylor
445 Park Ave.
New York, NY 10022
(212) 326-9100
Human Resources Director:
Christine Martin

LCF&L Inc.
260 Madison Ave.
New York, NY 10016
(212) 213-4646
VP, General Manager: Patti Ransom

The Lord Group
810 7th Ave.
New York, NY 10019
(212) 408-2100
Director of Personnel: Mercedes Colon

The Lowe Group
1114 6th Ave.
New York, NY 10017
(212) 403-7000
Director of Personnel: Ms. Pat Peltola

McCann Erickson
750 3rd Ave.
New York, NY 10017
(212) 697-6000
Personnel Director: Donna Borseso

Messner Vetere Berger McNamee Schmetterer
350 Hudson St.
New York, NY 10014
(212) 886-4100
Human Resources: Debra Breslin

Mezzina/Brown
410 Park Ave. South
New York, NY 10016
(212) 251-7700
VP, Director of Administration:
Margaret Williams

Ogilvy & Mather
309 W. 49th St.
New York, NY 10019
(212) 237-4000
Human Resources Director:
Patricia Enright

Partners & Shevak
1211 6th Ave.
New York, NY 10036
(212) 596-0200
Human Resources Director:
Susan Scaglione

Saatchi & Saatchi Advertising
375 Hudson St.
New York, NY 10014
(212) 463-2000
Human Resources Director: Joe Sansaverino

TBWA/Chiat Day
180 Maiden Lane, 38th Floor
New York, NY
(212) 804-1000
Human Resources Director: Mia Salibello

Thompson, J. Walter
466 Lexington Ave.
New York, NY 10017
(212) 210-7000
Director of Human Resources: Roni Elson

Wells, Rich, Greene BDDP
11 Madison Ave.
New York, NY 10019
(212) 590-7000
Director of Human Resources: Patti Ransom

Wunderman Cato Johnson
675 6th Ave.
New York, NY
(212) 941-3000
Senior VP, Human Resources: Judy Magnus-Jackson

Young and Rubicam
285 Madison Ave.
New York, NY 10017
(212) 210-3000
Director of Human Resources:
Virginia Hancher

Connecticut Employers:

Blau, Barry, & Partners
241 Danberry Rd.
Wilton, CT 06897

(203) 834-6900
Director of Human Resources: Jill Franzon

Clarion Marketing and Communications
Greenwich Office Park #5
Greenwich, CT 06831
(203) 862-6000
Director of Human Resources: Mary Mahon

New Jersey Employers:

Ferguson, Thomas G., Associates
30 Lanidex Plaza W.
Parsippany, NJ 07054
(201) 884-2200
Human Resources: Susan Didonato

Aerospace/Aviation

WEB SITES:

**Aeronautics/Aviation Career Search
Resources**
http://www.lmsc.lockheed.com/aiaa/sf/
career/search.html

American Aerospace Industries Association
http://www.well.com/user/css/aia.html

Aviation Links
http://www.air-transport.org/net_1.htm

AviationNet
http://www.aeps.com/aeps/avnethm.html

PROFESSIONAL ORGANIZATIONS:

For networking in aerospace and related
fields, check out the following local
professional organizations listed in
Chapter 5:
**IEEE Aerospace and Electronics Systems
    Society**
Wings Club

For additional information, you can
contact:

Aerospace Education Foundation
1501 Lee Highway
Arlington, VA 22209
(703) 247-5839

**Aerospace Industries Association of
America**
1250 I St., NW
Washington, DC 20005
(202) 371-8400

Air Transport Association of America
http://www.air-transport.org
1301 Pennsylvania Ave., NW, Suite 1100
Washington, DC 20004

**American Association of Airport
Executives**
http://www.airportnet.org
4212 King St.
Alexandria, VA 22302
(703) 824-0500

**American Institute of Aeronautics and
Astronautics**
http://www.lmsc.lockheed.com/aiaa/sf/
career.html
370 L'Enfant Promenade, SW, The
Aerospace Center
Washington, DC 20024
(703) 264-7500

**Int'l. Association of Machinists &
Aerospace Workers**
9000 Machinists Place
Upper Marlboro, MD 20772
(301) 967-4500

**National Air Traffic Controllers
Association**
http://home.natca.org
1150 17th St., NW, Suite 701
Washington, DC 20036
(202) 223-2900

Society of Senior Aerospace Executives
P.O. Box 151736
Chevy Chase, MD 20825
(301) 652-3381

Women in Aerospace
922 Pennsylvania Ave., SE
Washington, DC 20003
(202) 547-9451

PROFESSIONAL PUBLICATIONS:

Aerospace America
Aerospace Daily
Aerospace Engineering
Air & Space/Smithsonian
Air Jobs Digest
Air Line Pilot
Air Progress
Air Transport World
Aviation Week & Space Technology

DIRECTORIES:

Aerospace Facts & Figures (Aerospace
  Industries Assn. of America, Washington, DC)
*Aircraft Owners & Pilots Association
  Airport Directory* (Aircraft Owners &
  Pilots Association, Hagerstown, MD)
*Aviation Maintenance Foundation Job
  Opportunities Listing* (Aviation Maintenance Foundation Intl., Seattle, WA)
*Aviation Week & Space Technology,
  Marketing Directory Issue* (McGraw-
  Hill Publishing Co., New York, NY)
World Aviation Directory and Buyers Guide
  (McGraw-Hill, Washington, DC)

New York Employers:

BH Aircraft Company
441 Eastern Parkway
Farmingdale, NY 11735
(516) 249-5000
Personnel Director: Nancy Crimmins
Airplane/aerospace systems and equipment.

Cox & Company
200 Varick St., 4th Floor
New York, NY 10014
(212) 366-0200
Director of Human Resources:
John Matuzsa
Manufactures aircraft equipment.

Edo Corporation
14-04 111th St.
College Point, NY 11356
(718) 321-4000
Benefits Manager: Vincent DeMonte

International Telephone and Telegraph
1330 Avenue of the Americas
New York, NY 10019
(212) 258-1000
Director of Personnel: Robert W. Brokaw
Manufactures and develops UHF,VHF
radio transmission equipment, ground-
to-air tactical radio equipment, air traffic
control radio equipment. The defense-
space arm of the technology group is
located in Nutley, NJ, (201) 284-0123.

Lawrence Aviation Industries
Sheep Pasture Road
Port Jefferson Station, NY 11776
(516) 473-1800
Director of Human Resources: Carolyn
Bowen

Monitor Aerospace Corporation
1000 New Horizons Blvd.
Amityville, NY 11701
(516) 957-2300
Director of Human Resources: Rich
Dallari

National Helicopter Corp.
North Ave.
Garden City, NY
(718) 925-8807

**Northrup-Grumman Aerospace
Corporation**
South Oyster Bay Road
Bethpage, NY 11714
(516) 575-0571
Human Resources Director: Mr. Pat Lloyd
Military parts, services, and systems for
the aerospace and aircraft industries. Also
develops and manufactures energy
conservation devices.

Sequa Corporation
200 Park Ave.
New York, NY 10166

(212) 986-5500
Personnel Specialist: Carolyn Celechko,
location: 3 University Plaza,
Hackensack, NJ 07601, (201) 343-1122.
Aerospace systems.

Connecticut Employers:

Dow-United Technology
15 Sterling Drive
Wallingford, CT 06492
(203) 949-5000
Director of Human Resources: Fred
Boratynski

Kaman Aerospace Corp.
Old Windsor Road
Bloomfield, CT 06002
(860) 242-4461
Director of Personnel: Amanda Lindberg

United Technologies Corporation
United Technologies Building
Hartford, CT 06101

(860) 728-7000
Human Resources Manager: April Woods

New Jersey Employers:

Allied Signal
101 Columbia Road
Morristown, NJ 07962
(201) 455-2000
Director of Personnel: Louise Monahan
Airplane/aerospace systems.

Curtiss-Wright Flight Systems
300 Fairfield Road
Fairfield, NJ 07004
(201) 575-2200
Manager, Employee Relations: Joe
Sangregorio

Gec-Marconi Aerospace
110 Algonquin Parkway
Whippany, NJ 07981
(201) 428-9898
Personnel Director: Russ Stehn

Apparel/Textiles

WEB SITES:

Apparel Exchange
http://apparelex.com/

Textile Information Management System
http://www.unicate.com/

Textile Institute—Virtual Library
http://texi.org/library.htm

PROFESSIONAL ORGANIZATIONS:

For networking in the apparel and textile industries and related fields, check out the following local professional organizations listed in Chapter 5:
American Fur Industry
Apparel Guild
Career Apparel Institute
Ladies Apparel Contractors Association
Men's Fashion Association of America
Young Menswear Association

For additional information, you can contact:

American Apparel Manufacturers Association
2500 Wilson Blvd., Suite 301
Arlington, VA 22201
(703) 524-1864

Association of Bridal Consultants
200 Chestnutland Road
New Milford, CT 06776
(203) 355-0464

Career Apparel Institute
1156 Ave. of the Americas
New York, NY 10036
(212) 575-2847

Chamber of Commerce of the Apparel Industry
570 7th Ave., 10th Floor
New York, NY 10018
(212) 354-0907

Council of Fashion Designers of America (CFDA)
1412 Broadway
New York, NY 10018
(212) 302-1821

Educational Foundation for the Fashion Industries
227 W. 27th St.
New York, NY 10001
(212) 760-7641

International Association of Clothing Designers
475 Park Ave. S.
New York, NY 10016
(212) 685-6602

Professional Apparel Association
2017 Walnut St.
Philadelphia, PA 19103
(215) 569-3650

Sportswear Apparel Association
450 7th Ave.
New York, NY 10123
(212) 564-6161

Textile Distributers Association
45 W. 36th St., 3rd Floor
New York, NY 10018
(212) 563-0400

Textile Research Institute
P.O. Box 625
Princeton, NJ 08540
(609) 924-3150

PROFESSIONAL PUBLICATIONS:

Accessories
Apparel Industry Magazine
ATI—America's Textiles International
Fashion Accessories
Home Textiles Today
Textile Manufacturing
Textile World
Women's Wear Daily

DIRECTORIES:

American Apparel Manufacturers Association Directory of Members and Associate Members (American Apparel Manufacturers Association, Davison Publishing Co., Ridgewood, NJ)

Apparel Digest (Institute of Textile Technology)

Apparel Trades Book (Dun & Bradstreet, New York, NY)

Directory of Apparel Specialty Stores (Chain Store Guide Information Services, Tampa, FL)

Fashion Market Directory (Fashion Market Directory Group Ltd., New York, NY)

Phelon's Womens Apparel & Accessory Shops (Phelon, Sheldon & Marsar, Inc., Fairview, NJ)

New York Employers:

Bally Inc.
1 Bally Place
New Rochelle, NY 10801
(914) 632-4444
VP, Human Resources: Karen O'Mara

Bartlett, John
150 W. 28th St. 10001
New Rochelle, NY 10801
(212) 647-9409

Beacon Looms
261 5th Ave.
New York, NY 10016
(212) 685-5800
Personnel Director: Irma Farnsworth
Produces a wide range of textiles for sale to retailers nationwide.

Belding Hemingway
1430 Broadway
New York, NY 10018
(212) 944-6040
VP, Human Resources: Susan Brofsky
One of the largest textile and home sewing manufacturers in the country. Manufactures industrial yarns and threads, notions, zippers, buttons, and threads for home sewing.

Blass, Bill, Ltd.
550 7th Ave.
New York, NY 10018
(212) 221-6660
Controller: Michael Groveman

Bonjour International Ltd.
1411 Broadway
New York, NY 10018
(212) 398-1000
Personnel Director: Ms. Chris Miller

Boss, Hugo, USA
645 5th Ave.
New York, NY
(212) 940-0800

Brittania Sportswear
1411 Broadway
New York, NY 10018
(212) 921-0060
Personnel Director: Christy Gillihan, 500 Naches Ave., SW, Renton, WA 98055

Burlington Industries
1345 Avenue of the Americas
New York, NY 10105
(212) 621-3000
Personnel Director: Janice Jarsky
Textiles and home apparel fabrics; draperies, upholstery, carpets. New York office includes marketing, advertising, sales, and support services.

Chanel, Inc.
9 W. 57th St.
New York, NY 10019
(212) 688-5055

Chaus, Bernard
1410 Broadway
New York, NY 10018
(212) 354-1280
Director of Human Resources: Robin Santelia

Claiborne, Liz
1441 Broadway
New York, NY 10018
(212) 354-4900
Director of Human Resources: Elaine Jackler

Collins and Aikman
200 Madison Ave.
New York, NY 10016
(212) 578-1200
Personnel Director: Marie Dendrinos
Specialty fabrics, including fabricated and
non-fabricated textile products and wall
coverings.

Concord Fabrics
1359 Broadway
New York, NY 10018
(212) 760-0300
Personnel Director: Martin Wilson
Designer of woven and knitted fabrics for
sale to manufacturers and retailers. New
York office includes administration,
design, merchandising, and marketing.

Cygne Designs
1372 Broadway
New York, NY 10018
(212) 354-6474
Director of Personnel: Marcy Manna

Danskin Inc.
111 W. 40th St.
New York, NY 10018
(212) 764-4630
Personnel Director: Amy Baron

Dolce and Gabbana
532 Broadway
New York, NY 10003
(212) 966-2868

Ellis, Perry
1114 6th Ave.
New York, NY 10018
(212) 221-6795
Send resume to individual departments:
design, marketing, sales.
Human Resources Director: Geraldine
Collins

Ermenegildo Zegna Corp.
743 5th Ave.
New York, NY
(212) 751-3468

Evan-Picone Sportswear
1411 Broadway

New York, NY 10018
(212) 536-9500
President: Ellen Daniels

Forstmann & Co.
1155 6th Ave.
New York, NY 10036
(212) 642-6900
Administration Assistant: Barbara Coover

G-III Apparel Group
345 W. 37th St.
New York, NY 10018
(212) 944-6230
Personnel Department: Andrea Schaffer

Galey & Lord
980 6th Ave.
New York, NY 10018
(212) 465-3000
Personnel Director: Bill Odalen

Garan, Inc.
350 5th Ave.
New York, NY 10118
(212) 563-2000
Personnel Director: Dana Gleason

Gotham Apparel Corp.
1384 Broadway
New York, NY 10018
(212) 921-8800
Director of Personnel: Michael Schulman

Hilfiger, Tommy
25 W. 39th St.
New York, NY 10018
(212) 840-8888
Human Resources Director: Michelle
Falbo

Johnson, Betsey
498 7th Ave., 21st Floor
New York, NY 10018
(212) 244-0843
Human Resources: Kim Hingley

Jones Apparel Group
1411 Broadway
New York, NY 10018
(212) 642-3860
Director of Personnel: Ida Tejtro-DeColli

Jordache Enterprises
226 W. 37th St.
New York, NY 10018
(212) 643-8400
Director of Personnel: Judy Bratg

Karan, Donna
550 7th Ave.
New York, NY 10018
(212) 789-1500
Training Manager: Jennifer Cox

Klein, Anne, & Co.
11 W. 42nd Street
New York, NY 10036
(212) 626-6000
Personnel Director: Ruth McMomigle

Klein, Calvin
205 W. 39th St.
New York, NY 10018
(212) 719-2600
Personnel Director: Tina Olson

Lauren, Ralph
550 7th Ave.
New York, NY 10019
(212) 857-2500
Contact Human Resources

Liberty Fabrics of New York
295 5th Ave., 11th Floor
New York, NY 10016
(212) 684-3100
Personnel Director: Norma Broomfield
Knitted lace and elastic fabrics.

Maidenform, Inc.
90 Park Ave.
New York, NY 10016
(212) 953-1400
Resumes to: Human Resources, 154 Ave.
E., Bayonne, NJ 07002

Miller, Nicole
527 7th Ave.
New York, NY 10018
(212) 719-9200

**Milliken and Company Apparel/
Fabric Sales**
1045 Avenue of the Americas
New York, NY 10018

(212) 819-4200
Personnel Director: Tom O'Neill
Textile yarns and fabrics, apparel, and
related chemical and packaging products.

Missoni
836 Madison Ave.
New York, NY
(212) 826-6515

Nantucket Hosiery
Division Nantucket Industries
180 Madison Ave., Suite 1403
New York, NY 10016
(212) 889-5656
Office Manager: Cecilia Roote
Men's and women's undergarments and
hosiery.

Oldham, Todd
120 Wooster St.
New York, NY 10012
(212) 219-3531
Personnel Director: Tony Longoria

Patou, Jean
29 W. 57th St.
New York, NY 10019
(212) 688-5568

Phillips-Van Heusen Corporation
1290 Avenue of the Americas
New York, NY 10104
(212) 541-5200
Personnel Director: Barbara Burkepile

Romeo Gigli & Spazio
21 E. 69th St.
New York, NY 10021
(212) 744-9121

Russ Toggs
1450 Broadway
New York, NY 10018
(212) 626-5800
Personnel Manager: Donna Herman

Salant Corporation
1114 Avenue of the Americas
New York, NY 10036
(212) 221-7500
Personnel Manager: Geraldine Collins

Sam and Libby
1414 6th Ave., 7th Floor
New York, NY 10019
(212) 371-3770

Schumacher, F., and Company
79 Madison Ave.
New York, NY 10016
(212) 213-7900
Director of Emloyee Relations: Gail Maddox

Stock, Robert, Ltd.
350 5th Ave.
New York, NY 10016
(212) 947-2895

Warnaco Inc.
90 Park Ave.
New York, NY 10016
(212) 661-1300
Personnel Director: Richard Mitchell

Connecticut Employers:

Playtex Apparel
700 Fairfield Ave.
Stamford, CT 06902
(203) 356-8000
Personnel Director: Susan Amann

New Jersey Employers:

Benard, Harve, Ltd.
225 Meadowlands Parkway
Secaucus, NJ 07094
(201) 319-0909
Address resume to individual departments

Maidenform—Bayonne
154 Avenue E
Bayonne, NJ 07002
(201) 436-9200
Contact Human Resources

Contracting for a career on 7th Avenue

We asked Gary Randazzo, president of Geeankay Dress Company, a mid-sized contractor of women's apparel, to explain the lines of distribution in the apparel, or garment, industry. "Contractors are the first step in a long and often confusing line of distribution for a garment," says Randazzo. "Contractors put the goods together for manufacturers who do not have their own shops. This is what is known as piece work, assembling garments that have been cut and need only to be sewn together. Some contractors do the actual cutting of the material and construct the garment from the pattern to finished product. The public is generally not aware that contractors even exist, but they are a very important part of the chain.

"Once a garment has been finished, it is usually sent back to the manufacturer for sale to a wholesaler. It is then sold to the retail market. In some instances, large apparel companies can be considered wholesalers and manufacturers. They may also operate retail arms."

We asked if working for a contractor can help round out your experience in the garment industry. "Absolutely. After working for even a small contractor you can move to quality control, product management, and even inventory control for manufacturers or wholesalers. Also, you learn the business from the ground up: working on the shop floor examining dresses, dealing with employees, making contacts with wholesalers and manufacturers. That experience is invaluable in any part of the industry."

Architecture

WEB SITES:

ADAM: Art, Design, Architecture and Media Information Gateway
http://adam.ac.uk/

ArchiTech
http://www.archiweb.com/new/index.html

Job Hunting in Planning, Architecture, and Landscape Architecture
http://www.lib.berkeley.edu/ENVI/jobs.html

PROFESSIONAL ORGANIZATIONS:

For networking in architecture and related fields, check out the following local professional organizations listed in Chapter 5. Also see "Construction" and "Engineering."
American Institute of Architects
American Society of Civil Engineers
Architectural League of New York

For additional information, you can contact:

American Institute of Architects
http://www.aia.org
Long Island Chapter
(516) 294-0971
New Jersey Chapter
(609) 393-5690
Connecticut Chapter
(203) 865-2195

National Organization of Minority Architects
P.O. Box 535
Bellwood, IL 60104
(708) 544-3333

Society of American Registered Architects
303 S. Broadway
Tarrytown, NY 10591
(914) 631-3600

Women in Architecture Leadership Network
American Institue of Architects/NY Chapter
200 Lexington Ave.
New York, NY 10016
(212) 683-0023

PROFESSIONAL PUBLICATIONS:

AIA Journal
Architectural Record
Architecture
Building Design
Building Design & Construction
Contract Design
Progressive Architecture

DIRECTORIES:

American Institute of Architects Membership Directory (American Institute of Architects, Washington, DC)
Architects Directory (American Business Directories, Inc., Omaha, NE)

Landscape Architects Directory (American Business Directories, Inc., Omaha, NE)

ProFile Directory of U.S. Architectural Design Firms (American Institute of Architects, Washington, DC)

Society of American Registered Architects National Membership Directory (Society of American Registered Architects, Lombard, IL)

New York Employers:

Barth, David, Architects
133 5th Ave., 4th Floor
New York, NY 10003
(212) 529-4865

Beyer Blinder Belle
41 E. 11th St., 2nd Floor
New York, NY 10017
(212) 777-7800
Personnel Director: Jennie Pocock

Brennan Beer Gorman Architects
515 Madison Ave.
New York, NY 10022
(212) 888-7663

Ehterkrantz and Eckstut
23 E. 4th St.
New York, NY 10003
(212) 353-0400
Principal: Bill Donohoe

Haines Lundberg Waehler
115 5th Ave.
New York, NY 10003
(212) 353-4600
Office Manager: Mary Jane Beatty

Hardy Holzman Pfeiffer Assoc.
902 Broadway
New York, NY 10010
(212) 677-6030
Personnel Director: Victor Gong

Kliment, RM and Halsband, Frances Architects
255 W. 26th St.
New York, NY 10001
(212) 243-7400
Personnel Director: Alex Diez

Mancini Duffy
2 World Trade Center
New York, NY 10048
(212) 938-1260
Personnel Director: Donna Carpenter

Meli Borelli Associates
352 Park Ave. S.
New York, NY 10010
(212) 213-6824
Personnel Director: Jennifer Causch

Perkins Eastman Architects PC
437 5th Ave.
New York, NY 10016
(212) 889-1720
Personnel Director: Ms. Arnhild Buckhurst

Platt and White Associates
111 Broadway
New York, NY 10006
(212) 564-4100
Personnel Director: Esther Lee

Rogers Burgun Shahine and Deschler
150 Nassau St.
New York, NY 10038
(212) 571-0788
Principal: Dr. Agha

Silver and Ziskind
233 Park Ave. S., 4th Floor
New York, NY 10003
(212) 477-1900
Personnel Director: Rose Mulcahey

Swanke Hayden Connell Ltd.
295 Lafayette St.
New York, NY 10012
(212) 226-9696
Personnel Director: Joseph Pirrotta

Vinoly, Rafael Architects PC
50 Vandam St.
New York, NY 10013
(212) 924-5060
Personnel Director: Jay Bargmann

WalkerGoup/CNI
320 W. 13th St.
New York, NY 10014
(212) 206-0444
Personnel Director: Charles Baran

Wank Adams Slavin Associates
740 Broadway
New York, NY 10003
(212) 420-1160
Director, Financial Services: Hassan
Sharas

Weidlinger Associates.
375 Hudson Street
New York, NY 10014
(212) 367-3000
Personnel Director: Helen Pelekanos

Connecticut Employers:

Pelli, Cesar and Associates
1056 Chapel St.
New Haven, CT 06510
(203) 777-2515
Personnel Director: Carolann Morrissey

New Jersey Employers:

ABB Lummus Crest
1515 Broad St.
Bloomfield, NJ 07003
(201) 893-1515
Contact Human Resources

Berger, Louis, International
100 Halsted St.
P.O. Box 270
East Orange, NJ 07019
(201) 678-1960
Human Resources Director: Richard
Bergailo

EI Associates
115 Evergreen Pl.
East Orange, NJ 07018
(973) 672-5100
Personnel Director: Marty Brizzi

Automotive

WEB SITES:

AutoCenter
http://autocenter.com

Ward's Communications Online
http://www.wardsauto.com/

PROFESSIONAL ORGANIZATIONS:

For information on the automotive
industry, you can contact:

Automotive Service Industry Association
25 NW Point
Elk Grove Village, IL 60007
(847) 228-1310

**National Marine Manufacturers
Association**
401 N. Michigan Ave., Suite 1150
Chicago, IL 60611
(312) 836-4747

Society of Automotive Engineers
400 Commonwealth Drive
Warrendale, PA 15096
(412) 776-4841

PROFESSIONAL PUBLICATIONS:

AAA Motorist
Automobile Magazine
4-Wheel & Off Road
Motor Age
Motor Magazine
Motor Trend
Tow Times
Trux
Ward's Automotive Reports

DIRECTORIES:

Automotive News, Market Data Book Issue
  (Crain Communications, Detroit, MI)
Directory of Automotive Aftermarket

Suppliers (Chain Store Guide Information Services, Tampa, FL)

Fleet Association Directory (Bobit Publishing Company, Long Beach, CA)

Recreational Vehicle Directory (Hanley Publishing Co., Chicago, IL)

Ward's Automotive Yearbook (Ward's Communications, Detroit, MI)

New York Employers:

General Motors Corporation
767 5th Ave.
New York, NY 10153
(212) 418-6100
Personnel Director: R. James Kraus

Grumman Allied Industries
111 Stewart Ave.
Bethpage, NY 11714
(516) 575-0574
Major government contractor for aerospace and aircraft parts and bodies, as well as a manufacturer of automobile and truck bodies.

Harley Davidson of New York
686 Lexington Ave.
New York, NY
(212) 355-3003

Standard Motor Products
37-18 Northern Blvd.
Long Island City, NY 11101
(718) 392-0200
Personnel Director: Mr. Sandy Kay

Connecticut Employers:

Stanadyne Automotive Corporation
92 Deerfield Road
Windsor, CT 06095
(860) 525-0821
Human Resources Manager: Phillip Ricki

New Jersey Employers:

Allied-Signal
101 Columbia Road
Morristown, NJ 07960
(201) 455-2000
Sr. VP, Human Resources: Donald Redlinger
Manufacturer of electronic diagnostic equipment and automotive and aerospace parts.

General Automotive Specialty Co.
P.O. Box 6010, U.S. Route 1 and 130
N. Brunswick, NJ 08902
(908) 545-7000
Personnel Director: Joe Hammerman

Ingersoll-Rand Co.
200 Chestnut Ridge Road
Woodcliff Lake, NJ 07675
(201) 573-0123
Personnel Director: Marilyn Rossier

Jaguar Cars
555 MacArthur Blvd.
Mahwah, NJ 07430
(201) 818-8500
Personnel Director: Warren Luther

Mercedes-Benz of North America
1 Mercedes Drive
Montvale, NJ 07645-0350
(201) 573-0600
Personnel Director: Robert Erzen

Rolls-Royce Motor Cars
140 E. Ridgewood Ave.
Paramus, NJ 07652
(201) 967-9100
Personnel Director: Mary Hayes

Volvo Cars of North America
7 Volvo Drive
Rockleigh, NJ 07647
(201) 768-7300
Personnel Director: Wayne L'Heureux

Banking

WEB SITES:

National Banking Network—Jobs
http://banking-financejobs.com/

US Bank Homepages
http://www.wiso.gwdg.de/ifbg/
bank_usa.html

PROFESSIONAL ORGANIZATIONS:

For networking in the banking industry
and related fields, check out the following
local professional organizations listed in
Chapter 5. Also see "Stock Brokers/
Financial Services."
**Financial Women's Association of New
 York**
**New York Credit and Financial
 Management Association**
New York Society of Security Analysts
New York State Bankers Association

For additional information, you can
contact:

American Bankers Association
1120 Connecticut Ave., NW
Washington, DC 20036
(202) 663-5000

Bank Marketing Association
1120 Connecticut Ave.
Washington, D.C. 20036
(202) 663-5422

**Independent Bankers Association of
America**
1 Thomas Circle, NW, Suite 950
Washington, DC 20005
(202) 659-8111

**Mortgage Bankers Association of
America**
1125 15th St., NW
Washington, DC 20005
(202) 861-6500

National Bankers Association
1513 P St., NW

Washington, DC 20009
(202) 588-5432

New Jersey Bankers Association
P.O. Box 573
Princeton, NJ 08542
(609) 924-5550

**Savings and Community Bankers of
America**
900 19th St., NW
Washington, DC 20006
(202) 857-3100

PROFESSIONAL PUBLICATIONS:

ABA Bankers Weekly
ABA Banking Journal
American Banker
http://www.americanbanker.com
America's Community Banker
Bank Management
Bank Marketing Magazine
Bankers Magazine
Barron's
http://www.barrons.com
Bank Tellers Report
Mortgage Banking
Savings Institutions

DIRECTORIES:

American Bank Directory (McFadden
 Business Publications, Norcross, GA)
Callahan's Credit Union Directory
 (Callahan and Associates, Washington,)
Financial Institutions Directory (American
 Bankers Association, Washington, DC)
Financial Yellow Book (Leadership
 Directories, Inc., New York, NY)
McFadden American Financial Directory
 (McFadden Pubs., Atlanta, GA)
Moody's Bank and Finance Manual (Moody's
 Investors Service, New York, NY)
Polk Bank Directory, International Edition
 (R.L. Polk, Nashville, TN)
Rand McNally Bankers Directory (Rand
 McNally, Chicago, IL)

Savings and Loan Association Directory
(American Business Directories, Omaha,
NE)

Shesunoff 1,000 Largest U.S. Banks (Shesunoff
Information Services, Austin, TX)

Thompson Bank Directory (Thompson
Financial Publishers, Skokie, IL)

U.S. Savings Institutions, The (Thompson
Financial Publishers, Skokie, IL)

U.S. Savings and Loan Directory (Rand
McNally, Chicago, IL)

Who's Who in International Banking (Reed
Reference Publishing, New Providence, NJ)

New York Employers:

Amalgamated Bank of New York
11-15 Union Square
New York, NY 10003
(212) 255-6200
Personnel Director: Patricia Klepaci

Apple Bank for Savings
Wall St. Plaza, Maiden Lane and Water St.
New York, NY 10038
(212) 472-4545
Personnel Director: Mary O. Sullivan

Astoria Federal Savings
1 Astoria Federal Plaza
Lake Success, NY 11042
(516) 327-3000
Personnel Director: Gary Zimbalatti

Bank of New York
48 Wall St.
New York, NY 10286
(212) 495-1784
Personnel Director: Thomas Angers

Bank of Tokyo Trust
1251 Avenue of the Americas
New York, NY 10020
(212) 782-4000
Personnel Director: Sheryl Riceman

Bankers Trust New York Corp.
280 Park Ave.
New York, NY 10017
(212) 250-2500
Managing Director, Human Resources:
Mark Bieler

Chase Manhattan Corp.
1 Chase Manhattan Plaza, 27th Floor
New York, NY 10081
(212) 552-2222
Jobline: (800) JOBLINE
Resumes to: 4 Metrotech Center, Brooklyn, NY, (718) 242-7537.

Citicorp
399 Park Ave.
New York, NY 10043
(800) 285-3000
Resumes to: Search and Staffing, 1 Court
Sq., Long Island City, NY 11120

Dime Bancorp/Dime Savings Bank of NY
589 5th Ave.
New York, NY 11530
(800) 843-3463
Human Resources Director: Chenetta
Hagin

Emigrant Savings Bank
5 E. 42nd St.
New York, NY 10017
(212) 850-4000
Senior VP, Personnel: Edward Tully

European American Bank
1 EAB Plaza
Uniondale, NY 11555
(516) 296-5555
Senior VP, Human Resources: Raul Cruz

First Empire State Corp./East NY Savings Bank
350 Park Ave.
Uniondale, NY 10022
(212) 293-5507

Fleet Bank
515 7th Ave.
New York, NY 10018
(212) 764-7060
Recruiter: Sharon Lancone

Greater New York Savings Bank
1 Penn Plaza
New York, NY 10019
(212) 613-4000
Human Resources: John Dresch

Green Point Savings Bank
41-60 Main St.
Brooklyn, NY 11355
718-670-7500
Human Resources Director: Eugene
Philippi

IBJ Schroeder Bank & Trust Co.
1 State St. Plaza
New York, NY 10004
(212) 858-2000
Human Resources Director: Keith Darcy

Independence Savings Bank
195 Montague Street
Brooklyn, NY 11201
(718) 624-6620
Human Resources Director: Rosemary
Trainn

Industrial Bank of Japan
245 Park Ave.
New York, NY 10167
(212) 764-0776

Long Island Savings Bank
201 Old Country Road
Melville, NY 11747
(516) 547-2000
VP, Director of Personnel: Donna Kelly

Morgan, J.P., & Co.
23 Wall St.
New York, NY 10260
(212) 483-2323
Contact Human Resources

Republic Bank for Savings
452 5th Ave.

New York, NY 10018
(212) 525-5000
Resumes to Human Resources

Connecticut Employers:

Fleet Bank
777 Main St.
Hartford, CT 06115
(860) 986-2000
Human Resources Director: Kathleen
McManus

People's Bank
850 Main St.
Bridgeport, CT 06604
(203) 338-7171
Director of Personnel: Betty Garcia

New Jersey Employers:

First Fidelity Bank
550 Broad St.
Newark, NJ 07102
(201) 565-3200
Senior VP, Human Resources: Chuck
Schwenk

PNC National Bank
2 Tower Center Blvd.
E. Brunswick, NJ 08816
(908) 220-4444

National Westminster Bank
10 Exchange Place Center
Jersey City, NJ 07302
(908) 253-4000
Contact employment and training center

Broadcasting: TV and Radio

WEB SITES:

Radio Guide to WWW (Yahoo Server)
http://www.yahoo.com/Entertainment/
Radio

Television Guide to WWW (Yahoo Server)
http://www.yahoo.com/Entertainment/
Television

TV Jobs
http://www.tvjobs.com/

PROFESSIONAL ORGANIZATIONS:

For networking in radio, television, and related fields, check out the following local professional organizations listed in Chapter 5:
American Women in Radio and Television
Newswomen's Club of New York
Society of Motion Picture and Television Engineers

For additional information, you can contact:

American Federation of Television and Radio Artists
260 Madison Ave.
New York, NY 10016
(212) 532-0800

Academy of Television Arts and Sciences
5220 Lankershim Blvd.
North Hollywood, CA 91601
(818) 754-2800

American Radio Association
17 Battery Place, Rm. 1443
New York, NY 10004
(212) 809-0600

Association of America's Public Television Stations
1350 Connecticut Ave., NW, Suite 200
Washington, DC 20036
(202) 887-1700

Association of Independent Television Stations
1320 19th St., NW, Suite 300
Washington, DC 20015
(202) 887-1970

National Academy of Television Arts and Sciences
111 W. 57th St.
New York, NY 10019
(212) 586-8424

National Association of Broadcasters
http://www.nab.org
1771 N St., NW
Washington, DC 20036
(202) 429-5300

National Cable Television Association
http://www.cable-online.com
1724 Massachusetts Ave., NW
Washington DC 20036
(202) 775-3550

National Radio Broadcasters Association
2033 M St., NW
Washington, DC 20036
(202) 429-5420

Radio-Television News Directors Association
1000 Connecticut Ave. NW, Suite 615
Washington, DC 20036
(202) 659-6510

Society of Broadcast Engineers
http://www.sbe.org
8445 Keystone Crossing, Suite 140
Indianapolis, IN 46240
(317) 253-1640

Women in Cable and Telecommunications
230 W. Monroe St.
Chicago, IL 60606
(312) 634-2330

PROFESSIONAL PUBLICATIONS:

American Radio
Billboard
Broadcasting and Cable
Broadcasting Magazine
Broadcast News
Broadcast Technology
Cable World
Communications News
Communications Technology
Radio World
Ross Reports
Television Broadcast
TV Radio Age
Variety

DIRECTORIES:

Broadcasting Cable Sourcebook (Broadcasting Publishing Co., Washington, DC)
Broadcasting and Cable Yearbook (Reed Elsevier Directories, New Providence, NJ)
Gale Directory of Publications and Broadcast Media (Gale Research, Detroit, MI)
New York Publicity Outlets (Public Relations Plus, Washington Depot, CT)
Radio Stations & Broadcasting Companies (American Business Information, Inc., Omaha, NB)
Radio & Television Career Directory (Gale Research Inc., Detroit, MI)
Television and Cable Fact Book (Warren Publishing, Washington, DC)
Working Press of the Nation, Vol. III, TV & Radio Directory (Reed Elsevier Directories, New Providence, NJ)

Television Employers:

Television is a huge business with a wide variety of jobs. We've decided to list the personnel people and others as contacts to focus your search. However, it would be more helpful to contact the business manager of a particular show. They are the people on the staff of network-produced shows that oversee budgets and allocation of funds. It's a more direct way to find out if positions exist and if you're qualified.

American Broadcasting Company— Capitol Cities (ABC)
77 W. 66th St.
New York, NY 10023
(212) 456-7777
Director, Employee Relations: Brendan Burke

CBS Television Network
51 W. 52nd St.
New York, NY 10019
(212) 975-4321
Sr. VP, Human Resources: Joan Showlater

Educational Broadcasting Corp.
356 W. 58th St.
New York, NY 10019
(212) 560-2000
Director of Human Resources: Mark Morales

Fox Broadcasting Company
1211 Avenue of the Americas
New York, NY 10021
(212) 556-2400
Resumes to: P.O. Box 900, Beverly Hills, CA 90213

King World Productions
1700 Broadway
New York, NY 10019
(212) 315-4000
Personnel Manager: Ms. McCreery

National Broadcasting Company (NBC)
30 Rockefeller Plaza
New York, NY 10112
(212) 664-4444
Employment Manager: Judith Sullivan

New Jersey Network
CN 777
Trenton, NJ 08625
(609) 777-5000
Personnal Manager: Kim Burnett

Times Broadcast TV Group
Subsidiary of Times Mirror Co.
2 Park Ave., 8th Floor
New York, NY 10016
(212) 448-2900
Human Resources Director: Mike Valenti
(800) 528-4637

Viacom International
1515 Broadway
New York, NY 10036
(212) 258-6000
Director of Personnel: John Warrack
Video/communications company.

Worldwide Television News
1995 Broadway
New York, NY 10023
(212) 362-4440
VP: Mr. Terry O'Reilly

WABC-Channel 7
7 Lincoln Square
New York, NY 10023
(212) 456-7777
Director, Employee Relations: Brendan
Burke

WCBS-Channel 2
524 W. 57th St.
New York, NY 10019
(212) 975-4321
Human Resources Director: Linda Kalarchian

WNET Channel 13
356 W. 58th St.
New York, NY 10019
(212) 560-2000
Recruitment Manager: Ingrid Jones
Public broadcasting station.

WNYW-Channel 5
205 E. 67th St.
New York, NY 10021
(212) 452-5555
Personnel Director: Iris Sierra

WPIX-TV (Tribune Broadcasting Co.)
220 E. 42nd St.
New York, NY 10017
(212) 949-1100
Manager of Recruiting: Donna Coles
Independent television broadcaster.

WWOR-TV (BHC Communications)
9 Broadcast Plaza
Secaucus, NJ 07096
(201) 348-0009
Human Resources Director: Michael
DiLaura
Independently owned television station.

WXTV (Univision Station Group)
24 Meadowland Parkway
Secaucus, NJ 07094
(201) 348-4141
Personnel Director: Norma Hanley

Cable TV Employers:

A&E Arts and Entertainment Network
235 E. 45th St.
New York, NY 10017
(212) 661-4500
VP, Human Resources: Rosalind Clay
Carter

Bravo
3 Crossways Park W.
Woodbury, NY 11797
(516) 364-2222
Personnel Director: Pat Colon

Cable News Network
5 Penn Plaza
New York, NY 10001
(212) 714-7800

CNBC
2200 Fletcher Ave.
Ft. Lee, NJ 07024
(201) 585-2622
Human Resources: Margaret Lazo

Crosswalks Television Network
1 Centre St., 28th Floor
Tech II Bldg., Suite 222
Municipal Bldg.
New York, NY 10007
(212) 669-7400
Genera l Manager: Chip Benson
Cable TV network of NYC.

ESPN
ESPN Plaza
Bristol, CT 06010
(860) 585-2000
Resumes to Human Resources

fX
212 5th Ave.
New York, NY 10010
(212) 802-4000
Contact: Marge Curtis

Home Box Office
Division of Time, Inc.
1100 Avenue of the Americas
New York, NY 10036
(212) 512-1000

Lifetime Television
309 W. 49th St.
New York, NY 10019
(212) 424-7000
Human Resources Director: Deborah
Henderson

MTV Networks, Nickelodeon, VH-1
1515 Broadway
New York, NY 10036
(212) 258-8000

Madison Square Garden Network
2 Pennsylvania Plaza, 14th Floor
New York, NY 10121
(212) 465-6000
Human Resources Coordinator: Marilyn
Housner
The sports arena's in-house cable channel.

News 12 Long Island
1 Media Crossways
Woodbury, NY 11797
(516) 496-1200

News 12 Westchester
6 Executive Plaza
Yonkers, NY 10701
(914) 378-8916

NY 1 News
460 W. 42nd St.
New York, NY 10036
(212) 465-0111
Human Resources Director: Elizabeth
Sanfant

Showtime/The Movie Channel
1633 Broadway, 15th Floor
New York, NY 10019
(212) 708-1600
Contact 1 of 5 appropriate HR directors

Sports Channel New York
200 Crossways Park Drive
Woodbury, NY 11797
(516) 393-4100

Time Warner Entertainment Co.
75 Rockefeller Plaza
New York, NY 10019
(212) 484-8000
Contact individual departments

Univision Television Group
605 3rd Ave., 12th Floor
New York, NY 10158
(212) 455-5227
Office Manager: Ms. Elidieth Stern

USA Network
1230 Avenue of the Americas
New York, NY 10020
(212) 408-9100
Manager, Human Resources: Wendy
Charesp

Radio Employers:

ABC Radio Network
77 W. 66th St.
New York, NY 10023
(212) 456-7777
Personnel Director: Brendan Burke

CBS Radio Network-AM
524 W. 57th St.
New York, NY 10019
(212) 975-4321
Human Resources Director: Linda
Kalarchian

Breaking into broadcasting

Susan Symington is an executive at a New York radio station. We asked her how to get started in broadcasting.

"Persevere," she says. "One of my first interviews was with the personnel director of a television station in Albany.

'Do you realize,' he said, 'that SUNY graduated 800 communications majors last year alone? There aren't that many jobs in the whole state.'

"That was a sobering thought. It discourages a lot of people. But you have to keep in there. Send out resumes, read the trades, see who's switching formats, and all that. Do anything on the side that might result in a good lead. The year after I graduated from college, I took a news writing course taught at the New School. In New York there are a lot of broadcasting professionals teaching all over the city; taking a course from a working professional can lead to valuable contacts.

"Another important point is to treat your contacts with respect. Broadcasting is a volatile business. You can't afford to burn a lot of bridges or alienate a lot of people. Somebody can be your assistant one day and your boss the next."

Voice of America
26 Federal Plaza, Room 30-100
New York, NY 10278
(212) 264-2345
Resumes to: Personnel, Room 1543,
330 Independence Ave. SW, Washington,
DC 20547

Wall Street Journal Radio Network
200 Liberty St., 14th Floor
New York, NY 10281
(212) 416-2381
Nat'l Radio Program Sales Manager:
Anne Su

Westwood One
1675 Broadway
New York, NY 10019
(212) 247-1600
Personnel Director: Hannah McGinniss

WABC
2 Penn Plaza, 17th Floor
New York, NY 10121
(212) 613-3800
Resumes to: Brendan Burke, Director,
Employee Relations,
77 W. 66th St., New York, NY 10023

WBLS (Inner City Broadcasting Corp.)
3 Park Ave., 41st Floor
New York, NY 10016
(212) 447-1000
Personnel Director: Beverly Osborn

WCBS (CBS Inc.)
51 W. 52nd St.
New York, NY 10019
Resumes to: Human Resources, 524 W.
57th St., New York, NY 10019

WFAN (Infinity Broadcasting Corp.)
34-12 36th St.
Astoria, NY 11106
(212) 869-6660 (New York City number)
Personnel Director: Alice McNamara

WHTZ (Shamrock Broadcasting)
230 Park Ave., Suite 605
New York, NY 10169
(212) 826-6161
Personnel Director: Nadej Halperin

WINS (Group W)
888 7th Ave.
New York, NY 10106
(212) 397-1010
Personnel Director: Cecilia Quintero

WKTU (Evergreen Media Corp.)
525 Washington Blvd.
Jersey City, NJ 07310
(201) 420-3700
General Manager: John Fullam

WLTW (Viacom International)
1515 Broadway
New York, NY 10036
(212) 258-7000
Director of Personnel: John Warrack

WNYC
1 Centre St.
New York, NY 10017
(212) 669-7800
Personnel Director: Geraldine Ippolito

WOR (Buckley Broadcasting Corp.)
1440 Broadway
New York, NY 10018
(212) 642-4500
Human Resources Director: Judy Pasch

WPAT (Spanish Broadcasting System)
26 W. 56th St.
New York, NY 10019
(212) 246-9393

WPLJ (Capitol Cities/ABC)
2 Penn Plaza
New York, NY 10121
(212) 613-8900
Resumes to: Employee Relations, 77 W.
66th St.,13th Floor, New York, NY 10023

WQCD (Tribune Broadcasting Corp.)
220 E. 42nd St., Suite 400
New York, NY 10017
(212) 210-2800

WQEW (The New York Times Co.)
122 5th Ave.
New York, NY 10011
(212) 633-7600
General Manager: Warren Bodow

WQHT (Emmis Broadcasting)
395 Hudson St., 7th Floor
New York, NY 10014
(212) 229-9797
Assistant to Business Manager: Julie Soler

WQXR (New York Times Co.)
122 5th Ave.
New York, NY 10011
(212) 633-7600
Human Resources: Carol Haftel

WRKS (Summit Broadcasting Corp.)
395 Hudson St., 7th Floor
New York, NY 10014
(212) 229-9797
Personnel Director: Gladis Levy

WSKQ (Spanish Broadcasting Systems)
26 W. 56th St.
New York, NY 10019
(212) 279-1679

WXRK (Infinity Broadcasting Corp.)
40 W. 57th St.
New York, NY 10019
(212) 314-9200
Personnel Director: Tom Gesimondo

Chemicals

WEB SITES:

American Chemical Society
http://nearnet.gnn.com/wic/chem.06.html

Chemical companies and sites
http://www.yahoo.com/
Business_and_Economy/Companies/
Chemicals/

PROFESSIONAL ORGANIZATIONS:

For networking in the chemical industry and related fields, check out the following local professional organizations listed in Chapter 5:

American Institute of Chemical Engineers

Association of Consulting Chemists and Chemical Engineers

Chemists' Club

Drug, Chemical and Allied Trades Association

For additional information, you can contact:

American Chemical Society
1155 16th St., NW
Washington, DC 20036
(202) 872-4600

Chemical Manufacturers Association
1300 Wilson Blvd.
Arlington, VA 22209
(703) 741-5000

National Organization for the Professional Advancements of Black Chemists and Chemical Engineers
525 College St., NW
Washington, D.C. 20059
(202) 667-1699

PROFESSIONAL PUBLICATIONS:

Chemical Business
Chemical Industry Update
Chemical Week

DIRECTORIES:

Chem Sources-U.S.A. (Chemical Sources International, Clemson, SC)

Chemclopedia (American Chemical Society, Washington, DC)

Chemical and Engineering News, Career Opportunities Issue (American Chemical Society, Washington, DC)

Chemical Week, Buyer's Guide Issue (McGraw-Hill, New York, NY)

Chemical Week, Financial Survey of the 300 Largest Companies (McGraw-Hill, New York, NY)

New York Employers:

Aceto Corp.
1 Hollow Lane, Suite 201
New Hyde Park, NY 11042
(516) 627-6000
Office Manager: Patricia Miller
Industrial, organic, and inorganic chemicals.

Affrimet-Indussa
1212 Avenue of the Americas
New York, NY 10036
(212) 764-0880
Personnel Director: Lisa Calabro
Allied chemicals and metals manufacturers.

Bamberger Polymers
1983 Marcus Ave.
Lake Success, NY 11042
(516) 328-2772
Personnel Director: Andrea Lichtman
A major distributor of plastics and resins.

Ciba Corporation
444 Saw Mill River Road
Ardsley, NY 10502
(914) 228-4195
VP, Human Resources: Stanton H. Goldberg
Pharmaceutical, specialty, and agricultural chemicals, resins, and plastics manufacturers. Company headquarters.

Grow Group
200 Park Ave.
New York, NY 10166
(212) 599-4400
Director of Human Resources: Frank
Esser

Hoechst-Celanese
3 Park Ave.
New York, NY 10016
(212) 251-8000
Human Resources Director: Cathy Parys

ICD Group
600 Madison Ave.
New York, NY 10022
(212) 644-1500
Resumes to Human Resources
Exports and imports chemicals.

Manheimer, J.
47-22 Pearson Pl.
Long Island City, NY 11101
(718) 392-7800
Personnel Manager: Lynn Mallon
Marketer of raw materials for food
products, flavors, and fragrances.
Company headquarters.

Stinnes Corp.
120 White Plains Road
Tarrytown, NY 10591
(914) 366-7200
Contact department heads
Distributor of industrial chemicals.

Transammonia, Inc.
350 Park Ave.
New York, NY 10022
(212) 223-3200
Contact Human Resources
Exporter/importer of industrial chemicals.

Connecticut Employers:

Crompton and Knowles Corporation
1 Station Place Metro Center
Stamford, CT 06902
(203) 353-5400
Personnel Director: Gene Holmes
Manufacturer of specialty chemicals,
plastics, and related products.

Union Carbide
39 Old Ridgebury Road
Danbury, CT 06817
(203) 794-2000
Contact Human Resources

New Jersey Employers:

Allied Signal
10 N. Ave. E
Elizabeth, NJ 07201
(908) 354-3215
Personnel Director: Liz Leven

American Cyanamid Co.
1 Campus Drive
Parsippany, NJ 07054
(973) 683-2000
Personnel Director: Lois Springstead
Manufacturers of pharmaceuticals,
chemicals, fibers, and consumer health
products.

American Gas and Chemical Co. Ltd.
220 Pegasus Ave.
Northvale, NJ 07647
(201) 767-7300
Personnel Director: Melanie Kershaw
Manufactures chemical and electronic
leak detectors.

BASF Corporation/Chemicals Division
3000 Continental Drive N.
Mount Olive, NJ 07828
(201) 426-2600
Sr. VP, Human Resources: Norman Maas

Cytec Industries
5 Garret Mountain Plaza
West Paterson, NJ 07424
(201) 357-3100
VP, Employee Resources: James W. Hirsch

Degussa Corp.
65 Challenger Road
Ridgefield Park, NJ 07660
(201) 641-6100
Human Resources: Elaine Woodworth

Drew Chemical Corporation
1 Drew Plaza
Boonton, NJ 07005
(201) 263-7602

Human Resources: Ralph Piano
Leading supplier of specialty chemicals
and services to the international maritime
industry and other industrial markets
worldwide.

GAF Chemicals Corporation
1361 Alps Road
Wayne, NJ 07470
(201) 628-3000
Personnel Manager: Gary Schneid
Manufacturer of specialty chemicals and
building materials.

Huls America
Turner Place
Piscataway, NJ 08855
(908) 981-5000
Personnel Director: Esther Wolff
Manufacturer of coating chemicals and
colorants.

NAPP Chemicals
299 Market St., 4th Floor
P.O. Box 893
Saddlebrook, NJ 07663
(201) 773-3900
Personnel Director: Marie Galdo
Medical chemicals and bulk pharmaceuticals.

**National Starch and Chemical
Corporation**
10 Finderne Ave.
Bridgewater, NJ 08807
(908) 685-5033
Director of Employment: Ingrid Brase
Industrial chemical manufacturer,
producing adhesives, resins, starches, and
specialty chemicals.

Oakite Products
50 Valley Road
Berkeley Heights, NJ 07922
(908) 464-6900

Personnel Director: Bill Wenhold
Manufacturer of chemicals used for
industrial and institutional cleaning and
metal conditioning.

Penick Corporation
158 Mt. Olivet Ave.
Newark, NJ 07114
(201) 621-2822
Director of Human Resources: Elaine
Reilly
Producer of chemicals and pesticides.

Rhone-Poulenc
CN 5266
Princeton, NJ 08543-5266
(908) 297-0100
Senior VP, Human Resources: Robert C.
Machin, CN 7500, Cranberry, NJ 08512-
7500
Producer of chemicals and related
products.

Sequa Corporation
3 University Plaza
Hackensack, NJ 07601
(201) 343-1122
VP, Human Resources: Jesse Battino

Sun Chemical Corporation
222 Ridge Plaza S.
Fort Lee, NJ 07024
Personnel Director: Thomas Witkowski

United Mineral and Chemical Corp.
1100 Valley Brook Ave.
Lyndhurst, NJ 07071
(201) 507-3300
Office Manager: Elena Boroweic
Manufacturer of high-purity metals and
industrial chemicals for use in water
treatment and rubber curing. Corporate
headquarters.

Computers: Hardware/Software

WEB SITES:

Web Developer's Virtual Library
http://www.stars.com

ZDNet
http://www.zdnet.com/

PROFESSIONAL ORGANIZATIONS:

For networking in the computer industry, check out the following local professional organizations listed in Chapter 5. See also "Computers: Information Services/Multimedia" and "Electronics/Telecommunications."
Association for Computing Machinery
New York New Media Association
Women in Data Processing

For additional information, contact:

Association of Online Professionals
6096 Franconia Road, Suite D
Alexandria, VA 22310
(703) 924-5800

Association of Computer Professionals
9 Forest Drive
Plainview, NY 11803
(516) 938-8223

Association for Women in Computing
P.O. Box 68
Newton Upper Falls, MA
(617) 924-2468

Computer and Communications Industry Association
666 11th St., NW
Washington DC 20001
(202) 783-0070

Software Publishers Association
1730 M St., NW, Suite 700
Washington, DC 20036
(202) 452-1600

PROFESSIONAL PUBLICATIONS:

Business Software News
http://www.softwarenews.ezin.net/

BYTE Magazine
Computer World
InfoWorld
PC Computing
PC Magazine
PC Week
Windows

DIRECTORIES:

Computer Directory (Computer Directories, Inc., Cypress, TX)
Computer Industry Almanac (Simon & Schuster, Inc., New York, NY)
Computers & Computing Information Resources Directory (Gale Research, Detroit, MI)
Data Communications Buyers Guide (McGraw-Hill, New York, NY)
Data Processing Service Directory (American Business Directories, Omaha, NE)
Datapro Directory of Microcomputer/Software (Datapro Research Corp., Delran, NJ)
Directory of Computer Software (National Technical Information Service U.S., Arlington, VA)

New York Employers:

ACT Computer
150 Pearl St.
New York, NY
(212) 609-5959

American Telephone and Telegraph (AT&T)
295 Maple Ave.
Baskin Ridge, NJ 07920
(212) 387-5400 (New York City number)
Senior VP, Human Resources: Harold Burligame

Apple Computer
153 E. 53rd. St., 29th Floor
New York, NY 10022
(212) 339-3700
Resumes to: Staffing, 1 Infinite Loop, Cupertino, CA 95014

Computer Associates International
1 Computer Associates Plaza
Ilandia, NY 11788
(516) 342-5224
Senior VP, Human Resources: Deborah
Coughlin
The second largest software development
company in the country.

Computer Horizons Corporation
747 3rd Ave.
New York, NY 10017
(212) 371-9600
Director of Personnel: Ann Martone
Software consultants.

Digital Equipment Corporation
2 Penn Plaza
New York, NY 10121
(212) 856-2000
Director of Human Resources: Eileen
Jacobs
One of the world's largest manufacturers
of minicomputers, microcomputers,
mainframe computer systems, terminals,
word processors, small business computers, networks, and complete office
information systems. The company
maintains sales, service, and support
offices in New York, Long Island, and
northern New Jersey.

Doundless Data Systems
100 Marcus Blvd.
Hauppague, NY 11788
(516) 342-7400
Personnel Director: Paul Hiber
Cathode ray terminals and data display
equipment.

Grumman Corporation
S. Osyster Bay Road
Bethpage, NY 11714
(516) 575-0574
Manager of Employment: Janet Blume
Software development, largely for
government contracts.

Information Builders
1250 Broadway
New York, NY 10001
(212) 736-4433

Director of Personnel: Lila Goldberg
Software development.

Interactive Business Systems
380 Madison Ave. 7th Floor
New York, NY 10017
(212) 856-4499

International Business Machines (IBM)
New Orchard Road
Armonk, NY 10504
(914) 288-5701
Resumes to: Dennis Gallagher, Route 9,
Town of Mount Pleasant, Sleepy Hollow,
NY 10591
World's largest manufacturer of data
processing machines, telecommunications
systems, and information processing
systems.

International Business Machines
44 S. Broadway
White Plains, NY 10601
(914) 288-3000
(800) 964-4473 Employment Line

Megadata TSD
35 Orville Drive
Bohemia, NY 11716
(516) 589-6800
Personnel Director: Herb Shaver
Application-oriented computer terminals.

Microsoft
825 8th Ave.
New York, NY 10019
(212) 245-2100
Personnel: 9 Hillside Ave., Waltham, MA
02154

NEC America
8 Corporate Center Drive
Melville, NY 11747
(516) 753-7000
Manager, Human Resources: Marie
Speranza

NCR Corporation
111 Fulton St., 4th Fl.
Ilandia, NY 10033
(212) 484-5400
A leading manufacturer of computers for
home and office.

Booting up big $$$ in computer sales

Philip Daniels competes in the fast lane as a computer sales engineer. His clients are Fortune 500 companies, and his products are communications boards, controllers, and disk and tape subsystems manufactured by a relatively new specialty company. "It's an emotionally and physically stressful environment where I constantly have to prove myself," says Philip.

We asked how he got there and what keeps him successful.

"I use every skill and all the experience I've ever had," said the former teacher and editorial assistant for a steel company's community relations department. "When I decided to go back to school for an associate's degree in computers, I needed a job as well. So I sold cars, and that provided invaluable marketing and people experience, plus communications skills that are absolutely essential in my present business.

"Once I got into computer courses, I realized I couldn't settle for a $25,000 programming job and began laying more plans. And, incidentally, you must prepare yourself for the entry position in this field. My first job—strictly commission—was with a small systems house, and within a year I was director of marketing with a sales staff of six. I got a total overview of the business so that I could talk from that perspective on my next round of interviews.

"I used an employment agent who specializes in computer sales to get this position and was very specific with him about my requirements."

Asked to explain his current success, Philip responds: "I'd have to say the number one factor is technical expertise—with sales ability second. I read, listen, and pick brains to stay on top of the products and a changing market place so that my company provides a service to the client by sending me. By the way, with little more education than a $25,000 programmer, I'll make at least three times that this year. And the perks are great, too."

New York is the place to be for employement in the computer industry. The city's fastest growing occupations through 2005 are computer engineers (8.4%), systems operators (7.5%), and systems analysts (6.9%).

Oracle Corporation
520 Madison Ave.
New York, NY 10022
(212) 508-7700

Pencom Systems
40 Fulton St.
New York, NY 10038
(212) 513-7777
Contact: Cliff Kahan

Periphonics Corporation
4000 Veterans Memorial Highway
Bohemia, NY 11716
(516) 467-0500
Senior Administrator: Janet Anderson
Voice-controlled computer systems.

Software Engineering of America
1230 Hempstead Turnpike
Franklin Square, NY 11010
(516) 328-7000
Personnel Director: Thomas Mulvey

Wang Laboratories
150 E. 58th St.
New York, NY 10155
(212) 644-62-4
Personnel Representative: Stephanie Fields
A major manufacturer of office automation systems, data processing and word processing equipment.

Connecticut Employers:

Executive Business Machines
2 Post Road
Fairfield, CT 06430
(203) 254-8500
Personnel Director: Norma Brown

Perkin-Elmer
761 Main Ave.
Norwalk, CT 06859
(203) 762-4210
Personnel Director: Paul Palermo

XEROX
P.O. Box 1600
800 Long Ridge Road

Stamford, CT 06902
(203) 968-3000
Call for individual departmental mailing addresses

New Jersey Employers:

ADP (Automatic Data Processing)
2 Journal Square Plaza
Jersey City, NJ 07306
(201) 714-3000
Human Rersources: Bill Brenner
Computer services company.

Concurrent Computer Corporation
2 Crescent Place
Oceanport, NJ 07757
(908) 870-4500
(800) 666-4544 Employment Line
Personnel Director: Donna Bean
Computer systems equipment manufacturer.

Global Turnkey Systems
20 Waterview Blvd.
Parsippany, NJ 07054,
(201) 331-1010
Resumes to Human Resources
Sales and service of computer software and hardware.

Hewlett-Packard
150 Green Pond Road
Rockaway, NJ 07866
(201) 627-6400
Human Resources: Sandy Carr
Produces computer-controlled data acquisition, test, and control systems, system components and DC systems, and laboratory power supplies.

Unisys Corporation
2 Oak Way
Berkeley Heights, NJ 07922
(908) 771-5150
Recruiting and Staffing: Gary Cozin
Formed from the merger of Burroughs Corporation and Sperry Corporation. A leading producer of information processing systems and services, as well as electronic systems for defense and aerospace.

Computers: Information Services/Multimedia

WEB SITES:

Careers in computer consulting
http://www.acm.ndsu.nodak.edu/
~acmco/

News update on the information services industry
http://204.252.76.40/0002c2a.html

Assocation of Online Professionals
http://www.wdn.com/aop/

National Multimedia Association of America
http://www.nmaa.com

@NY (The New York Internet newsletter)
http://www.news-ny.com/news

PROFESSIONAL ORGANIZATIONS:

For local networking groups, see preceding section, "Computers: Hardware/Software." For additional information, contact the following organizations:

American Society for Information Science
8720 Georgia Ave., Suite 501
Silver Spring, MD 20910
(301) 495-0900

Association of Independent Information Professionals
234 W. Delaware Ave.
Pennington, NJ 08534
(609) 730-8759

IEEE Computer Society
1730 Massachusetts Ave., NW
Washington, DC 20036
(202) 371-0101

Information Industry Association
1625 Mass Ave., Suite 700
Washington, DC 20036
(202) 986-0280

Information Technology Association of America
1616 N. Ft. Myer Drive, Suite 1300
Arlington, VA 22209
(703) 522-5055

ITI Information Technology Industry Council
1250 I St., NW, Suite 200
Washington, DC 20005
(202) 737-8888

National Association for Information Services
1250 Connecticut Ave., NW, Suite 600
Washington, DC 20036
(202) 833-2545

Society for Information Management
401 N. Michigan Ave.
Chicago, IL 60611
(312) 644-6610

Special Interest Group on Data Communication
Association for Computing Machinery
1515 Broadway
New York, NY 10036
(212) 869-7440

Women in Information Processing
P.O. Box 39173
Washington, DC 20016
(202) 328-6161

PROFESSIONAL PUBLICATIONS:

CIO: The Magazine for Information Executives
Computer Communications Review
Computerworld: Newsweekly for Information Systems Management
Data Communications
Database Magazine
Datamation
http://www.datamation.com
EDI News
Information Processing and Management

InformationWEEK
Internet Business Report
Link-Up
Network World
Networking Management
Online

DIRECTORIES:

*Computers and Computing Information
Resources Directory* (Gale Research,
Detroit, MI)
Data Sources (Ziff-Davis Publishing, New
York, NY)
Directory of Top Computer Executives
(Applied Computer Research, Phoenix, AZ)
Information Industry Directory (Gale
Research, Detroit, MI)
Information Sources (Information
Industry Association, Washington, DC)

Employers:

(Also see "Multimedia Employers" list
following.)

CGI Systems
500 5th Ave., 32nd Floor
New York, NY 10110
(212) 575-2400
Human Resources Manager: Paul
Sheridan
Information resource consulting,
including systems planning, analysis, and
design.

Computer Associates International
Fort Lee Executive Park
2 Executive Drive
Fort Lee, NJ 07024
(201) 592-0009
Personnel Director: Gary Johnson
Builds on-line systems, offers technical
support for networking and database
communications.

Computer People
11 Penn Plaza, Suite 920
New York, NY 10001
(212) 279-8600
Branch Manager: Tom Meola
Information technology services.

Comtex Information Systems
40 Broad St.
New York, NY 10004
(212) 480-2609

Consortium, The
1156 Avenue of the Americas, 4th Fl.
New York, NY 10036
(212) 221-1544
Human Resources: Russ Notaro
Services for large mainframes, Unix,
and PCs.

DMRS
333 7th Ave.
New York, NY 10010
(212) 465-0814
Personnel: Ms. Grossman
Designs and develops marketing databases.

Dow Jones Markets
Harborside Financial Center, 600 Plaza 2
Jersey City, NJ 07311
(201) 938-4000
Staffing Director: Joe Njitray

Forsythe & Lincoln Associates
50 Broadway
New York, NY 10004
(212) 425-2668
President: Robert Patterson

Glasgal Communications
151 Veterans Drive
Northvale, NJ 07647
(201) 768-8082
Personnel Director: Mary Simon
Designs computer networks.

IDD Information Services
2 World Trade Center
New York, NY 10048
(212) 432-0045
Specializes in financial information
services.

I.M.A.G.E. Inc.
45 E. 30th St., 15th Floor
New York, NY 10016
(212) 843-8700
New Media Sales and Marketing: Alex
Betancur

Provides systems and database integration, on-line delivery, Web site construction, customized and corporate training.

Interim Technology
9 Polito Ave.
Lindhurst, NJ 07071-3406
(201) 392-0800
Human Resources Manager: Carolyn Cox
Computer operations and technical support.

MISI Company
350 Park Ave., 4th Floor
New York, NY 10022
(212) 355-5585
Recruiting Director: Christine DeStefano
Experts in application programming.

MMS International
65 Broadway, 19th Fl.
New York, NY 10006
(212) 770-4343

Prodigy Services Co.
445 Hamilton Ave.
White Plains, NY 10601
(914) 448-8000
VP, Human Resources: Nick Latko

RCG Information Technology
379 Thornall St.

Edison, NJ 08837
(212) 642-6000
Human Resources Director: Donna Gabinnella

Real Decisions Corporation
Gartner Group
56 Top Gallant Road
Stamford, CT 06904
(203) 964-0096
Recruiter: Jack Sia
Information management consultants.

VNU Business Information Services
11 W. 42nd St.
New York, NY 10036
(212) 789-3680
Personnel Director: Debbie Morise

Volt Information Sciences
1221 Avenue of the Americas, 47th Floor
New York, NY 10020
(212) 704-2400
Recruiter: Irving Proger

XTend Communications
171 Madison Ave.
New York, NY 10016
(212) 725-2000
Contact individual department of interest. Computer consultants, specializing in integration of facilities and services.

For gettogethers in cyberspace try these sites:
Cybersuds: New York New Media Association's "schmooze-o-rama"
(212) 459-4649

2600 Magazine holds monthly hacker invasion of pay-phone bank in Citicorp Center lobby
(516) 751-2600
meeting@2600.com

The New York Software Industry Association offers free advice to young software companies and professionals:
(516) 822-9100, etx. 232
NQFH71A@prodigy.com

Webgrrls: Networking for cyberfemales
(212) 642-8012
www.webgrrls.com

@NY holds monthly events, conferences and seminars relating to the city's cyberscene.
(212) 425-8201
http://www.news-ny.com/news

Multimedia Employers:

What is multimedia? According to the National Multimedia Association of America, multimedia is "a computer-related process that improves the transfer of information by involving two or more of the participant's senses."

Ad One
361 Broadway
New York, NY 10012
(212) 965-2900

Addison-Wesley Longman
170 5th Ave.
New York, NY
(212) 782-3300
Personnel: Susan Lowe

Agency.com
655 Broadway, 9th Floor
New York, NY 10012
(212) 358-8220
Personnel: Gerri Maquet

Concrete Media
580 Broadway
New York, NY 10012
(212) 334-8181
Personnel: Jane Mount

Hyperspace Cowgirls
857 Broadway
New York, NY 10012
(212) 741-1350
Personnel: Conrad Cummings

Jupiter Communications
627 Broadway
New York, NY 10012
(212) 780-6060
Personnel: Amy Bromberg

KinderActive
11 W. 19th St.
New York, NY 10011
(212) 352-1000

The Mining Company
220 E. 42nd St.
New York, NY 10017
(212) 849-2000
Personnel: Bill Day

Netcast
55 Broad St.
New York, NY
(212) 248-2989

Preiss, Byron, Multimedia
24 W. 25th St.
New York, NY 10001
(212) 645-9870
Personnel: Clarice Levin

R/GA Interactive
350 W. 39th St.
New York, NY 10018
(212) 946-4000
Personnel: Kailtyn Lynch

Red Herring
449 Washington
New York, NY 10013
(212) 219-0557
Personnel: Carol Bobolts

Site Specific
132 W. 21st St.
New York, NY 10011
(212) 206-6600
Personnel: Shirley Coke

Touchscreen Media Group
1674 Broadway

New York, NY
(212) 262-7015
Personnel: Dennis McCole

US Interactive
49 W. 27th St.
New York, NY 10001
(212) 685-3727
Personnel: Mary Garland

Construction

WEB SITES:

BuildingWeb
http://www.buildingweb.com

BuildNET—The Building Industry Online
http://www.abuildnet.com

Contractor Net
http://www.contractornet.com/list.html

PROFESSIONAL ORGANIZATIONS:

For networking in the construction industry and related fields, check out the following local professional organizations listed in Chapter 5. Also see "**Engineering.**"
American Society of Civil Engineers
Professional Women in Construction

For additional information, you can contact:

Associated Builders and Contractors
http://www.abc.org
1300 N. 17th St., 8th Floor
Rosslyn, VA 22209
(703) 812-2000

Associated General Contractors of America
http://www.agc.org
1957 E St., NW
Washington, DC 20006
(202) 393-2040

Construction Managers Association of America
12355 Sunrise Valley Drive
Reston, VA 22091
(703) 356-2622

National Association of Home Builders of the U.S.
1201 15th St., NW
Washington, DC 20005
(202) 822-0200

National Association of Minority Contractors
1333 F St., NW, Suite 500
Washington, DC 20004
(202) 347-8259

National Association Of Women in Construction
841 Worcester Road, Suite 101
Natick, MA 01760
(617) 325-3866

New York State Building and Construction Trades Council
211 E. 43rd St.
New York, NY 10017
(212) 682-7184

PROFESSIONAL PUBLICATIONS:

Better Homes and Gardens Building Ideas
Builder
Builder and Contractor
Building Contractors
Building Design and Construction

Building Systems Magazine
Construction Review
Constructor

DIRECTORIES:

Associated Builders & Contractors
 Membership Directory (Associated
 Builders & Contractors, Washington,
 DC)
Associated General Contractors Member-
 ship Mobile Directory (Washington, DC)
Builder/Dealer Manufacturers Directory
 (Corry Publishing, Erie, PA)
Building Contractors Directory (American
 Business Directories, Omaha, NE)
Construction Equipment, Buyers Guide
 Issue (Reed Elsevier Business Informa-
 tion, Chicago, IL)
Constructioneer, Directory Issue (HES,
 Inc., New Haven, CT)
Constructor, Directory Issue (Associated
 General Contractors of America,
 Washington, DC)
ENR Directory of Contractors (McGraw-
 Hill, New York, NY)
Cultural Institutions (Museums, Arts,
 Music)

New York Employers:

AMREP Corp.
641 Lexington Ave., 6th Floor
New York, NY 10022
(212) 705-4700
Personnel Director: Denise Williams

Fischbach Corporation
7 Hanover Sq.
New York, NY 10004
(212) 440-2100
Personnel Director: Steve Biskup

Herbert Construction Co.
770 Lexington Ave., 13th Fl.
New York, NY 10021
(212) 207-8576
Personnel Director: Evelyn Breiner

Kajima USA
320 Park Ave., 26th Floor
New York, NY 10022

(212) 355-4571
Personnel Director: Mr. Akira Goto

Lehrer McGovern Bovis
387 Park Avenue S.
New York, NY 10016
(212) 576-4000
Vice President: Ralph W. Bever

Morse/Diesel International
1633 Broadway
New York, NY 10019
(212) 484-0300
Director of Human Resources: Irwin
Wecker

NAB Construction Corp.
11-20 14th Ave.
College Point, NY 11356
(718) 762-0001
Personnel Director: Michelle Cote

NYC School Construction Authority
3030 Thomson Ave.
Long Island City, NY 11101
(718) 472-8000
Human Resources Director: Louise
Nicolazzi-Shapiro

Pormatech Inc.
225 W. 34th St.
New York, NY 10122
(212) 714-2140
President: Yvette Streahle

Saturn Construction Co.
115 Stevens Ave.
Valhalla, NY 10595
(914) 747-2727
President: Luca A. Cappelli

Starrett Housing Corp.
909 3rd Ave.
New York, NY 10022
(212) 751-3100
Personnel Director: Kelvin Rodrigeuz

Turner Corp.
375 Hudson St.
New York, NY 10014
(212) 229-6000
Personnel Director: Richard Esau
Nonresidential construction.

Connecticut Employers:

Atlas Construction
P.O. Box 2099
Stamford, CT 06906
(203) 327-0330
Personnel Director: Bill Cross

Morganti Group
100 Mill Plain Road
Ridgefield, CT 06811
(203) 743-2675
Personnel Director: Maida Hyde

Tomlinson-Hawley-Patterson
2225 Reservoir Ave.
Trumbull, CT 06611

(203) 777-6978
Personnel Director: Dick Jagoe

New Jersey Employers:

Foster Wheeler USA
Perryville Corporate Park
Clinton, NJ 08809
(908) 730-4000
Human Resources Director: Richard
Lively

Torcon Inc.
P.O. Box 609
Westfield, NJ 07091
(908) 232-8900
Personnel Director: George Saliola

Cosmetics/Perfume/Toiletries

WEB SITES:

Cosmetic company links
http://www.yahoo.com/text/
Business_and_Economy/
Products_and_Services/Personal Care/
Cosmetics/

PROFESSIONAL ORGANIZATIONS:

For networking in cosmetics and related
fields, check out the following local
professional organizations listed in
Chapter 5:
Cosmetic Executive Women
Drug, Chemical and Allied Trades
  Association
Fragrance Foundation
Society of Cosmetic Chemists

For more information you can contact:

**Cosmetic, Toiletry and Fragrance
Association**
1101 17th St., NW, Suite 300
Washington, DC 20036
(202) 331-1770

PROFESSIONAL PUBLICATIONS:

Beauty Fashion
CFTA Newsletter
Cosmetic World News
Cosmetics and Toiletries
Soap/Cosmetics/Chemical Specialties
*Toiletries, Fragrances and Skin Care: The
  Rose Sheet*

DIRECTORIES:

Beauty Fashion, Fragrance Directory Issue
  (Beauty Fashion, Inc. New York, NY)
Cosmetics & Perfume Dealers (American
  Business Information, Inc., Omaha, NB)
Fragrance Foundation Reference Guide
  (Fragrance Foundation, New York, NY)
*Who's Who: The CFTA Membership
  Directory* (Cosmetic, Toiletry and
  Fragrance Association, Washington, DC)

New York Employers:

Almay, Inc.
Division of Revlon
625 Madison Ave., 8th Floor
New York, NY 10022

(212) 527-4700
Human Resources: Sally Dickinson

American Home Products Corp.
5 Giralda Farms
Madison, NJ 07940
(973) 660-5000
Human Resources Director: Louis
Springstead

Arden, Elizabeth
1345 Avenue of the Americas, 35th Floor
New York, NY 10105
(212) 261-1000

Aveda
233 Spring St.
New York, NY 10003
(212) 807-1492

Avon Products
1345 Avenue of the Americas
New York, NY 10105
(212)282-5000
Director of Personnel: Cindy Drankowski

Bristol-Myers
345 Park Ave.
New York, NY 10154
(212) 546-4000

Carter-Wallace
1345 Avenue of the Americas
New York, NY 10105
(212) 339-5000
Personnel Manager: Anastasia Kehoe

Chanel, Inc.
9 W. 57th St.
New York, NY 10019
(212) 688-5055
Personnel Director: Marilyn Marino

Clarins USA
135 E. 57th St., 15th Floor
New York, NY 10022
(212) 980-1800
Personnel Director: Lilly Dobler

Clinique Laboratories
Division of Estee Lauder
767 5th Ave.

New York, NY 10153
(212) 572-3800
Contact Human Resources

Colgate-Palmolive
300 Park Ave.
New York, NY 10022
(212) 310-2000
Personnel Director: Douglas Reid
Manufacturer of soaps and cosmetics.

Cosmair, Inc. (Lancome, L'Oreal, Ralph Lauren, Redkin)
575 5th Ave.
New York, NY 10017
(212) 818-1500
Sr. VP, Human Resources: Robert Nile

Coty Division
237 Park Ave.
New York, NY 10017
(212) 850-2300
Director of Personnel: Eileen Harris

Del Laboratories
565 Broad Hollow Road
Farmingdale, NY 11735
(516) 293-7070
Personnel Director: Charles Schneck

Estee Lauder
767 5th Ave.
New York, NY 10153
(212) 572-4200
VP, Human Resources: Marian Beatty
Diversified manufacturer and marketer of cosmetics under the Lauder and Clinique names.

Florasynth, Inc.
300 North St.
Teeterboro, NJ 07608
(201) 288-3200
Personnel Manager: Ted Stuart

Guerlain, Inc.
444 Madison Ave.
New York, NY 10016
(212) 751-1870

International Flavors and Fragrances
521 W. 57th St.
New York, NY 10019
(212) 765-5500
Personnel Director: Eric Campbell

Lever Brothers Company
390 Park Ave.
New York, NY 10022
(212) 688-6000
Personnel Director: Alexandria Tow

Philippe, Jean, Fragrances
551 5th Ave.
New York, NY 10176
(212) 983-2640
Human Resources Director: Henry
Dominigez

Revlon, Inc. (Almay, Charles of the Ritz, Ultima II)
625 Madison Ave.
New York, NY 10022
(212) 572-5000
Senior VP, Human Resources: Ron
Dunbar

St. Laurent, Yves
40 W. 57th St.
New York, NY 10019
(212) 621-7300

Shiseido Cosmetics
178 Bauer Drive
Oakland, NJ 07436
(201) 337-3750
Contact Human Resources

Whitehall Laboratories
Division of American Home Products
5 Giralda Farms
Madison, NJ 07940
(973) 660-5000
Human Resources Director: Louis
Springfield

Connecticut Employers:

Bristol-Myers Squibb Co.
1 Blachley Road
Stamford, CT 06992
(203) 357-0000

Chesebrough-Pond's USA
33 Benedict Place
Greenwich, CT 06830
(203) 661-2000
VP, Personnel: James McCall
Cosmetics, pharmaceuticals.

Clairol, Inc.
345 Park Ave.
New York, NY 10154
(212) 546-5000
Personnel Director: Sandra Holleran

Conair Corporation
1 Cummingspoint Road
Stamford, CT 06904
(203) 351-9000
Director of Human Resources: Barbara
Melbourne

Educational Institutions

WEB SITES:

Academe This Week
http://chronicle.merit.edu/

Collegiate.Net
http://www.collegiate.net/

Peterson's Education Guide
http://www.petersons.com

PROFESSIONAL ORGANIZATIONS:

For networking in education and related fields, contact the following local organizations listed in Chapter 5.
Institute of International Education
National Resource Center for Parapro-
   fessionals in Education
New York Alliance of Black School
   Educators

For more information you can contact:

American Association of School
Administrators
1801 N. Moore St.
Arlington, VA 22209
(703) 528-0700

Association of Graduate Schools
1 Dupont Circle, NW
Washington, DC
(202) 466-5032

Association for Supervision and
Curriculum Development
http://www.ascd.org
1250 N. Pitt St.
Alexandria, VA 22314
(703) 549-9110

Connecticut Education Association
21 Oak St , Capitol Place, Suite 500.
East Hartford, CT 06106
(860) 525-5641

National Education Association of the U.S.
http://www.nea.org/
1201 16th St., NW

Washington, DC 20036
(202) 833-4000

New Jersey Association of School
Administrators
920 W. State St.
Trenton, NJ 08618
(609) 599-2900

New Jersey Education Association
180 W. State St.
Trenton, NJ 08607
(609) 599-4561

PROFESSIONAL PUBLICATIONS:

AACC (American Association for Career
   Education) Careers Update
AAHE (American Association for Higher
   Education) Bulletin
Academe
American Educator
American Teacher
Basic Education
Chronicle of Higher Education
Education Forum
Education Today
Instructor
School Administrator
Today's Catholic Teacher

DIRECTORIES:

American Trade Schools Directory (Croner
   Publications, Inc., Queens Village, NY)
Bricker's International Directory, Univer-
   sity-Based Executive Programs (Peterson's
   Guides, Princeton, NJ)
Patterson's American Education (Educa-
   tional Directories, Mt. Prospect, IL)
Patterson's Elementary Education (Educa-
   tional Directories, Mount Prospect, IL)
Patterson's Schools Classified (Educational
   Directories, Mount Prospect, IL)
Peterson's Annual Guide to Graduate Study
   (Peterson's Guides, Princeton, NJ)
Peterson's Annual Guide to Undergraduate
   Study (Peterson's Guides, Princeton, NJ)

Peterson's Guide to Four-Year Colleges
(Peterson's Guides, Princeton, NJ)
Peterson's Guide to Independent Secondary
Schools (Peterson's Guides, Princeton, NJ)

Who's Who in American Education (Marquis
Who's Who, New Providence, NJ)

A quick tip

If you are interested in an academic position with a college or university, it sometimes helps to contact the Dean of your discipline as well as the personnel office. Contact local boards of education for information on local schools.

Colleges and Universities, New York Employers:

Adelphi University-Main Campus
South Ave.
Garden City, NY 11530
(516) 877-3000
Assoc. VP of Human Resources and Labor
Relations: Donald H. Flanders

Baruch, Bernard M., College
17 Lexington Ave. (mailing address)
New York, NY 10010
(212) 387-1060
Personnel Director: Ms. Ronny Widener

Bronx Community College
181st and University Ave.
Bronx, NY 10453
(718) 289-5100
Personnel Director: Shelly Levey

City University of New York (CUNY)
535 E. 80th St.
New York, NY 10021
(212) 794-5555

College of Staten Island
2800 Victory Blvd., 1A-204
Staten Island, NY 10314
(718) 982-2000
Personnel Director: Evelyn Conti

Columbia University
116th St. and Broadway, 209 Dodge Hall
New York, NY 10027
(212) 870-2403

Cooper Union
30 Cooper Square
New York, NY 10003
(212) 353-4151
Personnel Director: John Maher

Fashion Institute of Technology (SUNY)
236 W. 27th St.
New York, NY 10001
(212) 217-5703
Personnel Director: Elaine Maceuli

Fordham University
E. Fordham Road
Bronx, NY 10458
(212) 636-6000

Hofstra University
1000 Fulton Ave.
Hempstead, NY 11550
(516) 463-6859
Human Resources Director: Janet
Lenaghan

Hunter College
695 Park Ave.
New York, NY 10021
(212) 772-4000
Personnel Director: Charles Hayes

Iona College
715 North Ave.
New Rochelle, NY 10801
(914) 633-2000
Director of Human Resources: Donald
Herring

Jay, John, College of Criminal Justice
445 W. 59th St.
New York, NY 10019
(212) 237-8000
Director of Human Resources: Margaret Shultzee

Kingsborough Community College
2001 Oriental Blvd.
Brooklyn, NY 11235
(718) 368-5000
Associate Personnel Director: Jan Baybusky

La Guardia Community College
31-10 Thomson Ave.
Long Island City, NY 11101
(718) 482-7200
Deputy Director of Personnel: Linda Johnson

Lawrence, Sarah, College
1 Meadway
Bronxville, NY 10708
(914) 395-2510
Personnel Director: Julie Auster

Long Island University
University Center, Northern Blvd.
Greenvale, NY 11548
(516) 299-0200
Director of Personnel: Howard White

Manhattan Community College
199 Chambers St.
New York, NY 10007
(212) 346-8000
Personnel Director: Ms. Alyne Coy

Manhattanville College
Purchase St.
Purchase, NY 10577
(914) 694-2200
Personnel Director: Elizabeth Capua

Marymount College
221 E. 71st. St.
New York, NY 10021
(212) 517-0400
Personnel Director: Christina Flanagan

Molloy College
1000 Hempstead Ave.
Rockville Center, NY 11570
(516) 678-5000
Academic Dean: Sister Patricia Morris

Nassau Community College (SUNY)
Stewart Ave., 1 Education Drive
Garden City, NY 11530
(516) 572-7501
Personnel Director: Fred Downs

New School for Social Research
66 W. 12th St.
New York, NY 10011
(212) 229-5600
Personnel Director: Pamela Landberg

New York Institute of Technology
Old Westbury Campus
Old Westbury, NY 11568
(516) 686-7516
Personnel Director: Rosalyn Marett

New York University
32 Washington Place
Washington Square
New York, NY 10003
(212) 998-1250
Assoc. Dean for Faculty: W. Gabreil Carras

Pace University
1 Pace Plaza
New York, NY 10038
(212) 346-1200
Personnel: Yvonne Ramierez
Campuses also in Pleasantville and White Plains.

Polytechnic Institute of New York
333 Jay St.
Brooklyn, NY 11123
(718) 260-3600
Director of Human Resources: Sharon Lax

Pratt Institute
200 Willoughby Ave.
Brooklyn, NY 11205
(718) 636-3600
Jobline: (718) 636-3742
Director of Human Resources: Dian Jones

Queens College
65-30 Kissena Blvd.
Flushing, NY 11367
(718) 997-4455
Contact individual department of interest

Queensborough Community College
222-05 56th Ave.
Bayside, NY 11364
(718) 631-6262
Contact Office of Academic Affairs

St. John's University
Grand Central and Utopia Parkways
Jamaica, NY 11439
(718) 990-1865
Campus also on Staten Island

School of Visual Arts
209 E. 23rd. St.
New York, NY 10010
(212) 592-2000
Personnel Director: Laurie Pearlberg

State University at Purchase (SUNY)
735 Anderson Hill Road
Purchase, NY 10577
(914) 251-6000
Personnel Director: Peter Brown

State University at Stony Brook (SUNY)
Nicolls Road
Stonybrook, NY 11794
(516) 689-6000
Director of Personnel: Gary Matthews
Jobline: (516) 632-9222

Westchester Community College
75 Grasslands Road
Valhalla, NY
(914) 785-6600
Contact chairperson of individual
department

Colleges and Universities, Connecticut Employers:

Fairfield University
N. Benson Road
Fairfield, CT 06430
(203) 254-4000
Academic VP: Dr. Robert Wall, Canisius
Hall

Wesleyan University
70 Wyllis Ave.
Middletown, CT 06459
(203) 685-2100
Contact individual departments
Jobline: (203) 785-2921 for non-academic
jobs.

Yale University
155 Whitney Ave.
New Haven, CT 06511
(203) 432-9321
Contact individual departments

Colleges and Universities, New Jersey Employers:

Drew University
36 Madison Ave.
Madison, NJ 07940
(201) 408-3739

New Jersey Institute of Technology
University Heights
Newark, NJ 07102
(201) 596-3140
Contact individual departments

Princeton University
9 Nassau Hall
Princeton, NJ 08544
(609) 258-3020
Dean of Faculty: Robert Gunning
Jobline: (609) 258-6130 for non-academic
jobs.

Rutgers University
P.O. Box 1360
Piscataway, NJ 08855
(908) 445-3020
Campus in New Brunswick; contact
individual department of interest

Seton Hall University
400 S. Orange Ave.
South Orange, NJ 07079
(201) 761-9178
Contact individual department of interest

Local Boards of Education:

Information on individual schools in an area can be obtained by contacting Boards of Education, which often have listings of current openings in their systems. Also available are directories for all *Non-Public Schools and Administrators* and *Public Schools and Administrators* published annually by the New York State Education Department, Information on Education, Albany, NY.

Archdiocese of New York
1011 1st Ave.
New York, NY 10022
(212) 371-1000, ext. 2876
Teacher Recruitment: Nancy Albizuri
Recruitment Center for Catholic elementary and high schools in NYC and neighboring counties.

Board of Cooperative Educational Services, Nassau
Salsbury Center
Valentine and Plain Road
Westbury, NY 11590
(516) 997-8700
Provides special education services for 57 school districts.

Board of Cooperative Educational Services, Northern Westchester and Putnam Counties
200 BOCES Drive
Yorktown Heights, NY 10598
(914) 245-2700

Board of Cooperative Educational Services, Southern Westchester County No. 2
17 Berkley Drive
Rye Brook, NY 10580
(914) 937-3820

Connecticut State Board of Education
165 Capital Ave., Room 322
Hartford, CT 06106
(203) 566-7822

New Jersey State Board of Education
225 E. State St., CN500
Trenton, NJ 08625
(609) 292-4444

New York City Board of Education
210 Livingston St.
Brooklyn, NY 11201
(718) 935-2000

Private Schools, New York:

Bank Street School
610 W. 122th St.
New York, NY 10025
(212) 875-4420

Berkeley Carroll School
181 Lincoln Pl.
Brooklyn, NY 11217
(718) 789-6060

Birch Walthen Lenox School
210 E. 77th St.
New York, NY 10021
(212) 861-0404

Brearley School
610 E. 83 St.
New York, NY 10028
(212) 744-8582

Columbia Grammar and Preparatory School
5 W. 93rd St.
New York, NY 10025
(212) 749-6200

Dalton School
108 E. 89th St.
New York, NY 10128
(212) 423-5200

Hackley School
293 Benedict Ave.
Tarrytown, NY 10591
(914) 631-0128

Hewitt School
45 E. 75th St.
New York, NY 10021
(212) 288-1919

Horace Mann School
231 W. 246th St.
Riverdale, NY 10471
(718) 548-4000

Packer Collegiate Institute
170 Joralemon St.
Brooklyn, NY 11201
(718) 875-6646

Rye County Day School
Boston Post Road at Cedar St.
Rye, NY 10580
(914) 967-1417

Staten Island Academy
715 Todt Hill Road
Staten Island, NY 10304
(718) 987-8100

Town School
New York, NY 10021
(212) 288-4383

Trinity School
139 W. 91st St.
New York, NY 10024
(212) 873-1650

United Nations International School
24-50 FDR Drive
New York, NY 10010
(212) 684-7400

Winston Preparatory School
4 W. 76th St.
New York, NY 10023
(212) 496-8400

York Preparatory School
116 E. 85th St.
New York, NY 10028
(212) 628-1220

**Private Schools,
Connecticut:**

Greenwich Academy
200 N. Maple Ave.
Greenwich, CT 06830
(203) 625-8985

Greenwich Country Day School
Old Church Road
Greenwich, CT 06830
(203) 622-8500

King and Low-Heywood Thomas School
1450 Newfield Ave.
Stamford, CT 06905
(203) 322-3496

**Private Schools,
New Jersey:**

Dwight-Englewood School
315 E. Palisade Ave.
Englewood, NJ 07631
(201) 569-9502

Montclair Kimberly Academy
201 Valley Road
Montclair, NJ 07042
(201) 509-7930

Newark Academy
915 Orange Ave.
Livingston, NJ 07039
(201) 992-7000

Electronics/Telecommunications

WEB SITES:

Consumer Electronics Cyberspace Companion
http://www.eia.org/cema

SemiConductors—Discover a New World of Opportunity
http://www.4chipjobs.com/index.html

Telecom Information Resources on the Internet
http://www.spp.umich.edu/telecom/telecom-info.html

Telecom Information Resources on the Internet
http://www.spp.umich.edu/telecom/online-pubs.html

Telecommunication Links
http://www.utsi.com/telecomm.html

WWW Virtual Library: Electrical Engineering
http://arioch.gsfc.nasa.gov/wwwvl/ee.html

PROFESSIONAL ORGANIZATIONS:

For networking in electronics, telecommunications, and the office automation systems field, you can contact the following local organization listed in Chapter 5. Also see "Computers."
Institute of Electrical and Electronics Engineers (IEEE)
For more information you can contact:

Alliance for Telecommunications Industry
1200 G St., NW, Suite 500
Washington, DC 20005
(202) 628-6380

American Electronics Association
http://www.aeanet.org
5201 Great American Pkwy., Suite 520
Santa Clara, CA 95054
(408) 987-4200

Cellular Telecommunications Industry Association
1250 Connecticut Ave., NW, Suite 200
Washington, DC 20036
(202) 785-0081

Electronics Industries Association
http://www.eia.org
2500 Wilson Blvd.
Arlington, VA 22201
(703) 907-7500

The Electronics Service Association of Connecticut
P.O. Box 227
Ledyard, CT 06339
(860) 536-1520

Institute of Electronic and Electrical Engineers (IEEE)
http://www.ieee.org/
1730 Massachusetts Ave., NW
Washington, DC 20036
(202) 371-0101

Multimedia Telecommunications Association
2000 M St., NW, Suite 550
Washington, DC 20036
(202) 296-9800

North American Telecommunications Association
2000 M St., NW, Suite 550
Washington, DC 20036
(202) 296-9800

Telecommunications Industry Association
http://www.tiaonline.org
2001 Pennsylvania Ave., NW, Suite 800
Washington, DC 20006
(202) 457-4912

United States Telephone Association
http://www.usta.org
1401 H St., NW, Suite 600
Washington, DC 20005
(202) 326-7300

PROFESSIONAL PUBLICATIONS:

Cellular Business
Communications News
Communications Week International
CTI For Management
Electronic Components
Electronics Week
Electrical World
tele.com
Telecommunications Magazine
Telephony
Wireless

DIRECTORIES:

American Electronics Association Directory
  (American Electronics Association,
  Santa Clara, CA)
*Defense Communications & Electronics
  Directory* (Phillips Business Information,
  Inc., Hagerstown, MD))
*Directory of Consumer Electronics Retailers
  & Distributors* (Chain Store, Guide
  Information Services, Tampa, FL)
*Directory of Contract Electronics Manufac-
  turers—North American Edition* (Miller
  Freeman, Inc., San Francisco, CA)
*Electronics Industries Association Trade
  Directory and Membership List*
  (Electronics Industries Association,
  Washington, DC)
Electronics Manufacturers Directory
  (Harris InfoSource International,
  Twinsburg, OH)
Telecommunications Directory (Gale
  Research, Detroit, MI)
Telecommunications Sourcebook (North
  American Telecommunications
  Association, Washington, DC)
Telephone Companies Directory (American
  Business Directories, Omaha, NE)
U.S. Electronic Industry Directory (Harris
  Publishing Co., Twinsburg, OH)

New York Employers:

**American Telephone and Telegraph
(AT&T)**
32 Avenue of the Americas
New York, NY 10013

(212) 387-5400
Jobline: (800) 222-0400
Personnel Office: 1200 Peachtree St. NE,
Promenade 1 Rm. 7075, Atlanta, GA
30309
Telephone, telegraph, satellite communi-
cations, and computer systems. One of the
largest long-distance carriers in the world.

AMNEX Inc.
6 Nevada Drive
Lake Success, NY 11042
(516) 326-2540
Personnel: 100 W. Lucerne Circle,
Orlando, FL 32801

Arrow Electronics
25 Hubb Drive
Melville, NY 11747
(516) 391-1300
VP, Human Resources: Tom Hallam

Bell Atlantic Mobile Systems
180 Washington Valley Road
Bedminster, NJ 07921
(908) 306-7000
Resumes to Human Resources

Canon USA
1 Canon Plaza
Lake Success, NY 11042
(516) 488-6700
Assistant Director, Human Resouces:
Marylou Ponzi

Concord Electronics Corporation
30 Great Jones St.
New York, NY 10012
(212) 777-6571
Personnel Director: Josie Wheaton
Electronics manufacturing firm.

Digital Equipment Corporation
2 Penn Plaza
New York, NY 10121
(212) 856-2763
Human Resources Department: Bob
Maher
One of the largest manufacturers of office
automation systems equipment and
computer equipment.

Eagle Electric Manufacturing Company
45-31 Court Sq.
Long Island City, NY 11101
(718) 937-8000
Personnel Director: Mr. Gerry Rocker
Manufactures electrical wiring devices.

Eaton Corporation/AIL Division
Commack Road
Deer Park, NY 11729
(516) 595-5000
Director of Personnel: Ms. Pat Comiskey
Engineers and manufactures electronic
systems, including defensive avionics, etc.

Executone Information Systems
3 Expressway Plaza
Roslyn Heights, NY 11577
(516) 625-9100
Human Resources: 478 Wheelers Farms
Road, Milford, CT 06460, (203) 876-7600.
Telecommunications systems.

Frontier Corporation
122 E. 42nd St., Suite 710
New York, NY 10168
(212) 984-8604
Director of Sales: Diane Lepore
Revenues of $2.6 billion, 5th largest long
distance company.

Gem Electric Manufacturing Company
390 Vanderbilt Motor Parkway
Hauppauge, NY 11788
(516) 273-2230
Manufactures electrical wiring devices.

Gull Electronic Systems
300 Marcus Blvd.
Smithtown, NY 11787
(516) 231-3737
Personnel Associate: Carol Costello
Digital electronic conversion devices.

Hitachi America
50 Prospect Ave.
Tarrytown, NY 10591
(914) 332-5800
Human Resources Manager: Masaaki
Aoyama

**International Business Machines
Corporation (IBM)**
Route 100
Somers, NY 10589
(914) 766-1900
(800) 964-4473 (Employment Line)
Handles IBM employment. The world's
largest producer of office automation
systems, telecommunications systems, and
computers.

**International Telephone and Telegraph
World Communications**
1330 Avenue of the Americas
New York, NY 10019
(212) 258-1000
Personnel Director: Rob Brokaw
Company headquarters for this worldwide
communications firm. ITT is involved in
the development and implementation of
long distance telephone and wireless
systems.

Levitton Manufacturing Company
59-25 Little Neck Parkway
Little Neck, NY 11362
(718) 229-4040
Director of Human Resources: Joyce
Bloom
Manufactures electrical wiring devices.

Loral Corporation
600 3rd Ave.
New York, NY 10016
(212) 697-1105
Contact Personnel Department
Telecommunications. Company headquarters.

MCI Telecommunications
2 International Drive
Rye Brook, NY 10573
(914) 937-3444
Recruitment Manager: George Niwinsky

Monroe Systems for Business
3 Park Ave.
New York, NY 10016
(800) 955-2252
Contact Personnel
Office automation systems.

Closing the deal on sales

Jerry Packer put in a long and successful stint as a salesman for Xerox, then got an MBA and went to work as district manager for a comparatively risky, aggressive new electronics manufacturing company. We asked him about the differences between selling for a giant and taking a risk with a relatively unknown firm.

"Xerox is probably typical of any large corporation," says Jerry, "in that they are very structured. It was a good place to work, but it didn't provide much opportunity for individual decision making. A new company offers a fantastic chance to exercise some entrepreneurial skills. The corporation sets general goals, but it's up to me how I meet them. I can try out different marketing techniques, divide up the territory in new ways, create teams, whatever. It's neat to be able to exercise that kind of flexibility."

We asked Jerry what it takes to be a good salesperson. "A lot of folks think that salespeople are forever buying lunches for clients and playing golf," says Jerry. "But in order to be really successful, you have to work hard. I don't necessarily mean 80 hours a week. But you need to put in sufficient time to do the things that are necessary. A second important requirement is an absolutely thorough understanding of the products you're selling. Not only your own products but also your competitors'.

"In high-level selling, sales people have to be especially sharp in terms of interpersonal skills. There's an old saying, and it's true: people don't buy from companies, they buy from people. When you're selling systems that range upward of $5 million, you're also selling yourself. It's important that your clients feel you'll be around after the sale to handle any problems that might come up. To establish that kind of rapport, you have to act responsibly and be very articulate. It also helps if you have good written communication skills."

North American Communications Control
114 E. 32nd St., Suite 401
New York, NY 10016
(212) 447-6262
Executive VP: Frank Caccamo

Northern Telecom
330 Madison Ave.
New York, NY 10017
(212) 856-7300
(888) 628-4473 (Jobline)
Telecommunications and telephone service.

NYNEX Corporation
1095 Avenue of the Americas
New York, NY 10036
(212) 395-2121
(800) 511-8086 (Employment Line)
Managing Director, Human Resources:
James Wooster,1113 Westchester Ave.,
White Plains, NY 10604
Executive offices of New York's telephone
service.

Pickering and Company
101 Sunnyside Blvd.
Plainview, NY 11803
(516) 349-0200
Personnel Manager: Virginia Rumpler
Manufactures a variety of electronics
audio equipment.

RCN
1133 Avenue of the Americas
New York, NY 10036
(212) 376-7400
RCN is the nation's first and largest
facilities-based telecommunications
company to offer competitive local
telephone, long distance, cable television,
and Internet access to the residential
market over advanced fiberoptic networks.

Signal Transformer/Division of Insilica
500 Bayview Ave.
Inwood, NY 11096
(516) 239-5777
Personnel Director: Florence Rosenberg
Manufactures and distributes transformers.

Sprint
1 Manhattanville Road
Purchase, NY 10577
(914) 935-7000
Personnel: (800) 655-4748

TCG Teleport Communications Group
One World Trade Center, Suite 5121
New York, NY 10048
(212) 478-8092
TCG is the nation's oldest and largest
competitive local exchange carrier for
businesses in 57 major metropolitan
markets nationwide.

Teleport Communications Group
2 Teleport Drive, 3rd Floor
Staten Island, NY 10311
(718) 983-2000
Personnel Manager: Wayne Balnicki
Telecommunications service.

TDK Electronics
12 Harbor Park Drive
Port Washington, NY 11050
(516) 625-0100
Human Resources: Nicole Brumfield

WinStar
380 Lexington Ave., Suite 815
New York, NY 10168
(212) 551-7828

WorldCom
380 Madsion Ave.
New York, NY 10017
(212) 766-0644
The nation's fourth largest, facilities-based
telecommunications carrier, and the
world's #1 international private-line
provider.

Connecticut Employers:

Amphenol/Danbury
1 Kennedy Ave.
Danbury, CT 06810
(203) 743-9272
Personnel Director: Keitha Keene
Producer of connectors, microwave
coaxial switches, and fiber optic intercon-
nect devices.

Framatome Connectors
55 Walls Drive, Suite 304
Fairfield, CT 06432
(203) 319-3940
Personnel Manager: Ms. Sandy D'Alene
Designs, manufactures, and sells electrical
and electronic connectors and allied
products.

General Electric Company
3135 Easton Turnpike—W2L2
Fairfield, CT 06431
(203) 373-2211

Senior VP, Human Resources:
William Conaty
Researches, develops, manufactures, and
markets electrical, electronic, chemical,
microelectronic products.

General Signal Corporation
High Ridge Park
P.O. Box 10010
Stamford, CT 06904
(203) 329-4100
Human Resources: Elizabeth Conklyn

Gestetner Corporation
599 W. Putnam Ave.
Greenwich, CT 06836
(203) 625-7600
Personnel Director: Dennis Murphy
Leading manufacturer of office computing, accounting, and copier equipment.

GTE Corporation
1 Stamford Forum
Stamford, CT 06904
(203) 965-2000
Director of Staffing and Development:
Phillip WHite
Corporate headquarters.

New Haven Manufacturing Corporation
446 Blake St.
New Haven, CT 06515
(203) 387-2572
Human Resources: Carla DeVita
Electronic hardware.

Pitney Bowes
1 Elmcroft Road
Stamford, CT 06926
(203) 356-5000
Director of Professional Employment:
Gus Stepp

Siemens Rolm
101 Merrid 7 Road, 6th Floor
Norwalk, CT 06851
(203) 840-3400
Telecommunications systems.
Human Resources Director: Janet Sage

New Jersey Employers:

ABB
1460 Livingston Ave.
N. Brunswick, NJ 08902
(908) 932-6000
Industrial electric power equipment.

AT&T Corp.
100 Southgate Plaza
Morristown, NJ 07960
(201) 898-8981
Jobline: 1-800-562-7288

Bell Atlantic NYNEX Mobile
2000 Corporate Drive
Orangeburg, NY 10962
(914) 365-7508

Dewey Electronics Corporation
27 Muller Road
Oakland, NJ 07436
(201) 337-4700
Systems-oriented civilian and military
electronics development, design, engineering, and manufacturing firm.
Human Resources Director: Thom Velto

Dialight Corporation
1913 Atlantic Ave.
Manasquan, NJ 08736
(908) 223-9400
Personnel Manager: Scott Ernst
Operations in consumer products and
services, electrical/electronic components,
and professional equipment.

Electronic Measurements
405 Essex Road
Neptune, NJ 07753
(908) 922-9300
Personnel Manager: Brenda Oakes
Manufacturer of DC power supplies.

GEC-Marconi Electronic Systems
164 Totowa Road
Wayne, NJ 07474-0975
(201) 633-6000
Personnel Director: Jan DeGennaro

LDDS World Com
1 Meadowlands Plaza
East Rutherford, NJ 07073
(201) 804-6400
Human Resources: Ms. Terry Caputo
Fourth largest long distance carrier in the
United States.

Matsushita Electric Corporation
1 Panasonic Way
Secaucus, NJ 07094
(201) 348-7000
Asst . General Manager of Personnel:
Robert Ohme

MCI Telecommunications
201 Centennial Ave.
Piscataway, NJ 08859
(908) 885-4000
Human Resources Director: Jeff Previte

Ricoh Corporation
5 Dedrick Pl.
Caldwell, NJ 07006
(201) 882-2000
Human Resources: JoAnne Ehman

Sharp Electronics Corp.
Sharp Plaza
P.O. Box 650
Mahwah, NJ 07430
(201) 529-8200
Personnel Director: David Alai

Siemens Corporation
1301 Avenue of the Americas
New York, NY 10019
(212) 258-4000
VP, Human Resources: Mitch Senker

Sony Corporation of America
1 Sony Drive
Park Ridge, NJ 07656
(201) 930-1000
Staffing Manager, College Relations:
Charles Gregory

Totaltel Inc.
150 Clove Road, 8th Floor
Little Falls, NJ 07424
(201) 812-1100
The fastest growing telecommunications
company in the Bell Atlantic region; 100%
growth past 3 years in a row.

Engineering

WEB SITES:

Job-search page
http://www.webcreations.com/bolton/

PROFESSIONAL ORGANIZATIONS:

For networking in engineering and related fields, check out the following local profesional organizations listed in Chapter 5. Also see "Construction."
American Society of Civil Engineers
American Society of Mechanical Engineers
Institute of Electrical & Electronics Engineers
Society of Women Engineers

For more information, you can contact:

Connecticut Society of Professional Engineers
2600 Dixwell Ave.
Hamden, CT 06514
(203) 281-4322

Institute of Mechanical Engineers
345 E. 47th St.
New York, NY 10017
(212) 705-7722

National Society of Professional Engineers
1420 King St.
Alexandria, VA 22314
(703) 684-2800

New York State Society of Professional Engineers
150 State St., 3rd Floor
Albany, NY 12207
(518) 465-7386

PROFESSIONAL PUBLICATIONS:

Building Design and Construction
Chemical Engineering Progress
Civil Engineering Magazine
Electronic Engineering Times
Engineering News Record

DIRECTORIES:

Directory of Contract Service Firms (C.E. Publications, Kenmore, WA)
Engineering, Science and Computer Jobs (Peterson's Guides, Princeton, NJ)
IEEE Membership Directory (Institute of Electrical and Electronics Engineers, New York, NY)
Official Register (American Society of Civil Engineers, New York, NY)
Professional Engineering Directory (National Society of Professional Engineers, Alexandria, VA)
Who's Who in Technology Today (Technology Recognition Corp., Pittsburgh, PA) Washington, DC)

New York Employers:

Ammann and Whitney
96 Morton St.
New York, NY 10014
(212) 524-7200
Personnel Director: Mike Simon
Civil engineers.

ATC Environmental
104 E. 25th St., 10th Floor
New York, NY 10014
(212) 353-8280
Contact Human Resources

Ebasco Services
2 World Trade Center
New York, NY 10048
(212) 839-1000
Personnel contact: Laura Golluscio

Flack and Kurtz Consulting Engineers
475 5th Ave., 8th Floor
New York, NY 10017
(212) 532-9600
Director of Personnel: Donna Astolfi
Civil engineers.

Gibbs and Cox
50 W. 23rd St.
New York, NY 10010
(212) 366-3900
Employment Manager: Louise Richardson
Marine engineers.

Hazen and Sawyer P.C.
730 Broadway, 6th Floor
New York, NY 10003
(212) 777-8400
Personnel Manager: Lianne Ruvbo

North American Phillips Corporation
100 E. 42nd St.
New York, NY 10017
(212) 850-5000
Human Resources: Jim Miller

Parsons, Brinckerhoff and Quade
1 Penn Plaza
New York, NY 10119
(212) 465-5000
Personnel Director: John Ryan

Pirnie, Malcolm
104 Corporate Park Drive
White Plains, NY 10604
(914) 694-2100
Personnel Director: Jack O'Neil
Environmental engineers.

Pitkin, Lucien
50 Hudson St.
New York, NY 10013
(212) 233-2737
Vice President: Mr. A. J. Vecchio

Seelye Stevenson Value and Knecht
225 Park Ave. S.
New York, NY 10003
(212) 777-4400
Contact individual department

Syska & Hennessy
11 W. 42nd St., 6th Floor
New York, NY 10036
(212) 921-2300
Personnel Director: Diane Morley

Tams Consultants
655 3rd Ave., 4th Floor
New York, NY 10017
(212) 867-1777
Personnel Assistant: Margie Ortiz

Vollmer Associates
50 W. 23rd St.
New York, NY 10010
(212) 366-5600
Contact Human Resources

Connecticut Employers:

Analysis and Technology
240 Oral School Road
Mystic, CT 06510
(860) 572-9600
Personnel Director: Ginny Fabianski
Headquarters: Route 2, P.O. Box 220,
North Stonington, CT 06359.

CNF Industries
355 Research Parkway
Meriden, CT 06450
(203) 237-5580
Human Resources Director: Liliana Audi

New Jersey Employers:

ABB Lummus Crest
1515 Broad St.
Bloomfield, NJ 07003
(201) 893-1515
Contact Human Resources

**Air and Water Technologies Corp./
Cottrell Research**
Route 22 West
Somerville, NJ 08876
(908) 685-4600
Personnel contact: Carol Ames
Environmental and pollution control
engineering.

Foster Wheeler Corp.
Perryville Corporate Park
Clinton, NJ 08809
(908) 730-4000
Personnel Director: James Cheffler

Entertainment

WEB SITES:

Entertainment industry companies
http://www.ern.com/ern.htm

Entertainment and music industries
http://www.ose.com/ose/

Theater, film, television, and music industries
http://www.fleethouse.com/fhcanada/western/bc/van/entertan/hqe/vrhq-lnk.htm

Theater resources
http://www.ircam.fr/divers/theatre-e.html

PROFESSIONAL ORGANIZATIONS:

For networking in the entertainment industry, check out the following local professional organizations listed in Chapter 5:

American Society of Composers, Authors and Publishers (ASCAP)
New York Council of Motion Picture and Television Unions
Society of Motion Picture and Television Engineers

For more information, you can contact:

Academy of Motion Picture Arts and Sciences
8949 Wilshire Blvd.
Beverly Hills, CA 90211
(310) 247-3000

American Film Institute
Kennedy Center for the Performing Arts
Washington, DC 20566
(202) 828-4000

Film Arts Foundation
346 9th St., 2nd Floor
San Francisco, CA 94103
(415) 552-8760

New York Women in Film
6 E. 39th St., 12th Floor
New York, NY 10016
(212) 679-0870

Recording Industry Association of America
1330 Connecticut Ave. NW, Suite 300
Washington, DC 20036
(202) 775-0101

PROFESSIONAL PUBLICATIONS:

American Theatre
Backstage
Billboard
Daily Variety: News of the Entertainment Industry
On Location Magazine
Show Business News
Stage Managers Directory
Theater Times
Variety

DIRECTORIES:

Back Stage Film/Tape/Syndication Directory (Back Stage Publications, New York, NY)
Blue Book (Hollywood Reporter, Hollywood, CA)
Film Producers, Studios, and Agents Guide (Lone Eagle, Beverly Hills, CA)
Music Address Book: How to Reach Anyone Who's Anyone in the Music Business (HarperCollins, NY)
Music Business Handbook & Career Guide (Sherwood Co., Los Angeles, CA)
New York Theatrical Sourcebook (Broadway Press, Shelter Island, NY)
Who's Who in the Motion Picture Industry (Packard House, Beverly Hills, CA)
Who's Who in Television (Packard House, Beverly Hills, CA)

Broadway Theater Employers:

Most of New York's Broadway theaters are run by large production companies or theater chains. Two of the largest are the Nederlander Theatre Group and the Shubert Organization Corporation. Employment decisions for all the theaters in a chain are made by the theater group's personnel office. A few Broadway theaters are independently owned, and the house manager usually makes all employment decisions.

Nederlander Productions
810 7th Ave.
New York, NY 10019
(212) 262-2400
Personnel Director: Kathleen Raitt
Brooks-Atkinson
Gershwin
Lunt-Fontanne
Marriott Marquis
Minskoff
Nederlander Theater
Neil Simon
Palace
Richard Rodgers

Shubert Organization Corporation
234 W. 44th St.
New York, NY 10036
(212) 944-3700
Personnel Director: Elliot Greene
Ambassador
Barrymore
Belasco
Booth
Broadhurst
Broadway
Cort
Golden
Imperial
Longacre
Lyceum
Majestic
Plymouth
Royale
Shubert
Winter Garden Theatre

Independent Theater Employers:

Beck, Martin, Theatre
302 W. 45th St.
New York, NY 10036
(212) 239-6200

Hayes, Helen, Theatre
240 W. 44th St.
New York, NY 10036
(212) 944-9450

Music Box Theatre
239 W. 45th St.
New York, NY 10036
(212) 239-6200

New Victory Theatre
209 W.42 St.
New York, NY 10036
(212) 382-4000

O'Neill, Eugene, Theatre
230 W. 49th St.
New York, NY 10019
(212) 239-6200

Roundabout Theatre
1530 Broadway
New York, NY 10036
(212) 719-9393

St. James Theatre
246 W. 44th St.
New York, NY 10036
(212) 398-0280

Off-Broadway Theater Employers:

Astor Place Theatre
434 Lafayette St.
New York, NY 10003
(212) 254-4370

Circle in the Square
159 Bleeker St.
New York, NY
(212) 254-6330

Kaufman Theatre
534 W. 42nd St.
New York, NY 10036
(212) 563-1684

Orpheum Theatre
126 2nd Ave.
New York, NY 10003
(212) 477-2477

i. Papp, Joseph, Public Theatre
425 Lafayette St.
New York, NY 10003
(212) 260-2400

Sullivan Street Playhouse
181 Sullivan St.
New York, NY 10012
(212) 674-3838

Motion Picture Companies:

Columbia Pictures International
711 5th Ave.
New York, NY 10022
(212) 751-4400

Disney, Walt
500 Park Ave.
New York, NY 10022
(212) 593-8900
Office Manager: Kitty Mincuso

King World Productions
1700 Broadway
New York, NY 10019
(212) 315-4000

MGM
1350 Avenue of the Americas
New York, NY 10019
(212) 708-0500

New Line Cinema Corp.
888 7th Ave.
New York, NY 10019
(212) 649-4900
Contact Human Resources

Paramount Communications
1633 Broadway, 16th Floor
New York, NY 10019
(212) 654-1000
Employment Manager: Ms. Randi Kester

Twentieth Century Fox
1211 Avenue of the Americas, 3rd Floor
New York, NY 10036
(212) 556-2400
Resumes to: Human Resources, P.O. Box
900, Beverly Hills, CA 90213

**Warner Brothers Distributing
Corporation**
1325 Avenue of the Americas
New York, NY 10019
(212) 636-5000
Senior Administrator, Human Resources:
Ann Quasarano

Breaking into film production

Tracey Barnett was working in public relations when she decided to break into film production. Although she didn't know anyone in the industry when she began, today she is a successful freelance production manager. We asked her how she did it.

"Most important was my desire to do it," says Tracey, "and I didn't get discouraged. I began by making a few contacts in the industry through people I knew in related fields. Then I set up interviews with these contacts. At the end of each interview, I asked for the names of three to five other contacts. This strategy opened a lot of doors for me. I followed up each interview with a phone call. I also kept in touch with my contacts on a monthly basis."

We asked Tracey what jobs are available for beginners in the film business and what qualifications are needed for those jobs.

"Entry-level positions include production assistant, stylist, assistant wardrobe manager, and grip," says Tracey. "There are no special requirements for these jobs. You don't need a degree in film to work in the business. In fact, people with film degrees begin at the same level as everybody else. What does count is intelligence and the ability to get things done quickly and efficiently. You need to think on your feet and be able to anticipate what needs to be done."

According to Tracey, freelance production assistants begin at about $75-$100 per day. More experienced production assistants can make as much as $175 per day. "But keep in mind that as a freelancer, you don't have the security of a regular paycheck," says Tracey. "You may not work every day." She advises those who need a more reliable income to look for a staff position in the industry.

Tracey advises those who want to break into the film business to keep at it: "Don't count your inexperience as a negative. Tenacity and enthusiasm will get you the first job. Approach your contacts and keep approaching them—over and over and over again."

Recording Companies:

A&M Records
595 Madison Ave.
New York, NY 10022
(212) 826-0477

Arista Records
6 W. 57th St.
New York, NY 10019
(212) 489-7400
Human Resources Director: Yvonne Lung

Arkadia Entertainment
34 E. 23rd St.
New York, NY 10011
(212) 533-0007

Atlantic Records
1290 Avenue of the Americas
New York, NY 10104
(212) 275-2000
Personnel Director: Lisa Swill

BMG Records
1540 Broadway
New York, NY 10036
(212) 930-4000
Contact Human Resources

Castle Records
352 Park Ave. S.
New York, NY 10010
(212) 685-6303

Eight Ball Records
50 W. 17th St.
New York, NY 10011
(212) 337-1200

Elektra Records
75 Rockefeller Plaza
New York, NY 10019
(212) 275-4000
Personnel contact: Mary Ann Mastropaolo

EMI Music Worldwide
1290 Avenue of the Americas
New York, NY 10019
(212) 492-1200
Personnel Director: Ms. Anthe Siaflas

Epic Records
A division of Sony Music Entertainment
51 W. 52nd St.
New York, NY 10019
(212) 833-8000
Resumes to: Recruitment Dept., 2nd Floor
550 Madison Ave., New York, NY 10022

Island Records/Polygram Records
825 8th Ave.
New York, NY 10019
(212) 333-8000

Matador Records
625 Broadway
New York, NY 10003
(212) 995-5882

Servisound, Inc.
35 W. 45th St.
New York, NY 10036
(212) 921-0555
Personnel Director: Rick Elliker
Sound for commercials, television, film,
industrial shows, and multimedia.

Sony Music Entertainment
550 Madison Ave.
New York, NY 10101
Resumes to: Recruitment Office, 2nd
Floor
(212) 833-3000

Triton-Sound
123 W. 43rd St.
New York, NY 10036
(212) 575-8055
Contact: David Smith
Recording studios for radio and television
commercials.

Other Employers:

Aqueduct Race Track
Rockaway Blvd.
Ozone Park, NY 11417
(718) 641-4700
Personnel Director: Sal Cartagine

Big Apple Circus
35 W. 35th St., 9th Floor
New York, NY 10001
(212) 268-2500
Personnel Director: Tanya Santiago

Bronx Zoo
Wildlife Conservation Society
2300 Southern Blvd.
Bronx, NY 10460
(718) 220-5100
Human Resources Director: Charles
Vassar

Brooklyn Academy of Music
30 Lafayette Ave.
Brooklyn, NY 11217
(718) 636-4100
Personnel Manager: Liz Sharp

Carnegie Hall
881 7th Ave.
New York, NY 10019
(212) 903-9601
Personnel Director: Joan Goldstone

Central Park Conservancy
1 E. 104th St.
New York, NY 10029
(212) 315-0385
Personnel Director: George Kellogg

Lincoln Center for the Performing Arts
70 Lincoln Center Plaza
New York, NY 10023
(212) 875-5000

Director of Personnel: Jay Spivack
Includes Alice Tully Hall, the Vivian
Beaumont Theatre, Avery Fisher Hall, the
Metropolitan Opera House, and New York
State Theatre. Contact personnel offices of
individual theaters.

Madison Square Garden
2 Penn Plaza
New York, NY 10121
(212) 465-6741
Director of Personnel: Marilyn Hausner
Major center for sports events, live
concerts, circuses, national and international sports meets. Houses the Knicks
and Rangers.

Metropolitan Opera Association
Lincoln Center
New York, NY 10023
(212) 799-3100
Personnel Director: Linda Freitag

**New Jersey Sports and Exposition
Authority/Meadowlands**
50 State Route 120
E. Rutherford, NY 07073
(201) 935-8500
Personnel Director: Robert Jennings

New York Botanical Garden
Southern Blvd. at 200th St.
Bronx, NY 10458
(718) 817-8700
Personnel Manager: Karen Yesnick

New York Shakespeare Festival
425 Lafayette St.
New York, NY 10003
(212) 260-2400
General Manager: Joey Parnes

Radio City Music Hall
1260 Avenue of the Americas
New York, NY 10020
(212) 632-4000
Personnel Director: Keith Wheeler

Shea Stadium
Roosevelt Ave. at 126th St.
Flushing, NY 11368
(718) 507-6387
Personnel Director: Russ Richardson
Home of the New York Mets.

United States Tennis Association
70 W. Red Oak Lane
White Plains, NY 10604
(914) 696-7000
Personnel Director: Dario Otero
Home of the United States Open Tennis
Championship at Flushing Meadow Park.

Yankee Stadium
River Ave. at 161st St.
Bronx, NY 10451
(718) 293-4300
Personnel Director: Harvey C. Winston

Environmental Services

WEB SITES:

EcoNet
http://www.econet.apc.org/econet

EnviroLink Library
http://www.envirolink.org/
EnviroLink_Library/

PROFESSIONAL ORGANIZATIONS:

For networking in environmental fields, check out the following local professional organizations listed in Chapter 5. See also "Engineering."
Environmental Action Coalition
Environmental Defense Fund
NYZS/The Wildlife Conservation Society
Women's Environment and Development Organization

For additional information, you can contact:

Alliance for Environmental Education
Marshall, VA 20115
(540) 364-9283

Environmental Careers Organization
286 Congress St., 3rd Floor
Boston, MA 02210
(617) 426-4783
apply@eco.org

National Wildlife Federation
1400 16th St., NW
Washington DC 20036
(202) 797-6800

Sierra Club
http://www/sierraclub.org
85 2nd St., 2nd Floor
San Francisco, CA 94105
(415) 977-5500

Water Environment Federation
601 Wythe St.
Alexandria, VA 22314
(703) 684-2400

PROFESSIONAL PUBLICATIONS:

Atmospheric Environment
Audubon
Conservation Issues
E, The Environmental Magazine
Ecology
Environ: A Magazine for Ecologic Living & Health
Environment
Environment Today
Environmental Action
Environmental Engineer
Environmental Forum
Environmental Management
Environmental Solutions
Friends of the Earth Newsmagazine
Greenpeace

DIRECTORIES:

Complete Guide to Environmental Careers, The (The CEIP Fund, Island Press, Washington, DC)
Conservation Directory (National Wildlife Federation, Washington, DC)
Directory of Environmental Organizations (Educational Communications, Long Beach, CA)
Directory of National Environmental Organizations (U.S. Environmental Directories, St. Paul, MN)
Environmental Career Guide, The (John Wiley & Sons, New York, NY)
Environmental Directory (Carroll Publishing Co., Washington, DC)
Gale Environmental Sourcebook (Gale Research, Detroit, MI)
Green at Work: Finding a Business Career That Works for the Environment (Island Press, Washington, DC)

Employers, Private Sector:

AMREP Solutions
10 Columbus Circle, Suite 1300
New York, NY 10019

(212) 541-7300
President: Harvey W. Schultz

Allee King Rosen & Fleming
117 E. 29th St.
New York, NY 10016
(212) 696-0670
Senior Manager: Peggy Rosenblatt

Atlas Paper Stock
585 Washington St.
New York, NY 10014
(212) 925-3280
President: John Pasquale
Paper recycling, commercial carting &
sanitation, waste management.

Berger, Louis, International
100 Halsted St.
E. Orange, NJ 07019
(973) 678-1960
Human Resources Director: Richard
Bergailo

Ecology and Environment
641 Lexington Ave, 6th Floor
New York, NY 10022
(212) 705-4747
Human Resources Director: Janet
Steinbruckner

Eder Associates
480 Forest Ave.
Locust Valley, NY 11560
(516) 671-8440
Human Resources Director: Bert
Weinstein

Environmental Labs
W. 142nd and North River
New York, NY
(212) 694-0360

Environmental Management Solutions
286 5th Ave.
New York, NY 10003
(212) 239-7358
Human Resources Director: Sue Youseff

Environmental Services of America
937 E. Hazelwood Ave.
Rahway, NJ 07065

(908) 381-9229
Human Resources Director: Sue Youseff

Handex Environmental Recovery
500 Campus Drive
Morganville, NJ 07751
(908) 536-8500
Human Resources Director: Doreen
France

Hazen and Sawyer
730 Broadway
New York, NY 10003
(212) 777-8400
Personnel Manager: Lianne Rubbo

Holzmacher, McLendon and Murrell
575 Broad Hollow Road
Melville, NY 11747
(516) 756-8000
Human Resources Director: Liz Davis

Killam Associates
27 Bleeker St.
Milburn, NJ 07041
(201) 379-3400
Personnel Manager: Phyllis Carroll

Lawler, Matusky & Skelly Engineers
1 Blue Hill Plaza
Pearl River, NY 10965
(914) 735-8300
Human Resources Director: Dan Lamperti

URS Consultants
1 Penn Plaza, Suite 610
New York, NY 10119
(212) 736-4444

Employers, Government Agencies:

Department of Environmental Protection
59-17 Junction Blvd.
Corona, NY 11206
(718) 595-3383

Environmental Protection Agency
290 Broadway
New York, NY 10007
(212) 637-3550
Personnel Director: John Henderson

New York State Department of
Environmental Conservation
47-40 21st St.
Long Island City, NY 11416
(718) 482-4900
Adminstrative Assistant: Mario Serrano

U.S. Department of Energy
201 Varick St.
New York, NY 10014
(212) 620-3607
Personnel Management Specialist:
Beatrice Cassidy

Employers, Non-Profit Organizations:

Environmental Action Coalition
625 Broadway
New York, NY 10012
(212) 677-1601

Environmental Defense Fund
257 Park Ave. S.
New York, NY 10010
(212) 505-2100

National Audubon Society
700 Broadway
New York, NY 10003
(212) 979-3000

National Resources Defense Council
40 W. 20th St.
New York, NY 10011
(212) 727-2700

Nature Conservancy, The
570 Seventh Ave.
New York, NY 10018
(212) 997-1880

Wildlife Conservation Society
2300 Southern Blvd.
Bronx, NY 10460
(718) 220-5100

A "growth" industry

An environmental consultant friend of ours says the enforcement of federal regulations and emphasis on compliance with hazardous waste removal and clean air and water acts has put increased demands on her office. Opportunities for lawyers, engineers, and environmentalists are growing in large corporations and non-profit organizations. As she says, "It's a growth industry."

Food/Beverage Producers and Distributors

WEB SITES:

Food Marketing Institute
http://www.fmi.org

Snack Food Association
http://www.snax.com

PROFESSIONAL ORGANIZATIONS:

For information about the food industry and related fields, contact the following professional organizations. Also see "Hospitality" and, for grocery chains, "Retailers."

American Dairy Association
10255 W. Higgins Road, Suite 900
Rosemont, IL 60018
(708) 803-2000

American Institute of Food Distribution
28-12 Broadway
Fairlawn, NJ 07410
(201) 791-5570

Association of Food Industries
5 Ravine Drive
Matawan, NJ 07747
(908) 583-8188

Connecticut Food Association
55 Farmington Ave., Suite 306
Hartford, CT 06105
(860) 247-8384

Distilled Spirits Council of the U.S.
1250 I St., NW, Suite 900
Washington, DC 20005
(202) 628-3544

Food Marketing Institute
800 Connecticut Ave., NW
Washington, DC 20006
(202) 452-8444

National Association of Beverage Retailers
5101 River Road, Suite 108

Bethesda, MD 20816
(301) 656-1494

National Association for the Specialty Food Trade
120 Wall St.
New York, NY 10005
(212) 482-6440

National Frozen Foods Association
4755 Linglestown Road
Harrisburg, PA 17112
(717) 657-8601

National Grocers Association
1825 Samuel Morse Drive
Reston, VA 22090
(703) 437-5300

National Soft Drink Association
1101 16th St., NW
Washington, DC 20036
(202) 463-6732

New York State Food Merchants Association
130 Washington Ave.
Albany, NY 12210
(518) 434-1900

Roundtable for Women in Foodservice
80 8th Ave., Suite 303
New York, NY 10011
(212) 807-5677

Wine & Spirits Wholesalers of America
850 15th St., NW, Suite 430
Washington, DC 20005
(202) 371-9792

PROFESSIONAL PUBLICATIONS:

American Wine & Food
Bakery Production and Marketing
Beverage World
Brewing Industry News
Concessionaire
Food Arts Magazine
Food and Beverage Marketing

Food Business
Food Distributor
Food and Drink Weekly
Food Management
Food Manufacturing
Food and Wine
Grocery Marketing
Market Watch
National Grocer
Wines and Vines

DIRECTORIES:

Directory of the Canning, Freezing, Preserving Industry (Edward E. Judge, Sons, Inc., Westminster, MD)
Food and Beverage Market Place (Grey House Publishing, Hartford, CT)
Food Master (Reed Elsevier Business Info, Radnor, PA)
Grocery Commercial Food Industry Directory (GroCom Group, Inc., Clearwater, FL)

Impact Yearbook: A Directory of the Wine and Spirits Industry (M. Shanken Communications, New York, NY)
Modern Brewery Age Blue Book (Business Journals, Inc., Norwalk, CT)
National Beverage Marketing Directory (Beverage Marketing Corp., New York, NY)
National Food Brokers Association Directory (National Food Brokers Association, Washington, DC)
National Food Processors Association Membership Directory (National Food Processors Association, Washington, DC)
National Frozen Food Association Directory (National Frozen Food Association, Harrisburg, PA)
Thomas Food Industry Register (Thomas Publishing Co., New York, NY)
Wines and Vines Directory of the Wine Industry in North America (Hiaring Co., San Rafael, CA)

Mouth–watering opportunities in food service management

Kate Williams, manager of the dietary department of a suburban hospital, sees the food service industry as a growing field with tremendous potential. The many hospitals in the New York area offer varied opportunities in food services, according to Kate. Some of the jobs, such as clinical or administrative dietitian, require a college degree in nutrition. But many do not.

"Some employees have experience working at a fast-food restaurant," says Kate. "Others just learn on the job. Still others have completed one- or two-year programs in food service offered by various colleges."

Besides registered dietitians, Kate's staff includes food service supervisors, who manage the personnel who prepare food; diet technicians, who prepare and implement menus based on information about the patient; diet aides, who perform such tasks as delivering meals to patients; a chef and cooking staff; and a food purchasing agent.

Kate is optimistic about employment prospects in the food service industry as a whole. "There are tremendous opportunities for those with culinary arts skills, as well as for hotel or restaurant food service managers. Opportunities exist in food equipment companies, public and private schools, contract food companies, and food service consulting firms. Right now the possibilities in food marketing are phenomenal.

"The nutritional needs of the growing elderly population," Kate adds, "will also create many new jobs in the food service business as hospitals and other organizations become involved in long-term care."

New York Employers:

Boar's Head Provision Co.
24 Rock St.
Brooklyn, NY 11206
(718) 456-3600
Human Resources Director: Josephine Sedda

Brooklyn Brewery
118 N. 11th St.
Brooklyn, NY 11211
(718) 486-7422

CPC Baking Business
55 Paradise Lane
Bayshore, NY 11706
(800) 356-3314
Human Resources Manager: Frank McNamee

Chock Full O'Nuts Corp.
370 Lexington Ave.
New York, NY 10017
(212) 532-0300
Human Resources Director: Peter Baer

Culbro Corporation
387 Park Ave. S.
New York, NY 10016
(212) 561-8700
Personnel Manager: Mary Raffaniello
Snack foods.

Dannon Company
120 White Plains Road
Tarrytown, NY 10501
(914) 366-9700
VP, Human Resources: Rick Corcoran

Dellwood Foods
170 Saw Mill River Road
Yonkers, NY 10701
(914) 948-3314
Personnel Director: Barbara Begamy

Domino Sugar Corporation
1114 Avenue of the Americas
New York, NY 10036
(212) 789-9700
Manager, Employee Benefits: Rod Hebert

Ferrero USA
600 Cottontail Lane
Sommerset, NJ 08873
(908) 764-9300
Human Resources Director: Joan Ferrero

Kraft General Foods Corporation
A division of Phillip Morris
250 North St.
White Plains, NY 10625
(914) 335-2500
Resumes to Human Resources
One of the world's largest producers of dry and processed foods.

Krasdale Foods
400 Food Center Drive
Bronx, NY 10474
(718) 378-1100
Personnel Manager: Ralph Zampini

Lever Brothers Company
390 Park Ave.
New York, NY 10022
(212) 688-6000
Contact Human Resources

Nestle Beverages
250 Fulton Ave.
Garden City Park, NY 11040
(516) 294-8282
Personnel Director: Janeth Phihower

Ogden/Allied Food Service
2 Penn Plaza
New York, NY 10121
(212) 868-6000
Director of Employment: Norm Jenkins
Provides food service to business and
industry. Also serves the sports, recreation,
travel, and entertainment industries.

PepsiCo, Inc.
700 Anderson Hill Road
Purchase, NY 10577
(914) 253-2000
Human Resources: Tracy Simmons
One of the world's largest producers of
snacks, soft drinks, and convenience
foods.

Pepsicola Company
1 Pepsi Way
Somers, NY 10589
(914) 767-6000

Philip Morris
120 Park Ave.
New York, NY 10017
(212) 880-5000
Human Resources Director: Timothy
Sompolski
A major producer of soft drinks, food
products, and cigarettes.

Pollio Dairy Products
120 Mineola Blvd.
Mineola, NY 11501
(516) 741-8000
Human Resources Manager: Eileen
McTiernan

Porto Rico Importing Company
201 Bleecker St.
New York, NY 10003
(212) 477-5421

RJR Nabisco Brands
1301 6th Ave.
New York, NY 10019
(212) 258-5600
Human Resources: Rosemarie Tice

Seagram, Joseph E., and Sons
800 3rd Ave.
New York, NY 10022
(212) 572-7900
Personnel Director: Yvonne Shaw
Alcoholic beverages.

Snapple Beverage Corp.
1500 Hempstead Turnpike
East Meadow, NY 11554
(516) 872-4272

Stella D'Oro Biscuit Co.
184 W. 237th St.
Bronx, NY 10463
(718) 549-3700
Personnel Director: Joe Golio

Connecticut Employers:

A & W Brands
6 High Ridge Park
Stamford, CT 06905
(203) 329-0911
Senior VP, Human Resources: Pam Cook

American Brands
1700 E. Putnam Ave.
Old Greenwich, CT 06870
(203) 698-5000
Manager, Corporate Personnel: : Robert
M. Garber

CPC Baking Business
10 Hamilton Ave.
Greenwich, CT 06830
(203) 531-2000
Human Resources: Tracy Felino

Cadbury Beverages
6 High Ridge Park
Stamford, CT 06905
(203) 329-0911
VP, Human Resources: Pam Cook

Carvel Corporation
20 Batterson Park Road
Farmington, CT 06032
(860) 677-6811
Personnel Director: Ken Ward

Pepperidge Farm
595 Westport Ave.
Norwalk, CT 06851
(203) 846-7000
VP, Human Resources: Dennis Dougherty

Perrier Group of America
777 W. Putnam Ave.
Greenwich, CT 06830
(203) 531-4100
Human Resources Manager: Christine
Walchuk

Peter Paul
889 New Haven
Naugatuck, CT 06770
(203) 729-0221
Human Resources Director: Janie Ellis
Confectionery products.

Tetley, Inc.
100 Commerce Drive, P.O. Box 856
Shelton, CT 06484
(203) 929-9200
Manager Compensation and Staffing:
Edward Schuler

New Jersey Employers:

American Home Food Products
5 Giralda Farms
Madison, NJ 07940
(201) 660-5000
Director, Corporate Human Resources:
Shawn Powell

Anheuser-Busch
200 Highway 1
Newark, NJ 07101
(201) 645-7700
Personnel Director: John Listinsky

Best Foods
180 Baldwin Ave.
Jersey City, NJ 07306
(201) 653-3800
Manager of Human Resources: Tom
Martin

Campbell Soup Company
Campbell Place
Camden, NJ 08103
(609) 342-4800
Resumes to: Human Resources, Box 35D.

CPC International
International Plaza, P.O. Box 800
Englewood Cliffs, NJ 07632
(201) 894-4000
Human Resources Director: Pat Biale
Food products manufacturers, including
Hellmann's mayonnaise and Skippy
peanut butter products.

Great Bear Spring Company
Division of Perrier
Great Bear Plaza
Teterboro, NJ 07608
(800) 950-9399
Resumes to: 460 Kingsland Ave., Brooklyn,
NY 11222

Lipton, Thomas J.
800 Sylvan Ave.
Englewood Cliffs, NJ 07632
(201) 567-8000
Contact Personnel Department

Marathon Enterprises
66 E. Union Ave.
E. Rutherford, NJ 07073
(201) 935-3330
Personnel Director: Bruce Dalessio
Manufacturer of provisions and baked
goods.

Mars, Inc.
800 High St.
Hackettstown, NJ 07840
(908) 852-1000
Contact Human Resources
International company manufacturing
and marketing food products.

Nabisco Brands
Nabisco Brands Plaza One

7 Campus Drive
Parsippany, NJ 07054
(973) 682-5000

Tuscan Foods/Dairylea
750 Union Ave.
Union, NJ 07083
1-800-526-4416
VP, Personnel: Don Griffin
Office also in Jamaica, NY:
(718) 899-9300.

Foundations/Philanthropies

WEB SITES:

Community Career Center
http://www.nonprofitjobs.org/

Internet Nonprofit Center
http://www.nonprofits.org/

Philanthropy Journal Online
http://www.philanthropy-journal.org/

PROFESSIONAL ORGANIZATIONS:

For information on foundations and
philanthropies, you can contact the
following local organization listed in
Chapter 5:
**Women and Foundations/Corporate
    Philanthropy**

For additional information on foundations and related fields you can contact:

Council on Foundations
1828 L St., NW, Suite 300
Washington, DC 20036
(202) 466-6512

The Foundation Center
79 5th Ave.
New York, NY 10003
(212) 620-4230

National Charities Information Bureau
19 Union Sq. W., 6th Floor
New York, NY 10003
(212) 929-6300

National Federation of Non-Profits
815 15th St., NW, Suite 322
Washington, DC 20005
(202) 628-4380

PROFESSIONAL PUBLICATIONS:

Advocate
Charities USA
Chronicle of Philanthropy
Community Action
Community Jobs
Foundation News
The Humanist
Nonprofit Times
Opportunities In Non-profit Organizations

DIRECTORIES:

*Corporate 500: The Directory of Corporate
    Philanthropy* (Gale Research, Detroit, MI)
Foundation Directory and *Corporate
    Foundation Profiles* (Foundation Center,
    New York, NY)
National Directory of Corporate Giving and
    New York State Foundations (Foundation
    Center, New York, NY)

New York Employers:

Carnegie Corporation of New York
437 Madison Ave.
New York, NY 10022
(212) 371-3200
Personnel Director: Idalia Holder
Philanthropic fund; grants to education
projects.

Ford Foundation
320 E. 43rd St.
New York, NY 10017
(212) 573-5000
Director of Human Resources: Bruce Steckey
Grants primarily to institutions for experience, demonstration, and development efforts within the foundation's major areas of interest: urban poverty, improvement of secondary education, education programs for disadvantaged youth and welfare recipients, child care, health and nutrition services, reduction of street crime and arson, housing rehabilitation, and research on urban problems.

Hearst Foundation
888 7th Ave.
New York, NY 10106
(212) 586-5404
Executive Director: Robert Frehse
Programs to aid poverty-level and minority groups, education programs, health delivery systems and medical research, and cultural programs with records of public support.

March of Dimes Birth Defects Foundation
1275 Mamaroneck Ave.
White Plains, NY 10605
(914) 428-7100
Human Resources Director: Susan Sachs

Mellon, Andrew W., Foundation
140 E. 62nd St.
New York, NY 10021
(212) 838-8400
Human Resources: T. Dennis Sullivan
Grants for higher education, medical and public health education and population research, cultural affairs, and the performing arts.

MS. Foundation for Women
120 Wall St, 33rd Floor
New York, NY 10005
(212) 742-2300
Personnel: Stephanie VanVelos

New York Community Trust
2 Park Ave., 24th Floor
New York, NY 10016
(212) 686-0010
VP, Fiannce and Administration: Karen Metcalf
Grants to charitable organizations; priority given to projects having significance for New York City area.

Reader's Digest Foundation
Reader's Digest Road
Pleasantville, NY 10570
(914) 238-1000
Senior VP, Human Resources: Glenda K. Burkhart
Particularly interested in journalism and education.

Rockefeller Foundation
420 5th Ave.
New York, NY 10018
(212) 869-8500
Personnel Manager: Charlotte Church
Active in six fields: agricultural sciences, population sciences, health sciences, equal opportunity, international relations, and arts and humanities.

Sloan, Alfred P., Foundation
630 5th Ave.
New York, NY 10111
(212) 649-1649
Financial VP: Stuart Campbell
Grants in science, technology, education, economics, management.

Texaco Philanthropic Foundation
2000 Westchester Ave.
White Plains, NY 10650
(914) 253-4000
Human Resource Representative: Alida Davis
Supports cultural programs, social welfare and civic organizations, hospitals, and health agencies.

United Jewish Appeal-Federation of Jewish Philanthropies of New York
130 E. 59th St.
New York, NY 10022
(212) 980-1000
Human Resources: Carol Troum

United States Committee for UNICEF
333 E. 38th St.
New York, NY 10016
(212) 686-5522
Director, Human Resources and Personnel: Les Williams

Walker Foundation, Madam C.J.
341 Madison Ave., 18th Floor
New York, NY 10017
(212) 697-1263
Contact: Brenda Dugue
A human policy research organization which acts as a leadership forum to enhance and encourage entrepreneurial talent.

Connecticut Employers:

GTE Foundation
1 Stamford Forum
Stamford, CT 06904
(203) 965-3620
VP: Maureen Gorman

Xerox Foundation
P.O. Box 1600
800 Long Ridge Road
Stamford, CT 06904
(203) 968-3000
Director: Evelyn Shockley

New Jersey Employers:

Exxon Education Foundation
P.O. Box 101
Florham Park, NJ 07932
(973) 765-7000

Johnson, Robert Wood, Foundation
P.O. Box 2316
Princeton, NJ 08543
(609) 452-8701
Director, Personnel and Administration: Linda Curran

Nabisco Foundation
Nabisco Brands Plaza
Parsippany, NJ 07054
(201) 682-7175

Prudential Foundation
15 Prudential Plaza
Newark, NJ 07101
(201) 802-7354

Government

WEB SITES:

Green book of New York City government offices
http://www.pubadvocate.nyc.gov/
~advocate/greenbook/greenbook.html

America's Job Bank (AJB)
http://www.ajb.dni.us

Federal Jobs Digest
http://www.jobsfed.com/

Fedworld Jobs, Labor, and Management Web Page
http://www.fedworld.gov/jobs.htm

Internet Job Source—State/Federal Jobs
http://www.statejobs.com/

PROFESSIONAL ORGANIZATIONS:

For networking in government and related fields, contact the following local professional organizations listed in Chapter 5.

American Society for Public Administration
Institute of Public Administration

For additional information about jobs in government and related fields, you can contact the following organizations:

American Federation of State, County and Municipal Employees
http://www.afscme.org/
1625 L St., NW
Washington, DC 20036
(202) 452-4800

American Society for Public Administration
1120 G St., NW, Suite 700
Washington, DC 20005
(202) 393-7878

Civil Service Employees Association
P.O. Box 7125, Capitol Station
Albany, NY 12210
(518) 434-0191

Federally Employed Women, NY Chapter
c/o Prnuella Washington
106 Reis Ave.
Englewood, NJ 07631

National Association of Government Employees
317 S. Patrick St.
Arlington, VA 22314
(703) 979-0290

PROFESSIONAL PUBLICATIONS:

AFSCME Leader
Beacon
Capital Source
City and State
Federal Jobs Digest
Federal Times
FedNews
Government Executive
Government Manager
Municipal World
Public Employee Newsletter
Public Employment
Public Management
Public Works

DIRECTORIES:

Braddock's Federal-State-Local Government Directory (Braddock Communications, Alexandria, VA)
City of New York Official Directory (Citybooks, New York, NY)
Federal Yellow Book (Monitor Publishing Co., New York, NY)
New York City Greenbook (City Publishing Center, New York, NY)
New York State Directory (Robert M. Walsh, San Mateo, CA)
New York Red Book (New York Legal Publishing Corporation, Guilderland, NY)

City Government Employers:

Department of Correction
225 Broadway, 13th Floor

New York, NY 10007
(212) 374-2288
Contact: Alan Vengersky

Department of Cultural Affairs
2 Columbus Circle
New York, NY 10019
(212) 841-4100
Personnel Director: Sara Gage

Department of Health
125 Worth St., Rm. 908
New York, NY 10013
(212) 788-4810
Personnel Director: Maureen Sealy

Department of Social Services
271 Church St., 4th Fl.
New York, NY 10013
(212) 274-5400

Economic Development Corp.
110 William St.
New York, NY 10038
(212) 312-3583
Contact: Hilda Lamas

Fire Department
250 Livingston St.
Brooklyn, NY 11201
(718) 694-2000
Director of Personnel: Sherry Ann Kavaler

Housing Preservation and Development
100 Gold St.
New York, NY 10038
(212) 386-6700
Contact: Margie Mack

NYC Department of Transporation
40 Worth St., Rm. 801
New York, NY 10013
(212) 442-6565

Parks and Recreation
16 W. 61 St.
New York, NY 10023
(212) 830-7851
Director of Personnel: David Terhune

Police Department
1 Police Plaza
New York, NY 10038
(212) 374-5000

County Government Employers:

Nassau County
To apply for a job with Nassau County, you must apply to the Department of Personnel, 1 West St., Mineola, NY 11501, (516) 571-4247. You will also need to take the civil service exam, available at the Nassau County Civil Service Commission, 140 Old Country Road, Mineola, NY 11501, (516) 571-2511.

Nassau County: Commerce and Industry
1550 Franklin Ave., Rm. 139
Mineola, NY 11501
(516) 571-4159

Nassau County: County Clerk's Office
240 Old Country Road
Mineola, NY 11501
(516) 571-2663

Nassau County: Department of Health
240 Old Country Road, 5th Floor
Mineola, NY 11501
(516) 571-3410

Nassau County: Department of Labor
1550 Franklin Ave.
New York, NY 11501
(516) 571-3095

Nassau County: Department of Public Works
1 West St.
Mineola, NY 11501
(516) 571-4150

Nassau County: Division of Public Transportation
400 County Seat Drive
Mineola, NY 11501
(516) 571-5836

Westchester County
To apply for a job with Westchester County, you must first apply to the Department of Personnel, 148 Martine Ave., White Plains, NY 10601, (914) 285-2103. They offer the civil service evam in several places and will notify applicants of the location.

Westchester County: County Clerk's Office
110 Grove St.
White Plains, NY 10604
(914) 285-3080

Westchester County: County Executive Office
148 Martine Ave., Building 1
White Plains, NY 10601
(914) 285-2900

Westchester County: District Attorney
111 Grove St.
White Plains, NY 10601
(914) 285-2000

Westchester County: Environmental Facilities
M.O.B. 148 Martine Ave., Rm. 400
White Plains, NY 10601
(914) 285-2450

Westchester County: Finance Department
148 Martine Ave.
White Plains, NY 10601
(914) 285-2756

Westchester County: Health Department
19 Bradhurst Ave.
Hawthorne, NY 10532
(914) 593-5100

State of New York Employers:

To apply for a job with a state employer, contact the New York State Civil Service, Announcement Section, Bldg. 1 Basement, State Office Building Campus, Albany, NY 12239. They will inform you of job openings and exam dates.

Assembly
270 Broadway
New York, NY 10017
Contact personnel in Albany:
(518) 455-4100

Attorney General
120 Broadway
New York, NY 10271
(212) 416-8806

Contact personnel in Albany:
(518) 474-7808

Banking Department
2 Rector St.
New York, NY 10006
(212) 618-6445
Contact Human Resources

Commerce Department
1515 Broadway, 53rd Floor
New York, NY 10036
(212) 930-0350
Contact Human Resources

Controller
633 Third Ave., 31st Fl
New York, NY 10017
(212) 681-4491
Contact personnel in Albany:
(518) 474-3594

Court Administration
25 Beaver St.
New York, NY 10004
(212) 428-2600
Personnel Director: Michael Miller

Department of Health
5 Penn Plaza
New York, NY
(212) 613-4310
Personnel Director: Ronald Rothfeld

Department of State
270 Broadway
New York, NY 10011
(212) 417-5800
Must take exam at : Clayton Powell State Office Bldg., 163 W. 125th St.

Economic Development
633 Third Ave.
New York, NY 10017
(212) 803-2200
Contact personnel in Albany:
(518) 474-4628

Empire State Development Corp.
1515 Broadway, 53rd Floor
New York, NY 10036
(212) 930-9000
Contact Human Resources

Environmental Conservation
47-40 21st St.
Long Island City, NY 11101
(718) 482-4949
Contact: Maria Serrano

Insurance Department
160 W. Broadway
New York, NY 10013
(212) 480-6400
Personnel Director: Mr. Jan Gorski

Labor Department
247 W. 54th St.
New York, NY 10019
(212) 265-2700
(212) 265-2700 (personnel)

Metropolitan Transportation Authority
347 Madison Ave.
New York, NY 10017
(212) 878-1000
Assistant Manager of Staffing: Jessie
Crawford

**Parks Recreation and Historic
Preservation**
New York City Regent Headquarters
915 Broadway, 7th Floor
New York, NY 10011
(212) 387-0271

United States Government Employers:

To apply for a position with the federal
government, you must appear in person at
the Office of Personnel Management,
Federal Job Information and Testing
Center, 26 Federal Plaza, New York, NY
10278. Job listings are available at the
plaza and the application process is
explained. We've listed some of the larger
government agencies that maintain offices
in the metropolitan area.

Army, Office of Human Resources
26 Federal Plaza
New York, NY 10278
(212) 264-0200

Commerce, Department of
26 Federal Plaza
New York, NY 10278
(212) 264-3860

Drug Enforcement Administration
99 10th Ave.
New York, NY 10011
(212) 337-3900

Environmental Protection Agency
290 Broadway
New York, NY 10007
(212) 637-3000

Federal Bureau of Investigation
26 Federal Plaza
New York, NY 10278
(212) 384-1000

Federal Communications Commission
201 Varick St.
New York, NY 10014
(212) 620-3438

Internal Revenue Service
120 Church St.
New York, NY 10008
(212) 264-2190

Justice, Department of
100 Church St., 18th Floor
New York, NY 10007
(212) 791-0008
Contact: Gwendolyn Massey

Labor Department
345 Hudson St.
New York, NY
(212) 352-6000
Director of Personnel: Antonio Murphy Jr.

Marine Corps
605 Third Ave.
New York, NY 10158
(212) 755-7846
Personnel: Captain Scott Cubbler

Peace Corps Recruiting
6 World Trade Center, Rm. 611
New York, NY 10048
(212) 466-2477

**Personnel Management, Office of
Federal Job Information and Testing
Center**
26 Federal Plaza
New York, NY 10278
(212) 264-0422

Postal Service
Applications and Examinations
341 9th Ave.
New York, NY
(212) 330-4000
(800) 725-2161

Secret Service
7 World Trade Center, 9th Floor
New York, NY 10048
(212) 637-4500
Contact: Maggie Quinn

Securities and Exchange Commission
7 World Trade Center
New York, NY
(212) 748-8022
Contact Personnel

Small Business Administration
26 Federal Plaza
New York, NY 10278
(212) 264-4354

State, Department of
270 Broadway

New York, NY 10007
(212) 417-5724

**Transportation, Department of
Commander (PC)**
MLCA Building 400L
Governors Island, NY 10004
(212) 668-3458

**Treasury Department
Bureau of Alcohol, Tobacco and
Firearms**
6 World Trade Center
New York, NY 10048
(212) 466-4487

**U.S. Department of Housing and Urban
Development**
26 Federal Plaza
New York, NY 10278
(212) 264-0782
Contact: Vida Mack, Rm. 35-130

Veterans Affairs
Regional Office
245 W. Houston St.
New York, NY 10014
(212) 807-7229

Voice of America Radio
26 Federal Plaza
New York, NY 10278
(212) 264-2345 New York Bureau

Health Care

WEB SITES:

Call24 Online
http://www.call24online.com/
Includes jobs in the health care industry,
as well as links to licensing and professional associations

Hospital Web
http://neuro-www.mgh.harvard.edu/
hospitalweb.nclk

MedSearch
http://www.medsearch.com/

Mental Health Net
http://www.cmhc.com/

PROFESSIONAL ORGANIZATIONS:

For networking in health care and related
fields, check out the following local
professional organizations listed in
Chapter 5:
**International Academy of Health Care
  Professionals**
National Health Career Association
National League for Nursing
**New York City Health and Hospitals
  Corporation**

For additional information, you can
contact:

American Association of Nursing
1 Dupont Circle, NW, # 530
Washington, DC 20036
(202) 463-6930

American Dental Association
211 E. Chicago Ave.
Chicago, IL 60611
(312)440-2500

American Health Care Association
1201 L St., NW
Washington, DC 20005
(202)842-4444

American Hospital Association
1 N. Franklin St.
Chicago, IL 60606
(312) 422-3000

American Medical Association
http://www.ama-assn.org
515 N. State St.
Chicago, IL 60610
(312) 464-5000

American Public Health Association
http://alpha.org
1015 15th St. NW
Washington, DC 20005
(202) 789-5600

Connecticut Public Health Association
30 Dwight Drive
Middlefield, CT 06455
(203) 673-4612

Group Health Association of America
1129 20th St., NW, Suite 600
Washington, DC 20036
(202) 778-3200

Home Healthcare Nurses Association
437 Twin Bay Drive
Pensacola, FL 32534
(904) 474-1066

National Association for Home Care
228 7th St. SE
Washington, DC 20003
(202) 547-7424

**National Council of Community Mental
Health Centers**
12300 Twinbrook Parkway, Suite 320
Rockville, MD 20852
(301) 984-6200

**New York State Association of Health
Care Providers**
90 State St., Suite 522
Albany, NY 12207
(518) 463-1118

PROFESSIONAL PUBLICATIONS:

American Dental Association News (ADA News)
American Journal of Medicine
American Journal of Nursing
American Journal of Public Health
Dental Assistant
Healthcare Executive
HMO Magazine
Hospitals
Hospital Business
Hospital and Healthcare
Journal of the American Medical Association (JAMA)
Managed Care Outlook
Modern Healthcare
Nations Health
Nursing Outlook

DIRECTORIES:

AMCRA's Managed Health Care Directory (American Managed Care and Review Association, Washington, DC)
American Hospital Association (AHA) Guide to the Health Care Field (American Hospital Association, Chicago, IL)
Directory of Hospital Personnel (Medical Economics Data, Montvale, NJ)
Dun's Guide to Healthcare Companies (Dun's Marketing Services, Parsippany, NY)
Dun's Healthcare Reference Book (Dun's Marketing Services, Parsippany, NY)
Health Organizations of the U.S., Canada and the World (Gale Research, Detroit, MI)
Managed Care 1500, The (Faulkner & Gray Healthcare Information Center, Washington, DC)
Medical & Healthcare Marketplace Guide (IDD Enterprises, New York, NY)
Medical and Health Information Directory (Gale Research Co., Detroit, MI)
National Directory of HMO's (GHAA, Washington, DC)

New York Employers:

Aetna Health Plans
2700 Westchester Ave.
Purchase, NY 10577
(914) 251-0600
Personnel Director: Sandy Jackson

Bellevue Hospital Center
1st Ave. and 27th St.
New York, NY 10016
(212) 562-4141
Asst. Director of Human Resources:
Brenda Chapman

Beth Israel Medical Center
1st. Ave. at E. 16th St.
New York, NY 10003
(212) 387-6900

Catholic Medical Center of Brooklyn and Queens
88-25 153rd St.
Jamaica, NY 11432
(718) 558-6900
Employment Manager: Bill Morse

CIGNA HealthCare
195 Broadway
New York, NY 10007
(800) 462-7486

Columbia Presbyterian Medical Center
622 W. 168th St
New York, NY 10032
(212) 305-2500
Human Resources: Dean Cividello

Empire Blue Cross/Blue Shield
622 3rd Ave.
New York, NY 10017
(212) 476-1000
Human Resources Director: S. Tyrone Alexander

Group Health
441 Ninth Ave.
New York, NY 10001
(212) 615-0000
Employment Manager: Nicholas Sinisgalli

Health Insurance Plan of Greater New York
7 W. 34th St.
New York, NY 10001
(212) 630-5000
VP: Fred Blickman

Kings County Hospital Center
451 Clarkson Ave.
Brooklyn, NY 11203
(718) 245-3131

Long Island Jewish Medical Center
270-05 76th Ave.
New Hyde Park, NY 11040
(718) 470-7000
Employment Manager: Marie Murtha,
410 Lakeville Road
New Hyde Park, NY 11040

MagnaCare
100 Garden City Plaza
Garden City, NY 11530
(516) 294-0700
VP, Operations: Ellen Kaplan

Memorial Sloan Kettering
1275 York Ave.
New York, NY 10021
(212) 634-3479

MetLife HealthCare Network
2929 Express Drive, N.
Hauppauge, NY 11787
(516) 348-7200

MetraHealth Care Plan of New York
2 Penn Plaza
New York, NY 10121
(212) 216-6400

Montefiore Hospital and Medical Center
111 E. 210th St.
Bronx, NY 10467
(718) 920-4321
Human Resources Director: Jack Berg

Mt. Sinai Medical Center
1 Gustave Levy Place
New York, NY 10029
(212) 241-6500

Multiplan Inc.
115 5th Ave.
New York, NY 10003
(212) 780-2000
Human Resources Director: Amanda
Rubin

NYLCARE
75-20 Astoria Blvd.
Jackson Heights, Queens 11370
(718) 899-5200
Human Resources Director: Mr. Loran
Couch

New York Hospital-Cornell Medical Center
525 E. 68th St.
New York, NY 10021
(212) 746-5454
Human Resources Director: Regina Allen

New York Hospital Medical Center of Queens
56-45 Main St.
Flushing, NY 11355
(718) 670-1333

Oxford Health Plans
1133 Avenue of the Americas
New York, NY 10036
(212) 805-3400
Human Resources Manager: Audrey Julian

Preferred Health Network
45th Ave. at Parson Blvd.
Flushing, NY 11355
(718) 497-4455

Presbyterian Hospital
622 W. 168th St.
New York, NY 10032
(212) 305-2500

Private HealthCare Systems
330 Madison Ave.
New York, NY 10017
(212) 983-5160

Prudential Health Care Plan
400 Rella Blvd., Suite 300
Suffern, NY 10901
(914) 368-4497
Human Resources: Patty North

St. Luke's Roosevelt Hospital Center
555 W. 57th St., 18th Fl.
New York, NY 10019
(212) 523-7180
Human Resources: Josephine Simpson

Careers in health care

"If you wish to work in the hospital field, it's important to pick a speciality and pursue it as early as possible," said Carl Martino, former director of personnel at Booth Memorial Medical Center (now NY Hospital Medical Center of Queens), when we asked him about the hospital industry. "Most hospital professions are very specialized and require a great deal of education. Many hospitals recruit right from high school or college if they operate training programs in allied health fields.

"Once you've been working for a while," adds Martino, "I would suggest to anyone, whether in the business or medical end of the hospital industry, that it's a good idea to join an association or society representing your occupation. The industry is known for its networking, and many associations have placement services. I rarely use an employment agency or place an ad in the paper to fill a position. Trade associations have been more helpful and more effective in filling any opening I might have. Also, for the job hunter, their services are confidential and fairly quick."

St. Vincent's Hospital and Medical Center of NY
153 W. 11th St.
New York, NY 10011
(212) 604-7887
Director of Employment: Susan Roti

U.S. Healthcare
333 Earle Ovington Blvd.
Nassau Omni W.
Uniondale, NY 11553
(516) 229-2500
Human Resources: Ann Druck, 55 Lane Road, Fairfield, NJ 07004

Visiting Nursing Service of New York
350 5th Ave.
New York, NY 10118
(212) 560-3370
Jobline: (212) 560-3342
Contact: Recruitment and Staffing Department

Connecticut Employers:

Cigna Health Corporation
900 Cottage Grove Road
Bloomfield, CT 06002
(860) 726-6000
Manager, Corporate Staffing: Mark Jacobs

Hartford Hospital
80 Seymour St.
Hartford, CT 06102
(860) 545-5555
VP, Human Resources: Richard McAloon

Yale-New Haven Hospital
20 York St.
New Haven, CT 06504
(203) 785-4242
VP, Human Resources: Ellen Andrews

New Jersey Employers:

Hackensack Medical Center
30 Prospect Ave.

Hackensack, NJ 07601
(201) 996-2000

Memorial Health Alliance
175 Madison Ave.
Mount Holly, NJ 08060
(609) 261-7011
Human Resources Director: Erich
Florentine

St. Joseph's Hospital and Medical Center
703 Main St.
Paterson, NJ 07503
(201) 977-2000
Human Resources Director: Georgette
Deroche

Hospitality: Hotels and Restaurants

WEB SITES:

Bon Appetit
http://www.epicurious.com/epicurious/
ba/ba.html

Hospitality Management Homepage
http://bizpubs.corp.com/magazine.html

Hospitality Net
http://www.hospitalitynet.com

New York City hotels
http://anansi.panix.com/clay/nyc/
hotels.html

PROFESSIONAL ORGANIZATIONS:

For networking in the hospitality industry
and related fields, check out the following
local professional organization listed in
Chapter 5:
New York State Restaurant Association

For more information, you can contact:

American Hotel & Motel Association
1201 New York Ave., NW, Suite 600
Washington, DC 20005
(202) 289-3100

Chefs de Cuisine Association of America
155 E. 55th St., Suite 302B
New York, NY 10022
(212) 832-4939

Connecticut Hotel-Motel Association
3 Waterville Road
Farmington, CT 06032
(860) 678-7299

**Hotel Sales & Marketing Association
International**
1300 L St., NW, Suite 800
Washington, DC 20005
(202)789-0089

**International Association for Exposition
Management**
P.O. Box 802425
Dallas, TX 75380
(317) 871-7272

**International Chefs Association, Big
Apple Chapter**
23 Home Place
Lodi, NJ 07644
(973) 340-9856
Chefs, cooks, and pastry chefs in
Connecticut, New Jersey, and New York.

International Special Events Society
9202 N. Meridian St., Suite 200
Indianapolis, IN 46260
(317) 571-5601

**Long Island Restaurant and Caterers
Association**
640 Fulton St., Suite 4
Farmingdale, NY 11735
(516) 752-0707

Meeting Professionals International
1950 Stemmons Freeway, Suite 5010
Dallas, TX 75207
(214) 712-7700

National Council of Chain Restaurants
1200 19th St., NW, #300

Washington, DC 20036
(202) 429-5152

National Restaurant Association
1200 17th St., N. W.
Washington, DC 20036
(202) 331-5900

New Jersey Hotel-Motel Association
196 W. State St.
Trenton, NJ 08608
(609) 278-9000

New Jersey Restaurant Association
Executive Sq. 1
1 Executive Drive, Suite 100
Somerset, NJ 08873
(908) 302-1800

New York Hotel and Motels Trade Council
707 8th Ave.
New York, NY 10036
(212) 245-8100

Restaurant Association of New York
505 8th Ave.
New York, NY 10018
(212)714-1330

PROFESSIONAL PUBLICATIONS:

Business Traveler Magazine
Club Management
Food Management
Food and Wine
Holiday and Travel News
Hotel Business
Hotel and Motel Management
Hotel and Resort Industry
Hotels and Motels
Lodging Magazine
Meetings and Conventions
Nation's Restaurant News
Restaurant Business
Restaurant Hospitality
Restaurants and Institutions
Restaurants USA
Successful Meetings

DIRECTORIES:

Directory of Chain Restaurant Operators (Chain Store Guide Information Services, Tampa, FL)
Directory of High Volume Independent Restaurants (Chain Store Guide Information Services, Tampa, FL)
Restaurant Hospitality, Hospitality 500 Issue (Penton/IPC, Inc., Columbus, OH)
Directory of Hotel and Motel Companies (American Hotel Association Directory, Washington, DC)
Hotel and Motel Redbook (American Hotel and Motel Association, Washington, DC)
Hotels & Motels Directory (American Business Directories, Omaha, NE)
Meetings and Conventions Magazine, Directory Issue (Murdoch Magazines, New York, NY)
Restaurants & Institutions, 400 Issue (Cahners Publishing, Des Plaines, IL)
Successful Meetings, International Convention Facilities Directory Issue (Bill Communications, New York, NY)

Hotel Employers:

Carlyle Hotel
35 E. 76th St.
New York, NY 10021
(212) 744-1600
General Manager: Dan Camp

Drake Hotel
440 Park Ave.
New York, NY 10022
(212) 421-0900
Human Resources Director: Carmen Galiano

Essex House
160 Central Park S.
New York, NY 10019
(212) 247-0300
Personnel Director: Leigh Russo

Four Seasons Hotels
57 E. 57th St.
New York, NY 10022
(212) 758-5700
Director of Human Resources: Jackie Nixon

Grand Hyatt Hotels
Park Ave. at Grand Central
New York, NY 10017
(212) 883-1234
Human Resources Director: Nancy
McCormick

Helmsley Hotels
680 Madison
New York, NY 10022
(212) 838-3000

Hotel Intercontinental, NY
111 E. 48th St.
New York, NY 10017
(212) 755-5900
Contact Human Resources

Le Parker Meridien
118 W. 57th St.
New York, NY 10019
(212) 245-5000
Human Resources Director: Janna
Lebowich

Marriott Marquis
1535 Broadway
New York, NY 10036
(212) 398-1900
Human Resources Director: Raymond
Falcone

New York Hilton Hotel
1335 Avenue of the Americas
New York, NY 10019
(212) 586-7000
Human Resources: Lou Stoltz

New York Palace
455 Madison Ave. (at 50th St.)
New York, NY 10022
(212) 888-7000
Human Resources Director: Lynn
Bushover

Omni Park Central Hotel
870 7th Ave.
New York, NY 10019
(212) 247-8000
Personnel Director: Joshua Wirshba

Peninsula Hotel
700 5th Ave.
New York, NY 10019
(212) 247-2200
Director of Personnel: Fanchea
Clarke-Brown

Pierre Hotel
A Four Seasons Hotel
5th Ave. at 61st St.
New York, NY 10021
(212) 838-8000
Director of Human Resources: Sandra
Finlay

Plaza Athenee
37 E. 64th St.
New York, NY 10021
(212) 734-9100

Plaza Hotel
768 5th Ave.
New York, NY 10019
(212) 759-3000
Director of Human Resources: George
Dertouzas

Hotel management: more than puttin' on the Ritz
With a little more than two years' experience in the hotel
business, our friend Kirk landed a job as sales manager for
a Midtown hotel. We asked him for an overview of the
hospitality industry.

"If you want to move up quickly," says Kirk, "this industry
is the place to be. It's anything but a dead-end business.
Some people stay with the same organization for most of

their careers. But I'd say the average is probably around five years with any given company. People are constantly calling and making job offers.

"I studied hotel management and general business. But you can't just walk out of college and into a middle-management position. I started as a receptionist at the Plaza. Then I became a secretary. I don't know anyone who hasn't paid dues for a year or two. If you're interested in food or beverages, you might start out as a dining room assistant. Essentially, you'd be doing the same thing as a secretary—typing up contracts or menus, that sort of thing. You really have to learn the business from the bottom up.

"In sales you move from secretarial work to a full-fledged sales position. I was a sales representative, then was promoted to sales manager. The next step might logically be director of sales or marketing, where I'd be responsible for advertising and marketing strategies, developing budgets, and so on. An equivalent position would be director of food and beverages, the person who's responsible for all the food and drink served in the hotel, room service, all the dining rooms, special banquets, everything. After director of sales or food and beverages, you go on to general manager.

"I'd say the competition is about average—not nearly as fierce as the advertising industry, for example. Earning potential is pretty good, too, depending, of course, on the size of the hotel and the city you're in and what kind of company you're working for. You start out pretty low, maybe around $20,000 or $21,000 a year. But each time you move up, you get a hefty raise, or ought to."

Radisson Empire Hotel
44 W. 63rd St.
New York, NY 10023
(212) 265-7400
Contact Human Resources

Ritz Carlton
112 Central Park S.
New York, NY 10019
(212) 959-1900
Personnel: Anna Petrovich

ITT Sheraton
112 Central Park S.
New York, NY 10019
(212) 757-1900
Human Resources: Ann Petrovich

St. Moritz
50 Central Park S.
New York, NY 10019
(212) 755-5800
Human Resources Secretary: Hilda Dejesus

St. Regis–Sheraton
2 E. 55th St.
New York, NY 10022
(212) 753-4500
Manager: Rick Segal

Trump Park Plaza Hotel
106 Central Park S.
New York, NY 10019
(212) 308-8802
Must apply in person

Waldorf Astoria
Subsidiary of Hilton Hotels
301 Park Ave.
New York, NY 10022
(212) 355-3000
Director of Human Resources: Ann
Rubenzahl

Westbury Hotel
69th St. at Madison
New York, NY 10021
(212) 535-2000
Human Resources: Jacqueline Pucci

Restaurant Employers:

There are thousands of restaurants in the
New York metropolitan area. We have
chosen the cream of the crop. You will
find here restaurants rated three and four
stars by major restaurant critics, restaurant chains, and some of the most famous
of New York's eateries.

Aureole
34 E. 61st St.
New York, NY 10021
(212) 319-1660
Manager: Vincent Santoro

Becco
355 W. 46th Street
New York, NY 10036
(212) 397-7597

Le Bernadin
155 W. 51st St.
New York, NY
(212) 489-1515

Blimpie, Inc.
370 7th Ave.
New York, NY 10001
(212) 279-7100
Contact: Maria Rirzarry

Bouley
120 W. Broadway
New York, NY 10013
(212) 904-2525
Manager: Didier Domique

La Caravelle
33 W. 55th St.
New York, NY 10019
(212) 586-4252

Les Celebrities
160 Central Park S.
New York, NY
(212) 484-5113

Chanterelle
2 Harrison St.
New York, NY
(212) 966-6960
General Manager: Karen Waltuck

Le Cirque
58 E. 65th St.
New York, NY 10021
(212) 794-9292
Manager: Benito Sezzarin

La Côte Basque
60 W. 55th St.
New York, NY 10019
(212) 688-6525
Manager: Pasqual Fevrier

Daniel
20 E. 76th St.
New York, NY
(212) 288-0033

Felidia Ristorante
243 E. 58th St.
New York, NY 10022
(212) 758-1479

Four Seasons, The
99 E. 52nd St.

New York, NY 10022
(212) 754-9494
General Manager: Alex Von Bidder

Hudson River Club
4 World Financial Center, 250 Vesey St.
New York, NY
(212) 786-1500

Kentucky Fried Chicken
10 Bank St., Suite 780
White Plains, NY 10606
(914) 287-4122
Director of Human Resources: Herbert
Jackson

Lespinasse
2 E. 55th St.
New York, NY 10022
(212) 339-6719
General Manager: Rick Segal

Luger, Peter
178 Broadway
Brooklyn, NY
(718) 387-7400

Lutèce
249 E. 50th St.
New York, NY 10022
(212) 752-2225
General Manager: Eberhard Muller

March
405 E. 58th St.
New York, NY
(212) 838-9393

McDonald's Corp.
Regional Headquarters
1 Crossroads Drive, Building A
Bedminster, NJ 07921
(908) 658-4100
Human Resources Manager: Kim Casey

Montrachet
239 W. Broadway
New York, NY 10013
(212) 219-2777
Manager: Eric Rota

Nathan's Famous
1400 Old Country Road
Westbury, NY 11590
(516) 338-8500
Director of Personnel and Training: Karen
Brown

National Restaurant Management
162 W. 34th St.
New York, NY 10001
(212) 563-7440
Manages 200 restaurants within metropolitan New York area.

Le Perigord
405 E. 52nd St.
New York, NY 10022
(212) 755-6244
Manager: George Briguet

Petrossian
182 W. 58th St.
New York, NY 10019
(212) 245-2214
General Manager: Robin Hollis

Piccolino
8 E. 36th St.
New York, NY 10016
(212) 683-6444
Co-Owner: Alfonso Kimche

Planet Hollywood
140 W. 57th St.
New York, NY 10019
(212) 956-7628

Rainbow Room
30 Rockefeller Plaza
New York, NY 10020
(212) 632-5000
General Manager: Charles Baum

Restaurants Associates Industries
36 W. 44th St.
New York, NY 10036
(212) 789-7900
Restaurants and catering.

River Cafe, The
1 Water St.
Brooklyn, NY
(718) 522-5200
General Manager: John McFadden

Russian Tea Room
150 W. 57th St.
New York, NY 10019
(212) 580-1200
Reopening in 1999

San Domenico
240 Central Park S.
New York, NY 10019

(212) 265-5959
General Manager: Tony May

Tavern On The Green
Central Park West at W. 67th St.
New York, NY 10023
(212) 873-3200
Personnel Director: Bob Logan

"21" Club
21 W. 52nd St.
New York, NY 10019
(212) 582-7200
Director of Operations: Brian McGuire

Human Services

WEB SITES:

Community Career Center
http://www.nonprofitjobs.org/

Journals, newsgroups, and listserves
http://lib4.fisher.su.oz.au/Social_Work/
socwkls.html

Links to social work sites
http://http.bsd.uchicago.edu/~r-tell/
socwork.html

Social work courses via the Internet
http://caster.ssw.upenn.edu/cont-ed/
index.html

PROFESSIONAL ORGANIZATIONS:

For networking in human services and
related fields, check out the following local
professional organizations listed in
Chapter 5. Also see **"Foundations"** and
"Health Care."
National Association of Black Social
   Workers
National Association of Social Workers,
   New York City Chapter
National League for Nursing

For more information, you can contact:

**American Association of Direct Human
Service Personnel**
1832 Little Road
Parma, MI 49269
(517) 531-5820

Community Action for Human Services
2225 Lodovick Ave.
Bronx, NY 10469
(718) 655-7700

Executive Women in Human Services
27 Barrow St.
New York, NY 10014
(212) 254-9283

National Association of Social Workers
750 1st St., NE
Washington, DC 20002
(202) 408-8600

**National Association of Social Workers:
Connecticut Chapter**
2139 Silas Dove Highway
Rocky Hill, CT 06067
(860) 257-8066

New Jersey Chapter
110 W. State St.
Trenton, NJ 09608
(609) 394-1666

Society for Human Resource Management
http://www.shrm.org
1800 Duke St.
Alexandria, VA 22314
(703) 548-3440

PROFESSIONAL PUBLICATIONS:

Advocate
American Rehabilitation
Child and Youth Services Review
Child Welfare Journal
Community Action
Community Jobs
Family Journal
Journal of Social Welfare
Society

DIRECTORIES:

Child Welfare League of America Directory
  (Child Welfare League of America, Inc.,
  Washington, DC)
Community Resources Directory (Gale
  Research, Inc., Detroit, MI)
Directory of Agencies (National Association
  of Social Workers, Washington, DC)
Human Services Organizations (American
  Business Information, Inc., Omaha, NB)
*National Directory of Children and Youth
  Services* (Marion Peterson Longmont, CO)
*National Directory of Private Social
  Agencies* (Croner Publications, Queens
  Village, NY)
Public Welfare Directory (American Public
  Welfare Association, Washington, DC)
Social Service Organizations (American
  Business Information, Inc., Omaha, NE)

Employers:

American Cancer Society
19 W. 56th St.
New York, NY 10019
(212) 586-8700
Administration Director: Frank Gulfin

**American Fund for Alternatives to
Animal Research**
175 W. 12th St., Suite 16G
New York, NY 10011
(212) 989-8073

American Red Cross
150 Amsterdam Ave.
New York, NY 10023
(212) 787-1000
Personnel Director: Maxine Teitler

**American Society for the Prevention of
Cruelty to Animals**
424 E. 92nd St.
New York, NY 10128
(212) 876-7700

**Association for Children with Retarded
Mental Development (ACRMD)**
345 Hudson St.
New York, NY 10014
(212) 741-0100
Employment Manager: Karen Mapp

**Association for the Help of Retarded
Children**
200 Park Ave. S.
New York, NY 10003
(212) 255-0351

Big Brothers, Big Sisters
223 E. 30th St.
New York, NY 10016
(212) 686-2042
Program Director: Emily Forman

Boy Scouts of America
345 Hudson St.
New York, NY 10014
(212) 242-1100
Personnel Director: Ledy Alvarado

Builders for Family and Youth
191 Joralemon St.
Brooklyn, NY 11201
(718) 722-6000
Personnel: Phillip Zalensi

Cancer Care, and the American Cancer Foundation
1180 Avenue of the Americas
New York, NY 10036
(212) 221-3300
Personnel Director: Loretta Dunn

Children's Aid Society
105 E. 22nd St.
New York, NY 10010
(212) 949-4800
Personnel Director: Jose Alfaro

Community Family Planning Council
184 5th Ave., 3rd Floor
New York, NY 10010
(212) 924-1400
Executive Director: Robin D. Lane

Covenant House
460 W. 41st St.
New York, NY 10036
(212) 613-0300
Personnel: Judy Mills

F.E.G.S.
114 5th Ave., 11th Floor
New York, NY 1001
(212) 366-8400
Human Resources: Nina Mondeleone

Gay Men's Health Crisis (GMHC)
119 W. 24th St., 9th Fl.
New York, NY 10011
(212) 367-1476
Jobline: (212) 337-1910
Personnel Director: Donna Dash

Girl Scout Council of Greater New York
43 W. 23rd St.
New York, NY 10010
(212) 645-4000
Personnel Director: Elisabeth Orozco

Heartshare Human Services of New York
191 Joralemon St., 10th Floor
Brooklyn, NY 11201
(718) 330-0600
Recruiter: Veronica Harris

International Rescue Committee
122 E. 42nd St.
New York, NY 10168
(212) 551-3017
Contact: Loiuse Shey

Jewish Board of Family and Children Services
120 W. 57th St.
New York, NY 10019
(212) 582-9100
Human Resources Manager: Richard Clausen

National Council on Alcoholism
12 W. 21st St., 7th Floor
New York, NY 10010
(212) 206-6770
Human Resources Asst.: Robert Pierce

National Urban League
120 Wall St., 8th Fl.
New York, NY 10005
(212) 310-9000
Director of Human Resources: Wanda Jackson

New York Association for New Americans
17 Battery Pl.
New York, NY 10004
(212) 425-2900
Human Resources Director: Nina Mondeleone

Planned Parenthood Federation of America
810 7th Ave.
New York, NY 10019
(212) 541-7800
VP, Human Resources: Pili Nunez

The Salvation Army of Greater New York
120 W. 14th St.
New York, NY 10011
(212) 337-7200

Selfhelp Community Services
440 9th Ave.

New York, NY 10001
(212) 971-7600
Senior Human Resources Specialist:
Robert Hinkelman

Services for the Underserved
305 7th Ave., 10th Floor
New York, NY 10001
(212) 633-6900
Director of Development: Judith Jackson

United Cerebral Palsy Association
330 W. 34th St.
New York, NY 10001
(212) 947-5770
Manager of Personnel: Janice Pshena

United Way-Greater New York Fund
99 Park Ave.
New York, NY 10016
(212) 973-3800
Senior VP, Human Resources: Margaret
Carter

United Way of Westchester and Putnam
336 Central Park Ave.
White Plains, NY 10606
(914) 997-6700
Human Resources Director: Kathi
Sokolowski

Victim's Services
2 Lafayette St., 3rd Floor
New York, NY 10003
(212) 577-7700
Human Resources: Donna Rey

Volunteers of America
340 W. 85th St.
New York, NY 10024
(212) 496-4313
Manager: Jill Roberts

Young Adult Institute
460 W. 34 St., 11th Floor
New York, NY 10001
(212) 563-7474
Human Resources: Jules Feiman

Young Men's Christian Association
333 7th Ave., 15th Floor
New York, NY 10001
(212) 630-9600
VP, Human Resources: Charles Wilkins

Young Women's Christian Association
610 Lexington Ave.
New York, NY 10022
(212) 755-4500
Human Resources Director: Patricia Butts

Insurance

WEB SITES:

Insurance Connections!
http://www.connectyou.com/ins/

InsuranceWeb
http://www.insweb.com

RISKWeb
http://www.riskweb.com/

SafeTNet
http://www.safetnet.com

PROFESSIONAL ORGANIZATIONS:

For networking in insurance and related fields, check out the following professional organizations listed in Chapter 5:
American Insurance Association
Insurance Society of New York
National Association of Insurance Women
Risk and Insurance Management Society

For more information, you can contact:

American Council of Life Insurance
1001 Pennsylvania Ave., NW, Suite 500
Washington, DC 20004
(202) 624-2000

American Insurance Association
1130 Connecticut Ave., NW
Washington, DC 20036
(202) 828-7100

Council of Insurance Agents & Brokers
316 Pennsylvania Ave., SE, Suite 400
Washington, DC 20003
(202) 547-6616

Insurance Association of Connecticut
55 Farmington Ave.
Hartford, CT 06105
(203) 547-0610

National Association of Independent Insurers
2600 River Road
Des Plaines, IL 60018
(847) 297-7800

National Association of Life Underwriters
1922 F St., NW
Washington, DC 20006
(202) 331-6000

National Association of Professional Insurance Agents
400 N. Washington St.
Alexandria, VA 22314
(703) 836-9340

Professional Insurance Agents of New York
25 Chamberlain, P.O. Box 997
Glenmont, NY 12077
(518) 434-3111

Society of Certified Insurance Counselors
P.O. Box 27027
Austin, TX 78755
(512) 345-7932

PROFESSIONAL PUBLICATIONS:

Actuarial Digest
American Agent & Broker
Best's Insurance Report
Best's Review
BestWeek
http://www.ambest.com/
Broker, The
Business Insurance
Claims
Health Insurance Underwriter
Independent Agent
Insurance
Insurance Advocate
Insurance Agent
Insurance Journal
Insurance & Technology
Insurance Times
National Underwriter

DIRECTORIES:

Insurance Almanac (Underwriter Publishing Co., Englewood, NJ)
Insurance Fact Book (American Council of Life Insurance, Chicago, IL)

National Association of Life Underwriters, Directory (Natl. Assn. of Life Underwriters (Washington, DC)

Roster of Membership (Risk and Insurance Management Society, Chicago, IL)

Who's Who in Risk Management (Underwriter Printing and Publishing Co., Englewood, NJ)

New York Employers:

Aetna Insurance
452 Fifth Ave.
New York, NY 10018
(212) 512-0700
Director of Human Resources:
Christopher Taylor

Alleghany Corp.
375 Park Ave., 32nd Fl.
New York, NY 10152
(212) 752-1356
President & CEO: John Burns, Jr.

AMBAC Inc.
1 State Street Plaza
New York, NY 10004
(212) 208-3357
Human Resources Director: Thomas Perry

American International Group (AIG)
72 Wall St., 11 Floor
New York, NY 10270
(212) 770-7000
Director, Corporate Staffing: Jacque Weiss
Property and casualty insurance.

Atlantic Mutual
100 Wall St.
New York, NY 10005
(212) 943-1800

Capital Reinsurance Corp.
1325 6th Ave.
New York, NY 10019
(212) 974-0100
Human Resources Manager: Ivana Grillo

Center Reinsurance Co. of NY
1 Chase Manhattan Plaza
New York, NY 10005
(212) 898-5300
Human Resources Director: Cheryl Rink

Constitution Reinsurance Corp.
110 William St.
New York, NY 10038
(212) 225-1000

Continental Insurance Companies
180 Maiden Lane
New York, NY 10038
(212) 440-3000
Personnel Director: Kim McNulcy
Property and casualty insurance.

Empire Blue Cross and Blue Shield
622 3rd Ave.
New York, NY 10017
(212) 476-1000

Equitable Variable Life Insurance Co.
1290 6th Ave.
New York, NY 10104
(212) 554-1234
Human Resources: John O'Hara

Guardian Life Insurance Co. of America
201 Park Ave. S.
New York, NY 10003
(212) 598-8000
VP, Staffing and Employee Relations:
Ms. Alix Kane

Leucadia National Corp.
315 Park Ave. S.
New York, NY 10010
(212) 460-1900
Human Resources Director: Laura Ulbrandt

MBIA Inc.
113 King St.
Armonk, NY 10504
(914) 273-4545
Human Resources Director: Kevin Silva

Merrill Lynch Life Insurance Co. of NY
225 Liberty St.
World Financial Center S. Tower, 11th Fl.
New York, NY 10080
(212) 236-8309
Recruting: Christopher Falvey

Metropolitan Life Insurance
1 Madison Ave.
New York, NY 10010
(212) 578-2211

Munich Re Group
560 Lexington Ave.
New York, NY 10022
(212) 310-1600

Mutual of America
320 Park Ave.
New York, NY 10022
(212) 399-1600
Human Resources: Diane Aramony

Mutual Life Insurance Company of New York
1740 Broadway
New York, NY 10019
(212) 708-2000
Manager, Human Resources: Nina Walters

New York Life Insurance Co.
51 Madison Ave.
New York, NY 10010
(212) 576-7000
Senior Human Resoures Asst.: Genevieve Kelley

North American Reinsurance
237 Park Ave., 13th Floor
New York, NY 10017
(212) 907-8000
Asst. VP of Employee Relations: Kenneth Robinson

Penncorp Financial Group
745 5th Ave.
New York, NY 10151
(212) 932-0700

Reliance Group Holdings
55 E. 52nd St.
New York, NY 10055
(212) 909-1100
Assistant Director, Human Resources: Ann Colleran

Risk Enterprise Management
59 Maiden Lane, 19th Floor
New York, NY 10038
(212) 530-6600
VP: Alice Geckeler

SCOR Reinsurance Corp.
2 World Trade Center
New York, NY 10048

(212) 390-5200
Human Resources: Matthew Jazynski

Sun Alliance USA
88 Pine St.
New York, NY 10005
(212) 753-8130
VP, Operations: Ava Penning

Swiss Re America
237 Park Ave.
New York, NY 10017
(212) 907-8000

Teacher's Insurance and Annuity Association
730 3rd Ave.
New York, NY 10017
(212) 490-9000
Exec. VP, Human Resources: Matina Horner

Transamerica Insurance Group
40 Fulton St.
New York, NY 10038
(212) 602-6400
Human Resources:5205 N. O'Connor Blvd.
Irving, TX 75039
Property and casualty insurance.

Travelers Group
388 Greenwich St.
New York, NY 10013
(212) 816-8000

U.S. Life Corp.
125 Maiden Lane
New York, NY 10038
(212) 709-6000
Human Resources Director: Jospehine Stith

Winterthur Reinsurance Corp. of America
225 Liberty St.
New York, NY 10281
(212) 416-5700
Human Resources Director: Lynn Distefano

Zurich Reinsurance
1 Chase Manhattan Plaza
New York, NY 10005
(212) 898-5000

Connecticut Employers:

Aetna Life and Casualty Company
151 Farmington Ave.
Hartford, CT 06156
(860) 273-7898
Director of Recruiting: Ellen Brown

Connecticut General Life (Cigna)
900 Cottage Grove Road
Bloomfield, CT 06002
(860) 726-6000
Recruiting Analyst: Fran Raisstanger

Travelers, The
1 Tower Sq.
Hartford, CT 06183
(860) 277-0111
Director, Staffing and Recruiting: Florence
Johnson

New Jersey Employers:

Chubb Group
15 Mountainview Road
Warren, NJ 07060
(908) 903-2000
Contact Human Resources

Mutual Benefit Life
520 Broad St.
Newark, NJ 07102
(201) 481-8000
Human Resources Director: Christine
Ertle

Prudential of America
213 Washington St.
Newark, NJ 07102
(201) 802-6000
Human Resources Director: Joan Ellen

Law Firms

WEB SITES:

Law Employment Center
http://www.lawjobs.com/
lawjoblistings.html

LawInfo
http://www.lawinfo.com/employment

LawJobs
http://www.lawjobs.com

LawLinks
http://www.counsel.com/lawlinks

NY State Trial Lawyers Association
http://www.nystla.org/

PROFESSIONAL ORGANIZATIONS:

For networking in law and related fields,
check out the following local professional
organizations listed in Chapter 5:
**International Federation of Women
  Lawyers**
Metropolitan Black Bar Association
National Conference of Black Lawyers

National Lawyers Guild
**New York Council of Defense Lawyers
  Educational Services**
New York County Lawyers Association
New York State Trial Lawyers Association
New York Women's Bar Association

For more information, you can contact:

American Bar Association
http://www.abanet.org
750 N. Lake Shore Drive
Chicago, IL 60611
(312) 988-5000

Association of Trial Lawyers of America
1050 31st St., NW
Washington, DC 20007
(202) 965-3500

**National Bar Association (Minority
Lawyers)**
1225 11th St., NW
Washington, DC 20001
(202) 842-3900

National Paralegal Association
6186 Honey Hollow Road
Solebury, PA 18963
(215) 297-8333

PROFESSIONAL PUBLICATIONS:

ABA Journal—The Lawyer's Magazine
Administrative Law & Practice
Affiliate
ALI Reporter (American Law Institute)
American Lawyer
*ATLA Advocate (Association of Trial
  Lawyers of America)*
Bar News
Business Law Today
Compleat Lawyer
Criminal Law Bulletin
For the Defense
Law Practice Management
Lawyer's Weekly Report
Legal Times
National Bar Association Magazine
*National and Federal Legal Employment
  Report*
Paralegal
Practical Lawyer
Student Lawyer
Trial

DIRECTORIES:

ABA Directory (American Bar Association,
  Chicago, IL)
Directory of Lawyer Referral Services
  (American Bar Association, Chicago, IL)
Law Firms Yellow Book (Leadership
  Directories, Inc., New York, NY)
Law & Legal Information Directory (Gale
  Research, Inc., Detroit, MI)
Martindale-Hubbell Law Directory
  (Martindale-Hubble, Summit, NJ)

New York Employers:

Brown & Wood
1 World Trade Center
New York, NY 10048
(212) 839-5300
Recruiting Coordinator: Maureen
McGovern

Cadwalader Wickersham & Taft
100 Maiden Lane
New York, NY 10038
(212) 504-6000
Human Resources Director: Anita Howell

Cahill Gordon & Reindel
80 Pine St.
New York, NY 10005
(212) 701-3000
Recruiting Director: Joyce Hilly

Chadbourne & Paarke
30 Rockefeller Plaza
New York, NY 10112
(212) 408-5100
Recruiting Director: Bernadette Miles

Cleary Gottlieb Steen and Hamilton
1 Liberty Plaza
New York, NY 10006
(212) 225-2000
Recruiting Director: Norma Cirincione

Cravath Swaine & Moore
825 8th Ave.
New York, NY 10019
(212) 474-1000
Recruiting Director: Lorraine Winheim

Davis Polk & Wardwell
450 Lexington Ave.
New York, NY 10017
(212) 450-4000
Recruiting Director: Bonnie Hurry

Debevoise and Plimpton
875 3rd Ave.
New York, NY 10022
(212) 909-6000
Recruiting Director: Ethel Leichti

Dewey Ballantine
1301 6th Ave.
New York, NY 10019
(212) 259-8000
Recruiting Director: Patrizia De Gennaro

Fried Frank Harris Shriver & Jacobson
1 New York Plaza
New York, NY 10004
(212) 859-8000
Director of Legal Personnel : Wendy Cox

Kaye Scholer Fierman Hays & Handler
425 Park Ave.
New York, NY 10022
(212) 836-8000
Recruiting Director: Wendy Evans

LeBoeuf Lamb Greene & MacRae
125 W. 55th St.
New York, NY 10019
(212) 424-8000
Recruiting Director: Yiba Ng

Millbank Tweed Hadley & McCloy
1 Chase Manhattan Plaza
New York, NY 10005
(212) 530-5000
Recruiting Director: Christine Wagner

Morgan Lewis & Bockius
101 Park Ave.
New York, NY 10178
(212) 309-6000
Recruiting Director: Brenda Ollman

Paul Weiss Rifkind Wharton & Garrison
1285 6th Ave.
New York, NY 10019
(212) 373-3000
Recruiting Coordinator: Joane Ollman

Proskauer Rose Goetz & Mendelsohn
1585 Broadway
New York, NY 10036
(212) 969-3000
Recruiting Director: Kristin Williams

Rogers & Wells
200 Park Ave.
New York, NY 10166
(212) 878-8000
Recruiting Coordinator: Ms. Kelly Murphy

Rosenman & Colin
575 Madison Ave.
New York, NY 10022
(212) 940-8800
Recruiting Director: Edmar Petterson

Shearman and Sterling
599 Lexington Ave.
New York, NY 10022
(212) 848-4000

Recruiting Coordinators: Jane Salvi
(paralegals)
Halle Schargel (attorneys)

Shearman & Sterling
599 Lexington Ave.
New York, NY 10022
(212) 848-4000
Human Resources Director: Brenda
Levengood

Simpson Thacher & Bartlett
425 Lexington Ave.
New York, NY 10017
(212) 455-2000
Director of Legal Employment: Dee Pifer

Skadden Arps Slate Meagher & Flom
919 3rd Ave.
New York, NY 10022
(212) 371-6000
Recruiting Director: Carol Sprague

Stroock & Stroock & Lavan
180 Maiden Lane
New York, NY 10038
(212) 806-5400
Recruiting Director: Diane Cohen

Sullivan & Cromwell
125 Broad St.
New York, NY 10004
(212) 558-4000
Recruiting Director: Maria Alkiewicz

Weil Gotshal & Manges
767 5th Ave.
New York, NY 10153
(212) 310-8000
Recruiting Administrator: Donna Lang

White & Case
1155 Avenue of the Americas
New York, NY 10036
(212) 819-8200
Recruiting Director: Vera Murphy

Willkie Farr & Gallagher
153 E. 53rd St.
New York, NY 10022
(212) 821-8000
Recruiting Director: Ms. Billie Kelly

Wilson Elser Moskowitz Edelman & Dicker
150 E. 42nd St.
New York, NY 10017
(212) 490-3000
Recruiting Director: Eileen Loffredo

Connecticut Employers:

Cummings & Lockwood
4 Stamford Plaza
Stamford, CT 06904
(203) 327-1700
Recruiting Director: Agnes Kong

Day Berry and Howard
185 Asylum St.
Hartford, CT 06103
(203) 275-0100
Recruiting Director: Laurie LaBrec

Robinson and Cole
P.O. Box 10305
Stamford, CT 06904
(203) 964-1200
Recruiting Director: Susan Oehlsen

New Jersey Employers:

McCarter and English
4 Gateway Center, 100 Mulberry St.
Newark, NJ 07102
(201) 622-4444
Recruiting Director: Sherelyn Kilar

Pitney Hardin Kipp and Szuch
P.O. Box 1945
Morristown, NJ 07962
(201) 966-6300
Recruiting Director: Marylin O'Live

Wilentz Goldman and Spitzer
90 Woodbridge Center Drive
Woodbridge, NJ 07095
(908) 636-8000
Managing Administrative Partner:
Stephen Barcan

Management Consultants

WEB SITES:

Business Magazines
http://www.geocities.com/WallStreet/
2172/busperiod.htm

**Institute of Management and
Administration**
http://www.ioma.com

Management Consulting Online
http://www.cob.ohio-state.edu/~fin/jobs/
mco/mco.html

PROFESSIONAL ORGANIZATIONS:

For networking in management consult-
ing and related fields, check out the
following local professional organizations
listed in Chapter 5:
American Management Association
**Association of Management Consultants
  (ACME)**
Consultants' Network

For more information, you can contact:

American Institute of Management
P.O. Box 7039
Quincy, MA 02269
(617) 472-0277

American Marketing Association
http://www.ama.org/hmpage.htm
250 S. Wacker Drive, Suite 200
Chicago, IL 60606
(312) 648-0536

**Association of Management Consulting
Firms (ACME)**
521 5th Ave.
New York, NY 10175
(212) 697-9693

Institute of Management Consultants
521 5th Ave.
New York, NY 10175
(212) 697-9693

National Management Association
2210 Arbor Blvd.
Dayton, OH 45439
(937) 294-0421

PROFESSIONAL PUBLICATIONS:

Academy of Management Journal
Academy of Management Review
ACME Newsletter
Business Quarterly
Consultants News
Executive
Harvard Business Review
Management Review

DIRECTORIES:

*Consultants and Consulting Organizations
  Directory* (Gale Research, Detroit, MI)
Dun's Consultants Directory (Dun &
  Bradstreet, Parsippany, NY)
*Dun's Reference Book of Corporate
  Managements* (Dun's Marketing
  Services, Parsippany, NY)
Who's Who in Association Management
  (American Society of Association
  Executives, Washington, DC)

Employers:

APM Inc.
1675 Broadway, 18th Floor
New York, NY 10019
(212) 903-9300
Recruiting Coordinator: Doris Kiefer

American Management Systems
1 Chase Plaza
New York, NY 10005
(212) 612-3600

Andersen Consulting
1345 Avenue of the Americas
New York, NY 10105
(212) 708-4000

Aon Consulting
2 World Trade Center
New York, NY 10048
(212) 441-2000

Booz Allen & Hamilton
101 Park Ave.
New York, NY 10178
(212) 697-1900
Director of Human Resources: Lonnie Nam

Buck Consultants
2 Penn Plaza
New York, NY 10121
(212) 330-1000

Coopers & Lybrand
333 E. River Drive, Suite 400
E. Hartford, CT 06108
(860) 290-6809
Human Resources Manager: Rick Valeriay

Deloitte & Touche Consulting Group
2 World Financial Center
New York, NY 10281
(212) 436-2000

Eisner, Richard & Co.
575 Madison Ave.
New York, NY 10022
(212) 355-1700

Ernst & Young LLP
787 7th Ave.
New York, NY 10019
(212) 773-3000

Gemini Consulting
25 Airport Road
Morristown, NJ 07960
(201) 285-9000
Recruiting Manager: Jennifer Wines

IBM Consulting Group
Route 9, Town of Mount Pleasant
Sleepy Hollow, NY 10591
(914) 332-3811

Jaspan, Norman, Associates
60 E. 42nd St., Suite 1825
New York, NY 10165
(212) 687-4611
VP: Mr. York

Juran Institute
11 River Road
Wilton, CT 06892
(203) 834-1700

Kearney, A.T.
153 E. 53rd St.
New York, NY 10022
(212) 751-7040

Kepner-Tregoe
17 Research Road
Princeton, NJ 08542
(609) 921-2806
Human Resources Director: Angelique
Bizzarri

KPMG Peat Marwick-Management Consultants
65 E. 55th St.
New York, NY 10022
(212) 909-5000

McKinsey and Company
55 E. 52nd St.
New York, NY 10022
(212) 446-7000
Personnel Director: Jerome Vascellaro

Mercer Management Consulting Group
1166 Avenue of the Americas
New York, NY 10036
(212) 345-3400
VP: Kimberly Sullivan

Milliman & Robertson
2 Penn Plaza
New York, NY 10121
(212) 279-7166

Mitchell Madison Group
520 Madison Ave.
New York, NY 10022
(212) 372-9000

Price Waterhouse
1177 Avenue of the Americas
New York, NY 10036
(212) 596-7000
Contact Human Resources

RCG Information Technology
379 Thornall St.
Edison, NJ 08837
(908) 744-3500

Sedgwick Noble Lowndes
3 Becker Farm Road
Roseland, NJ 07068
(201) 533-4500

The Segal Company
1 Park Ave.
New York, NY 10016
(212) 251-5000

Stone & Webster Management Consultants
1 Penn Plaza
New York, NY 10119
(212) 290-7190
Recruiting: Lorraine Perrucci

Towers Perrin
335 Madison Ave.

New York, NY 10017
(212) 309-3400

Walsh-Lowe & Associates
47 Newark St.
Hoboken, NJ 07039
(202) 216-1100

Watson Wyatt Worldwide
461 5th Ave.
New York, NY 10017
(212) 725-7550

Werner International
11 Madison Ave.
New York, NY 10018
(212) 909-2160
VP: Mary O'Rourke

Market Research Firms

WEB SITES:

American Marketing Association
http://www.ama.org/

Direct Marketing Web
http://www.sme.com/dmweb/

PROFESSIONAL ORGANIZATIONS:

For networking in market research and related fields, check out the following local professional organizations listed in Chapter 5. Also see "Advertising Agencies" and "Public Relations."
American Marketing Association
Direct Marketing Association

For more information you can contact:

Council of American Survey Research Organizations
3 Upper Devon, Belle Terre
Port Jefferson, NY 11777
(516) 928-6954

Marketing Research Association
2189 Silas Deane Highway, Suite 5

Rocky Hill, CT 06067
(860) 257-4008

National Association of Market Developers
1422 W. Peachtree, NW, Suite 500
Atlanta, GA 30309
(404) 892-0444

Sales and Marketing Executives International
Statler Office Tower, No. 458
Cleveland, OH 44115
(216) 771-6650

PROFESSIONAL PUBLICATIONS:

Direct Marketing Magazine
Industrial Marketing
Journal of Marketing
Journal of Marketing Research
Marketing News
Marketing Review
Marketing and Media Decisions
Marketing Times
Potentials in Marketing
Sales & Marketing Management

DIRECTORIES:

American Marketing Association
  Membership Directory & Marketing
  Services
Guide (American Marketing Association,
  Chicago, IL)
*Bradford's Directory of Marketing Research
  Agencies* (Bradford Publishing Co.,
  Fairfax, VA)
*Handbook of Independent Advertising and
  Marketing Services* (Executive Commu-
  nications, Inc., New York, NY)
*International Membership Directory and
  Marketing Services Guide* (American
  Marketing Association, Chicago, IL)
Membership Roster (American Marketing
  Association, Chicago, IL)
*Multinational Marketing and Employment
  Directory* (World Trade Academy Press,
  Inc., New York, NY)

Employers:

Arbitron Company
142 W. 57th St.
New York, NY 10019
(212) 887-1300
Human Resources Manager: Kathy Ross/
Glen Hernandez; (410) 512-8000

BAI
580 White Plains Road
Tarrytown, NY 10591
(914) 332-5300
Senior VP: Claire Braverman

Datatab
49 E. 21st St.
New York, NY 10010
(212) 228-6800

FIND/SVP
625 6th Ave.
New York, NY 10011
(212) 645-4500
Human Resources Director: Kristi
Johnston

Jupiter Communications
627 Broadway
New York, NY 10003

(212) 780-6060
Research and consulting firm specializing
in emerging consumer on-line and
interactive technologies.

Langer Assoc.
19 W. 44th St., Suite 1600
New York, NY 10036
(212) 391-0350
Contact: AnnMarie Brogan

Mendelsohn Media Research
841 Broadway
New York, NY 10003
(212) 677-8100
VP: Joel Zeiler

Neilson Media Research
299 Park Ave.
New York, NY 10171
(212) 708-7500
Human Services Rep.: Carolyn Thomas

Research International
466 Lexington Ave., 8th Floor
New York, NY 10017
(212) 973-2300
Contact Human Resources

Roper Organization, The
205 E. 42nd St.
New York, NY 10017
(212) 599-0700
Office Manager: Sara Cintron

Scarborough Research
11 W. 42nd St.
New York, NY 10036
(212) 789-3560

Siemens Corporate Research
755 College Road
Princeton, NJ 08540
(609) 734-6500
Human Resources: Walter Pruiksma

Simmons Market Research Bureau
309 W. 49th St.
New York, NY 10019
(212)373-8900
VP, Director of Administration: Rebecca
Mcpheters

Tribeca Research
90 Hudson St.
New York, NY
(212)431-8700

USA Data
363 7th Ave.
New York, NY
(212) 967-3000

Yankelovich Partners
101 Merritt 7 Corporate Park
Norwalk, CT 06851
(203) 846-0100
Human Resources Director: Sally
Summerlin

Museums/Art Galleries

WEB SITES:

CultureFinder: The Internet Address for the Performing Arts
http://www.culturefinder.com/

Galleries & Museums Yellow Pages
http://www.imagesite.com/muse/
museylpgs.html

The Museum Professional
http://www.sirius.com/~robinson/
musprof.html

PROFESSIONAL ORGANIZATIONS:

To network about running museums and art galleries, you can contact the following local professional organizations listed in Chapter 5:
Art Information Center
Public Art Fund

For more information, you can contact:

American Association of Museums
1575 I St., NW, Suite 400
Washington, DC 20005
(202) 289-1818

American Federation of Arts
41 E. 65th St.
New York, NY 10021
(212) 988-7700

Arts and Business Council
121 W. 27th St.
New York, NY 10001
(212) 727-7146

Association of Art Museum Directors
41 E. 65th St.
New York, NY 10021
(212) 249-4423

International Foundation for Art Research
46 E. 70th St.
New York, NY 10021
(212) 879-1780

Institute for Contemporary Art
46-01 21st St.
Long Island City, NY 11101
(718) 784-2084

Museum Computer Network
8720 Georgia Ave., Suite 501
Silver Spring, MD 20910
(301) 585-4413

National Assembly of Local Art Agencies
1420 K St., NW, Suite 204
Washington, DC 20005
(202) 371-2830

Women's Caucus for Art
P.O. Box 2646
New York, NY
(212) 689-0563

PROFESSIONAL PUBLICATIONS:

Art Business Magazine
http://www.ffa.ucalgary.ca/artbusiness
Art Calendar
Artfocus
Art in America

Art & Design News
Art Education Journal
Art Issues
Art Now Gallery Guide
Arts 'n Crafts ShowGuide
Art World
Museum News

DIRECTORIES:

American Art Directory (Reed Elsevier Directories, New Providence, NJ)
Art in America Annual Guide to Galleries, Museums, Artists (Brant Publications, Inc. , New York, NY)

Art & Antique Dealers League of America, Membership Directory (Art & Antique Dealers League of America, New York, NY)
Art Business News Buyers Guide (Brant Art Publications, New York, NY)
National Directory of Arts Internships (National Network for Artist Placement, Los Angeles, CA)
Official Museum Directory (Reed Elsevier Directories, New Providence, NJ)
Who's Who in American Art (Reed Elsevier Directories, New Providence, NJ)

For art's sake

The least expensive club you can join, if you want to network with New York's business and cultural elite, is an art museum. You'll be invited to "openings" and members' nights, where, between sips of white wine, you can introduce yourself to descendants of Rockefellers, Fricks, Whitneys, and Vanderbilts; and the members' dining rooms are lovely places to entertain your friends and colleagues with reasonably priced food and drink amidst beautiful surroundings.

Museum Employers:

American Museum of Natural History
Central Park West at 79th St.
New York, NY 10024
(212) 769-5100
Contact Personnel

Bronx Museum of the Arts
1040 Grand Concourse at 165th St.
Bronx, NY 10456
(718) 681-6000
Executive Director: Jane Delgado

Brooklyn Museum
200 Eastern Parkway
Brooklyn, NY 11238
(718) 638-5000
Personnel Director: Jack Ryan

Cooper-Hewitt Museum
2 E. 91 St.
New York, NY 10128
(212) 860-6868
Personnel Director: Lorna Hannah

Frick Collection, The
1 E. 70th St.
New York, NY 10021
(212) 288-0700
Curator: Edgar Munhall

Guggenheim, Solomon R., Museum
1071 5th Ave.
New York, NY 10128
(212) 360-3500

Guggenheim Museum, SoHo
575 Broadway (at Prince St.)
Personnel Manager: Laura Price

Hayden Planetarium at the American Museum of Natural History
Central Park West at 79th St.
New York, NY 10024
(212) 769-5900
Contact Personnel
Part of the American Museum of Natural History.

International Center of Photography
1130 5th Ave.
New York, NY 10128
(212) 860-1777
Personnel Manager: Louis Beck

Jewish Museum, The
1109 5th Ave.
New York, NY 10128
(212) 423-3200
Curator: Susan Goodman

Metropolitan Museum of Art
1000 5th Ave.
New York, NY 10028
(212) 879-5500
Contact Employment Services

Museum of American Folk Art
2 Lincoln Square
New York, NY 10023
(212) 595-9533
Director: Gerard C. Wertkin

Museum of Modern Art
11 W. 53rd St.
New York, NY 10019
(212) 708-9400
Founded by Abby Aldrich Rockefeller, this museum houses one of the world's leading collections of 19th and 20th century painting and sculpture.
Director of Personnel: Camille Gargiso

Museum of New York City
103rd St. at 5th Ave.
New York, NY 10029
(212) 534-1672
Personnel Director: Debbie Washington

Museum of Television and Radio
25 W. 52nd St.

New York, NY 10019
(212) 621-6600
Director: Robert Batscha

Noguchi, Isamu, Museum
33rd Road and Vernon Blvd.
Long Island City, NY
(718) 204-7088
Personnel Director: Lawry Stone

Queens Museum
The New York City Building
Flushing Meadow-Corona Park
Flushing, NY 11368
(718) 592-2405
Exec. Director: Carma Fauntolroy

South Street Seaport Museum
207 Front St.
New York, NY 10038
(212) 669-9400
President: Peter Neal

Whitney Museum of American Art
945 Madison Ave.
New York, NY 10021
(212) 570-3600
Personnel Director: Hillary Blass

Art Gallery Employers:

Alexander, Brooke
59 Wooster St., 4th Floor
New York, NY 10012
(212) 925-4338
Contact: Carolyn Alexander

Artists' Space
38 Greene St., 3rd Floor
New York, NY 10013
(212) 226-3970
Contact: Austin Thomas

Boone, Mary
417 W. Broadway
New York, NY 10012
(212) 752-2929

Castelli, Leo, Gallery
420 W. Broadway
New York, NY 10012
(212) 431-5160
Director: Susan Brundage

Christie's Fine Art Auctioneers
55 E. 59th St.
New York, NY 10022
Mailing Address: 502 Park Ave.
New York, NY 10022
(212) 546-1000
Personnel Director: Martin Phillips

Cooper, Paula
155 Wooster St.
New York, NY 10012
(212) 674-0766
Gallery Director: Paula Cooper
Gallery also at 980 Madison Ave.

Dia Center for the Arts
542 W. 22nd St.
New York, NY 10011
(212) 989-5566
Contact Personnel Department

Emmerich, Andre, Gallery
41 E. 57th St.
New York, NY 10022
(212) 752-0124
Personnel: Contact Sotheby's personnel,
606-7000

Gagosian
980 Madison Ave.
New York, NY 10021
(212) 744-2313
Personnel: Melisssa Lazaroz
Gallery also at 136 Wooster St.

Marlborough
40 W. 57th St.

New York, NY 10019
(212) 541-4900
Administrator: John Helmrich

Pacewildenstein
32 E. 57th St.
New York, NY 10022
(212) 421-3292
Operations Director: Cay Rose
Gallery also at 142 Greene St.

Painewebber
1285 Avenue of the Americas
New York, NY 10019
(212) 713-2885

Sonnabend
420 W. Broadway
New York, NY 10012
(212) 966-6160

Sotheby Galleries
1334 York Ave.
New York, NY 10021
(212) 606-7000
Personnel Director: Daryl Krimsky

Sperone Westwater
142 Greene St.
New York, NY 10012
(212) 431-3685
Personnel Director: David Leiber

Weber, John
142 Greene St.
New York, NY 10012
(212) 691-5711

Oil/Gas/Plastics

WEB SITES:

Oil and Gas Journal
http://www.pennwell.com/ogj.html

OilNetwork
http://www.oilnetwork.com

PROFESSIONAL ORGANIZATIONS:

For networking in oil, gas, plastics, and related fields, check out the following local professional organizations listed in Chapter 5. Also see "Chemicals" and "Engineering."

American Institute of Chemical Engineers
Association of Consulting Chemists and Chemical Engineers
Plastic Soft Materials Manufacturers Association
Society of the Plastics Industry

For more information, you can contact:

American Gas Association
1515 Wilson Blvd.
Arlington, VA 22209
(703) 841-8400

American Petroleum Institute
1220 L St., NW
Washington, DC 20005
(202) 682-8000

Empire State Petroleum Association
33 W. Main St.
Elmsford, NY 10523
(203) 921-1975

New York Gas Group
500 5th Ave., Suite 1650
New York, NY 10110-0469
(212) 354-4790

Petroleum Industry Research Foundation
122 E. 42nd St.
New York, NY 10168
(212) 867-0052

Society of Plastics Engineers
14 Fairfield Drive
Brookfield, CT 06804
(203) 775-0471

Society of the Plastics Industry
1801 K St., NW, Suite 600
Washington, DC 20005
(202) 974-5200

PROFESSIONAL PUBLICATIONS:

Drilling Contractor
Engineering & Mining Journal
Gas Industries Magazine
Lundberg Letter
Modern Plastics
National Petroleum News
Oil Daily
Oil and Gas Journal
Petroleum Marketer
Pipeline
Plastics World
Solar Energy
Solar Today Magazine
World Oil

DIRECTORIES:

Energy Job Finder (Mainstream Access, New York, NY)
Gas Industry Training Directory (American Gas Association, Arlington, VA)
International Petroleum Encyclopedia (PennWell Publishing Co., Tulsa, OK)
Modern Plastics, Encyclopedia Issue (McGraw-Hill, New York, NY)
Oil and Gas Directory (Geophysical Directory, Inc., Houston, TX)
Plastics World, Directory Issue (PTN Publishing Co., Newton, MA)
Solar Electricity Today (PV Network News, Santa Fe, NM)
USA Oil Industry Directory (Penwell Books, Tulsa, OK)

Employers:

Acrilex Inc.
230 Culver Ave.
Jersey City, NJ 07305
(800) 222-4680
President: Harold Sarvetnick
Custom plastics fabrication.

AIN Plastics
P.O. Box 151
Mount Vernon. NY 10550
(914) 668-6800
Personnel Director: Adrian Bonfiglio

Amerada Hess
1185 Avenue of the Americas
New York, NY 10036
(212) 997-8500
Recruiting Director: Laurine Fox
Company headquarters.

Castle Oil Corp.
500 Mamaroneck Ave.
Harrison, NY 10528
(914) 381-6500
Personnel Director: Theresa Delgado

Chevron Companies
1325 Avenue of the Americas
New York, NY 10019
(212) 424-2400
Personnel in San Francisco Headquarters,
225 Bush St., San Francisco, CA 94104,
(415) 894-2552 (job holine)
One of the largest refiners and manufacturers of petroleum products in the
country.

Commerical Plastics and Supply
98-31 Jamaica Ave.
Richmond Hills, NY 11418
(212) 477-5000
Personnel Director: Tom Boney

Dande Plastics
216 North Ave.
Dunnellen, NJ 08812
(800) 448-8947
Personnel Director: Tom DeMateo

Eagle Plastics Corp.
45-31 Court Sq.
Long Island City, NY 11101
(718) 937-8000
Human Resources Director: Jerry Rocker

E&T Plastic Manufacturing Company
45-45 37th St.
Long Island City, NY 11101
(718) 729-6226
Plant Manager: Mr. Jan Gorski

Emco Industrial Plastics
24 Just Road
Fairfield, NJ 07004
(800) 292-9906
Personnel Director: Sandra Karchmas

Exxon Corp.
180 Park Ave.
Florham Park, NJ 07932
(201) 765-7000
The largest petroleum refiner and
manufacturer of pretroleum products in
the world.

Gary Plastic Packaging Corp.
770 Garrison Ave.
Bronx, NY 10474
(718) 893-2200
Human Resources: Mark Varela

GE Plastics
3135 Easton Turnpike
Fairfield, CT 06431
(203) 373-2211
Resumes to: Robert Muir, 1 Plastics Ave.,
Pittsfield, MA 01201

Getty Petroleum Corp.
125 Jericho Turnpike
Jericho, NY 11753
(516) 338-6000
Human Resources Director: Carol-Ann
Gaites

Goldmark Plastic Compounds
Nassau Terminal Road
New Hyde Park, NY 11040
(718) 343-7600

Heller, H., and Company
707 Westchester Ave.
White Plains, NY 10604
(914) 682-0010
Plastics suppliers, processors,
compounders, and distributers.
Human Resources Director: Joe Orlando

Hillside Industries
405 Park Ave.
New York, NY 10022
(212) 935-6090
Plastic products.

Innovative Plastics Corp.
400 Route 303
Orangeburg, NY 10962
(914) 359-7500

Just Plastics
250 Dyckman St.
New York, NY 10034
(212) 569-8500
Director of Personnel: Lois Vermann

Nichimen America
1345 6th Ave.
New York, NY 10105
(212) 698-5000
Director of Personnel: Gary Ferraro

Petro
55-60 58th St.
Msaspeth, NY 11378
(718) 628-3300
Director of Personnel: Patty Gilhooky,
(516) 686-1619

Streamline Plastics
1112 Brook Ave.
Bronx, NY 10456
(718) 588-1211
Personnel Director: Bea Bartner

Sunrise Plastics
124 57th St.
Brooklyn, NY 11220
(718) 492-6355
Personnel Director: Anna Pedri

Texaco, Inc.
2000 Westchester Ave.
White Plains, NY 10650
(914) 253-4000
Recruitment: Alida Davis
Major refiner and manufacturer of
petroleum products.

Paper and Allied Products

WEB SITES:

Pulp and Paper Net
http://www.pulpandpaper.net/

Technical Association of the Paper and Pulp Industry
http://www.tappi.org

PROFESSIONAL ORGANIZATIONS:

For more information about the paper industry, you can contact:

American Forest and Paper Association
1111 19th St. NW, Suite 1700
Washington, DC 20036
 (800) 878-8878

American Paper Institute
260 Madison Ave.
New York, NY 10016
(212) 340-0600

National Paper Trade Association
http://www.papertrade.com/
111 Great Neck Road, # 418
Great Neck, NY 11021
(516) 829-3070

New York Paper Merchants Association
185 Madison Ave.
New York, NY 10016
(212) 867-9660

Paper Industry Management Association
1699 Wall St., Suite 212
Mount Prospect, IL 60056
(847) 956-0250

Sales Association of the Paper Industry
P.O. Box 21926
Columbus, OH 43221
(614) 326-3911

Technical Association of the Pulp and Paper Industry
http://www.tappi.org/
Technology Park, Box 105113
Atlanta, GA 30348
(614) 446-1400

PROFESSIONAL PUBLICATIONS:

Good Packaging Magazine
Packaging
Paper Age
Paper Sales
Pulp and Paper

DIRECTORIES:

Directory of the Forest Products Industry
   (Miller Freeman Publications, San
   Francisco, CA)
International Pulp and Paper Directory
   (Miller Freeman, San Francisco, CA)
*Lockwood-Post's Directory of the Paper and
   Allied Trades* (Miller Freeman, New
   York, NY)
*Paper Industry Management Association
   Membership Directory* (Paper Industry
   Management Association, Mt. Prospect, IL)
Paper Yearbook (Harcourt Brace
   Jovanovich, New York, NY)
Pulp and Paper, Buyer's Guide Issue
   (Miller Freeman, San Francisco, CA)
*Walden's ABC Guide and Paper Production
   Yearbook* (Walden-Mott Corp., Ramsey, NJ)
Western Packaging Directory (Good
   Packaging Magazine, Pacific Trade
   Journals San Jose, CA)

Employers:

Champion International Paper
1 Champion Plaza
Stamford, CT 06921
(203) 358-7000
Manager, Human Resources: Kay Combs

Gilman Paper Co.
111 W. 50th St.
New York, NY 10020
(212) 246-3300
VP, Human Resources: John Faiella

Gould Paper Corp.
315 Park Ave. S.
New York, NY 10010
(212) 505-1000
Human Resources Director: Susan Cassola

Imperial Paper Box Corp.
252 Newport St.
Brooklyn, NY 11212
(718) 346-6100
Personnel Manager: Ms. Dee Harrison

International Paper Company
2 Manhattanville Road
Purchase, NY 10577
(914) 397-1500
Major manufacturer of paper and allied products.
VP, Human Resources Director: Robert Byrnes

Millar, George W., and Company
Division of Marquardt
161 Avenue of the Americas, 2nd Floor
New York, NY 10013
(212) 645-7200
Office Manager: Jerry St. John

New York Envelope Corporation
29-10 Hunters Point Ave.
Long Island City, NY 11101

(718) 786-0300
Plant Manager: Carl Mezella
Office Manager: Myrna Toboroff

Paper Corporation of U.S.
161 Avenue of the Americas
New York, NY 10013
(212) 645-5900
Personnel: Lee Nordstrom, (860) 298-3218

Royal Paper Corporation
185 Madison Ave.
New York, NY 10016
(212) 684-1200
Human Resources: Gloria Gregg, (610) 667-9210

Websource
Subsidiary of Alco Standard Corporation
161 Avenue of the Americas
New York, NY 10013
(212) 255-1600
Personnel Director: Maryann Daviou

Pharmaceuticals/Biotechnology

WEB SITES:

BIO on-line
http://www.bio.com

Bio-Space Career Center
http://www.biospace.com/career/

Pharmaceutical Information Network
http://pharminfo.com/pharmmall/
pm_hp.html

PROFESSIONAL ORGANIZATIONS:

For networking in the drug industry and
related fields, check out the following local
professional organizations listed in
Chapter 5:
Drug, Chemical and Allied Trades
  Association
New York Biotechnology Association

For additional information you can
contact:

American Foundation for
Pharmaceutical Education
1 Church St., Suite 202
Rockville, MD 20850
(301) 738-2160

American Pharmaceutical Association
2215 Constitution Ave., NW
Washington, DC 20037
(202) 628-4410

Biotechnology Industry Organization
1625 K St., NW, Suite 1100
Washington, DC 20006
(202) 857-0244

Connecticut Pharmaceutical Association
35 Cold Spring Road, Suite 125
Rocky Hill, CT 06067
(860) 563-4619

National Association of Pharmaceutical
Manufacturers
320 Old Country Road
Garden City, NY 11530
(516) 741-3699

National Wholesale Druggists' Association
1821 Michael Faraday Drive
Reston, VA 22090
(703) 787-0000

New Jersey Pharmacists Association
38 Maurlin Drive
Robbinsville, NJ 08691
(609) 394-5596

Pharmaceutical Manufacturers Association
1100 15th St., NW
Washington, DC 20005
(202) 835-3400

Pharmaceutical Research and
Manufacturers of America
1100 15th St., NW, Suite 900
Washington, DC 20005
(202) 835-3400

Pharmaceutical Society of the State of
New York
Pine W. Plaza IV
Washington Ave. Extension
Albany, NY 12205
(800) 632-8822

PROFESSIONAL PUBLICATIONS:

American Druggist
Bio/Technology
Biotechnology Business
Drug Store News
Drug Topics
Journal of Pharmaceutical Marketing and
  Management
Journal of Pharmaceutical Sciences &
  Technology
Pharmaceutical Executive
PMA Newsletter

DIRECTORIES:

Biotechnology in the U.S. Pharmaceutical
  Industry (Oryx Press, St. Paul, MN)
Directory of Custom Pharmaceutical
  Manufacturers (Delphi Marketing
  Services Inc., New York, NY)

Directory of Drug Store & HBC Chains
 (Chain Store Guide Information
 Services, Tampa, FL)
National Association of Chain Drugstores
 (NACDS) Membership Directory
 (National Association of Chain
 Drugstores, Arlington, VA)
National Wholesale Druggists Association
 (NWDA) Membership & Executive
 Directory (National Wholesale Druggists
 Association, Reston, VA)
Pharmaceutical Manufacturers of the U.S.
 (Noyes Data Corp., Park Ridge, NJ)
Pharmaceutical Marketers Directory (CPS
 Communications, Boca Raton, FL)

New York Employers:

Altana, Inc.
60 Baylis Road
Melville, NY 11747
(516) 454-7677
Contact Human Resources

Bristol-Myers Squibb Co.
345 Park Ave.
New York, NY 10154
(212) 546-4000
Human Resources Department: Julie
Mark

Carter-Wallace
1345 Avenue of the Americas
New York, NY 10105
(212) 339-5000
Director of Human Resources: Anastasia
Kehoe
Company headquarters.

Ciba Specialty Chemicals
540 White Plains Rd.
Tarrytown, NY 10591
(914) 785-2000
VP, Human Resources: Stanlet Kose

Circa Pharmaceutical
33 Ralph Ave.
Copiague, NY 11726
(516) 842-8383
Personnel Director: Angela DeRosa

Del Pharmaceuticals
163 E. Bethpage Road
Plainview, NY 11803
(516) 844-2020
Personnel Director: Charles Schneck

Dupont Pharmaceuticals
1000 Stewart Ave.
Garden City, NY 11530
(516) 832-2210
Personnel Director: Barbara Mandello

Enzo Biochem
60 Executive Blvd.
Farmingdale, NY 11735
(516) 755-5500, (800) 221-7705
Personnel Director: Debbie Sonner

Forest Laboratories
909 3rd Ave.
New York, NY 10022
(212) 421-7850
Director of Human Resources: Bernard
McGovern

ImClone Systems
100 Varick St.
New York, NY 10014
(212) 645-1405
Personnel Director: Lisa Camony

Lederle Laboratories
Division of American Cyanamid
401 N. Middletown Road
Pearl River, NY 10965
(914) 732-5000
Personnel Manager: Dave Barnhill

Marlop Pharmaceuticals
5704 Mosholu Ave.
Bronx, NY 10471
(718) 796-1570
President: Ruben Delgado

Novartis Corp.
608 5th Ave.
New York, NY 10020
(212) 307-1122
Human Resources: (908) 277-5000

Pfizer, Inc.
235 E. 42nd St.
New York, NY 10017
(212) 573-2323, ext. 4150 (jobline)

Regeneron Pharmaceuticals
777 Old Saw Mill River Road, Suite 10
Tarrytown, NY 10591
(914) 347-7000
Personnel Director: Vicki Gaddy

Taro Pharmaceuticals USA
5 Skyline Drive
Hawthorne, NY 10532
(914) 345-9001
Director of Human Resources: Bernard J.
Schoenfeld

Connecticut Employers:

Boehringer Ingelheim Pharmaceuticals
900 Ridgebay Rd.
Ridgefield, CT 06877
(203) 798-9988
Director of Human Resources: Ms. Sandie
Nikituk

Frederick, Purdue Co.
100 Connecticut Ave.
Norwalk, CT 06850
(203) 853-0123
Sr. Personnel Director: Danielle Nelson

International Biotechnologies
4 Science Park West
New Haven, CT 06511
(203) 786-5600
Personnel Director: Hector Chavez

New Jersey Employers:

American Home Products
5 Giralda Farms
Madison, NJ 07470
(973) 83-2000
Personnel Director: Anne Schram

Bio-Technology General Corp.
70 Wood Ave. S.
Iselin, NJ 08830
(908) 632-8800
Personnel Director: Leah Berkovits

Hoechst-Roussel Pharmaceuticals
30 Independence Blvd.
Warren, NJ 07059
(908) 231-2000
Director of Human Resources: Antonette
D'Angelo

Hoffman-La Roche
340 Kingsland St.
Nutley, NJ 07110
(201) 235-5000
Director of Human Resources: Al Vinson

Johnson and Johnson
1 J&J Plaza
New Brunswick, NJ 08933
(908) 524-0400
Contact Recruitment Office

Merck and Company
P.O. Box 100
White House Station, NJ 08889
(908) 423-1000
Resumes to Personnel Department

Novartis Pharmacueticals
59 Route 10
E. Hanover, NJ 07936
(201) 503-7500
Director of Human Resources: Joe Sebra

Ortho Biotech
700 Route 202 S.
Raritan, NJ 08869
(908) 704-5000
Personnel Director: Marilyn Thompson

Ortho-McNeil Pharmaceutical
US Route 202
Raritan, NJ 08869
(908) 218-6000
Contact recruitment office at Johnson and
Johnson

Schering Corp.
2000 Gallopin Hill Road
Kenilworth, NJ 07033
(908) 298-4000
VP: Mary Duffy

Warner-Lambert
201 Tabor Road

Morris Plains, NJ 07950
(201) 540-2000
VP, Human Resources: Mr. Kees Hulstein

Whitehall Laboratories
Division of American Home Products
5 Giralda Farms

Madison, NJ 07940
(212) 878-5500 (New York City number)

Zenith Laboratories
140 LeGrand Ave.
Northvale, NJ 07647
(201) 767-1700
Personnel Director: Winifred Stavros

Printing

WEB SITES:

American Printer Online
http://www.americanprinter.com/

DesignSphere Online
http://www.dsphere.net/

PROFESSIONAL ORGANIZATIONS:

For networking in printing and related
fields, check out the following local
professional organizations listed in
Chapter 5:
Association of Graphic Arts
Graphic Arts Professionals
International Association of Printing
    House Craftsmen, NY Chapter
Type Directors Club
Women in Production

For more information, you can contact:

International Association of Graphic
Arts Professionals
84 Park Ave.
Flemington, NJ 08822
(908) 782-4635

National Association of Printers and
Lithographers
780 Palisade Ave.
Teaneck, NJ 07666
(201) 342-0700

Printing Industries of America
100 Daingerfield Road
Alexandria, VA 22314
(703) 519-8100

Printing Industry of Connecticut
P.O. Box 144
Milford, CT 06460
(203) 874-6793

Technical Association of the Graphic Arts
68 Lomb Memorial Drive
Rochester, NY 14623
(716) 475-7470

PROFESSIONAL PUBLICATIONS:

American Printer
Graphic Arts Monthly
Print
Printing Impressions
Printing News
Who's Printing What

DIRECTORIES:

Blue Book of Printing and Graphic Arts Buyers,
    The (A.F. Lewis & Co., New York, NY)
Design Firms Directory (Wefler and
    Associates, Evanston, IL)
Graphic Arts Monthly, Printing Industry
    Sourcebook (Cahners Magazines, New
    York, NY)
Printing Industry Goldbook (North American
    Publishing Co., Philadelphia, PA)
Typographers Directory (American
    Business Directories, Omaha, NE)

Employers:

Allied Printing
280 Midland Ave.
Saddle Brook, NJ 07663
(201) 794-0400
Personnel Director: Robert Masucci
Newspapers and circulars.

American Bank Note
200 Park Ave., 49th Fl.
New York, NY 10166
(212) 582-9200
Engraving and printing of foreign
currency.

American Standard
1 Centennial Ave.
Piscataway, NJ 08855
(908) 980-6000
Personnel Director: John Adams

Applied Graphics Technology
463 Barell Ave.
Carlstadt, NJ 07072
(201) 935-3200
Human Resources Dept.: Lori Force

Berlin & Jones Company
2 E. Union Ave.
E. Rutherford, NJ 07070
(201) 933-5900
Contact: Walter Lypowi

Blumberg, Julius
62 White St.
New York, NY 10013
(212) 431-5000
Human Resources Manager: Jerry Mason
Legal printers.

Bowne and Company
345 Hudson St.
New York, NY 10014
(212) 924-5500
Personnel Director: Cathy Bristow
Financial and corporate printing.

Coronet Graphics
250 Hudson St.
New York, NY 10013
(212) 727-3666
Vice President: Moses Elkaim

Danbury Printing and Lithogrpahy
1 Prindle Lane
Danbury, CT 06811
(203) 792-5500
Personnel Director: Frances Winfree

Depthography
122 E. 27th St.
New York, NY 10016
(212) 679-8101
Manufacturer of 3-D animated images,
products, and art.

Donnelly, R.R., and Sons
75 Park Pl.
New York, NY 10007
(212) 233-9600
Human Resources Coordinator: Nancy
Cortez
Books, magazines, catalogs, and tabloids.

Enquire Printing
47-15 33rd St.
Long Island City, NY 11101
(212) 581-5050
Direct mail, books, newspapers, catalogs,
and financial printing.

Gibson, C.R., Company
225 5th Ave.
New York, NY 10010
(212) 532-0420

Ivy Hill Corp.
375 Husdon St., 7th Floor
New York, NY 10014
(212) 741-1404
Offset lithographer
Personnel: Maureen Cordero

Kinko's Copies
16 E. 16th St., 2nd Floor
New York, NY 10003
(212) 254-2399

Lehigh Press
11 Penn Plaza, 5th Floor
New York, NY 10001
(212) 946-2605
Resumes to: Tom Walker, East Coast
Sales Mgr.

Meehan Tooker
25 E. Union Ave.
E. Rutherford, NJ 07073
(201) 933-9600
Human Resources Director: Diane
Caivano
Office also in NYC.

Miller Printing
225 Varick St.
New York, NY 10014
(212) 929-0344
Personnel Director: Mitchell Krantz

National Envelope Corp.
99 Kero Road
Carlstadt, NJ 07072
(201) 935-9400
Personnel Director: John Pachon
Office also in NYC.

New York Copy Center
204 E. 11 St.
New York, NY 10003
(212) 673-5628
Digital output, image scanning, OCR
conversion, offset printing.

Photo Comp Press
408 West St.
New York, NY 10014
(212) 675-0606

Sales Manager: Nels Anthony
Offset printing.

Thebault, L.P., Company
249 Pomeroy Road
Parsippany, NJ 07054
(201) 884-1300
Personnel Director: Mike Konnopinsky
Office also in NYC.

Wilson, H.W., and Company
950 University Ave.
Bronx, NY 10452
(718) 563-1060
Personnel Director: Harold Regan
Book printing.

World Color Press
1155 6th Ave., 11th Floor
New York, NY 10036
(212) 354-3355
Offset, gravure, and letterpress.
Personnel: (203) 532-4200

Public Relations

WEB SITES:

Public Relations Online Resources and Organizations
http://www.impulse-research.com/
impulse/resource.html

Public Relations Society of America
http://www.prsa.org/

PROFESSIONAL ORGANIZATIONS:

For networking in public relations and related fields, check out the following local professional organization listed in Chapter 5. Also see "Advertising Agencies" and "Market Research Firms."
Public Relations Society of America

For more information, you can contact:

Women Executives in Public Relations
P.O. Box 609
Westport, CT 06881
(203) 226-4947

Women in Communications
10605 Judicial Drive Suite A-4
Arlington, VA 22004
(703) 920-5555

PROFESSIONAL PUBLICATIONS:

Communication World
Inside PR
O'Dwyer's PR Services Report
PR Reporter
Promo Magazine
Public Relations Journal
Public Relations News
Publicist

DIRECTORIES:

Bacon's Publicity Checker (Bacon's Publishing Company, Chicago, IL)
National Directory of Corporate Public Affairs (Columbia Books, Washington, DC)
O'Dwyer's Directory of Public Relations Firms (J.R. O'Dwyer Co., New York, NY)

Public Relations Career Directory (Gale Research, Detroit, MI)
Public Relations Journal, Register Issue (Public Relations Society of America, New York, NY)
Who's Who in P.R. (P.R. Publishing Co., Exeter, NH)

New York Employers:

Burson-Marsteller
230 Park Ave. S.
New York, NY 10003-1566
(212) 614-4000
Contact: Maria Fornario

Cohn & Wolfe
225 Park Ave. S., 17th Floor
New York, NY 10003
(212) 598-3600
Office Manager: Milly Bach

Creamer Dickson Basford
350 Hudson St.
New York, NY 10014
(212) 367-6800
Personnel Director: Maria Tassone

Dewe Rogerson
850 3rd Ave.
New York, NY 10022
(212) 688-6840

Dorf & Stanton Communications
111 5th Ave., 3rd Fl.
New York, NY 10003
(212) 420-8100

Edelman, Daniel J.
1500 Broadway, 33rd Floor
New York, NY 10036
(212) 768-0550
Contact Personnel

Factor, Mallory, Inc.
555 Madison Ave., 27th Floor
New York, NY 10022
(212) 350-0000
Contact: Michael Cassady

Fleishman-Hillard
1330 Avenue of the Americas
New York, NY 10019
(212) 265-9150
Director of Administration: Joann Divito

GCI Group
777 3rd Ave.
New York, NY 10017
(212) 546-2200
Contact: Dan Relton

Georgeson & Company
88 Pine St., Wall Street Plaza
New York, NY 10005
(212) 440-9800
Personnel Dept.: Delores Phlan

Gibbs & Soell
600 3rd Ave.
New York, NY 10016
(212) 697-2600
Personnel Director: Lillie Clarke

Hill and Knowlton
466 Lexington Ave., 3rd Floor
New York, NY 10017
(212) 885-0300
Human Resources Recruiter: Gladys
Maddon

KCSA Public Relations
800 2nd Ave., 5th Floor
New York, NY 10017
(212) 682-6300
Managing Partner: Joe Mansi

Ketchum Public Relations
220 E. 42nd St.
New York, NY 10017
(212) 878-4600
Office Manager: Merle Leung-Chung

King, D.F., & Co.
77 Water St.
New York, NY 10005
(212) 269-5550
VP: Frank Spina

Klores, Dan, Associates
386 Park Ave. S.
New York, NY 10016

(212) 685-4300
Personnel Director: Stacey Krinsky

Lobsenz-Stevens
460 Park Ave. S., 11th Floor
New York, NY 10016
(212) 684-6300
Office Manager: Ruth Ost

Makovsky & Co.
575 Lexington Ave.
New York, NY 10022
(212) 508-9600
Human Resources: Mary Tompkins

Manning, Selvage and Lee
79 Madison Ave.
New York, NY 10016
(212) 213-0909
Personnel Manager: Miriam Coleman

Marston, Robert, and Associates
485 Madison Ave.
New York, NY 10022
(212) 371-2200
Human Resources: Collene Byrnes

Morgen-Walke Associates
380 Lexington Ave
New York, NY 10168
(212) 850-5600
Human Resources Director: Riva Gruen

Ogilvy Adams and Reinhart
708 3rd Ave.
New York, NY 10017
(212) 880-5200
Personnel Director: Alisa Brussel

Porter/Novelli
437 Madison Ave.
New York, NY 10022
(212) 872-8000
Recruiter: Jackie Herman

Robinson, Lake, Sawyer, Miller
Bozell Public Relations
640 Fifth Ave.
New York, NY 10019
(212) 445-8100
Human Resources Director: Lisa Welsh

Rowland Co.
1675 Broadway
New York, NY 10019
(212) 527-8800

Rubenstein, Howard J., Associates
1345 Avenue of the Americas
New York, NY 10105
(212) 489-6900
Human Resources: Robbin Jordan

Ruder Finn
301 E. 57th St.
New York, NY 10022
(212) 593-6400

Shandwick USA
111 5th Ave.
New York, NY 10003
(212) 420-8100

Softness Group, The
381 Park Ave. S.
New York, NY 10016
(212) 696-2444
Personnel Director: Cathy Peck

Connecticut Employers:

Block & Nardizi
1 Stamford Landing
Stamford, CT 06902
(203) 969-1311
Office Manager: Lisa Martragono

Martin, Peter, Associates
1200 High Ridge Road
Stamford, CT 06905
(203) 322-4700

New Jersey Employers:

MCS
86 Summit Ave.
Summit, NJ 07901
(908) 273-9626
Office Manager: Janice Karlen

MWW/Stretegic Communications
1 Meadowlands Plaza, 6th Floor
E. Rutherford, NJ 07073
(201) 507-9500
Office Manager: Denise Masanko

Publishers, Book/Literary Agents

WEB SITES:

Acq Web's Directory of Publishers and Vendors
http://www.library.vanderbilt.edu/law/acqs/pubr.html#links

American Booksellers Association
http://www.bookweb.org/aba

The Inkspot: Resources for Writers
http://www.inkspot.com/

Writers Guild of America List of Agents and Agencies
http://www.wga.org/agency.html

PROFESSIONAL ORGANIZATIONS:

For networking in book publishing and related fields, check out the following local professional organizations listed in Chapter 5. Also see "Publishers, Magazine and Newspapers."
Association of Authors' Representatives
Association of Business Publishers
Publishers Publicity Association
Women's National Book Association

For additional information, you can contact:

American Booksellers Association
http://www.bookweb.org/aba
828 S. Broadway
Tarrytown, NY 10591
(914) 591-2665

Association of American Publishers
71 5th Ave.
New York, NY 10003
(212) 255-0200

Book Industry Study Group
160 5th Ave.
New York, NY 10010
(212) 929-1393

National Association of Independent Publishers
P.O. Box 430
Highland City, FL 33846
(941) 648-4420

National Directory Publishing Association
http://www.idpa.org
c/o Warren Publishing
02115 Ward Court, NW
Washington, DC 20037
(202) 342-0250

Periodical and Book Association of America
120 E. 34th St., Suite 7-K
New York, NY 10016
(212) 689-4952

Women's National Book Association
160 5th Ave., Room 604
New York, NY 10010
(212) 675-7805

PROFESSIONAL PUBLICATIONS:

American Bookseller
Columbia Journalism Review, The
Editor and Publisher
http://www.mediainfo.com/ephome/
Folio
Library Journal
Literary Market Place
Multimedia Week
Publishers Weekly
Publishing Essentials
Publishing & Production Executive
Publishing Systems
Small Press
Writer's Digest

DIRECTORIES:

American Book Trade Directory (Reed Elsevier Directories, New Providence, NJ)
Editor and Publisher International Yearbook (Editor and Publisher, New York, NY)

Literary Agents of North America (Author/ Aid Research Associates., New York, NY)

Literary Market Place (Reed Elsevier Directories, New Providence, NJ)

Publisher's Directory (Gale Research, Detroit, MI)

Publishers, Distributors, and Wholesalers of the United States (Reed Elsevier Directories, New Providence, NJ)

Small Press Center Directory (Small Press Center, New York, NY)

Writer's Market (F&W Publications, Cincinnati, OH)

New York Employers, Book Publishers:

(Literary Agents list follows.)

Avon Books
Division of Hearst Corporation
1350 Avenue of the Americas
New York, NY 10019
(212) 261-6800
Asst. Personnel Director: Cecile Grant

Bantam Doubleday Dell
1540 Broadway
New York,NY 10036
(212) 354-6500
Director of Personnel: Robert Sherwood
Trade publisher. Imprints include
Delacorte Press and Delta Books.

Barrons Educational Series
250 Wireless Blvd.
Happaugue, NY 11788
(516) 434-3311
Personnel Director: Dan Panessa
Educational and business publisher.

Bender, Matthew, & Company
2 Park Ave.
New York, NY 10016
(212) 448-2000
Personnel Director: Marie Mann
Publisher of law-related titles.

Cambridge University Press
40 W. 20th St.
New York, NY 10011
(212) 924-3900
Personnel Director: Carol New

Columbia University Press
562 W.113th St.
New York, NY 10025
(212) 666-1000
Human Resources Director: Grace
Dronzek, 136 S. Broadway, Irvington, NY
10533, (914) 591-9111

Dekker, Marcel
270 Madison Ave.
New York, NY 10016
(212) 696-9000
Personnel Director: Jennifer Foo

Elsevier Science
655 Avenue of the Americas
New York, NY 10010
(212) 989-5800
Personnel Director: Linda Stone
Technical and scientific books.

Facts on File
11 Penn Plaza, 15th Floor
New York, NY 10001
(212) 967-8800
Personnel Director: Rhonda Shahin

Harlequin/Silhouette Books
300 E. 42nd St.
New York, NY 10017
(212) 682-6080
Personnel Director: Linda Kleinman
Romance fiction publishers.

HarperCollins Publishers
10 E. 53rd St.
New York, NY 10022
(212) 207-7000
Trade publisher.

Hearst Books Group
1350 Avenue of the Americas
New York, NY 10019
(212) 261-6500

Holt, Henry, and Co.
115 W. 18th St.
New York, NY 10011
(212) 886-9200
Personnel Director: Maria Ferrel

Macmillan Publishing Co.
1230 Avenue of the Americas
New York, NY 10020

(212) 698-7000
Call (212) 698-7136 for name of appropriate division contact.
Trade publisher. Imprints include Atheneum, Charles Scribner's Sons, Four Winds Press, Dillon Press, New Discovery, Schirmer Books, and Collier Books.

McGraw-Hill
1221 Avenue of the Americas
New York, NY 10020
(212) 512-2000
Placement Specialist: Denise Scheer
Trade publisher. Divisions include Osborne/McGraw-Hill and TAB Books.

Morrow, William
1350 6th Ave.
New York, NY 10019
(212) 261-6500

New York Law Publishing Company
345 Park Ave. S.
New York, NY 10016
(212) 779-9200
Law books, CD-ROMs, legal newsletters, periodicals, and other products on everything from criminal law to multimedia, torts to Internet and on-line law.

New York University Press
70 Washington Square S.
New York, NY 10003
(212) 998-2575

Oxford University Press
198 Madison
New York, NY 10016
(212) 726-6000
Personnel Director: Nancy O'Connor

Pearson Inc.
30 Rockefeller Plaza, 5th Fl.
New York, NY 10020
(212) 713-1919

Penguin USA
375 Hudson St.
New York, NY 10014
(212) 366-2000
Personnel Manager: Shelly Sadler
Imprints include Dial Books, Dutton, and Viking.

Plenum Publishing
233 Spring St.
New York, NY 10013
(212) 620-8000
Personnel Director: Veronica Gallwey

Putnam Berkely Group, The
200 Madison Ave.
New York, NY 10016
(212) 951-8800
Personnel Director: Grace Schlemm

Random House
201 E. 50th St.
New York, NY 10022
(212) 751-2600
Contact Human Resources
Imprints include: Alfred A. Knopf, Ballantine, Crown, Del Rey, Fawcett, Pantheon, Clarkson N. Potter, Times Books, Villard, and Vintage.

Reader's Digest General Books
261 Madison Ave.
New York, NY 10016
(212) 907-6671
Human Resources Director: Kathy Marshall (914) 244-5877
Trade publisher.

St. Martin's Press
175 5th Ave.
New York, NY 10010
(212) 674-5151
Personnel Director: Carolyn Jensen

Schirmer, G., Inc. and Associated Music Publishers
257 Park Ave. S.
New York, NY
(212) 254-2100
Biographies, catalogs, program notes, performance calendars, news, and repertory for a variety of music functions.

Scholastic
555 Broadway
New York, NY 10012
(212) 343-6100
Director of Human Resources: Jan Lorimer
Educational publisher.

Simon and Schuster
1230 Avenue of the Americas
New York, NY 10020
(212) 698-7000
Call (212) 698-7136 for name of appropriate division contact.
Leading trade publisher. Imprints include Paramount, Pocket Books, Prentice Hall, and Silver Burdett Press.

Sterling Publishing Company
387 Park Ave. S.
New York, NY 10016
(212) 532-7160
Editorial Director: John Woodside

Van Nostrand Reinhold
115 5th Ave.
New York, NY 10003
(212) 254-3232
Personnel Manager: Amy Walen
Trade publisher.

Warner Books
1271 Avenue of the Americas
New York, NY 10020
(212) 522-7200
Personnel Director: Ann Cruz

Wiley, John, and Sons
605 3rd Ave.
New York, NY 10158
(212) 850-6000
Director of Staffing and Training: Linne Salisbury
Trade and educational publisher.

Connecticut Employers, Book Publishers:

Thompson Corporation
1 Station Place
Stamford, CT 06902
(203) 969-8700
Human Resources Director: Mr. T. Hoffman

New Jersey Employers, Book Publishers:

Bowker, R.R., Co. (Reed Publishing)
121 Chanlon Road

New Providence, NJ 07974
(908) 464-6800
VP, Human Resources: Ilene Purelis
Publishes books, magazines, and related media such as *Publishers Weekly, Literary Market Place, Books in Print,* and *Library Journal.*

Peterson's Guides
P.O. Box 2123
Princeton, NJ 08543
(609) 243-9111
VP, Human Resources: Thomas McGee

Employers, Literary Agents:

Borchardt, Georges
136 E. 57th St.
New York, NY 10022
(212) 753-5785
Contact: Ann Borchardt

Brandt and Brandt Literary Agents
1501 Broadway
New York, NY 10036
(212) 840-5760
Personnel Manager: Gabe Szabo

Brown, Curtis, Ltd.
10 Astor Place
New York, NY 10330
(212) 473-5400
Office Manager: Elizabeth Knowlton
Literary and dramatic agents.

Carlton, Royce, Inc.
866 UN Plaza
New York, NY 10017
(212) 355-3210
Contact: Lucy Lepage
Agents and managers for lectures, lecture brokerage services, teleconferencing, and performing arts.

Donadio, Candida, and Ashworth
121 W. 27th St., Suite 704
New York, NY 10001
(212) 691-8077
Contact: Neil Olson

International Creative Management
40 W. 57th St.

New York, NY 10019
(212) 556-5600
Director of Operations/Personnel:
Andrew Suss

International Management Group (IMG)
22 E. 71st. St
New York, NY 10021
(212) 772-8900
Human Resources Director: Deborah Dash

Janklow, Nesbit Associates
598 Madison Ave.
New York, NY 10022
(212) 421-1700
Office Manager: Alice Drucker

Markson, Elaine, Literary Agency
44 Greenwich Ave.
New York, NY 10011
(212) 243-8480
Contact: Elaine Markson

Miller, Peter, Agency
Subsidiary of Lion Entertainment
132 W. 22nd St., 12th Fl.
New York, NY 10011
(212) 929-1222
Contact: Peter Miller

Morris, William, Agency
1325 Avenue of the Americas
New York, NY 10019
(212) 586-5100
Personnel Director: Ms. Pat Galloway

Sterling Lord Agency
65 Bleecker St.
New York, NY 10012
(212) 780-6050

Writers and Artists Agency
19 W. 44th St., Suite 1000
New York, NY 10036
(212) 391-1112
Personnel Director: Alyssa Tullin

Publishers, Magazine and Newspaper

WEB SITES:

Acq Web's Directory of Publishers and Vendors
http://www.library.vanderbilt.edu/law/acqs/pubr.html#links

The Inkspot: Resources for Writers
http://www.inkspot.com/

Journalism-Related Job Openings
http://eb.journ.latech.edu/jobs/jobs_home.html

Virtually all large companies, as well as major newspapers, magazines, and reference publishers, have an electronic publishing division. Check out the homepage of the publication or business of interest to learn about their electronic division.

PROFESSIONAL ORGANIZATIONS:

For networking in the magazine and newspaper publishing business, check out

the following local professional organizations listed in Chapter 5. Also see "Broadcasting" and "Publishers, Book/Literary Agents."
American Society of Composers, Authors and Publishers (ASCAP)
American Society of Magazine Editors
Magazine Publishers Association
Multimedia Publishers Group
Newswomen's Club of New York
New York Association of Black Journalists

For additional information, you can contact:

Association of American Publishers
71 5th Ave.
New York, NY 10003
(212) 255-0200

Electronic Publishers Association
609 Pacific Ave. , #204
Santa Cruz, CA 95060
(408) 423-8580

Magazine Publishers of America
919 3rd Ave., 22nd Floor
New York, NY 10022
(212) 872-3700

National Association of Independent Publishers
P.O. Box 430
Highland City, FL 33846
(941) 648-4420

National Directory Publishing Association
http://www.idpa.org
c/o Warren Publishing
02115 Ward Court, NW
Washington, DC 20037
(202) 342-0250

National Newspaper Association
1525 Wilson Blvd.
Arlington, VA 22209
(703) 907-7900

Newsletter Publishers Association
1501 Wilson Blvd., Suite 509
Arlington, VA 22209
(703) 527-2333

Newspaper Features Council
37 Arch St.
Greenwich, CT 06830
(203) 661-3386

Periodical and Book Association of America
120 E. 34th St., Suite 7-K
New York, NY 10016
(212) 689-4952

Society of Professional Journalists
16 S. Jackson
Greencastle, IN 46135
(317) 653-3333

Suburban Newspapers of America
401 N. Michigan Ave.
Chicago, IL 60611
(312) 644-6610

Writers Guild of America, East
555 W. 57th St.
New York, NY 10019
(212) 767-7800

PROFESSIONAL PUBLICATIONS:

Columbia Journalism Review, The
Editor and Publisher
http://www.mediainfo.com/ephome/
Folio
Literary Market Place
Multimedia Week
Publishing Essentials
Publishing & Production Executive
Publishing Systems
Writer's Digest

DIRECTORIES:

American Newspaper Representatives Directory of Community Newspapers (American Newspaper Representatives Inc., Troy, MI)
Bacon's Newspaper/Magazine Directory (Bacon's Information International, Ltd., Chicago, IL)
Editor and Publisher International Yearbook (Editor and Publisher, New York, NY)
Gale Directory of Publications and Broadcast Media (Gale Research, Inc., Detroit, MI)
Literary Market Place (Reed Elsevier Directories, New Providence, NJ)
Magazine Career Directory (Gale Research, Detroit, MI)
Newspapers Career Directory (Gale Research, Detroit, MI)
New York Publicity Outlets (Public Relations Plus, Washington Depot, CT)
Oxbridge Directory of Magazines (Oxbridge Communications, New York, NY)
Oxbridge Directory of Newsletters (Oxbridge Communications, Inc., New York, NY)
Publisher's Directory (Gale Research, Detroit, MI)
Publishers, Distributors, and Wholesalers of the United States (Reed Elsevier Directories, New Providence, NJ)
Standard Periodical Directory (Oxbridge Communications, Inc., New York, NY)

Ulrich's International Periodicals Directory (Reed Elsevier Directories, New Providence, NJ)

Writer's Market (F&W Publications, Cincinnati, OH)

New magazines mean new jobs

Times Mirror is contemplating a new men's outdoor adventure title with a tentative launch date in early 1999, and "we'd obviously be doing a lot of hiring," according to one VP. Hearst Magazines is planning a women's financial magazine entitled *Money Minded*. McGraw Hill is waiting for the green light on a small business spin-off of *Business Week*, and The American Express Publishing Company, managed by Time Inc., is set to launch its new quarterly title, *Travel & Leisure Golf*. A new weekly tabloid magazine on the Internet industry is on the horizon for early 1998, to be published by the International Data Group.

Magazine Employers:

Archie Comics Publishers
325 Fayette Ave.
Mamaroneck, NY 10543
(914) 381-5155
Send resumes to individual departments of interest.

Billboard Publications
1515 Broadway
New York, NY 10036
(212) 764-7300
Personnel Manager: Deborah Kahlstrom

Bride's Magazine
140 E. 45th St.
New York, NY 10017
(212) 880-8800
Editor: Millie Martini Bratten

Business Week
McGraw-Hill Building
1221 Avenue of the Americas
New York, NY 10020
(212) 512-2000
Managing Editor: Mark Morrison

Conde Nast Publications
360 Madison Ave.
New York, NY 10017
(212) 371-1330
Publisher of a broad range of nationally distributed magazines: *Vanity Fair, Vogue, Glamour, Self,* and *Gentleman's Quarterly.*

Consumers Union of US
101 Truman Ave.
Yonkers, NY 10703
(914) 378-2000
Human Resources Director: Richard Lustig
Publishers of *Consumer Reports* magazine.

Cosmopolitan
224 W. 57th St.
New York, NY 10019
(212) 649-2000
Editor: Helen Gurley Brown
Monthly magazine with features on glamour, fashion, and women's issues.

Country Living
224 W. 57th St., 10th Floor
New York, NY 10019
(212) 649-2000
Contact Human Resources

Crain's NY Business
220 E. 42nd St.
New York, NY 10017
(212) 210-0277
Editor: Greg David

DC Comics Group
1700 Broadway
New York, NY 10019
(212) 636-5400
Personnel Director: Vivian Ayala, 1345 6th
Ave., New York, NY 10019

Detour
34 W. 22nd St., 23rd Floor
New York, NY 10010
(212) 675-3680
Bureau Chief: Long Hguyen
Entertainment and style.

Esquire
250 W. 55th St., 8th Floor
New York, NY 10019
(212) 649-4020
Managing Editor: Linda Nardi

Essence
1500 Broadway
New York, NY 10036
(212) 642-0600
Editor: Susan Taylor

Family Circle
110 5th Ave.
New York, NY 10011
(212) 499-2000
VP, Human Resources: Kathy Cashion

Field and Stream
2 Park Ave.
New York, NY 10016
(212) 779-5000
Editor: Duncan Barnes

Food and Wine
1120 6th Ave.
New York, NY 10036
(212) 382-5600
Editor: Dana Cowin

Forbes Magazine
60 5th Ave.

New York, NY 10011
(212) 620-2200
Editor: James Michaels

Fortune
Time & Life Building
Rockefeller Center
New York, NY 10020
(212) 522-1212
Contact Human Resources

Gentlemen's Quarterly
350 Madison Ave.
New York, NY 10017
(212) 880-8800
Editor: Arthur Cooper

George
1633 Broadway
New York, NY 10019
(212) 767-6100
Executive Editor: Elizabeth Mitchell

Geyer-McCallister Publications
51 Madison Ave.
New York, NY 10010
(212) 689-4411
Personnel Director: Katherine Nicra

Glamour
350 Madison Ave.
New York, NY 10017
(212) 880-8800
Editor: Ruth Whitney

Golf Magazine
2 Park Ave.
New York, NY 10016
(212) 779-5000
Editor: George Peper

Harper's
666 Broadway, 11th Floor
New York, NY 10012
(212) 614-6500
Managing Editor: Ellen Rosenbush

Harper's Bazaar
1700 Broadway
New York, NY 10019
(212) 903-5000
Editor: Elizabeth Tilberis

Hearst Corporation
224 W. 57th St.
New York, NY 10019
(212) 649-2000
Human Resources Director: Ruth Diem

House Beautiful
1700 Broadway
New York, NY 10019
(212) 903-5000
Editor: Louis Oliver Gropp

Jane
1025 Lexington Ave.
New York, NY
(212) 772-7710
Editor-in-Chief: Jane Pratt

Ladies Home Journal
125 Park Ave.
New York, NY 10017
(212) 557-6600
Editor: Myrna Blyth

LIFE
Time & Life Building
Rockefeller Center
New York, NY 10020
(212) 522-1212
Editor: Jay Lovinger

Mademoiselle
350 Madison Ave.
New York, NY 10017
(212) 880-8800
Managing Editor: Faye Haun

Marvel Entertainment Group
387 Park Ave. S.
New York, NY 10016
(212) 696-0808
Human Resources: Mary Sprowls

Maxim
1040 6th Ave.
New York, NY 10018
(212) 302-2626
Editor-in-Chief: Clare McHugh
Men's magazine.

McCall's
375 Lexington Ave.

New York, NY 10017
(212) 499-2000
Editor: Sally Koslow

Mirabella
1633 Broadway
New York, NY 10019
(212) 767-6000
Eidtor in Chief: Roberta Myers

Modern Bride
249 W. 17th St.
New York, NY 10011
(212) 462-3400
Editor: Cele Lalli

Money
Time Life Building, Rockefeller Center
New York, NY 10020
(212) 522-1212
Editor: Frank Lalli

Ms. Magazine
135 W. 50th St.
New York, NY 10020
(212) 445-6100
Personnel: Barbara Lane

Nation, The
72 5th Ave.
New York, NY 10011
(212) 242-8400
Contact Human Resources

New Woman
2 Park Ave.
New York, NY 10016
(212) 251-1500
Editor in Chief: Betsy Carter

New York Magazine
444 Madison Ave.
New York, NY 10022
(212) 880-0700
Editor: Caroline Miller

New Yorker, The
20 W. 43rd St.
New York, NY 10036
(212) 840-3800
Personnel Director: Anthony Pisano

Newsweek
251 W. 57th St.
New York, NY 10019
(212) 445-4000
Human Resources Director: Jean Varish

Notorious
37 E. 28th St., Suite 906
New York, NY 10016
(212) 759-4554
Executive Editor: Scott Baldinger
Entertainment magazine.

Oneworld
73 Spring St., Suite 501
New York, NY 10012
(212)941-1325
Publisher: John Pasmore

Outdoor Life
2 Park Ave.
New York, NY 10016
(212) 779-5000
Editor: Todd Smith

Paper
365 Broadway
New York, NY 10013
(212) 226-5929
Associate Publisher: Sharon Phair
New York living.

Parade Publications
711 3rd Ave.
New York, NY 10017
(212) 450-7000
Human Resources Director: Carol Unger

Parents Magazine
375 Lexington Ave.
New York, NY 10017
(212) 499-2209
Editor-in-Chief: Ann Murphy

People
Time and Life Building
1271 Avenue of the Americas
New York, NY 10020
(212) 522-1212
Editor: Carol Wallace

Popular Photography
1633 Broadway
New York, NY 10019
(212) 767-6000
Editor: Jason Schneider

Popular Science
2 Park Ave.
New York, NY 10016
(212) 779-5000
Editor: Fred Abatemarco

Premiere
1633 Broadway, 41st Fl.
New York, NY 10016
(212) 767-6000
Managing Editor: Howard Karen

Psychology Today
49 E. 21st St., 11th Floor
New York, NY 10010
(212) 260-7210
Managing Editor: Lisa Dagliantori

Reader's Digest Association
Reader's Digest Road
Pleasantville, NY 10570
(914) 238-1000
Human Resources Director: Kathy
Marshall

Redbook
224 W. 57th St.
New York, NY 10019
(212) 649-2000
Editor: Kate White

Rolling Stone
1290 6th Ave.
New York, NY 10104
(212) 484-1616
Human Resources Director: Pam Fox

Sassy
230 Park Ave.
New York, NY 10169
(212) 935-9151
Editor in Chief: Jane Pratt

Scholastic Magazines
555 Broadway
New York, NY 10012

(212) 343-6100
Personnel: Jan Lorimer

Scientific American
415 Madison Ave.
New York, NY 10017
(212) 754-0550
Editor: John Rennie

Self
350 Madison Ave.
New York, NY 10017
(212) 880-8834
Editor: Rochelle Udeii

Seventeen
850 3rd Ave.
New York, NY 10022
(212) 407-9700
Managing Editor: Michelle Wolf

Sports Illustrated
1271 Avenue of the Americas
New York, NY 10020
(212) 522-1212
Managing Editor: Bill Colson

Swing
342 Madison Ave., Suite 1402
New York, NY 10017
(212) 490-0525
Executive Editor: Megan Liberman
Magazine for 20-something generation.

Time
Time & Life Building
Rockefeller Center
New York, NY 10020
(212) 522-1212
Managing Editor: Walter Isaacson

Town and Country
1700 Broadway
New York, NY 10019
(212) 903-5000
Managing Editor: Susan Jenett Bleecker

Travel & Leisure
1120 Avenue of the Americas
New York, NY 10036
(212) 382-5600
Editor: Nancy Novoerod

TV Guide
1211 6th Ave.
New York, NY 10036
(212) 852-7500
Managing Editor: Jack Curry

U.S. News & World Report
599 Lexington Ave.
New York, NY 10022
(212) 326-5350
Editor: Richard Thompson

Vanity Fair
Conde Nast
350 Madison Ave.
New York, NY 10017
(212) 880-8800
Editor: E. Graydon Carter

Vogue
350 Madison Ave.
New York, NY 10019
(212) 880-8800
Editor: Anna Wintour

Woman's Day
1633 Broadway
New York, NY 10019
(212) 767-6000
Editor: Jane Chestnut

Working Woman
135 W. 50th St., 16th Floor
New York, NY 10020
(212) 445-6100
Editor: Nancy Smith

Ziff Davis Publishing Company
1 Park Ave.
New York, NY 10016
(212) 503-3500
Ziff-Davis publishes a variety of computer magazines including *PC Computers*, *PC Week*, and *Macuser*.

Newspaper Employers, New York:

Barron's Financial Weekly
200 Liberty St.
New York,NY 10281
(212) 416-2700
Contact: Edwin Finn Jr.

China Daily Distribution
One World Trade Center, Suite 3369
New York, NY 10048
(212) 488-9677
Contact: Lingling Sun
The only English-language daily paper
from China with business and financial
information.

Crain Communications
220 E. 42nd St.
New York, NY 10017
(212) 210-0100
Contact: Kevin McCullough
Trade publisher and business newspapers.

El-Diario Prensa
143-155 Varick St.
New York, NY 10013
(212) 807-4600
Personnel Manager: Elisha Piaeyro
Newspapers for the Spanish-speaking
population of New York.

Gannett Westchester Newspapers
1 Gannett Drive

White Plains, NY 10604
(914) 694-9300
News Editor: Toni Davenport
Chain of suburban newspapers.

Investor's Business Daily
19 W. 44th St., Suite 804
New York, NY 10036
(212) 626-7676
Contact: Sharon Scott

The Jewish Post of New York
130 W. 29th St.
New York, NY 10001
(212) 967-7313
Publisher: Henry J. Levy

New York Daily News
450 W. 33rd St., 3rd Floor
New York, NY 10001
(212) 210-2100
Human Resources: Franz Martin
Mass circulation newspaper that publishes
Manhattan, Queens, and Long Island
editions.

Getting the scoop on a newspaper career

Jeff Canning was a high school student when he began
working part time for the Gannett Westchester newspaper
chain. He enjoyed the work so much that he returned to
Gannett Westchester after serving in the armed forces.
Today, Canning serves as a senior news editor for the chain.
We asked him about his career path in the news business.

"I've done everything from cub reporter to working the
copy desk to serving as the chief of the metro desk," says
Canning. "Now I'm a senior news editor. The important
thing is that each time I made a move, I became more
valuable to the company or any company that would have
hired me."

Canning offers the following advice to people who want
to break into the news business. "I always tell young
people who express an interest in the business to do two
things: get some writing samples together—even if they are
only articles in a school or community newspaper—

anything to show you can handle the English language. Then, try to gain some work experience. College newspapers, local weekly suburban newspapers, and local feature magazines are sometimes understaffed and willing to give newcomers a try.

"When you begin looking for a full-time job, hit every publication in the area. It's a good idea to send your resume to the news editor instead of the managing editor or editor-in-chief. The latter are certainly good choices, but if a paper has a senior news editor, he or she may not receive as much mail as other editors on staff. News editors will usually forward any resumes to the proper people, along with a personal note.

"After you've been working for at least a year, you can consider moving around. Most newspapers like to see two to three years' experience in one area, and some positions require as much as five to seven years' experience. Keep that in mind if you get tired of covering a beat you really don't like. You have to pay your dues. When you are ready to move, you can check trade journals like *Editor and Publisher,* although they list primarily entry-level jobs. Your contacts and word of mouth will get you the jobs you really want. So make networking one of your priorities right from the beginning."

New York Newsday
235 Pinelawn Road
Melville, NY 11747
(516) 843-2020
Managing Editor: Howard Schneider
Long Island's leading daily newspaper.

New York Post
210 South St.
New York, NY 10002
(212) 815-8000

New York Press
295 Lafayette St.
New York, NY 10012
(212) 941-1130
Editor: Russ Smith

New York Times, The
229 W. 43rd St.
New York, NY 10036
(212) 556-1234
Jobline: (212) 556-1383
Managing Editor: Gene Roberts
The most respected New York daily newspaper.

Resident Publications
215 Lexington Ave, 13th Floor
New York, NY 10016
(212) 679-4970
Editor in Chief: Karen Smilk
Uptown, Downtown, Eastside, and Westside weeklies.

Staten Island Advance
950 Fingerboard Road
Staten Island, NY 10305
(718) 981-1234
Editor: Arthur Silverstein

Village Voice
36 Cooper Sq.
New York, NY 10003
(212) 475-3300
Personnel Administrator: Terry West
Weekly newspaper covering the arts and
local feature news.

Wall Street Journal
200 Liberty St., Tower A
New York, NY 10281
(212) 416-2000
Contact Employee Relations
Business newspaper published Monday
through Friday.

Newspaper Employers, Connecticut:

Connecticut Post
410 State St.
Bridgeport, CT 06604
(203) 333-0161
Managing Editor: Michael Daly

Danbury News Times
333 Main St.
Danbury, CT 06810
(203) 744-5100
Managing Editor: Paul Steinmetz

Newspaper Employers, New Jersey:

Bergen Record
150 River St.
Hackensack, NJ 07601
(201) 646-4000, (212) 279-8484
Editor: Vivian Waixel

Newark Star–Ledger
1 Star Ledger Plaza
Newark, NJ 07102
(201) 877-4141
Managing Editor: Charles Harrison

**News Services and
Feature Syndicates, Employers:**

Associated Press
50 Rockefeller Plaza
New York, NY 10020
(212) 621-1500
Contact Human Relations

Dow Jones & Company
Harbor Side Financial Center
600 Plaza 2
Jersey City, NJ
(212) 416-2471
Human Resources Director: Susan Phipps

Entertainment News Syndicate
P.O. Box 20481
Dag Hammarskjold Communications
Center
New York, NY 10017
(212) 223-1821
Editor-in-Chief: Robert Michael

Fairchild News Syndicate
7 W. 34th St.
New York, NY 10001
(212) 630-4000
Director of Human Resources: Sharon
Thorn

Global Information Network
275 7th Ave., Rm. 1206
New York, NY 10001
(212) 647-0123
Executive Editor: Lisa Vives

Hearst Newspapers
224 W. 57th St.
New York, NY 10019
(212) 649-2000
Contact Recruiting

Knight-Ridder Financial News Service
75 Wall St., 22nd Floor
New York, NY 10005
(212) 269-1110
Employment Manager: Julie Brown

Reuters America
1700 Broadway
New York, NY 10019
(212) 603-3300
Contact Human Resources

United Media Enterprises
200 Madison Ave., 4th Floor
New York, NY 10016
(212) 293-8500

News feature service. Owners of Newspaper Enterprise Association and United Feature Syndicate.

United Feature Syndicate
200 Madison Ave., 4th Floor
New York, NY 10016
(212) 293-8500
Human Resources Director: Carol Gershowitz

Real Estate

WEB SITES:

HomeNet
http://www.intertel.com/resident/
homepage.htm

Real Jobs
http://www.real-jobs.com/

Real estate agencies in New York City
http://www.nyrealty.com/

PROFESSIONAL ORGANIZATIONS:

To learn more about the real estate industry, you can contact the following local professional organizations listed in Chapter 5:
Bronx Board of Realtors
Institute of Real Estate Management
Long Island Board of Realtors

For more information, you can contact:

American Association of Certified Appraisers
800 Compton Road
Cincinnati, OH 45231
(513) 729-1400

American Society of Appraisers
535 Herndon Pkwy.
Herndon, VA 22070
(202) 478-2228

Building Owners and Managers
Association of Greater New York
11 Penn Plaza, Suite 1000
New York, NY 10001
(212) 239-3662

International Real Estate Institute
8383 E. Evans Road
Scottsdale, AZ 85260
(602) 998-8267

National Association of Realtors
http://www.realtor.com
430 N. Michigan Ave.
Chicago, IL 60611
(312) 329-8200

Women's Council of Realtors
430 N. Michigan Ave.
Chicago, IL 60611
(312) 329-8483

PROFESSIONAL PUBLICATIONS:

Appraiser News
Journal of Property Management
Journal of Real Estate Research
Mortgage Banking
National Real Estate Investor
Opportunities in Property Management
Real Estate Issues
Real Estate News
Real Estate Review
Real Estate Technology

http://www.brigadoon.com/newstand/ret/
Real Estate Today
Realty and Building

DIRECTORIES:

American Society of Real Estate Counselors
Directory (ASREC, Chicago, IL)
Directory of Certified Residential Brokers
(Retail National Marketing Institute,
Chicago, IL)
National Association of Real Estate
Appraisers-Directory of Members (Assn.
of Real Estate Appraisers, Phoenix, AZ)
National Real Estate Directory (Real Estate
Publications, Tampa FL)
National Real Estate Investor, Directory
Issue (Communications Channels Inc.,
Atlanta, GA)
National Roster of Realtors (Stamats
Communications, Cedar Rapids, IA)
Opportunities in Real Estate (VGM Career
Horizons, Lincolnwood, IL)
Real Estate Investments Directory (Ameri-
can Business Directories, Omaha, NB)
Real Estate Sourcebook (Reed Publishing,
Wilmette, IL)

Employers:

Adams and Company Real Estate
411 5th Ave.
New York, NY 10016
(212) 679-5500
Controller: Martin Radwell
Commercial management, leasing,
appraisals, consulting, and sales.

Axiom Real Estate Management
55 E. 59th St.
New York, NY 10022
(212) 759-9700
Human Resources: Laura Gifford

Brown Harris Stevens
71 Vanderbilt Ave.
New York, NY 10169
(212) 692-7400
Luxury homes and estates.

Century 21 of the Northeast
1 World Trade Center, #8735
New York, NY 10048
(800) 477-6628
Personnel Director: Carolyn Sullivan
Commercial and residential real estate
brokers.

Location, location, location

Bob Billingsley is a partner in a firm that leases office space
in Midtown Manhattan. We talked with him recently about
getting started in commercial real estate. "Leasing commercial real estate in New York is a very tough business," says
Billingsley. "You don't make any money during your first year
or two in the business. There's a very high attrition rate.

"But if you stick with it, you can make more money than
your peers in other fields ever dreamed of. Six-figure
incomes are not uncommon among people who have been
in the business only five years.

"At our firm, we don't hire people right out of school; we
look for people with some experience in the business world
and in real estate. But many of the larger firms will hire
recent grads and train them. In fact, some large firms have
formal training programs.

"If you're a young person just starting out, I'd suggest getting a job with a bigger firm. Then be like a blotter—soak up everything they can teach you. After a few years, reevaluate your position with the company. The problem with the bigger firms is that they sometimes tend to ignore you once they've trained you. In a smaller firm, the senior people see more of a relationship between your success and the overall success of the company. Also, there's a lot of competition within a large firm. It's easy to get lost in the shuffle."

We asked Billingsley what qualifications are needed to succeed in commercial real estate. "You have to be tough because you'll face a certain amount of rejection. You have to be hungry because this is an extremely competitive business. A college degree is helpful, but it isn't required. This business is basically sales—getting out and seeing people, convincing them that your skills and knowledge are up to snuff. When you're just starting out, it's also very important to have a mentor in the company—someone to help you and look out for you."

Century Paramount Assoc.
235 W. 46th St.
New York, NY 10036
(212) 764-5500
Human Resources: Lauren Brock

Chase Manhattan Bank
Commercial Real Estate Division
101 Park Ave.
New York, NY 10178
(212) 907-6000

Citibank
Real Estate Division
599 Lexington Ave.
New York, NY 10043
(212) 559-7249
Human Resources: Patti Mittelman

Colliers ABR
40 E. 52nd St.
New York, NY 10022
(212) 318-9716

Corcoran Group
645 Madison Ave.
New York, NY 10022
(212) 355-3550
Personnel Director: Ellen Rosenfeld

Cushman and Wakefield
51 W. 52nd St.
New York, NY 10019
(212) 841-7500
Employment Supervisor: Melissa Madden

Douglas Elliman Gibbons and Ives
575 Madison Ave.
New York, NY 10022
(212) 891-7000
Director, Human Resources: Joyce Sponholz
Sales and leasing of residential and commercial properties. Along with management, insurance, appraisals, and consulting.

Galbreath Co.
437 Madison Ave.
New York, NY 10022
(212) 644-7040

Garfield, Leslie J., & Company
654 Madison Ave.
New York, NY 10022
(212) 371-8200
Residential, commercial, and institutional
buildings.

Garrick-Aug Worldwide
360 Lexington Ave., 4th Floor
New York, NY 10017
(212) 557-9090
General Manager: Mr. Lee Stand

Gordon, Edward S.
200 Park Ave.
New York, NY 10166
(212) 984-8000
Human Resources: Dawn Groh

Green, S. L.
70 W. 36th St.
New York, NY 1008
(212) 594-2700
Human Resources: Linda Quinlan

Greenthal, Charles H., and Company
4 Park Ave.
New York, NY 10016
(212) 340-9300
Personnel Director: Barbara Rosenberg
Real estate management, sales, and
brokerage. Conversion specialists.

Greiner-Maltz Company
42-12 28th St.
Long Island City, NY 11101
(718) 786-5050
Personnel Director: Lisa Marino
Commercial properties, including
factories, warehouses, offices, sites, and
stores.

Grubb and Ellis Company
55 E. 59th St.
New York, NY 10022
(212) 838-2000
Contact Human Resources

Commercial and residential properties
and brokerage.

Hekemian and Co.
505 Main St.
Hackensack, NJ 07601
(201) 487-1500
Personnel Director: Renie Wilman

Helmsley Enterprises
60 E. 42nd St.
New York, NY 10165
(212) 687-6400
Commercial leasing, mortgages, appraisals, consulting, sales, and insurance.

James Lang Wooton USA
101 E. 52nd St.
New York, NY 10022
(212) 688-8181

Koll
140 E. 45th St.
New York, NY 10017
(212) 986-7878
Human Resources: Joe Owad

La Salle Partners
220 E. 42nd St.
New York, NY 10017
(212) 661-6161
Human Resources: Diana Torres

Mason, Alice F., Ltd.
635 Madison Ave., 14th Floor
New York, NY 10022
(212) 832-8870
Office Manager: Dominique Richard
Cooperatives, luxury rentals, town houses,
and furnished sublets.

Mendik Realty Co.
330 Madison Ave.
New York, NY 10017
(212) 557-1100
Human Resources: Sondra Berger

Newmark & Co. Real Estate
125 Park Ave.
New York, NY 10017
(212) 372-2000
Human Resources: Bruce Fuller

Pembrook Management
767 5th Ave.
New York, NY 10153
(212) 207-0200
Human Resources: Jeanine Mannow,
421-8200

Resnick, Jack, & Sons
110 E. 59th St.
New York, NY 10022
(212) 421-1300
Human Resources: Sherri Saturn

Rockefeller Group, The
1221 Avenue of the Americas
New York, NY 10020
(212) 698 8500
Employment Manager: Louise Ippolito
Real estate developers.

Sopher, J.I., and Company
425 E. 61st St.
New York, NY 10021
(212) 486-7000
Manager: Uval Greenblatt
Luxury apartment rental and sales agency.

Sylvan Lawrence and Company
100 William St.
New York, NY 10038
(212) 344-0044
Chief Financial Director: Barry
Aronowsky
Consulting, brokerage, and management
of commercial space.

Trump Organization
765 5th Ave.
New York, NY 10022
(212) 832-2000
Personnel Director: Rona Graff

Walters and Samuel
419 Park Ave. S.
New York, NY 10016
(212) 685-6200
Office Manager: Elena Zweisach

White, William A., Grubb and Ellis
55 E. 59th St.
New York, NY 10022
(212) 759-9700
Personnel Director: Virginia Bermo

Williams and Company
530 5th Ave.
New York, NY 10036
(212) 704-3500
Director of Operations: David Wolf
Managing agents of more than 200
commercial buildings.

Williamson Pickett Gross
85 John St.
New York, NY 10038
(212) 233-6810
Human Resources: Naomi Shafiroff

Retailers/Wholesalers

WEB SITES:

Internet Business Solutions
http://www.inetbiz.com/market

Merchandising Technologies
http://www.merchtech.com/

PROFESSIONAL ORGANIZATIONS:

For networking in retailing and wholesaling, check out the following local professional organizations listed in Chapter 5:
Apparel Guild
Retail, Wholesale and Department Store Union
For more information, you can contact:

General Merchandise Distributors Council
1275 Lake Plaza Drive
Colorado Springs, CO 80906
(719)576-4260

Manufacturers' Agents National Association
23016 Mill Creek Road
Laguna Hills, CA 92654
(714) 859-4040

National Association of Convenience Stores
1605 King St.
Alexandria, VA 22314
(703) 684-3600

National Retail Federation
325 7th St., NW, Suite 1000
Washington, DC 20004
(202) 783-7971

Wholesale Distributors Association
10875 Plano Road, Suite 115
Dallas, TX 75238
(214) 349-7100

PROFESSIONAL PUBLICATIONS:

Chain Store Age
Chain Store Age Executive
College Store Executive
Inside Retailing
Journal of Retailing
Merchandising
Merchant Magazine
Store Planning
Stores
Women's Wear Daily

DIRECTORIES:

American Wholesalers and Distributors Directory (Gale Research, Inc., Detroit, MI)
Convenience Stores Directory (American Business Directories, Omaha, NB)
Convenience Stores Membership Directory (National Association of Convenience Stores, Alexandria, VA)
Directory of Department Stores & Mail Order Firms (Chain Store Guide Information, Tampa, FL)
Directory of High Volume Independent Drug Stores (Chain Store Guide Information, Tampa, FL)
Directory of Major Malls (Directory of Major Malls, Inc., Spring Valley, NY)
National Association of Chain Drug Stores Membership Directory (National Association of Chain Drug Stores, Alexandria, VA)
Plunkett's Retail Industry Almanac (Plunkett Research, Ltd., Galveston, TX)
Sheldon's Major Stores and Chains (Phelon, Sheldon & Marsar, Inc., Fairview, NJ)
Sheldon's Retail Directory of the U.S. and Canada (PS & H, Inc., New York, NY)

Employers:

Abraham and Strauss
Division of Federated Department Stores
422 Fulton St.
Brooklyn, NY 11201
(718) 802-7500

American Retail Group
1114 Avenue of the Americas
New York, NY 10036
(212) 704-5300
Personnel Director: Steve Salk,
(770) 662-2816

Ann Taylor, Inc.
142 W. 57th St.
New York, NY 10019
(212) 541-3300
Director, Executive Placement: Susan
Vandow
Women's clothing chain.

Arden, Elizabeth
691 5th Ave.
New York, NY 10022
(212) 546-0200
Manager: Leah Zamuchansky
Women's specialty retail store chain.

Associated Merchandising Corp.
1440 Broadway
New York, NY 10001
(212) 596-4000
RecruitmentL Barbara Dugan

Barnes and Noble
120 5th Ave.
New York, NY 10003
(212) 633-3300
VP, Human Resources: Michelle Smith

Barney's, Inc.
575 5th Ave.
New York, NY 10017
(212) 450-8300
Corporate Recruiter: Clara Lopez
Women's and men's specialty retail store
chain.

Bendel, Henri
712 5th Ave.

New York, NY 10019
(212) 247-1100
Manager, Human Resources: Kathleen
Fitzgerald
Women's apparel retailer.

Bergdorf Goodman
754 5th Ave.
New York, NY 10019
(212) 872-8706
Personnel Rep.: Nicole Phillips
Apparel store catering to upper-income
customers.

Bloomingdale's
Division of Federated Department Stores
Lexington Ave. at 59th St.
New York, NY 10022
(212) 705-2000
Personnel Services: Margaret Hofbek
Major department store chain.

Bolton's
317 Madison Ave.
New York, NY 10017
(212) 557-5370
Personnel Director: Leah Dweck
Women's retailer.

Brittania Sportswear
1411 Broadway
New York, NY 10018
(212) 921-0060
Personnel Director: Dave Koons
Apparel manufacturer and wholesaler.

Brooks Brothers
346 Madison Ave., 8th Floor
New York, NY 10017
(212) 682-8800
VP, Human Resources: Elizabeth Wood
Men's and women's apparel retailer
known for its conservative, upper-income
clientele.

Bulova Corporation
1 Bulova Ave.
Woodside, NY 11377
(718) 204-3300
Personnel Director: Eleanor Smith

Burlington Coat Factory
263 W. 38th St.
New York, NY 10018
(212) 221-0010
Human Resources Director: Sara Orleck,
1830 Route 130, Burlington, NJ 08016

Cartier, Inc.
653 Fifth Ave.
New York, NY 10022
(212) 753-0111
Personnel Director: Ms. Teri Schaffer
Retailer of jewelry, silverware, crystal,
watches and clocks, stationery, gifts, and
china.

Century 21 Department Store
22 Cortlandt St.
New York, NY 10007
(212) 227-9092

Charivari Ltd.
2307 Broadway
New York, NY 10024
(212) 362-1212
Personnel Director: Howard Burner
Women's and men's specialty stores.

Chaus, Bernard, Inc.
1410 Broadway
New York, NY 10018
(212) 354-1280
Human Resources Director: Robin
Sancelia, (201) 863-4646

Coach Leatherware Company
516 W. 34th St.
New York, NY 10001
(212) 594-1850
VP, Human Resources: Maxine Fechter

Crew, J., Inc.
770 Broadway
New York, NY 10003
(212) 209-2500

Dalton, B, Bookseller
105 5th Ave.
New York, NY 10003
(212) 633-3300
VP, Human Resources: Michelle Smith,
(516) 338-8000

Farmhouse
860 Broadway
New York, NY 10003
(212) 477-9400
Personnel Director: Joseph Keller, Jr.
Discount department store chain.
Operates 41 stores in several states.

Filene's Basement
620 Avenue of the Americas
New York, NY
(212) 620-3100

Fortunoff
1300 Old Country Road
Westbury, NY 11590
(516) 832-1520
Executive Recruiter: Robyn Ornstein

G and G Shops
Division of Petrie Stores
520 8th Ave., 4th Floor
New York, NY 10018
(212) 279-4961
Personnel Director: Barbara McGregor
Women's specialty store. Operates a total
of 85 stores.

Garan, Inc.
350 5th Ave.
New York, NY 10118
(212) 563-2000
Personnel Director: Dana Therese
Apparel wholesaler.

Grand Union Co.
201 Willowbrook Blvd.
Wayne, NJ 07470
(201) 890-6000
Corporate VP, Personnel: Gil Vuolo
Large supermarket chain.

Great Atlantic and Pacific Tea Co.
2 Paragon Drive
Montvale, NJ 07645
(201) 930-4416
Manager Personnel Employment: Corinne
Blake
Major food retail chain.

Kinney Shoe Corporation
233 Broadway
New York, NY 10279
(212) 720-3700
VP, Human Resources: John Kozlowski
Women's specialty store chain that
operates 283 junior apparel stores
throughout the United States.

Lauren, Ralph, International Corp.
650 Madison, 6th Floor
New York, NY 10022
(212) 318-7000
Director of Recruiting: Michelle Prest

Lerner New York
460 W. 33rd St., 5th Floor
New York, NY 10001
(212) 736-1222
Director of Recruitment: Chris Grant
Women's and children's apparel retailer.
Operates 792 stores nationwide.

Loehmanns' Inc.
2500 Halsey St.
Bronx, NY 10461
(718) 409-2000
VP, Human Resources: Linda Merker

Lord and Taylor
424 5th Ave.
New York, NY 10018
(212) 382-7800
Personnel Director: Ned Fitch

Macy, R.H., and Company
151 W. 34th St.
New York, NY 10001
(212) 695-4400
Corporate headquarters for the Macy's
chain, which operates 17 stores in several
states.

Modell's
3424 Vernon Blvd.
Long Island City, NY 11106
(212) 822-1000
Personnel Director: Phylis Fietel
Discount sportswear. Operates 18 retail
outlets.

Neiman Marcus
Maple and Paulding Ave.
White Plains, NY 10601
(914) 428-2000
Human Resources Director: Rose Bennett

Petrie Stores Corp.
150 Meadowland Pkwy.
Secaucus, NJ 07094
(201) 866-3600
Senior VP, Human Resources: Tom
Bennett

Rolex Watch USA
665 5th Ave.
New York, NY 10022
(212) 758-7700
Personnel Director: Bob Krish

Saks Fifth Ave.
Division of Batus Retail
611 5th Ave.
New York, NY 10022
(212) 753-4000
Director Personnel: Deborah McRae
Exclusive apparel retailer known for its
showcase window displays on 5th Avenue.

Schwartz, FAO
767 5th Ave.
New York, NY 10153
(212) 644-9400
Personnel Director: Edward Gates
Toy retailer that operates 38 stores.

Swank, Inc.
90 Park Ave.
New York, NY 10016
(212) 867-2600
Office Manager: Ms. Jeffrie Leshinger
Retailer of jewelry for men, leather goods,
gifts, men's accessories, toiletries, and
perfume.

Tiffany and Company
727 5th Ave.
New York, NY 10022
(212) 755-8000
Director of Human Resources: Katheryn
Murphy

Toys "R" Us
461 From Road
Paramus, NJ 07652
(201) 262-7800
Director of Employment: Jim Gorenc

Waldbaum Inc.
1 Hemlock St.
Central Islip, NY 11722

(516) 582-9300
Director Human Resources: Bill Clark
Supermarket chain.

WaldenBooks
100 Greyrock Place
Stamford, CT 06901
(203) 358-8927
Human Resources: (313) 913-1100

Sports, Fitness, and Recreation

WEB SITES:

Fitness World
http://www.fitnessworld.com

Online Sports—Career Center
http://www.onlinesports.com/pages/
CareerCenter.html

SportsLink
http://www.sportsite.com/mac/allshop/
sgma/html/sgma_hp.html

PROFESSIONAL ORGANIZATIONS:

For networking in the sports and
recreation fields, check out the following
local professional organizations listed in
Chapter 5:
National Academy of Sports
People-to-People Sports Committee
Women's Sports Foundation

For more information, you can contact:

**Aerobics and Fitness Association of
America**
15250 Ventura Blvd.
Sherman Oaks, CA 91403
(818) 905-0040

**American Association for Leisure and
Recreation**
1900 Association Drive
Reston, VA 22091
(703) 476-3472

**IDEA: The International Association of
Fitness Professionals**
6190 Cornerstone Court E., Suite 204
San Diego, CA 92121
(800) 999-4332

**International Association of Fitness
Professionals**
6190 Cornerstone Court E., Suite 204
San Diego, CA 92121
(800) 999-4332

National Recreation & Parks Association
22377 Belmont Ridge Rd.
Ashborn, VA 20148
(703) 820-4940

National Sporting Goods Association
1699 Wall St.
Mt. Prospect, IL 60056
(847) 439-4000

Society of Recreation Executives
P.O. Drawer 17148
Pensacola, FL 35222
(904) 477-2123

PROFESSIONAL PUBLICATIONS:

American Fitness
Athletic Business
Athletic Management
Backroads—Walking & Hiking
Fitness Management
Parks and Recreation
Sporting Goods Dealer

Sporting Goods Market
Sporting Goods Retailers
Sports Industry News

DIRECTORIES:

American Fitness Association Directory
  (American Fitness Association, Long
  Beach, CA)
Athletic Business, Professional Directory
  Section (Athletic Business Publications,
  Madison, WI)
Fitness Management Source Book (Leisure
  Publications, Los Angeles, CA)
Health Clubs Directory (American
  Business Directories, Omaha, NE)
*New American Guide to Athletics, Sports,
  and Recreation* (New American Library,
  New York, NY)
Parks & Recreation Buyers Guide (National
  Recreation and Parks Association,
  Arlington, VA)
Recreation Centers Directory (American
  Business Directories, Omaha, NE)
Sporting Goods Retailers Directory
  (American Business Directories &
  Omaha, NE)
Sports Administration Guide and Directory
  (National Sports Marketing Bureau,
  New York, NY)
Who's Who in Recreation (Society of
  Recreation Executives, Pensacola, FL)
Who's Who in Sports and Fitness (American
  Fitness Association, Long Beach, CA)

Employers, Sports and Fitness:

Asphalt Green
555 E. 90th St.
New York, NY 10128
(212) 369-8890
Personnel Director: Pam Banks

Bally's Total Fitness/The Vertical Clubs
60 Merrick Rd.
Rockville Center, NY 11570
(516) 887-7500

Blue Velvet Boxing Club
23 W. 34th St.

New York, NY 10001
(212) 822-1960

Callanetics Studios of Manhattan
154 W. 57th St.
New York, NY 10019
(212) 765-2900

Cardio-Fitness Center
200 Park Ave.
New York, NY 10016
(212) 682-4440
Personnel Director: Juli Sutton

Chelsea Piers
Pier 62
New York, NY 10011
(212) 336-6666

City Climbers Club of New York
533 W. 59th St.
New York, NY 10019
(212) 974-2250

Crunch Fitness
88 University Place, 11th Floor
New York, NY 10003
(212) 620-7867
Personnel Director: Lizette Muñoz

Dolphin Gym
146 W. 23rd St.
New York, NY 10011
(212) 679-7300
Personnel: Mark Jones

Equinox Fitness Club
895 Broadway
New York, NY 10003
(212) 677-0180
Personnel Director: David Fowler

Gold's Gym
1657 Broadway
New York, NY
(212) 757-4653

Kingsway International Boxing
1 W. 28th St., 2nd Floor
New York, NY 10001
(212) 679-3427
Sr. Trainer: Michael Olajide Sr.

Madison Square Garden
2 Penn Plaza
New York, NY 10121
(212) 465-6741
Director of Personnel: Marilyn Hausner
Major center for sports events, live
concerts, circuses, national and international sports meets. Houses the Knicks
and Rangers.

**New Jersey Sports and Exposition
Authority/ Meadowlands**
50 Route 120
E. Rutherford, NY 07073
(201) 935-8500
Personnel Director: Robert Jennings

New York Health & Racquet Club
3 New York Plaza
New York, NY 10004
(212) 797-1500
Personnel Director: Ms. Lee Mathias

**The 92nd Street Y Center for Health,
Fitness and Sports**
1395 Lexington Ave.
New York, NY 10128
(212) 415-5729
Human Resources Director: Connie Zalk

Radu's Physical Culture Studio
24 W. 57th St.
New York, NY 10019
(212) 581-1995

Shea Stadium
Roosevelt Ave. at 126th St.
Flushing, NY 11368
(718) 507-6387
Personnel Director: Ray Scott
Home of the New York Mets.

Synergy Fitness Clubs
221 W. 57th St.
New York, NY 10019
(212) 262-5155
Downtown, Midtown, Upper East Side;
cardio, strength, aerobics, karate, yoga,
personal training.

**Town Sports International/New York
Sports Clubs**
888 7th Ave.
New York, NY 10106
(212) 246-6700
Personnel Director: Anthony Ancona

United States Tennis Association
70 W. Red Oak Lane
White Plains, NY 10604
(914) 696-7000
Personnel Director: Dario Otero
Home of the United States Open Tennis
Championship at Flushing Meadow Park.

Yankee Stadium
River Ave. at 161st St.
Bronx, NY 10451
(718) 293-4300
Personnel Director: Harvey C. Winston

YM-YWHA 92nd St. Y
1395 Lexington Ave.
New York, NY 10028
(212) 415-5729

YWCA
333 7th Ave.
New York, NY
(212) 630-9600
Personnel Director: Particia Butts

Employers, Recreation:

Aqueduct Race Track
Rockaway Blvd.
Ozone Park, NY 11417
(718) 641-4700
Personnel Director: Sal Cartagine

Belmont Race Track
Hempstead Turnpike and Plainfield Ave.
Belmont, NY 10003
(718) 641-4700
Personnel Director: Sal Cartagine

Big Apple Circus
35 W. 35th St., 9th Floor
New York, NY 10001
(212) 268-2500
Personnel Director: Tanya Santiago

Bronx Zoo
Wildlife Conservation Society
2300 Southern Blvd.
Bronx, NY 10460
(718) 220-5100
Human Resources Director: Charles
Vasser

Brooklyn Academy of Music
30 Lafayette Ave.
Brooklyn, NY 11217
(718) 636-4100
Personnel Manager: Liz Sharp

Carnegie Hall
881 7th Ave.
New York, NY 10019
(212) 903-9601
Human Resources Director: Joan
Goldstone

Central Park Conservancy
1 E. 104th St.
New York, NY 10029
(212) 315-0385
Personnel Director: George Kellogg

Lincoln Center for the Performing Arts
70 Lincoln Center Plaza
New York, NY 10023
(212) 875-5000

Director of Personnel: Jay Spivack
Includes Alice Tully Hall, the Vivian
Beaumont Theatre, Avery Fisher Hall, the
Metropolitan Opera House, and New York
State Theatre. Contact personnel offices of
individual theaters.

Metropolitan Opera Association
Lincoln Center
New York, NY 10023
(212) 799-3100
Personnel Director: Linda Freitag

New York Botanical Garden
Southern Blvd. at 200th St.
Bronx, NY 10458
(718) 817-8705
Personnel Manager: Karen Yesnick

New York Shakespeare Festival
425 Lafayette St.
New York, NY 10003
(212) 598-7100
General Manager: Joey Parnes

Radio City Music Hall
1260 Avenue of the Americas
New York, NY 10020
(212) 632-4000
Personnel Director: Keith Wheeler

Stock Brokers/Financial Services

WEB SITES:

Bank.Net
http://bank.net/home.rich.html

Investment Banks on the Web
http://www.cob.ohio-state.edu/~fin/cern/
invbank.htm

PROFESSIONAL ORGANIZATIONS:

For networking in finance and related
fields, check out the following local
professional organizations listed in
Chapter 5. Also see "Banking."
Association of Investment Brokers
Financial Women's Association of New
   York
New York Society of Security Analysts
Security Traders Association

For more information, you can contact:

American Financial Services Association
919 18th St., NW
Washington, DC 20006
(202) 296-5544

**Association for Investment Management
and Research**
http://www.aimr.com/aimr.html
5 Boar's Head Lane
Charlottesville, VA 22903
(804) 980-3668

Financial Analysts Federation
5 Boar's Head Lane
Charlottesville, VA 22903
(804) 977-8977

Financial Managers Society
8 S. Michigan Ave., Suite 500
Chicago, IL 60603
(312) 578-1300

Financial Women International
7910 Woodmont Ave.
Bethesda, MD 20814
(301) 657-8288

Institute of Certified Financial Planners
7600 E. Eastman Ave., Suite 301
Denver, CO 80231
(303) 751-7600

**International Association of Financial
Planning**
5775 Glenridge Drive NE, Suite B300
Atlanta, GA 30328
(404) 845-0011

**Investment Counsel Association of
America**
20 Exchange Place
New York, NY 10005
(212) 344-0999

**National Association of Personal
Financial Advisors**
350 West Dundee Road, Suite 200
Buffalo Grove, IL 60089
(847) 537-7722

**National Association of Securities
Dealers**
1735 K St., NW
Washington, DC 20006
(202) 728-8000

National Venture Capital Association
1655 N. Fort Meyer Drive
Arlington, VA 22209
(703) 351-5269

Securities Industry Association
635 Slaters Lane, Suite 110
Alexandria, VA 22314
(703) 683-2075

PROFESSIONAL PUBLICATIONS:

Barron's
Better Investing Magazine
CFO
CreditWeek
D & B Reports
Dun's Business Month
Financial Weekly

Financial World
Futures Magazine
Institutional Investor
Investment Advisor
Kiplinger's Mutual Funds
Mergers & Acquisitions
Registered Representative
Stock Market Magazine
Traders Magazine
Wall Street Letter

DIRECTORIES:

Complete Commodity Futures Directory
  (Christopher Resources, Inc., Frankfort, IL)
Corporate Finance Sourcebook (National
  Register Publishing, New Providence, NJ)
CUSIP Master Directory (Standard &
  Poor's, New York, NY)
Financial Yellow Book (Monitor Publishing
  Co., New York, NY)
*Handbook of Financial Markets and
  Institutions* (John Wiley and Sons, New
  York, NY)
Industry Review (Moody's Investors
  Service, Inc., New York, NY)
Investment & Securities Directory (Ameri-
  can Business Directories, Omaha, NE)
Securities Industry Yearbook (Securities
  Industry Association, New York, NY)
Security Dealers of North America
  (Standard and Poor's, New York, NY)
*Security Traders Association Traders
  Annual* (Security Traders Association,
  New York, NY)
*Standard & Poor's Security Dealers of
  North America* (Standard Poor's Corp.,
  New York, NY)
Who's Who in Finance and Industry (Reed
  Reference Publishing, New Providence, NJ)
Who's Who in the Securities Industry
  (Economist Publishing Co., Chicago, IL)

Employers:

Alliance Capital Management
1345 Sixth Ave.
New York, NY 10105
(212) 969-1000
Human Resources: Denise Bernardo

American Express
3 World Financial Center
New York, NY 10285
(212) 640-2000
Travel-related insurance, investment and
international banking services.
Manager: Rocco Cocchiarale

American Stock Exchange
86 Trinity Pl.
New York, NY 10006
(212) 306-1000
Employment Manager: Allison Katz
Stock exchange market for stocks and
bonds of mid-range growth companies.
Nation's third largest stock exchange.

Bear Stearns and Company
245 Park Ave.
New York, NY 10167
(212) 272-2000
Personnel Director: Anne Corwin
Worldwide securities trading and financial
services partnership.

Blackstone Group LP
345 Park Ave.
New York, NY 10154
(212) 935-2626
Personnel Director: Sylvia Moss

Blair, D.H., and Company
44 Wall St.
New York, NY 10005
(212) 495-4000
Assistant Director of Personnel: Ruth
Robles
One of New York's biggest investment
firms.

Bloomberg Financial Markets
499 Park Ave.
New York, NY 10022
(212) 318-2000
Human Resources: Lisa Schreier

CS First Boston
55 E. 52nd St.
New York, NY 10055
(212) 909-2000

Cantor Fitzgerald
1 World Trade Center
New York, NY 10048
(212) 938-5000
Recruiting Manager: Attn: Tara

Commodity Exchange
4 World Trade Center
New York, NY 10048
(212) 390-1420/748-1000
Human Resources Director: Paul
McCourt

Credit Suisse Asset Management
12 E. 49th St.
New York, NY 10017
(212) 238-5800

Dean Witter InterCapital
2 World Trade Center
New York, NY 10048
(212) 392-2222

Bullish on Wall Street

Lisa Marini, an options trader with a major New York firm,
gave us this rundown on New York's trading scene. "New
York is the equities market capital of the world. On the
trading floor, what you see is the most naked form of
supply and demand in action. It's an outcry market. Floor
traders literally shout out their bids on stocks, options,
commodities, metals, whatever.

"There are two classes of people in the market—the
traders and everybody else. You start out as a runner,
running orders to the floor traders, who are the only ones
who can actually bid. Next you become a phone clerk;
they're the people who answer the phones and give the
orders to the runners. From phone clerk you move up to
crowd assistant or market-maker clerk. A crowd assistant
helps the broker or trader execute the orders. A market-
maker clerk monitors a trader's position and risk in the
market.

"Many phone clerks earn upward of $75,000 a year. I
know one market-maker clerk who made $140,000 last year.
If you are very successful you may be able to buy equity
into the firm and become a market maker or floor trader,"
although that requires passing a standardized test and
certification.

Deutsche Morgan Grenfell
31 W. 52nd St.
New York, NY 10019
(212) 474-8000

Dillon Read and Company
535 Madison Ave.
New York, NY 10022
(212) 906-7000
Personnel Director: Laurie Connoloy
Investment banking firm.

Donaldson Lufkin and Jenrette
140 Broadway
New York, NY 10005
(212) 504-3000
Director of Human Resources: Gerald Rigg
International banking and securities firm.

Dreyfus Corp.
200 Park Ave., 7th Floor
New York, NY 10166
(212) 922-6000
Contact Corporate Human Resources

Dun & Bradstreet Corporation
1 Diamond Hill Rd.
Murray Hill, NJ 07974
(908)665-5000
Human Resources Director: Peter Ross
Financial information services.

First Boston Corporation
11 Madison Ave.
New York, NY 10010
(212) 909-2000
Recruiting Director: Kisha Coston
International banking firm.

First Investors Corporation
95 Wall St.
New York, NY 10005
(212) 858-8000

Goldman Sachs and Company
85 Broad St.
New York, NY 10004
(212) 902-1000
Employment Manager: Elizabeth Reese
Investment banking firm.

Gruntal & Company
14 Wall St.
New York, NY 10005
(212) 267-8800
Employment Manager: Bob Getcewich

HSBC Securities
250 Park Ave.
New York, NY 10177
(212) 808-0500

Kemper Securities Group
1 World Trade Center

New York, NY 10006
(212) 839-7500
Personnel Department: 77 W. Wacker
Drive, Chicago, IL 60601

Lazard Freres and Company
30 Rockefeller Plaza
New York, NY 10020
(212) 632-6000
Contact Personnel
Investment banking firm.

Lehman Brothers
3 World Financial Center
New York, NY 10285
(212) 526-7000
Contact: Rita Haring
Commission work in stocks, bonds, and
commodities.

MasterCard International
2000 Purchase St.
Purchase, NY 10577
(914) 249-3600

Merrill Lynch and Company
225 Liberty St.
World Financial Center, S. Tower
New York, NY 10080
(212) 449-1000
One of the nation's largest investment
banking and securities brokerage firms.

Morgan, J. P., and Company
60 Wall St.
New York, NY 10260
(212) 483-2323

Morgan Stanley Asset Management
1251 Avenue of the Americas
New York, NY 10020
(212) 703-4000
Personnel Director: William Higgins,
750 7th Ave., New York, 10019
Investment banking firm.

NASDAQ
33 Whitehall St.
New York, NY 10004
(212) 858-4409
Fast-growing exchange for lower capitali-
zation stocks, especially technology issues.

Neuberger & Berman
605 3rd Ave.
New York, NY 10015
(212) 476-9000
Human Resources Director: Barbara
Katersky

New York Stock Exchange
11 Wall St.
New York, NY 10005
(212) 656-3000
VP, Human Resources: Joseph Johnson
Principal marketplace for trading stocks
and bonds in the United States.

Oppenheimer Funds
2 World Trade Center
New York, NY 10048
(212) 323-0597
Personnel Director: Jim Phillips

PaineWebber Group
1285 Avenue of the Americas
New York, NY 10019
(212) 713-2000
Contact: Human Resources/Employment
Division
One of the world's largest investment
firms.

Primerica Financial Services
388 Greenwich St.
New York, NY 10016
(212) 816-8000
Senior VP, Human Resources: Barry
Mannes

Prudential Securities
199 Water St.
New York, NY 10292
(212) 778-1000
Senior Recruiter: Rosemary Albergo
International securities brokerage and
investment banking firm.

Quick and Reilly Group
26 Broadway

New York, NY 10004
(212) 747-1200
VP, Human Resources: Liz O'Hern

Salomon Brothers
7 World Trade Center
New York, NY 10048
(212) 783-7000
International investment banking and
research firm.

Scudder Stevens and Clark
345 Park Ave.
New York, NY 10154
(212) 326-6300
Personnel Director: Ms. Chris Irwin

Seligman, J. & W., & Co.
100 Park Ave.
New York, NY
(212) 850-1864

**Smith Barney Harris Upham and
Company**
338 Greenwich St.
New York, NY 10013
(212) 816-6000
Major international investment banking
firm.

Spear Leeds and Kellogg
120 Broadway
New York, NY 10006
(212) 433-7000
Stock brokerage firm.
Personnel Director: Beverly Fiorentino

Tiger Management Corp.
101 Park Ave.
New York, NY 10178
(212) 867-4350
Human Resources Director: Terry
Brennan

USB Securities
299 Park Ave.
New York, NY 10171
(212) 821-4000

Travel/Shipping/Transportation

WEB SITES:

Internet Guide to Transportation
http://www.iac.co.jp/~bobj/IGT/
index.html

Transport News
http://www.transportnews.com/

Travel Links
http://travellinks.com/

TruckNet
http://www.truck.net/

PROFESSIONAL ORGANIZATIONS:

To learn more about the travel, shipping, and transportation industries, you can contact the following local professional organizations listed in Chapter 5:
American Bureau of Shipping
American Society of Travel Agents
Association of Group Travel Executives
Association of Travel Marketing Executives
Greater Independent Association of National Travel Services

For more information, you can contact:

Air Transport Association of America
http://www.air-transport.org
1301 Pennsylvania Ave., Suite 1100
Washington, DC 20004
(202) 626-4000

American Public Transit Association
1201 New York Ave.,NW, Suite 400
Washington, DC 20005
(202) 898-4000

American Society of Travel Agents
1101 King St.
Alexandria, VA 22314
(703) 739-2782

American Trucking Association
2200 Mill Road
Alexandria, VA 22314
(703) 838-1700

Association of Retail Travel Agents
845 Sir Thomas Court, Suite 3
Harrisburg, PA 17109
(717) 545-9548

Institute of Transportation Engineers
525 School St., SW
Washington, DC 20024
(202) 554-8050

New York Shipping Association
2 World Trade Center, 20th Floor
New York, NY 10048
(212) 323-6600

Travel Industry Association of America
http://www.tia.org
1100 New York Ave., NW, Suite 450
Washington, DC 20005
(202) 408-8422

United States Tour Operators Association (USTA)
342 Madison Ave., Suite 1522
New York, NY 10173
(212) 750-7371

PROFESSIONAL PUBLICATIONS:

ASTA Travel News
Air Cargo USA
Air Traffic Management
Air Transport World
American Shipper
American Trucker
Aviation Digest
Aviation Week and Space Technology
Business and Commercial Aviation
Commercial Carrier Journal
Fleet Management News
Heavy Duty Trucking
Inside Trucking
Marine Log
Shipping & Receiving
Tours and Resorts
Travel Agent
Travel Trade: The Business Paper of the Travel Industry

Travel Weekly
Urban Transport News

DIRECTORIES:

American Motor Carrier Directory (K-III
Directory Corp., New York, NY)
*American Society of Travel Agents-
Membership Roster* (American Society of
Travel Agents, Inc., Arlington, VA)
Bus Industry Directory (Friendship
Publications, Inc., Spokane, WA)
Coast Marine & Transportation Directory
(Pacific Shipper, San Francisco, CA)
Job Opportunities Listing (Aviation Mainte-
nance Foundation Intl., Seattle, WA)
Moody's Transportation Manual (Moody's
Travel Service, New York, NY)
Motor Carrier Professional Services
Directory (American Trucking Assn.,
Arlington, VA)
Official Motor Carrier Directory (Official
Motor Freight Guide, Inc., Chicago, IL)
*Travel Industry of America Directory of
Membership & Services* (Travel Industry
of America, Washington, DC)
World Aviation Directory & Buyer's Guide
(McGraw-Hill Aviation Group,
Washington, DC)

Employers:

Air India
345 Park Ave.
New York, NY 10154
(212) 407-1300
Personnel Manager: Nicholas Metz
U.S. headquarters location.

Alitalia Airlines
666 5th Ave.
New York, NY 10103
(212) 903-3300
Contact: Selection and Training Department

American Airlines
Main St., 1 American Plaza
Hartford, CT 06103
(860) 520-6310
Human Resources Director: Nancy Taylor

**American Express Travel Related
Services**
3 World Financial Center
200 Vesey St.
New York, NY 10285
(212) 640-2000
International travel coordinator.

Amtrak
360 W. 31st St., 4th Fl.
New York, NY 10001
(212) 630-7150
Personnel Director: Haddie McCoy
Nation's only long-distance passenger
railroad.

Avis, Inc.
900 Old Country Road
Garden City, NY 11530
(516) 222-3000
Jobline: (516) 222-3399
Employment Manager: Cathy Lee Gibson

Blue Ocean Lines
40 Exchange Place
New York, NY 10004
(212) 943-1000
International shipping company specializing in worldwide transportation of full
container and LCL freight.

British Airways
75-20 Astoria Blvd.
Jackson Heights, NY 11370
(718) 397-4000
Personnel Director: Irv Rudowitz
One of the largest air carriers in the world;
wholly owned by the British government.

Club Med
40 W. 57th St.
New York, NY 10019
(212) 977-2100
Personnel Director: Maggie Maloney,
(602) 948-9190

Cook, Thomas, Travel Services
2 Penn Plaza, 18th Floor
New York, NY 10121
(212) 967-4390
Contact: John Harvey
One of the world's largest travel agencies.

Cunard Line
555 5th Ave.
New York, NY 10017
(212) 880-7500
Human Resources Director: Jane Duguid

Eastern Mediteranean Shipping
990 6th Ave., Suite 16H
New York, NY 10018
(212) 563-5001
President: Andy Sharma

Easy Travel
518 Broadway Mall
Hicksville, NY 11801
(516) 931-1717
Personnel Director: Karen Radecki

EL AL Israel Airlines
120 W. 45th St.
New York, NY 10036
(212) 7852-0625

Emery Worldwide Air Freight Corporation
184-54 149th Ave.
Springfield Gardens, NY 11413
(718) 995-6500
Contact: Jim Tracey, HR Dept., PO Box 3477, Portland, OR 97208
One of the world's largest air cargo carriers.

Farrell Lines
1 Whitehall St.
New York, NY 10004
(212) 440-4200
Human Resources Director: Richard Thompson
Major steamship service.

Federal Express
880 Third Ave.
New York, NY 10022
(800) 463-3339
Personnel: Joann Bourne
Transportation of packages and documents through a fleet of more than 60 aircrafts and numerous trucks and vans.

Green Bus Lines
165-25 147th Ave.
Jamaica, NY 11434
(718) 995-4700
Office Manager: Doris Drantch
Major bus transportation line servicing Queens and Manhattan.

Greyhound Corporation
625 8th Ave.
New York, NY 10018
(212) 971-6349
Contact Personnel
Holding company, operating several subsidiaries, including Greyhound Bus Lines, Greyhound Manufacturing Group, and Armour and Company.

Hertz Corporation
225 Brae Blvd.
Park Ridge, NJ 07656
(201) 307-2000
Human Resources Manager: Karry Guerriero

K International Transport Company
74 Trinity Place
New York, NY
(212) 267-6400
International freight forwarder, customs broker, export packing, air freight, and container services.

Liberty Lines Transit
475 Saw Mill River Road
Yonkers, NY 10701
(914) 969-6900
Human Resources Director: Neil Erickson
Commuter bus operation, servicing Yonkers and Westchester area.

Liberty Travel
440 Franklin Turnpike
Mahwah, NJ 07430
(201) 327-5695
Personnel Director: Ms. Pat Harmes

Long Island Railroad
Archer Ave. & Sutphin Blvd.
Jamaica, NY 11435
(718) 558-7400

Personnel Director: Roseann Neville
The country's largest commuter railroad.

Maritz Travel
330 Madison Ave.
New York, NY 10017
(212) 309-7400
Personnel Director: Jane Yarar
Fourth largest agency in the U.S.

McCallister Brothers
17 Battery Pl.
New York, NY 10004
(212) 269-3200
Personnel Director: Jean Brown
Major U.S. marine services firm. Operates
the largest fleet of tugs and barges on the
East Coast and in the Caribbean.

Metro North Commuter Railroad
347 Madison Ave.
New York, NY 10017
(212) 340-3000
Personnel Director: Celia Ussak

Metropolitan Suburban Bus Authority
700 Commercial Ave.
Garden City, NY 11530
(516) 542-0100
Human Resources Manager: Mary Lou
Saoanitri
Bus company that operates as part of the
Metropolitan Transportation Authority.

Metropolitan Transportation Authority
347 Madison Ave.
New York, NY 10017
(212) 878-7407
Manager Staffing and Employee Relations:
Sheldon Dixon
A public benefit transportation corpora-
tion whose subsidiaries include the New
York City Transit Authority, Manhattan
and Bronx Surface Transit Operations
Authority, the Staten Island Rapid Transit
Operating Authority, Metropolitan
Suburban Bus Authority, the Long Island
Railroad, Metro North Commuter Rails,
and the Triborough Bridge and Tunnel
Authority.

New Jersey Transit
180 Boyden Ave.
Maplewood, NJ 07040
(201) 378-6300
Human Resources Director: Jospeh Allen

New York Bus Tours
Interstate 95 at Exit 13
Bronx, NY 10475
(718) 994-5500
Contact: Tim Fitzgerald

New York City Transportation Authority
370 Jay St.
Brooklyn, NY 11201
(718) 330-3000
Employment Line: (718) 834-7074

Nippon Express USA
590 Madison Ave.
New York, NY 10022
(212) 758-6100
Asst. Manager: John DeLuca

Ocean Conco Line
19 Rector St.
New York, NY
(212) 747-1909
Offers a full freight fowarding shipping
service with routes to South America.

Omega World Travel
875 3rd Ave.
New York, NY 10022
(212) 753-4900
Fifth largest agency in the country.

**Port Authority of New York and New
Jersey**
1 World Trade Center, Suite 44N
New York, NY 10048
(212) 435-7000
Agency responsible for operation,
maintenance, and development of public
transportation facilities in New York and
New Jersey metropolitan area. Also
operates Kennedy, La Guardia, and
Newark airports; the Lincoln and Holland
tunnels; the George Washington Bridge;
Marine Terminals; Port Authority Bus
Terminal; World Trade Center; and PATH
Rapid Transit.

Swissair
41 Pinelawn Road
Mellville, NY 11747
(516) 844-4500

Transcontainer Transportation
39 Broadway
New York, NY 10038
(212) 425-2278
Ships any size container or shipment
anywhere in the world.

Triboro Coach Corporation
85-01 24th Ave.
Jackson Heights, NY 11369
(718) 335-1000
Personnel Director: Joe Ortiz

United Parcel Service
643 W. 43rd St.
New York, NY 10036
(212) 631-6441
Human Resources Representative: Eileen
Breen, 650 Winters Ave.,
Paramus, NJ 07652, (201) 330-2305
Parcel pick-up and delivery service, with
nationwide operations.

Universal Maritime Service Corporation
P.O. Box 880
Madison, NJ 07940
(201) 514-5000
Personnel: Brian Borchik
Major marine cargo handler.

Utilities

WEB SITES:

Electric Power NewsLink
http://www.powermag.com/

EnergyNet
http://www.energynet.com

PROFESSIONAL ORGANIZATIONS:

For information about the utilities
industry, contact the following organizations. See "Electronics/Telecommunica-
tions" for major phone and cellular
companies.

American Gas Association
1515 Wilson Blvd.
Arlington, VA 22209
(703) 841-8400

American Public Gas Association
11094 "D" Lee Highway
Fairfax, VA 22030
(703) 352-3890

American Public Power Association
2301 M St., NW
Washington, DC 20037
(202) 467-2900

Electrical Women's Round Table
c/o Ellen Katz
Consolidated Edison
4 Irving Place, Room 819
New York, NY 10003
(212) 460-4600 ext. 6506

Institute of Public Utilities
Michigan State University
410 Eppley Center
East Lansing, MI 48824
(517) 355-1876

New Jersey Utilities Associations
50 W. State St., Rm. 1106
Trenton, NJ 08608
(609) 392-1000

New York Gas Group
500 5th Ave., Suite 1650
New York, NY 10110
(212) 354-4790

PROFESSIONAL PUBLICATIONS:

American Gas
Electric Light and Power
Electrical World
Public Power
Public Utility Fortnightly
Transmission & Distribution World

DIRECTORIES:

American Public Gas Association Directory of Municipal Gas Systems (American Public Gas Association, Fairfax, VA)
Brown's Directories of North American Gas Companies (Edgel Communications, Cleveland, OH)
Directory of Municipal Gas Systems (American Public Gas Association, Vienna, VA)
Electrical World Directory of Electrical Utilities (McGraw-Hill, New York, NY)
Energy Job Finder (Mainstream Access, New York, NY)
Moody's Public Utility Manual (Moody's Investors Service, New York, NY)

Employers:

Brooklyn Union Gas
1 Metro Tech Center
Brooklyn, NY 11201
(718) 403-2000
Personnel Director: Arquelio Fraticelli
Natural gas company servicing Brooklyn and Long Island.

Connecticut Light and Power
107 Seldin St.
Berlin, CT 06037
(860) 947-2000

Consolidated Edison Company
4 Irving Place
New York, NY 10003
(212) 460-2014
Manager, Professional Recruitment: Loretta Vanacore
Electric power and gas supplier to most of New York City and Westchester County.

General Public Utilities Corp.
100 Interpace Parkway
Parsippany, NJ 07054
(201) 263-6500
Personnel Director: Richard Postweiler

Long Island Lighting Company
175 E. Old Country Road
Hicksville, NY 11801
(516) 755-6000
Employment Administrator: Carolyn Rubin
Major electric and gas supplier to Long Island.

Long Island Water Corporation
733 Sunrise Highway
Lynbrook, NY 11563
(516) 593-1000
Personnel Director: Ann Simmons
Water supplier to Long Island residents.

National Fuel Gas Company
30 Rockefeller Plaza
New York, NY 10112
(212) 581-0722

New York Power Authority
123 Main St.
White Plains, NY 10601
(914) 681-6200
Human Resources Specialist: Gerard Loughran
The nation's largest non-federal public power organization, providing more than one-third of the electricity for New York State.

New York Telephone
1095 Avenue of the Americas
New York, NY 10036
(212) 395-2552
Executive offices of New York's telephone service.

Northeast Utilities
P.O. Box 270
Hartford, CT 06141
(203) 665-5000
Senior VP, Human Resources: Cheryl Grise

Oil Burner Utility
44-39 Purvis
Long Island City, NY
(718) 729-0300

Orange and Rockland Utilities
1 Blue Hill Plaza
Pearl River, NY 10965
(914) 352-6000
VP, Human Resources: Nancy Jakobs

Public Service Electric & Gas Co.
80 Park Plaza
Newark, NJ 07101
(201) 430-7000
Human Resources Director: Martin
Mellett
Third largest combined gas and electric
company in the United States.

Employers Index

General Index

Boldface indicates employer listings